Great Thinkers in Economics

The famous historian, E.H. Carr once said that in order to understand history it is necessary to understand the historian writing it. The same could be said of economics. Famous economists often remark that specific episodes in their lives, or particular events that took place in their formative years attracted them to economics. Great Thinkers in Economics is designed to illuminate the economics of some of the great historical and contemporary economists by exploring the interaction between their lives and work, and the events surrounding them.

Giandomenica Becchio

Barbara Bergmann

An Intellectual Biography

palgrave
macmillan

Giandomenica Becchio
Department of ESOMAS
University of Torino
Torino, Italy

ISSN 2662-6276 ISSN 2662-6284 (electronic)
Great Thinkers in Economics
ISBN 978-3-032-18695-9 ISBN 978-3-032-18696-6 (eBook)
https://doi.org/10.1007/978-3-032-18696-6

Cover credit: Barbara Bergmann papers, box 7, David M. Rubenstein Rare Book & Manuscript Library, Duke University

This Palgrave Macmillan imprint is published by the registered company Springer Nature Switzerland AG
The registered company address is: Gewerbestrasse 11, 6330 Cham, Switzerland

This book is dedicated to my sons, Alessandro and Federico, who are my greatest love, joy, and pride.

Acknowledgments[1] I first came across the work of Barbara Bergmann many years ago, while writing my previous books on the history of feminist economics and on the doctrine of the separate spheres within the history of economic thought. I was immediately fascinated by the depth of Bergmann's insights and the originality of her approach to issues such as discrimination and gender inequality. Her sharp analytical style, lucid prose, and distinctive way of engaging with feminism immediately captured my attention and have continued to influence my thinking ever since.

I owe a special debt of gratitude to Steve Pressman, who first suggested me to undertake Bergmann's intellectual biography. His steady support and constant encouragement have been invaluable throughout this project.

I am also immensely grateful to Sarah Bergmann and David Bergmann, Barbara's children, who kindly accepted to speak with me. They answered my many questions with patience and openness, sharing personal recollections of their parents that enrich several sections of this book.

My thanks extend as well to several of Bergmann's friends and colleagues: Francine Blau, Amy Cross, Deborah M. Figart, Maria Floro, Thesia Garner, Heidi Hartmann, Marlene Kim, Mary King, and Myra H. Stober. I greatly appreciate the time and thought they devoted to writing down their memories of Barbara and allowing me to include them here.

My sincere thanks go to Bruce Caldwell for his kind support and help during my stay at Duke University. A special acknowledgment goes to Andy Armacost, Curator of Collections and Head of the Collection Development Department, for his generous help and time, as well as to all the staff of the David M. Rubenstein Rare Book & Manuscript Library at Duke University, where Bergmann's archive is held. I am also grateful to Edith Kuiper, who allowed me to consult some material from the IAFFE archive, housed in the same location.

[1] This research is part of the results of the University of Torino Research Unit of PRIN 2022KKWTTK The Economic Thought of Italian Women (1750–1999): Methodological Issues, Ideas, Impact, International Links, a Census and an Online Database.

Competing Interests The author has no competing interests to declare that are relevant to the content of this manuscript.

Contents

About the Author

Giandomenica Becchio (Ph.D. University of Florence) is Full Professor of History of Economic Thought at the University of Torino (ESOMAS Department), Italy. Her research field spans history of political economy, methodology of economics, feminist economics, and women's contributions to economic thought. Supported by research fellowships, she has been a visiting scholar/professor at the New School for Social Research (NSSR); Duke University; Yeshiva University (NYC); Hitotsubashi University (Tokyo); VSE University (Prague); Universidade Federal do Rio de Janeiro; the Gender Institute at the LSE; UTS (Sydney); Wirtschaftsuniversität Wien (Vienna). She is currently the National Secretary of AISPE (Italian Association for the History of Economic Thought). Her works include several articles published in major academic journals and three books, respectively on the philosophical origins of neoliberalism as developed within the history of economic thought (Routledge, 2017), on the history of feminist and gender economics (Routledge, 2020), and on the doctrine of separate spheres within political economy and economics (Palgrave Springer, 2024).

CHAPTER 1

Introduction: A Life in Economics, Feminism, and Public Engagement

Barbara Bergmann (New York 1927 – Bethesda, Maryland 2015) was an outstanding economist, a fierce feminist, and a tireless advocate for social reform. Her academic activity started in the 1960s and officially ended in 1988, although she continued to work and publish until her final days. In her life, Bergmann witnessed the economic, political, and social transformation of American society between the 1930s and the 2010s; the rise of civil rights and feminist movements; the institutionalization of women's studies and feminist economics; and the methodological debates that reconfigured the profession from the 1960s onward.

Economics served Bergmann as a tool to understand the origin and the effects of social inequality between groups in power and minorities in American society, which especially affected women and Black people. She insisted, throughout her life, that economics must serve the needs of people and must confront the injustices too often ignored by standard economists of her time.

Feminism pushed her to extend her research to a broader analysis of the economic conditions of women in both public and private spheres, i.e., the marketplace and the household.

Combining economics and feminism made her develop an economic vision shaped by the conviction that neither equality nor freedom was possible without access to earnings and employment: personal freedom depends on economic structures, not merely cultural norms, and

G. Becchio, *Barbara Bergmann*, Great Thinkers in Economics,
https://doi.org/10.1007/978-3-032-18696-6_1

economic independence depends on social norms, not merely individual preferences.

She never limited her contribution to abstract theories, rather she championed affirmative action, aimed at transforming people's lives, by publishing in major academic journals as well as in the national popular press, and by writing books, academic and popular, by serving as an expert in congressional hearings as well as in public debates.

She was one of a kind: witty, brilliant, and ironic, she combined a profound expertise in economic matters with the urgency to change what was wrong in a very pragmatic way, by proposing feasible solutions rather than ideological systems. She was funny, often irreverent, straight to the point, assertive, and open-minded. As her son David says, you either loved her or disliked her (see Chapter 9).

This biography reconstructs Bergmann's intellectual trajectory and offers some glimpses on her private persona. It is aimed at clarifying the enduring significance of her thought and her work, too often underappreciated, outside feminist economics. In fact, while the existing literature often frames her primarily as a feminist economist, this book emphasizes the broader scope of her contributions: her theoretical work on occupational segregation altered the way scholars understand the persistence of discrimination in the job market, and it represented the most vigorous alternative to the neoclassical labor economics as shaped by Jacob Mincer and Gary Becker; her approach to empirical analysis as well as her critique of neoclassical economics, too abstract and unable to scrutinize real dynamics behind decision-making processes, placed her at the forefront of methodological pluralism; her public engagement exemplified a model of the economist as a public intellectual committed to democratic governance.

This book is based on several sources: the analysis of her published works; the scrutiny of her entire archive, held at the David M. Rubenstein Rare Book & Manuscript Library, Duke University; unedited interviews and testimonies from her children and friends; and additional published material on her work. Her archive mainly contains research material, unpublished research proposals, almost everything she published, many private memoranda on the cases she was working on, many articles she wrote for the popular press, a few letters to journal editors, material from her hearings before Congress, a few printed emails (mainly related to submissions and referees' reports), awards and honors, as well as some photographs of her.

Taken together, these materials allow the reader to follow her professional trajectory as well as to get to know more about her private life and her exceptional personality. Each chapter, which is devoted to specific contributions by Bergmann, follows a chronological order aimed at presenting the evolution of her economic analysis, often influenced by her own life experience within and outside academia.

Chapter 2 is focused on her personal life. It starts from her youth, when she early experienced discrimination as a Jew and as a young girl in mid-century United States society, which informed her analysis of power dynamics within society throughout her life. Her early sense of being part of a double minority status provided a framework for understanding structural inequality long before the term intersectionality entered academic vocabulary. It continues by describing her academic trajectory as well as her constant commitment to promoting affirmative agenda up to the end of her life, by highlighting the way her personal experience occupied the center of her research (Bergmann, 2005, 2009a; Olson, 2007; Olson & Emami, 2002; Saunders & King, 2000; Strober, 1998).

Chapter 3 describes her early interest in and studies of structural unemployment and occupational segregation that led her to formulate the occupational crowding model, according to which, white men retained privileged access to high-wage positions by restricting women as well as Black workers to narrow, low-paid occupations. Against the neoclassical claim that discrimination was costly and would eventually disappear in competitive markets, Bergmann argued the opposite, i.e., discrimination could be efficient for dominant groups which tend to perpetuate the *status quo* by forcing disadvantaged groups into overcrowded jobs (Bergmann, 1971, 1974). She presented her theory of discrimination as analytically rigorous yet empirically rooted, and offered a structural account of institutions that explained not only why discrimination persisted, but also why it systematically reproduced itself across generations.

Chapter 4 highlights Bergmann's research on the origin and the effects of the economic emergence of women, i.e., the phenomenon of women entering the public sphere, identified with the market forces (Bergmann, 1986). Bergmann insisted on considering the difference between emergence and emancipation: although women emerged in the public sphere, real emancipation and gender equality were still far from being reached. Nonetheless, women's entering the public sphere led to a transformation of the internal dynamics of traditional families. Differently from Claudia

Goldin's notion of 'quiet revolution' (Goldin, 2006), women's revolution, according to Bergmann, was noisy and boisterous and led standard economists of the time to shape the New Home Economics, based on the reinforcement of the traditional family model based on a male breadwinner and a female caregiver, regarded as efficient for society as whole and grounded in personal preferences (Becker, 1981). To better fight against this analytically grounded revival of an obsolete family model, Bergmann expanded her research to the condition of women within their private sphere, i.e., the economics of the family, taking into account the constraints of full-time domestic labor, motherhood, and the role of cultural expectations. The economic effects of women's double burden, i.e., paid work combined with unpaid household responsibilities, were central to her explanation of women's persistently lowerwages, lower lifetime earnings, and weaker retirement security (Bergmann, 1981).

Taken together, Chapters 3 and 4 show the way Bergmann rejected standard economics' explanation of racial discrimination and gender discrimination in the job market, as well as the traditional division of labor within the household, as empirically inaccurate and ideologically conservative models. She argued that, far from being efficient, those models were characterized by unequal power, racism, chauvinism, asymmetric responsibilities, and legal structures that disadvantaged minorities on the basis of race and sex, as well as children.

Bergmann devoted herself to overcoming these structural inequalities by proposing effective affirmative action aimed at improving the condition of people of color, women, and children (Bergmann, 1996a), by constantly pointing out that solving issues of social inequality is not only a matter of economic efficiency, but also of fairness, which is systematically ignored by standard economics.

Chapter 5 is intended to show that Bergmann's goal was not merely to criticize standard economics, but to revise its methodological assumptions (Bergmann, 1989, 1995, 2009b). Her main target was the neoclassical approach to family behavior adopted by the New Home Economics, a critique that she shared with feminist economists, who between the 1980s and the 1990s converged toward the institutionalization of feminist economics as a new research field. She lamented the profession's reliance on rational choice models aimed at achieving states of equilibrium that treated individuals as atomistic and fully rational agents. Such models, she argued, ignored the complexity of real lives in social contexts. She publicly questioned whether business behavior, family behavior, and macroeconomic dynamics could be properly deduced from mathematical models. Instead, she promoted an empirically grounded approach, based on demographic and statistical as well as on computer microsimulation and experiments aimed at talking to people, observing institutions, and understanding constraints, in order to analyze real decision-making processes and the macrodynamics of society as a whole (Bergmann, 1987, 1988; 1990a, 1990b).

Her archive contains extensive datasets and reports on labor-force participation, marriage, divorce, fertility, and single-parenthood. Across her projects, some unpublished and presented here, she tried to build up a morerealistic economic theory aimed at providing concrete solutions. Her interest in microsimulation reflected that intent. Long before agent-based modeling became fashionable, Bergmann was building simulations to model poverty, the labor market, and the effects of social policies on household behavior and family decision-making, and to test possible policies aimed at addressing issues such as child support, welfare reforms, and social security.

Chapter 6 is devoted to describing Bergmann's major role in the emergence of feminist economics as an alternative approach that challenged the epistemological assumptions of the New Home Economics, as well as her role in building the International Association for Feminist Economics (IAFFE) and its journal, *Feminist Economics.* This chapter also highlights Bergmann's peculiar position within IAFFE as well as within the broader notion of 'feminist economics'. Barbara was, without any doubt, devoted to feminism and applied it to her economic analysis. Nonetheless, feminism is multifaceted, and differently from many feminist economists of her time, who have often placed themselves on the left wing of the ideological spectrum, Bergmann's position was more nuanced (Bergmann, 1990a).

She rejected Marxism and radical feminism that assumed capitalism as the main source of gender inequality and women's subjection, by calling for wholesale social transformation. Her approach might be situated within egalitarian liberalism, i.e., a belief in equality grounded in individual autonomy and freedom, combined with well-designed public policies aimed at reshaping structural inequalities, within a capitalistic system. One of her most provocative positions was her defense of the 'total commodification of family work' (Bergmann, 1998). She rejected the feminine notion of domestic labor as inherently morally superior to paid work and argued that care work should be moved into the market so that it could be distributed more equitably and remunerated appropriately. In her view, true gender equality requires dismantling the gendered division of labor, not accommodating it. Hence, she promoted policies aimed at implementing an equal division of household responsibilities between women and men. Her policy recommendations for expanded labor-force participation for women, social security, and enforcement of public child-care derived from this vision. She insisted that equality is not just a matter of cultural change, rather it requires structural interventions that alter the economic incentives and institutional settings within which households and markets operate (Bergmann, 1994).

Besides being a feminist economist, Bergmann was deeply influenced by institutionalism that served her to analyze not only discrimination in the job market, but also the origin ofpoverty which affected the weakest, such asBlacks, women, and children. She was constantly committed to scrutinizing the origin and the persistence of poverty within some specific social groups in order to find possible solutions that she proposed in her articulated policy plans.

Chapter 7 shows her affirmative action agenda which included public-child support enforcement and policies that facilitated women's entry into thelabor market as well as welfare reforms aimed at reducing poverty. Unlike many economists, who defended affirmative action in abstract terms, Bergmann advocated openly for quotas, arguing that they were necessary to break occupational monopolies. Without them, she warned, corporations would continue to recruit from shrinking pools of white male workers while excluding women and minorities. Her views reflected her structural approach to discrimination: without intervention, labor-market monopolies would persist. Her advocacy for universal child care was likewise central to her policy agenda. Long before this became a mainstream political issue, she argued that child care policy was essential to women's economic equality. She viewed child care not as merely a family issue, but as a macroeconomic policy instrument (Bergmann, 1996b). Against the universal basic income, she elaborated several possible welfare policies, by comparing data between some European countries, such as France and Sweden, and the United States.

Chapter 8 is dedicated to portraying Bergmann as a publicly engaged expert. In fact, she never confined her work to academia. Unlike many academic economists, Bergmann saw public engagement as a primary responsibility. She wrote prolifically for newspapers and magazines, most notably in her regular *New York Times* Sunday columns (1981–82),

Challenge, and *Los Angeles Times*, and many more. She testified before Congress, served as an expert in lawsuits, and engaged directly in public debates on many issues of her time. They included: Reaganomics, Bush's regressive fiscal policy, social security, affirmative action, welfare reform, sexual harassment in the workplaces, the decline of marriage, child care, abortion, college tuition, environmental issues, nurse shortage, which constantly affected the United States health system. Her final battle was for the right to a dignified death that might include a legalized assistedsuicide.

Her public voice, which contributed to her broad influence outside academia, was fortified by her clarity of writing. She prioritized intelligibility over technicality, and she believed economists should communicate in terms the public could understand, making economics useful for a significant improvement of society as a whole, against the attitude of the majority of economists who limit themselves to abstract models. She even promoted the abolition of the Nobel prize for economics, which tended to award that kind of abstraction rather than scholars involved in providing specific instruments to solve actual economic problems (Bergmann, 1999).

Chapter 9 represents a tribute to Bergmann as a private figure through the unedited testimonies of Barbara's children, who kindly accepted to be interviewed, and of some friends and colleagues of hers, who were available to share their thoughts for this book. Their unedited memories and reminiscences have been combined with the most significant celebrations of Barbara, which were published either during her life, for example on the occasion of a special issue of *Feminist Economics,* dedicated to her, or as tributes after she passed. Chapters 9 and 2 combined shed light on her unique personality.

Chapter 10 points out the importance of Bergmann as an economist and her multifaceted legacy within the history of economic thought as well. Although her contributions have been sometimes forgotten outside the feminist economics tradition, her analyses make her a central figure in the contemporary history of economic thought. As an economist, she reshaped understanding of discrimination, the segmentation of labor markets, and household dynamics. Furthermore, from a methodological perspective, she challenged the narrowing of standard economics and worked to broaden it by introducing alternative methods, based on empirical evidence. As a feminist economist and a public intellectual, she helped disseminate feminist economics to a wider audience by pressing and lobbying for policies that advanced gender and racial equality. Bergmann's professional life and civic commitment to economics, feminism, and feminist economics, cannot be better explained than by using her own words, she pronounced on the occasion of her 75th birthday, when IAFFE organized a party to celebrate her. Barbara concluded her final speech with the words:

> [Economics] is a profession where you can have a lot of fun, and I enjoyed it, and I certainly enjoyed my lifelong association with all of you. Thank you.[1]

Bergmann's private and professional life invites us to reconsider what economics can and should be: a discipline grounded in reality, committed to human equality, and at the service of those in need. Her legacy still challenges contemporary economists to restore the ties between theory and lived experience, between research and moral responsibility, and between institutions and the individuals they claim to serve.

References

Becker, G. (1981). *A treatise on the family*. Harvard University Press.

Bergmann, B. (1971). The effect on white incomes of discrimination in employment. *Journal of Political Economy, 79*(2), 294–313.

Bergmann, B. (1974). Occupational segregation, wages and profits when employers discriminate by race or sex. *Eastern Economic Journal, 1*(2), 103–110.

Bergmann, B. (1981). The economic risks of being a housewife. *American Economic Review, 71*(2), 81–86.

Bergmann, B. (1986). *The economic emergence of women*. Basic Books.

Bergmann, B. (1987). Measurement, or finding things in economics. *Journal of Economic Education, 18*(2), 191–201.

Bergmann, B. (1988). An experiment on the formation of expectations. *Journal of Economic Behavior and Organization, 9*, 137–151.

Bergmann, B. (1989). Why do most economists know so little about the economy? In S. Bowles, R. Edwards, & W. Shepard (Eds.), *Unconventional wisdom: Essays on economics in honor of John Kenneth Galbraith* (pp. 29–37). Houghton Mifflin Company.

[1] IAFFE archive, box 5. David M. Rubenstein Rare Book & Manuscript Library, Duke University.

Bergmann, B. (1990a). Feminism and economics. *Women Studies Quarterly, 18*(3/4), 68–74. Reprinted from *Academe: Bulletin of the American Association of University Professors, 69*(5), 22–25. (Original work published in 1983).

Bergmann, B. (1990b). Micro-to-macro simulation: A primer with a labor market example. *Journal of Economic Perspective, 4*(1), 99–116.

Bergmann, B. (1994). Curing child poverty in the United States. *American Economic Review, 84*(2), 76–80.

Bergmann, B. (1995). Becker's theory of the family: preposterous conclusions. *Feminist Economics, 1*(1), 141–150.

Bergmann, B. (1996a). *Saving our children from poverty: What the United States can learn from France*. Russell Sage Foundation.

Bergmann, B. (1996b). *In defense of affirmative action*. Basic Books.

Bergmann, B. (1998). The only ticket to equality: total androgyny, male style. *Journal of Contemporary Legal Issues, 9*, 75–86.

Bergmann, B. (1999). Abolish the Nobel Prize for economics. *Challenge, 42*(2), 52–57.

Bergmann, B. (2005). Pushing for a more humane society. *American Economist, 49*(2), 11–15.

Bergmann, B. (2009a). *Memorandum*. Barbara Bergmann's papers, box 8. David M. Rubenstein Rare Book & Manuscript Library Collections, Duke University.

Bergmann, B. (2009b). The economy and the economics profession: both need work. *Eastern Economic Journal, 35*(1), 2–9.

Goldin, C. (2006). The quiet revolution that transformed women's employment, education, and family. *American Economic Review, 96*(2), 1–21.

Olson, P. (2007). On the contributions of Barbara Bergmann to economics. *Review of Political Economy, 19*(4), 475–496.

Olson, P., & Emami, Z. (2002). Barbara Berman Bergmann. In *Engendering economics. Conversations with women economists in the United States* (pp. 53–72). Routledge.

Saunders, L., & King, M. (2000). An interview with Barbara Bergmann: leading feminist economists. *Review of Political Economy, 12*(3), 305–316.

Strober, E. A. (1998). Interview with Barbara Bergmann. *Feminist Economics, 4*(3), 5–6.

CHAPTER 2

Feminist, Economist, Activist

Barbara Bergmann was a fierce feminist, an outstanding economist, and a tireless activist for social reforms. She always fought for women's emancipation and empowerment. She published extensively in major academic economic journals, and wrote several pivotal books on racial and gender equality in the job market,child care, and social security. She was also engaged in spreading her progressive agenda outside academia, in the public arena.

This chapter provides a biography of Bergmann. It is based on the interview I conducted with her children, Sarah Bergmann and David Bergmann, on November 14, 2025; excerpts from David's eulogy for his mother; her most recent *Curriculum Vitae*, which David kindly sent to me; some unpublished archival material; and her published interviews and memoranda (Bergmann, 2005, 2009; Olson, 2007; Olson & Emami, 2002; Saunders & King, 2000; Strober, 1998). Major works published by Barbara are not mentioned here, as they are discussed across the Chapters 3–8.

Bergmann always defined herself as a feminist. She wrote:

> I became a feminist (a person who believes in working toward the equality of women and men) at age five, when it became obvious to me that you needed your own money to be an independent person, which was what I wanted to be when I grew up. (Bergmann, 2005, p. 11)

G. Becchio, *Barbara Bergmann*, Great Thinkers in Economics,
https://doi.org/10.1007/978-3-032-18696-6_2

As an economist, her *cursus honorum* spanned from her first job at the Bureau of Labor Statistics in 1948 to her status of Professor Emerita at American University (1988) and at the University of Maryland (1997).

Though, her feminist view and her commitment to economics were intertwined earlier than the official start of her career as an economist, as testified by Bergmann herself on January 4, 2003, on the occasion of the celebration of her 75th birthday organized by IAFFE (the International Association of Feminist Economics). On that occasion, she remembered some previously unknown episodes of her life, including when, as a graduate student, she went to a broker's office located on 17th Street in downtown Manhattan to invest some money for better financial security. She told him: "I have just come in with $5700 and I'd like your advice on what to invest in". The man took her hand and said: "Listen, this is not the time for a nice Jewish girl like you to put the money into distressed assets". With no more explanation, Bergmann left his office and decided that she wanted "to become an economist dedicated to making people's, and especially women's, lives better".[1]

The reason the broker emphasized Barbara's Jewishness is not explained by Bergmann, but it is a relevant element. As she always recounted in her autobiographical memoirs, being a Jewish woman provided her with a double minority status that was especially tough in the United States during her youth (1930s–1950s), and pushed her to focus her attention on one of the biggest topics of her lifelong research: the economics of discrimination on the basis of ethnicity and gender.

The economic analysis of discrimination led her to work outside academia, writing articles for newspapers and magazines, providing testimonies to Congress, and getting involved in lawsuits as an expert. Her intense activity in the public domain made her a tireless social reformer advocating for social welfare policies, capable of providing a better life for people in need.

[1] The episode is a transcription of the recorded video of Bergmann's celebration, held in IAFFE's archive, box 5. David M. Rubenstein Rare Book & Manuscript Library Collections.

2.1 Early Feminist, Brilliant Student

Barbara Rose Berman was a New Yorker. She was born on July 20, 1927, to Martin Berman and Nellie Wallenstein Berman in a Jewish neighborhood located in the Bronx. At 11, she moved to Queens, where she attended junior high school, in which she particularly excelled in algebra, and Forest Hill High School, both public schools.

Barbara's parents were Jewish immigrants.

Her mother, born in Romania, used to claim that she was a family member of the Grand Rabbi of Bucharest, a claim that Barbara was very doubtful about. Arriving in New York around 1903, with her five children and no husband, Barbara's maternal grandmother and her family settled down in the Lower East Side of Manhattan and all the children were sent to work: the girls, including her aunt and mother, worked in a trimming factory, never went to school, and never became citizens.[2]

Barbara's father was born in New York, but his parents were immigrants as well, coming from the Russian part of Poland. Their family name, Berman, is a typical Ashkenazi one, while Jews from Romania, like Barbara's mother, were usually Sephardic. Thus, Barbara inherited both sides of the main Jewish groups of the diaspora.

According to Barbara's memories, none of her three grandparents ever learned to speak English. This element illustrates the isolation of European immigrants of the time, as well as the difficulties of first generation immigrants in integrating into American society. Barbara's father was a typographer and typesetter who was able to get a decent salary (circa $50 a week) during the Great Depression of the 1930s, a period when poverty was widespread and unemployment was around 25%. Barbara was a kid at that time, and she remembered well people begging for money in her neighborhood, such as a talented fiddler, who, after having collected some money from a casual audience in the street, was willing to sell his violin to whoever would offer him a job.

[2] This was the time of the second major wave of immigration to the United States: immigrants were from Eastern and Southern European countries, either Jews (coming from Balkans, Galicia, and Russia) or Catholics (mainly coming from Italy). They tended to remain in the city and to live in the Lower East Side in overcrowded and poorly ventilated tenement buildings without indoor plumbing, which were inexpensive and allowed proximity to fellow immigrants. Tenements often doubled as sweatshops or warehouses where immigrant women worked under male supervision (Becchio, 2025; Blake, 2006; Dolkart, 2006).

Barbara's parents were strong supporters of the Democratic Party. Her father was a member of the typographers' union, and she was deeply affectionate toward the figure of Franklin Delano Roosevelt, whose death in 1945 was a shock for Barbara: "I felt like a father had disappeared" (Olson & Emami, 2002, p. 55). Barbara remembered that she had always been a genuine democratic progressive at heart. She wrote:

> My childhood during the Great Depression left me a strong believer in having government provide help when people face problems either beyond their power to control, as was the case during the Depression, or because they have made improvident choices, or because they have legitimate needs that they cannot supply out of their own resources. (Bergmann, 2005, p. 11)

Neither young Barbara was attracted to Marxism, albeit it was quite popular in her Bronx Jewish community, nor she was attracted to it later, in the 1970s, when the feminist movement often arose within a Marxist cultural and political framework. She used to place one of her worst memories on her visit to the World's Fair in 1939, where her teacher, a fanatic Marxist, forced the kids to spend all the time in the Soviet pavilion, where Barbara was "repulsed" by objects and manufactures celebrating Stalin's cult of personality (Olson & Emami, 2002, p. 56). In stark contrast, on that occasion, Barbara was amazed by the General Motors pavilion, which showed "the marvelous capitalistic world of the future" (Bergmann, 2005, p. 12).

Moreover, there was a time, when she was 17, when she:

> felt sure [that I would] earn during my glorious future career [and] hated the idea that the riches might be taxed away by the government and transferred to those less talented and less hardworking than I. (ibid)

Nonetheless, she soon moved past this attitude and adopted a genuine progressive position, believing in a capitalist society that continuously requires adjustments and reforms. She wrote:

> Even today, among many of the academic people I know, "capitalism" is a term of opprobrium, and they attribute to capitalism everything bad that happens. A lot of what is bad does come from capitalism, but that can be corrected by appropriate government regulations, and by the generous

government provision of important services and safety nets. But a lot of what is good and indispensable comes from capitalism too. (ibid, 12)

Barbara's parents split up during World War II, when she was a teenager. Her father quit his job and became a merchant seaman, but he passed away a few years later, at 45. Barbara had no siblings: she candidly admitted that her mother chose to have three abortions in order to prevent the family from getting into trouble due to lack of money. As we will see, Barbara was a fierce supporter of free choice in all matters, including abortion (see Chapter 8).

After her father left, Barbara and her mother moved to Queens and her mother started to work with her sister, Aunt Lena Wallenstein. Barbara's mother never stayed at home, not even when her husband was still in the picture. Her life experience, as a working woman and a single mother, had a profound influence on Barbara's interest in supporting affirmative action in favor of single mothers and fatherless children (see Chapter 7).

Although both uneducated, Barbara's parents were supportive of her decision to go to college, contrary to her high school teachers, who never suggested that a young woman pursue any career. Barbara's mother would have loved for her daughter to have a career as a piano soloist at Carnegie Hall, and provided Barbara with private lessons, but music was not Barbara's first choice. Although she later became an opera lover, she admitted she did not practice enough and preferred to focus on science and mathematics. Much later, she took classes in violin as an adult and involved the rest of the family in her passion for chamber music (see Chapter 9).

After the war, she applied to MIT and Cornell. MIT rejected her, probably because of genderdiscrimination: the guy who interviewed her found her decision to become a civil engineer ridiculous, in spite of her excellence in mathematics. She remembered: "the interviewer looked at me as though I were crazy" (Olson & Emami, 2002, p. 56). Cornell also excluded Barbara from the engineering school, though she was admitted to the School of Arts and Sciences, where she earned her BA in mathematics in 1948.

While in college, Barbara began to attend some courses in economics, mainly under the influence of Gunnar Myrdal's book, *An American Dilemma* (Myrdal, 1944), a book inspired by W.E.B. DuBois's ideas about the lack of education of Black people in the U.S., attributed to the perversity of the system, based on prejudice, racism, and segregation, as the main cause of their lower competitive standards in the job market. As we will see, Myrdal's idea was pivotal in Bergmann's first research on job discrimination against Blacks, that she later extended to gender discrimination in the marketplace (see Chapters 3 and 4). In a memorandum dated 2009, held in her archive, Bergmann wrote that she had been a member of theNational Association for the Advancement of Colored People (NAACP) since 1945,[3] and that she regretted not being more active in the civil rights battles of the time.

During college, Barbara added a second major in economics, being the only female student in her cohort. When she was asked why she chose economics she replied: "it's the enjoyment of petty mathematical triumphs" (Olson & Emami, 2002, p. 57). Barbara's sense of humor and self-irony were well known among those who knew her even superficially and pervaded almost every writing she published, as well as her interviews and public speeches.

After her graduation from Cornell, Barbara went back home to live with her mother, who seemed to be quite disappointed by the fact that she was not able to get a fiancé besides a degree. Apparently, Barbara realized that her mother actually encouraged her to go to college to increase her chances of finding a good husband.

Nevertheless, her mother's attitude reinforced Barbara's feminist desire to be independent. The situation in late 1940s was not easy for a young woman: the available positions for women were limited to maids, department store saleswomen, and clerical workers. In addition, as mentioned earlier, beingJewish made things harder. Out of necessity, Barbara accepted a job as a typesetter, but it lasted two days, and she stayed unemployed for 1 year. Then, under her mother's pressure, she attended Teachers College at Columbia University. Barbara remembered that decision as one of the worst of her life: the curriculum was "ridiculous", and she was asked to prepare kids to live under collectivism, something that really annoyed Bergmann, "given my anti-Marxist impetus" (ibid. p. 58).

In 1949, she applied for a job with the federal government and started to work at the New York Regional Office of the Bureau of Labor Statistics, although at the lowest professional level. She was placed in the unit

[3] NAACP was founded in 1909 in New York by W.E.B. Du Bois, Mary White Ovington, and Ida B. Wells to promote the advancement of Black people in terms of civil and political rights.

that answered inquiries from the public. A year later, she was appointed head of the unit. She worked there for 3 years, and that was a fundamental experience: at the Bureau she started to seriously work on data about discrimination against Blacks. Furthermore, there was only one Black employee in the office, and he was not allowed to sit with the rest of the staff to prevent people from seeing him. This circumstance made Barbara frustrated and furious. Nonetheless, she had the impression that government agencies were indeed useful for the benefit of the society as a whole.

It was at that time that, at her office, Barbara met an economist, who suggested that she go to graduate school. Her boss wrote a letter of recommendation, and Barbara applied for a Ph.D. in economics at Harvard and Cornell. That was the time when she wanted to make some extra money and went to the broker's office on 17th street, who refused to help her (see Chapter 1). She was accepted by both schools, and she chose Harvard, Radcliffe College, the college reserved for women. Among fifty Ph.D. students in economics, there were only four women. It was 1952, and she received no fellowship until 1 year later, but her mother backed her (Saunders & King, 2000, p. 307).

In 1953, Barbara got a teaching assistantship in economic statistics at the Sociology department, under Fred Mosteller's supervision, and she left the Bureau. She served as an instructor at Harvard University from 1953 to 1961. In the last academic year (1960–1961), she was appointed Senior Research Associate.

At Harvard, she was mainly influenced by three economists: Guy Orcutt, who introduced her to computer simulation; Alvin Hansen, who taught Keynesian macroeconomics, and was a fierce supporter of economic policy and government action; and Edward Chamberlin who taught models of imperfect competition by insisting on analyzing complex and real economic phenomena, such as oligopoly, as well as pioneering experimental economics. Under their influence, Barbara realized that economic theory may be extremely persuasive, yet misleading, and should always be confronted by empirical observation. Unlike the majority of her colleagues, she found Chamberlain's empirical methodology much more interesting than Wassily Leontief's advanced theory course. Furthermore, she attended Gottfried Haberler's course on business cycles and interacted with Fritz Machlup, too. Meanwhile, in 1954, she started to teach mathematical economics to graduate students, becoming a teaching assistant for both Leontief and Franco Modigliani.

Bergmann's Ph.D thesis was about an input/output model based on Leontief's work applied to the New York metropolitan area, a work "she was never proud of", supervised by a visiting professor, Edward Hoover (Saunders & King, 2000, p. 60), and published in 1961 (Berman et al., 1961).

In 1958, Bergmann earned her MA and Ph.D.

Although Barbara's training as an economist was entirely focused on empirical research, she had a hard time returning to the real world when she left Harvard: "I was reluctant to go out into real world. When I did, no one offered me a job" (ibid). She was also quite isolated, without a real social life, and not mentored by any of the big names of the time.

Between 1957 and 1961, she worked as an economist at the New York Metropolitan Regional Study, and between 1961 and 1962, she served as Senior Staff Economist at the Council of Economic Advisers, in the Executive Office of the President. After JFK's assassination, Barbara left Washington DC, and went back to academia: she moved to Massachusetts, where she got a non-tenured associate professorship position at Brandeis University (1962–1964), which never turned into a tenured one.

Meanwhile, between 1963 and 1965, back in Washington DC, Barbara worked at the Brookings Institution as a senior staff member: the position gave her the chance to travel to Bolivia and Peru to work on the consequences of creating new infrastructure, such as highways, for the development of Bolivia (Bergmann, 1966). Between 1966 and 1967 she was Senior Economic Advisor at A.I.D., in the U.S. Department of State.

Since its foundation, in 1966, Bergmann was a member of the National Organization for Women (NOW),[4] although she was not very active until her retirement, when she tried to involve NOW in lobbying for more money for government child care programs, unfortunately, as she wrote, "without any progress with it" (Bergmann, 2009, p. 3).

[4] Founded by Betty Friedan and Pauli Murray in 1966, NOW is a feminist organization in the United States that promotes gender equality and women's empowerment within the present political system.

2.2 The Economist Within and Outside Academia

In 1965, Bergmann was appointed Associate Professor of Economics at the University of Maryland. She taught graduate macro, graduate micro, graduate econometrics, and, in the early 1970s, she started a course on poverty and discrimination, which became her major research field that she actually never abandoned. She taught an undergraduate course on computer methods in economics, at a time when "computers were 'way out' [and] there were no PCs" (ibid). That was the very beginning of her work on microsimulation in economics that led her to publish on computer simulation of the U.S. economy, which "unfortunately fell into a black hole" (Bergmann, 2005, p. 62) (see Chapter 5).

In 1971 she became a full professor and remained in Maryland until 1988.

Meanwhile, at a party in New Haven, she had met Fred Heinz Bergmann, a genetic scientist, who worked at the National Institute of Health. They got married in 1965 and stayed together for almost 40 years, until Fred passed away in 2004. According to feminist economist Marianne Ferber, a close friend of the Bergmanns', they had had only one serious disagreement in their long and happy marriage: in adjacent columns in *Who's Who*, Barbara claimed to have been married on July 14, 1965, while Fred claimed they were married on July 16 (Ferber, 1998). Barbara admitted that while "pushing for women's equality [wa]s not a big thing in [her] husband's life", he always shared with her half of the housework and child care, allowing her to manage her own work (ibid, 3).[5]

The Bergmanns became parents of Sarah and David, "both feminists, of course", as pointed out by Barbara in a memorandum dated December 2004, (Bergmann, 2005, p. 2). Sarah was born during an academic leave (1967), when Barbara was working at the Agency for International Development as a senior economic advisor, while David was adopted one year later.

David Bergmann wonderfully described his parents' partnership in his eulogy to Barbara.[6] He wrote:

[5] Barbara Bergmann's papers, box 8. David M. Rubenstein Rare Book & Manuscript Library Collections.

[6] As mentioned earlier, David Bergmann kindly sent me the eulogy for his mother.

> [Fred was] her very best friend and life-partner (…) he was such an important part of her life for so many years, I felt it was important to include him. Fred was truly my mother's most favorite person ever. A lot of you knew him and can attest to the fact that he was genuinely one of the kindest, warmest, and most decent of people. I think he bears mention for the simple fact that he put up with my mom day-in and day-out for 46 years (…) and for those of you who knew my mom, and I'll be the first to say it, that wasn't always easy. I really think he balanced her out so well and his presence had a significant impact on the trajectory of her life. Professionally, he was a critical proofreader of her many manuscripts and articles. Domestically, he shared in the child-rearing and the housework (…) And I don't think he did this because he felt he had no choice being married to a woman who believed so strongly ingender equality. He did it because he himself also believed in equality. He was a lot of things to my mom: He was the family gardener and caretaker of the greenhouse. He cooked and cleaned, but mainly he was just a loyal and loving companion who knew better than anyone (and this was something he would remind me of often), *"that my mom's bark was always far worse than her bite"*. The fact that they shared similar perspectives and values in regards to politics, religion, and humanity in general, provided my mom with her favorite pastime of all: sitting with my dad at the table each morning over coffee, each with their newspaper, laughing and lamenting at what my mom thought was one of the most entertaining aspects of life (…) the absurd and sometimes tragic comedy of the human experience. (Bergmann, 2015)

Both Barbara and Fred worked full time: "I did not stay home with my children for 5 minutes" said Bergmann (Saunders & King, 2000, p. 312). They shared home responsibilities and decided to regularly hire housekeepers and nannies, with Barbara as "a great believer in commodification", albeit she claimed that the "whole nanny thing", the only option available at that time, "was a bad idea" that should be replaced by a system of public child care system. However, she had no regrets about their decision. With her usual sense of humor she declared: "my children weren't too badly damaged; they turned out to be Democrats" (Bergmann, 2005, p. 62).

Nonetheless, being a married woman and mother with a full time position was not easy. Fifteen years passed between Barbara's Ph.D. and her tenure. At a faculty party she noticed that a male colleague of hers, Norton Dodge, with whom she shared the same education (Ph.D. in Economics), schools (Cornell and Harvard), and even the same marriage year (1965), was far richer than her, having made his money in the stock market (perhaps recalling the episode of the broker in Manhattan who refused to help her in doing some financial investments). When she asked her husband Fred why so, he replied: "Barbara, you've gone as far from the Bronx as a girl can go in one generation!" (ibid, 61).

Barbara's bitter disappointment as well as Fred's sentence perfectly summarized gender barriers and biases of the time.

Barbara's decision to adopt commodification for child care and housekeeping in her own life was fundamental in her battle for affirmative action that continued until the end of her life (see Chapters 3 and 7) as well as for her ideas about care work (see Chapter 6). In 1998, for example, Barbara applied for and received a fellowship from the Rockefeller Foundation for working together with Suzanne Helburn on the manuscript "The Child Care Problem: Policies to Repair a Flawed System", aimed at formulating a new child care policy for the U.S., and discussing the political issues that involved in moving toward it. Their suggested policy included a major federal subsidy program, considerably beyond the suggestions that were recently made by President Clinton.

As reported in a memorandum, in the early 1970s, Bergmann started to battle the gender wage gap in her department of the University of Maryland (Bergmann, 1986) which affected her salary, despite her outstanding publications and her commitment within the major economic associations of the country (see Chapter 3). In fact, between 1970 and 1973, Barbara was a Board member of the *American Economic Review*, and between 1970 and 1971 she received the Ford Faculty Research Fellowship. In 1974, she was a founding member and first President of the Eastern Economic Association, and, in 1976, she was elected vice-president of the American Economic Association.

Furthermore, in the 1970s, Bergmann, was a leading member of the American Economic Association's Committee on the Status of Women in the Economics Profession (CSWEP). CSWEP was established in 1971 to address gender disparities in employment in economics departments, during a session on 'What Economic Equality for Women Requires', chaired by Barbara, at a meeting of the AEA in New Orleans (Becchio, 2020).[7] On that occasion, several resolutions were established to improve

[7] On that occasion the group of women economists, led by Carolyn Shaw Bell, worked overnight on a set of resolutions to be presented to President John Kenneth Galbraith, President-elect Kenneth Arrow, and the executive committee. AEA board members reacted favorably to their requests by establishing CSWEP, which aimed to monitor the progress

the status of women economists within academia.[8] Between 1970 and 1978, she was the Director and Principal Investigator of the Project on the Economics of Discrimination, at the University of Maryland.

As reported by Presser (1998), in the 1970s, Bergmann was actively involved in a successful feminist mobilization that led to the removal of the concept of the "head of household" from the U.S. decennial censuses beginning in 1980. The concept, adopted by the Bureau of the Census, but never measured or tested, resulted offensive to many people.[9] It was Bergmann's idea, in 1976, to create a small group of feminist social scientists, in the Washington area, to stop the Census Bureau from using the concept in the future. At that time, she was a member of the Census Advisory Committee of the American Economic Association.

Two meetings were held to achieve their purpose.

The first meeting occurred in early November 1976, when Bergmann raised the headship issue. Presser recalled that as feminists, they were sympathetic to the objections raised about its continued use; though as researchers, they were concerned about whether there would be an analytic cost to dropping the concept. On that occasion, the group converged on two resolutions: the formation of an organization called "Social Scientists in Population Research" (SSPR), "purposely not mentioning 'feminist' in our title, so that we would be taken more

of women economists within academic departments and to reduce the gender gap in the profession (Barlett, 1999). A year later, in 1972, CSWEP's first official document was published and signed by Walter Adams, Kenneth Arrow, Francine Blau, Martha Blaxall, Kenneth Boulding, Carolyn Shaw Bell, John Kenneth Galbraith, Collette Moser, Barbara Reagan, Myra Strober, and Phyllis Wallace. The document admitted that the origin of women's discrimination within the discipline was "a special case of a much larger process of role learning and role acceptance, which begins almost from the moment of birth" (Bell et al., 1973, p. 1049).

[8] Among them, Resolution I declared that AEA recognized "that economics is not exclusively a man's field" (Bell et al., 1973, p. 1053), and that no gender discrimination will be tolerated in admission, recruitment, salary, or financial aid. The Caucus also requested a formal commitment to promote equal opportunities, from early career encouragement to tenured positions, which led to the formation of 'Job Openings for Economists' (JOE) in 1974 (Becchio, 2020).

[9] The designation of a family head was used by the U.S. Bureau of the Census from 1790 through 1840. Between the 1850s and 1870s, names of everyone in the household were listed on the census schedule, with no head designated. From 1880 through 1930, all household members were listed by name along with their relationship to the head of the family. From 1940 through 1970, the decennial censuses used the designation of "head of household" rather than "head of family".

seriously"; and the arrangement to meet with two Census Bureau professionals, Arthur Norton, Chief of the Marriage and Family Statistics Branch, and Senior Demographer Paul Glick, to better understand the Bureau's resistance to dropping the headship designation, and what information (if any) would be lost without it.

In the second meeting, which occurred in late November 1976, Norton and Glick were invited, although "Norton refused to attend because he did not want to contend with a group of feminists". Glick pointed out that the headship concept was a pure indicator, aimed at facilitating written reports. Yet, the group noticed that the concept could lead to confusion. For instance, if a grandmother, a mother, and a child were living in a three-person household, and the grandmother reports herself as the head, it was unclear what that meant relative to a similar three-person household in which the mother reports herself as head.

More importantly, with regard to the usefulness of this concept for implementing government programs, Carolyn Shaw Bell pointed out that the term 'headship' was used to justify the denial of unemployment benefits to some women in some states, on the ground that they were not heads of their household (as reported in Bergmann, 1980).

After considerable discussion, the Committee passed the following resolution:

> We believe the term 'head of household' in the questionnaire and in the public tabulations is ambiguous, not currently descriptive of many households, and offends numbers of people. Elicitation of the information needed by users of the Census is feasible through other methods. We urge that the Census Bureau make the change in time for the 1980 Census. (Presser, 1998, p. 146)

In December 1976, Bergmann, along with three other members of the group (Wendy Baldwin, Heidi Hartmann, and Sandra Tangri) met with Congresswoman Patricia Schroeder, at that time Chair of the U.S. House Subcommittee on Population and the Census. The concept was finally dropped by the Bureau of the Census, though it continued to be used within some other data collection agencies.

As Bergmann wrote to the Director of the Bureau of the Census in 1980:

> I have just received the Census publication, *Money Income in 1978 of Households in the United States,* issued February 1980. I was distressed to see that the term "head of household" continues to be used in the body of the report, and that data continue to be tabulated by characteristics of the 'head'. My understanding was that the Bureau had undertaken to discontinue using the ambiguous, subjective and invidious term 'head'. Its use in this publication is rendered even more extraordinary by the fact that the questionnaire which collected the data and which is reproduced on the back of the report does not ask respondents to name the head of their household. It does ask respondents to name the 'person or one of the persons who (owns/rents) this home'. (Bergmann, 1980, in Presser, 1998, p. 152)

Throughout her life, Bergmann was committed to the policy-making arena and devoted enormous time and effort to providing leadership and working with organizations aimed at promoting social welfare (see Chapter 7).

From 1977 to 1988, she served on the Congressional Budget Office Panel of Economic Advisors, and periodically testified before Congress on race and gender issues. She served as a member of the following institutions: Advisory Board to the Women's Law Project (1974–1980); the Board of Directors, Public Interest Economics Center (1975–1976); the Congressional Budget Office Panel of Economic Advisors (1977–1988); the American Economic Association Advisory Committee to the Census Bureau (1977–1982); the Price Advisory Committee, U.S. Council on Wage and Price Stability (1979–1980); Chair of CSWEP (1983–1984); the Board of Directors, Economists Allied for Arms Reduction (1992); and as a Senior Research Associate at the Council on Contemporary Families (2003).

In 1985, Barbara was named Washington Woman Economist of the Year by the Washington Women Economists (WWE), a professional association founded in 1979 to promote the status of women economists.

Her activity in disseminating her economic policy ideas was intense: between 1981 and 1982, she became a regular contributor to the Sunday business section on economic affairs of the *New York Times*; she wrote in several other newspapers and magazines (see Chapter 8).

After spending 25 years at the University of Maryland, in 1988, Barbara left the institution as Professor Emerita and accepted a position as Distinguished Professor of Economics at the American University.

In Bergmann's archive, the hiring process of her move to the American University is well described. In a letter dated March 10, 1988, to Dean Betty Bennett, Barbara listed her conditions for accepting the position. They included: a retirement date at her option; participation in a system of annual merit and cost-of-living percentage increases in salary; a single-person office until retirement; access to any facilities after retirement; unlimited use of university's computers for research purposes before and after retirement; assignment of graduate assistant for all courses; a teaching load of three courses per year to be chosen among 'Computer Methods in Economic Research' (undergrad), 'Computer Simulation of Economic Systems' (grad), 'Sex Roles in Economic Life' (undergrad), and 'Dissertation Workshop' (grad); waiver of tuition for children; and extra funds for books, journals, and travel expenses. Dean Bennett's reply, dated May 25, 1988, confirmed Barbara's requests and added a personal note to express her and Provost Greenberg's delight in having Barbara aboard.[10]

As we can see, Bergmann made sure to include in her non-negotiables the possibility to teach gender issues in economics and computer simulations. The syllabus of Bergmann's course in 'Sex Roles in Economic Life' (Fall semester 1994), held in her archive, reveals her perspective in addressing gender inequality issues in economics: the underrepresented role ofwomen in the job market; the patriarchal attitudes of men who avoid any form of caring; and the defense of affirmative action, such as quotas, to ensure genderequality in parenting.[11] That course, introduced in late 1980s, became the vital groundwork for the creation of the Graduate Program on Gender Analysis in Economics (PGAE) at

[10] Letters are held at Barbara Bergmann's papers, box 8, David M. Rubenstein Rare Book & Manuscript Library Collections, Duke University.

[11] Here is the complete list of readings: "Why Men don't Rear Children. A Power Analysis" by M. Polatnik; "Sex Roles: the Argument from Nature" by J. Trebilcot; "Process of Occupational Sex-Typing" by S. Cohen; "Still a Chilly Climate for Women" by F. Flam; "Why I'm Leaving Standford: I Wanted My Dignity Back", by F. Conley; Johnson v. Transportation Agency, Santa Cruz County, CA; "Can Quota Be Defended", by B. Bergmann; "Shifting Perspective on Marital Law" by S. Westerback; "On Patriarchy Born: The Political Economy of Fertility Decisions" by N. Folbre; "International Traffic in Reproduction" by J.G. Raymond; "Father Participation in Paternal Leave", by I. Haas; "The Housewife: An Unjustified Financial Burden on the Community" by R. Culliver; "Child Care. The Key to End Child Poverty", by B. Bergmann; "Getting Tough on the Poor", by A. Hacker; "Sex Differences in Economic Well-Being" (statistical data). Barbara Bergmann's papers, box 8, David M. Rubenstein Rare Book & Manuscript Library Collections, Duke University.

the Economics Department of American University (see Chapter 9).[12] As reported in the American University newsletter (2010), Bergmann's tenure as a distinguished professor at AU from 1988–97 marked the beginning of incorporating gender issues into economic education. As soon as she arrived at AU, she introduced two courses (undergrad and grad) "in what was then called 'women and the economy'" (Tabak, 2010, p. 3).

Since 1963, Bergmann was a long-time activist with American Association of University Professors (AAUP), an association founded by John Dewey, who served as its first President in 1915. She was also involved with the Association's Special Committee on Athletics.

In 1975 she co-authored a report, published on the AAUP bulletin, *Academe*, on gender wage gap (Bergmann & Maxfield, 1975), and other issues, such as academic freedom and tenure (Bergmann & Poston, 1998), national health insurance (Bergmann, 1991a),[13] administrative spending (Bergmann, 1991b),[14] teaching evaluation (Gray & Bergmann, 2003),[15] and the quota system (see Chapter 7) in American academia.

[12] AU annually grants an award to a promising graduate student to support gender research in economics in the name of Fred and Barbara Bergmann. Retrieved on October, 2nd, 2025 from: https://www.american.edu/cas/economics/gender/.

[13] She argued that the U.S. must move to a national health-insurance system, even though many full-time professors currently benefit from employer-provided coverage. More than 30 million people lack insurance, including part-time faculty, small business owners, adult children, and workers without benefits, leaving many with no access to preventive care and forcing them to seek treatment in overcrowded public hospitals (1991a).

[14] She argued that the expansion of administrative spending in American higher education has seriously harmed campus life, academic work, and institutional efficiency by generating excessive bureaucracy (Bergmann, 1991b).

[15] The authors argued that at best, evaluations identified only the strongest and weakest teachers; they could not accurately distinguish among the large middle group. Their use in high-stakes decisions, such as tenure and raises, also harmed students' education. Faculty reported feeling pressured to water down content, inflate grades, or avoid innovative teaching methods for fear of lower ratings. Statistically, students' grade expectations strongly influenced their evaluations, encouraging grade inflation and ultimately undermining educational quality. Although many better measures of teaching existed, such as exam performance, mentoring, availability, curriculum development, and involvement in research, these required time and peer judgment, which administrators wished to avoid. Instead, they embraced a corporate model focused on "customer satisfaction," while using "below-average" ratings to limit tenure and salary increases. The evaluation process itself also damaged faculty–student relationships. Because evaluations could jeopardize careers,

Starting from data available at her own University of Maryland, she developed a model to study wage differentiation between male and female faculty members to be applied to any university where the salary information was available (Bergmann & Maxfield, 1975).[16]

In 1985, she wrote an article for *Academe* about thegender wage gap among college professors, by arguing that any differences across academic departments often reflect bias, especially sex discrimination, rather than legitimate market forces or differences in job requirements. She argued that many academic jobs involve similar responsibilities, such as teaching, research, advising, and service, so equal pay across departments should be the default. Therefore, correcting discriminatory differentials requires deliberate equity adjustments, funded either through increased budgets or by redistributing salary increases. Though costly, these changes are feasible and necessary (Bergmann, 1985).

Between 1990 and 1992, Bergmann served as President of the AAUP: "with Barbara as President, things will never be dull" as Mary Gray, chair of the nominating committee, said (AAUP, 1990, p. 1). On that occasion, Barbara stated that her main goal as President of AAUP would be:

> to improve higher education in our country on all levels, particularly in working to improve access for disadvantaged students; to increase freedom of speech for students and faculty; to prevent any form of sexual harassment; to introduce collective bargaining; to reduce administrative duties and expenditures in college administration, which waste money and faculty time with insatiable demands for paperwork. (ibid)

the system tempted faculty to cheat, prompting administrators to impose procedures that implicitly accused teachers of dishonesty. Furthermore, students were required to collect and deliver the forms, creating an atmosphere of suspicion that both parties felt but rarely acknowledged (Gray & Bergmann, 2003).

[16] Koch and Chizmar (1976) criticized the Bergmann–Maxfield salary model for examining sex discrimination in faculty pay without including measures of faculty productivity or performance. Because productivity often declines with age, they argued that a Bergmann–Maxfield "broad-brush" model unfairly favored older faculty and misidentified discrimination. Bergmann (1976) replied that while productivity data would be ideal, it was often impossible to gather in a usable form on most campuses. She also insisted that a "broad-brush" method was better than no analysis at all, especially since universities routinely lacked complete and unbiased data. Finally, Bergmann criticized the view that paying women less based on assumptions about lower future productivity (e.g., related to childbearing) violated the Equal Pay Act and emphasized that feasibility and fairness both required workable methods, not ideal but unattainable ones.

In 1994–1995, she served as President of the Society for the Advancement of Socio-Economics, and became a member of Sandia National Laboratories to work on a project of microsimulation modeling.

Earlier, in 1989, she was involved in two research projects that combined her lifelong interest: she became a member of the French-American Foundation to analyze French child care, and she participated in reviewing a model of the academic science and engineering labor market for DRI Data Resources at McGraw-Hill.

In 1992, Bergmann was among the founders of the International Association for Feminist Economics (IAFFE). The first annual meeting of IAFFE was held in 1992 at the American University, and she served as IAFFE's fourth President between 1998 and 1999 (see Chapter 6).[17]

Meanwhile, in the early 1990s, she joined the Economists' Group for Policy Issues that was a member of the National Council of Women's Organizations, based in Washington, D.C., an umbrella organization encompassing most women's groups of the time. Barbara, along with feminist economist Heidi Hartmann, was very committed to organizing it. The group was small, consisting of perhaps five or six feminist economists. They rated the presidential candidates (Clinton, G. Bush, and Perot) using a system that showed Clinton as the most favorable. The group and its rating, an early example of such an initiative, received considerable media attention.[18]

2.3 A Publicly Committed Emerita

In 1997, Bergmann retired from academia and became Emerita at the American University. She was already Emerita at the University of Maryland, since she left it in 1988. She never quit her research work, though. When, in 2000, she was asked which part of her work made her happiest, her reply was "social policy and the feminist policy", albeit she sadly noted that "the establishment rewards women whose work says that women earn less because women are different" (Saunders & King, 2000, p. 314).

During her life, Barbara received several awards. In 1995, she received AAUP's Georgina Smith Award for her advocacy for the status of women

[17] In 1998, Volume 4, issue 3 of *Feminist Economics* was entirely dedicated to Bergmann and her work (see Chapters 6 and 9).

[18] I owe this information to Heidi Hartmann, who kindly shared it with me in an email exchange in November 2025. See also Hartmann (1998).

in academia. In 1996, she received an Honorary Degree from De Montford University (UK); later, in 2000, she received another honorary degree from Muhlenberg College. In 2004 was awarded the Carolyn Shaw Bell Award. In the words of one of her nominators:

> Barbara fully lives up to your requirements of vision, intellectual curiosity, informed willingness to take risks, and most particularly determination to make the world a better place. Further, she always takes great joy in being able to do what she does.[19]

In the same year, she was also awarded the Eastern Economic Association award "for reminding those in her discipline that economics should be interdisciplinary, engage in methodological pluralism, and advocate policies that help people".[20]

In 2006, she was the recipient of the Charlotte Perkins Gilman Fellowship from the American Academy of Political and Social Sciences and spent a semester as a resident scholar in Bellagio (Como Lake). In the same year, she also began to work on the failure of competition in the labor market for nurses, hired by the Service Employees International Union (see Chapter 8).

Between 2007 and 2010, she worked on a project on poverty measurement and poverty policy promoted by the Stanford Center for the Study of Poverty and Inequality.

On February 19, 2010, the American University organized a tribute to Bergmann and launched in her honor a fundraising drive to establish a scholarship for research in gender issues in economics.

[19] The Carolyn Shaw Bell Award was created in January 1998 as part of the 25th Anniversary celebration of the founding of CSWEP. Carolyn Shaw Bell, the Katharine Coman Chair and Professor Emerita of Wellesley College, was the first Chair of CSWEP. The Bell award is given annually to an individual who has furthered the status of women in the economics profession, through example, achievements, increasing the understanding of how women can advance in the economics profession, or through mentoring of others. Retrieved on November 5th, 2025, from: https://web.archive.org/web/20120207033528/http://www.cswep.org/PDFs/Bell_announcement.pdf.

[20] Both awards are in the forms of plaques and are held at Barbara Bergmann's papers, box 8, David M. Rubenstein Rare Book & Manuscript Library Collections, Duke University.

In 2014, she was hired as a regular commentator by *HuffPost*.[21] She published only two blog posts: on single-parenthood and on climate change (see Chapter 8).

In her last 10 years, she became a supporter of Dignitas, an association founded in 1998 in Zurich, aimed at ensuring death with dignity for its members. In her archive there is the text of a testimony in support of the Maryland House Bill 1021, from the 2015 legislative session, which proposed the Richard Israel and Roger Moyer Death with Dignity Act, a bill to legalize physician-assisteddying.[22]

In her testimony Barbara wrote: "I am strongly in favor of getting this help to Maryland citizens". She emphasized that this has nothing to do with euthanasia for the disabled, which she would not be in favor of. Rather, this is a free individual act of liberty, and there is no evidence that a similar legislation had previously promoted any form of mistreatment of the disabled. She concluded:

> Another objection to this legislation is that God wants to choose the time of each person's death. Those who believe that will, of course, be free to avoid using this law. However terminal ill people who desperately want to limit their suffering, and who believe that God would not object, should be allowed to do so.[23]

On April 5, 2015, the "Betty Friedan of the economics profession", as Heidi Hartmann called her, passed away. Two obituaries, published respectively in *The New York Times* and *The Washington Post*, underlined her vigorous feminism and her role as one of the most influential figures in the economic world (Schwartz, 2015; Weil, 2015). Both obituaries recalled her as an enthusiastic and outspoken participant in policy debate as well as her visionary perspective and her commitment "to using economic knowledge for social betterment". Both obituaries recalled that her major book, *The Economic Emergence of Women* (1986; 2005), was a

[21] The agreement is held in her archive Barbara Bergmann's papers, box 4. David M. Rubenstein Rare Book & Manuscript Library Collections, Duke University.

[22] The bill was introduced in the Maryland General Assembly in 2019, and it would have allowed terminally ill adults to obtain a prescription from a physician to end their lives. Named after the late Marylanders Richard Israel and Roger Moyer, the act was patterned on Oregon's physician-assisted suicide law but ultimately did not pass.

[23] Barbara Bergmann's papers, box 4. David M. Rubenstein Rare Book & Manuscript Library Collections, Duke University.

groundbreaking work on questions of race and gender in the economy, on employment discrimination and on the underlying assumptions held by the majority of those in her profession, and a pivotal book in a research field "once shared by relatively few but now a recognized area of economic thought" (See Chapter 9).

References

AAUP (1990). New AAUP president, Barbara R. Bergmann. *Footnotes*. pp. 1–2.

Barlett, R. (1999). CSWEP: 25 Years at a time. *The Journal of Economic Perspectives, 12*(4), 177–183.

Becchio, G. (2020). *A history of feminist and gender economics*. Routledge.

Becchio, G. (2025). Economic ideas serving social reforms: The case of Lillian Wald and Mary K. Simkhovitch in the settlement movement (New York, 1880s–1920s). *History of Economic Ideas, 33*(2), 123–138.

Bell, C., et al. (1973). Findings of the American economic association committee on the status of women in the economics profession. *The American Economic Review, 63*(5), 1049–1061.

Bergmann, B. (1966). The Cochabamba-Santa Cruz highway in Bolivia. In G. W. Wilson et al. (Eds.), *The impact of highway investment on development* (pp. 17–54). Brookings Institution.

Bergmann, B. (1976). Correspondence: Bergmann replies. *Academe, 62*(1), 126–128.

Bergmann, B. (1980). Letter to Vincent F. Barabba, director, bureau of the census, March 19. As reported in Presser (1998).

Bergmann, B. (1985). Comparable worth for professors. *Academe, 71*(4), 8–10.

Bergmann, B. (1986). *Draft Statement*. Box 7. Barbara R. Bergmann papers, David M. Rubenstein Rare Book & Manuscript Library, Duke University.

Bergmann, B. (1991a). Professors should back national health insurance. *Academe, 77*(3), 62.

Bergmann, B. (1991b). Bloated administration. Blighted campuses. *Academe, 77*(6), 12–16.

Bergmann, B. (2005). Pushing for a more humane society. *American Economist, 49*(2), 11–15.

Bergmann, B. (2009). *Memorandum*. Barbara Bergmann's papers, Box 8. David M. Rubenstein Rare Book & Manuscript Library Collections, Duke University.

Bergmann, B., & Maxfield, M. (1975). How to analyze the fairness of faculty women's salaries on our own campus. *Academe, 61*(3), 262–265.

Bergmann, B., & Poston, M. (1998). Academic freedom and tenure: University of the District of Columbia: Massive terminations of faculty appointments. *Academe, 84*(3), 46–55.

Bergmann, D. (2015). *Barbara Rose Bergmann Eulogy.* Unpublished as stated.

Berman, B., Chinitz, B., & Hoover, E. (1961). *Projection of a metropolis: Technical supplement to the New York metropolitan region study*. Harvard University Press.

Blake, A. (2006). *How New York became American, 1890–1924*. John Hopkins University.

Dolkart, A. (2006). *Biography of a tenement house in New York City*. University of Virginia Press.

Ferber, M. (1998). Barbara Bergmann: Scholar, mentor and activist. *Feminist Economics, 4*(3), 3–4.

Gray, M., & Bergmann, B. (2003). Student teaching evaluations: Inaccurate, demeaning, misused. *Academe, 89*(5), 44–46.

Hartmann, H. (1998). The economic emergence of women: Bergmann's six commitments. *Feminist Economics, 4*(3), 169–180.

IAFFE (International Association for Feminist Economics. International Association for Feminist Economics records, David M. Rubenstein Rare Book & Manuscript Library, Duke University.

Koch, J., & Chizmar, J. (1976). The unfairness of how to analyze the fairness of women's salaries on your own campus. *AAUP Bulletin, 62*(1), 123–124.

Myrdal, G. (1944). *An American dilemma: The Negro problem and modern democracy*. Harper & Bros.

Olson, P. (2007). On the contributions of Barbara Bergmann to economics. *Review of Political Economy, 19*(4), 475–496.

Olson, P., & Emami, Z. (2002). Barbara Berman Bergmann. In P. Olson & Z. Emami (Eds.), *Engendering economics. Conversations with women economists in the United States* (pp. 53–72). Routledge.

Presser, H. (1998). Decapitating the U.S. Census Bureau's 'head of household': Feminist mobilization in the 1970s. *Feminist Economics, 4*(3), 145–158.

Saunders, L., & King, M. (2000). An interview with Barbara Bergmann: Leading feminist economists. *Review of Political Economy, 12*(3), 305–316.

Schwartz, N. (2015, April 11). Barbara Bergmann, trailblazer for study of gender in economics, is dead at 87. *New York Times,* A21.

Strober, E. A. (1998). Interview with Barbara Bergmann. *Feminist Economics, 4*(3), 5–6.

Tabak, J. (2010). Honoring pioneering feminist economist Barbara Bergmann. *American University Department of Economics Newsletter*.

Weil, M. (2015, April 13). Barbara Bergmann, leader in gender-based economics, dies at 87. *The Washington Post*, p B4.

CHAPTER 3

Race and Sex in the Job Market

Life's experience and intellectual research are often, maybe always, intertwined in a scholar's interest and work, and Bergmann's was not an exception. She faced discrimination as a Jew and as a woman in her job search as well as in her career (see Chapter 2). In fact, the economic analysis of discrimination was constantly at the center of her research from the beginning of her career to the end. In doing so, Bergmann fundamentally reshaped the way scholars and policymakers understood discrimination in the labor market. Her central contribution was the formalization of the crowding hypothesis, which she applied to the American job market. Her analysis of discrimination was first developed to understand the limited access that Black workers had to job opportunities, likely inspired by the episode at her job in the New York Bureau of Labor Statistics, where her Black male colleague was forced to stay at the rear to prevent customers from seeing him, as well as by reading Myrdal's pivotal book on racial discrimination (Myrdal, 1944). Later on, she extended her crowding hypothesis to the female workforce.

She interpreteddiscrimination not as a temporary inefficiency that a free competitive market would eliminate, as some neoclassical labor economists of the time, such as Gary Becker (1957), suggested, but rather as a structural mechanism that conferred tangible benefits to dominant groups, namely white men. Bergmann demonstrated that discrimination

G. Becchio, *Barbara Bergmann*, Great Thinkers in Economics,
https://doi.org/10.1007/978-3-032-18696-6_3

could, in fact, be efficient when viewed from the perspective of privileged groups: occupational crowding restricted minority workers, such as Blacks and women, to a narrow set of lower-remunerated jobs, and served to preserve higher wages and status for dominant workers while further pushing marginalized groups into overcrowded jobs (Bergmann, 1971, 1974a, 1980).

In Bergmann's analysis of women's participation in the labor market, she added the expectations of full-time domestic labor as mothers and homemakers to the crowding hypothesis that leads them to low wages, income, and pensions. This combination makes women face the double burden, as data revealed. Bergmann in fact constantly adopted an empirical approach that relied heavily on demographic data, including marriage and divorce rates, fertility patterns, and the relationship between education and family dynamics. This data-driven methodology enabled her to move beyond theoretical assertions and provide evidence thatdiscrimination was deeply embedded in both economic and social structures.

Likely, her personal choice to hire a full-time nanny may have been a consequence of her economic ideas on the double burden, or vice versa.

A key aspect of Bergmann's critique concerned the cultural stereotype that middle-class American women, being devoted full time to unpaid household work, should be satisfied with their roles because they enjoyed high standards of living. In her *American Economic Review* article, Bergmann (1981a) dismantled this myth by showing that many women's lived experiences contradicted the idealized image of the happy idealization of the American housewife (see Chapter 4). Instead, women faced significant economic dependency, limited career development, and reduced autonomy, conditions that could not be equated with genuine well-being.

Bergmann's agenda aimed at eliminating discrimination in the job market focused on affirmative action plans, especially those applied to big corporations. She wrote:

> Business executives have become increasingly conscious of the fact that white men now account for less than half the workforce, and that they will have an even smaller share in the labor market of the future, especially among young workers. If employers continued to allow white men to maintain their traditional monopolies over large segments of the job

> market, they would be forced to recruit important elements of their workforce from a smaller and smaller share of all workers. (Bergmann, 1996, p. 279)

Among affirmative action plans, Bergmann always supported quotas. She wrote:

> [Quota is] a word that apparently has strong negative connotations for most people. Most of those favoring affirmative action have denied that the label is apt. However, if paying attention to the race and sex of those being hired or promoted, and making sure that some unconventional candidates are successful implies that a quota system is being used, then it must be acknowledged that an affirmative action plan with goals and timetables has quota-like aspects. In fact, it is just these aspects that are necessary to enable a corporation to move forward toward integration. Without them very little change is likely. (ibid, p. 286)

By emphasizing the efficiency of exclusionary practices for dominant groups, Bergmann revealed why discrimination endured despite its social costs. Her empirical research provided a blueprint for subsequentfeminist economics and continues to inform debates on occupational segregation and the structural roots of gender inequality.

3.1 Understanding Structural Unemployment and Occupational Segregation

One of the major interests in Bergmann's economic perspective was to understand and overcome the phenomenon of structural unemployment, which was not merely an academic concept, but rather a social issue that eroded social welfare as well as the dignity of individuals.

While working at the Brookings Institution, Bergmann focused on the challenges of defining, measuring, and understanding this phenomenon (Berman, 1965[1]; Bergmann & Kaun, 1967). According to her, the most useful way to define structural unemployment is in terms of the consequences of policy actions. In other words, the definition should clarify

[1] At the time of this publication, Barbara was not married yet. Hence, when referring to this paper, I have adopted her maiden name, Berman, as it appears in that publication.

how unemployment responds, or fails to respond, to government policies, training programs, and economic expansions. She pointed out that structural unemployment arises because of heterogeneity in the labor force. Workers differ in their skills, education, demographic characteristics, and access to opportunities. Employers, likewise, differ in what kinds of skills they demand. When the supply of labor and the demand for labor do not align, some workers remain unemployed even during periods of economic growth. This mismatch is the essence of structural unemployment, and the main fault of economists is their tendency to regard workers as perfectly interchangeable without taking heterogeneity into account.

Berman presented a model of labor market flows. She depicted unemployment as a room with two entrances and two exits. Workers can enter unemployment either from previous jobs or from outside the labor force. Similarly, they can exit unemployment either by finding a job or by leaving the labor force altogether. This framework allows researchers to analyze how people move in and out of unemployment, and how mismatches affect those movements. For example, if many people enter unemployment from jobs, but few are able to exit back into jobs, this suggests that the demand for their specific skills has weakened. Alternatively, if people frequently move from unemployment to non-participation, it may mean that discouraged workers are giving up on the job search.

Both patterns reveal structural features of the labor market that cannot be explained by short-term fluctuations in demand alone. Furthermore, she introduced two key concepts: the employment expansion path, which describes how employment grows as demand increases, and theskill endowment point, which refers to the mix of skills that the labor force possesses. If the path of job creation and the distribution of worker skills do not match, structural unemployment results. This mismatch can occur even during periods of overall improvement in the labor market and, if it persists, structural unemployment will arise.

Berman cautioned against confusing structural unemployment with other causes of group-specific unemployment. For example,Black workers in the United States have historically experienced higher unemployment rates than white workers. While one explanation is that Black workers are overrepresented among the unskilled, another explanation is that discrimination pushes them to the "back of the hiring line", making them less likely to be hired, even when they have equivalent skills.

This distinction is crucial for policy. If unemployment stems from structural mismatches, the solution may involve retraining workers, improving education, or reshaping the economy's demand for labor. Ifunemployment stems from discrimination, the solution must involve stronger enforcement of anti-discrimination laws, changes in employer behavior, and broader social reforms.

Blurring the line between these causes can lead to misguided policies that fail to address the real source of the problem.

Hence, Berman insisted that policymakers should direct pay attention to reducing mismatches and distinguishing between mismatches, cyclical downturns, and discriminatory practices, by remaining cautious not to overgeneralize, as structural unemployment does not explain all disparities in the labor market, nor is it the only barrier to full employment.

In 1979, Bergmann wrote a paper for the National Commission on Employment and Unemployment Statistics calling for a major expansion and improvement of labor market data systems to better understand and combat employment discrimination against women and minorities (Bergmann, 1979). She emphasized that while the lack of data was not the main reason for slow progress in reducing discrimination, collecting and publishing relevant information was crucial for shaping national policy and enforcing anti-discrimination laws. Bergmann suggested reforms, based on publishing data cross-tabulated by race and sex, focused on labor turnover, i.e., hires and promotions rather than just total employment, and providing firm-level data for large companies. She highlighted that accurate data on unemployment rates, job distribution, wages, labor market experience, and turnover can help policymakers, researchers, and the public monitor to address discrimination effectively. Overall, Bergmann argued that better labor market information would not only improve anti-discrimination efforts but also enhance understanding of broader labor market issues, including unemployment and low-wage employment.

Bergmann began to work on the relationship between structural unemployment and discrimination against minorities in the job market, starting with the analysis of the situation of Black workers, which she later extended to women. Her main target wasBecker's idea of competition as a force that compels businesses to act in a nondiscriminatory way, "an idea that has been widely accepted as realistic by economists" (Bergmann, 1989a, p. 71). However, according to Bergmann, empirical observations of discrimination showed the contrary. Furthermore, Bergmann rejected Becker's human capital theory, which was adopted to explain wage differentiation, by pointing out that the overwhelming majority of empirical studies show that a large gender or racialpay gap cannot be attributed to minorities' lower job qualifications or performance, but rather to the effects of discrimination, regardless of the overall unemployment rate. As she wrote:

> Low unemployment rates, however, will not by themselves root out the employer practices which keep women, Blacks and Hispanics in inferior jobs at low pay. Likewise, high unemployment rates need not prevent progress in rooting them out. (Bergmann, 1981b, p. 30)

Hence, according to Bergmann, economists must recognize the existence of a considerable (if not absolute) segmentation of the labor market with respect to race and sex, which, according to her, must be distinguished from structural unemployment. Based on a Keynesian assumption, according to which unemployment is not determined only by the supply of workers, but also by the overall level of aggregate demand in the economy, Bergmann pointed out that reducing unemployment differences between groups (women, men, Blacks, and white people) would not necessarily reduce the overall average unemployment rate. In other words, simply moving women and minorities into jobs traditionally held by white men, is desirable, albeit it would not by itself create more total jobs, since the total volume of employment mainly depends on macroeconomic conditions, such as demand, spending, investment, and fiscal and monetary policy. However, economists should promote a more even distribution of labor market imbalances: if unemployment is more evenly spread across occupations, this can reduce inflationary pressures for a given average unemployment rate. In turn, that could encourage policymakers to adopt more expansionary policies, which might indirectly boost overall employment.

As it was pointed out, "the Bergmann criterion for underrepresentation (and overrepresentation) is more demanding than a simple comparison of proportions in the population and in occupations. When her index takes a value significantly below unity it signals the presence of discriminatory processes" (Gibson et al., 1998, p. 89). As Blau et al. (1998) explained, Bergmann's analysis of segregation allowed us to better understand the pay gap. Furthermore, Bergmann's articles on segregation published in the early 1970s "foreshadowed an entire generation of research that estimated the impact of the racial and gender composition of a job on earnings" (Lapidus & Figart, 1998, p. 7).

Later, in the 1980s and 1990s, feminist scholars extended Bergmann's results and strengthened them by analyzing accessible datasets, showing that implementing equal pay would appreciably narrow the race and gender-based wage gaps especially among women of color, who face a status of intersectional minority. As they wrote: "Bergmann's theoretical insights pointed us in just the direction we needed to go" (ibid, p. 8).

3.2 Discrimination on the Basis of Race

In the 1960s, the U.S. passed major civil rights legislation aimed not just at outlawing discrimination, but also at encouraging, and in some cases requiring, fairer hiring practices toward Black workers and other minorities, such as Executive Order 10925 (signed in 1961 by President Kennedy),[2] the Civil Rights Act of 1964 (Title VII),[3] Executive Order 11246 (1965),[4] and the Civil Rights Act of 1968,[5] signed by President Johnson. The first two acts did not directly incentivize employers with subsidies, rather they made discriminatory hiring illegal and exposed firms to lawsuits and sanctions if they failed to comply. The third one represented a shift from mere prohibition to proactive obligation by promoting affirmative action.

Although there were no straightforward financial incentives, like tax breaks or subsidies for hiring Black workers, the combination of legal prohibitions against discrimination and affirmative action requirements for federal contractors effectively pressured employers, especially those tied to government contracts, to expand opportunities for Black workers.

This set of federal legislation had two major consequences. First, it changed the dynamics of the job market in the United States. Second, it provoked a significant debate among economists of the time.

[2] It first introduced the idea of affirmative action for federal contractors, requiring them to ensure applicants were treated equally without regard to race, creed, color, or national origin.

[3] It prohibited employment discrimination on the basis of race, color, religion, sex, or national origin, and created the Equal Employment Opportunity Commission (EEOC) to enforce fair employment practices.

[4] It required federal contractors not only to avoid discrimination but also to actively take steps to hire and promote more Black workers and other minorities.

[5] Although it focused mainly on housing, it further expanded protections against discrimination in related domains, including access to credit and opportunities connected to residential segregation, which indirectly affected employment opportunities.

On one side, economists, such as Jacob Mincer (1963) and Gary Becker (1964), applied human capital theory to labor economics in order to explain that discrimination was mainly due to employers' preferences for hiring higher educated workers, i.e., white men, over lower skilled workers, i.e., Blacks and women. Nonetheless, according to human capital theorists, employers who discriminate would restrict their labor pools, raise their costs, and lose out to less biased competitors. Hence, government intervention would be unnecessary, or even distortive, because in the long run, the market itself would naturally eliminate these inefficiencies.

On the other side, economists such as Bergmann, showed an opposite view: discrimination was neither a matter of employers' preferences nor a temporary inefficiency, but rather a deeply embedded phenomenon that required legal intervention to address both wage disparities and occupational segregation, since the two mutually reinforced each another.

Hence, as mentioned, in the late 1960s and early 1970s, Bergmann started to work on discrimination in the job market on the basis of race (Bergmann, 1968, 1969a, 1969b, 1971; Bergmann & Lyle, 1971). In her early writings, she adopted the notion of human capital and admitted that the racial wage gap was mainly due to Black people's lower education and training. Nonetheless, she argued that Black people were actually less educated because of the role of institutionalized racism in the U.S., which included school segregation that represented a major determinant of this phenomenon. Furthermore, Black people's lower human capital was due to a deficient share in work experience. In fact, the formation of human capital takes place not only in schools, but also in workplaces where experience is gained. Hence, as she stated in a report submitted to the Congress of the United States, Black people's human capital must be increased by specific public investments in training (Bergmann, 1968).

In a paper she published in the *American Economic Review* (Bergmann, 1969b), Bergmann went further, exploring the growing intersection between urban economics and the pressing social issues facing American cities in the late 1960s. She observed that the field of urban economics had begun to shift its focus: from analyzing the size and structure of urban economies to addressing the urgent realities of the urban crisis, namely, poverty, racial inequality, crime, inadequate education, deteriorating housing, poor transportation, and strained municipal finances. Although these problems did not originate purely from economic processes, Bergmann argued that they were deeply intertwined with economic structures and performance. The social and environmental conditions of a city both influenced and were influenced by its economic activity, creating a complex web of mutual correlation.

Bergmann's primary goal was to propose a systematic framework for tracing the relationship between an urban area's economy and its social, environmental, and governmental (SEG) problems. Rather than developing a formal economic model based on a theoretical approach, she proposed adopting an accounting system based on available data, to be intended as a structured way to organize and integrate information about how different sectors of the urban economy affect the city's social conditions. Such a system would not explain causality in the strict theoretical sense, but it would allow policymakers and researchers to visualize connections, identify where data were missing or theories were misleading, and to estimate the cumulative effects of various economic activities on urban well-being.

Drawing an analogy to the National Income Accounts, Bergmann argued that her accounting system would serve a similar function for urban policy. Just as national income accounts help policymakers assess economic performance and sectoral imbalances, an urban accounting system could help identify which sectors of a city's economy were contributing to or alleviating urban problems. It would highlight which industries or institutions were lagging in addressing social and environmental issues and which were performing well. For Bergmann, the ultimate purpose of her accounting system was practical and political, and it should be aimed at mobilizing efforts to confront urban social and environmental challenges. While not a substitute for detailed research, it would encourage researchers to present their findings in a way that could be integrated with the work of others and used coherently in policy debates.

At the core of Bergmann's argument was the idea that business establishments, government agencies, and households all affected the urban crisis through their ordinary economic performance. Firms influenced urban problems through several channels. Firms' level of production influence the supply side of the market: for instance, construction companies affect the housing supply. Firms' hiring practices, such as whether they employed Black workers or excluded them, influence segmentation of the market. Firms' geographic location determines which jurisdiction received their tax payments. Finally, firms' production originates externalities, either negative, such as pollution, or positive, which affect the quality of life in the area. Even if firms' actions were not consciously designed to influence social or environmental outcomes, their effects were nonetheless significant. Similarly, governments and households played major roles through their employment decisions, consumption patterns, and residence choices, all of which shaped the economic and social geography of urban areas.

Bergmann thus called for a comprehensive system that treated businesses, households, and government agencies as interconnected components of the urban economy. Only by mapping their interactions systematically, she argued, could economists and policymakers begin to understand and address the structural roots of urban inequality and decline.

Her proposal represented an early attempt to bridge the gap between traditional economic analysis and the broader study of urban social problems, emphasizing that the 'urban crisis' was not only a moral and political issue but also an economic one, requiring rigorous, data-driven insight into how cities functioned as integrated systems.

In a paper co-authored with a Ph.D. graduate, Bergmann applied her accounting system to the racial segmentation within the job market, which was measured by an index that compared the different distributions of Blacks and Whites among occupations in 1966, computed for 67 industries and for 45 metropolitan areas. The index was computed separately for men and women and omitted domestic workers in private households.[6] Bergmann's aim was to estimate the extent to which discrimination was responsible for the inferior position of equally qualified Black workers in the job market. The results of their analysis showed that the racial occupational and wage gap could be only partially explained by the lower quality of education of Black workers and their suggestion was to encourage non-discriminatory behavior by employers, rather than rely on investments in higher education, transportation and so forth (Bergmann & Lyle, 1971).

In the same year (1971), Bergmann presented her crowding hypothesis applied to Black workers, who were relegated to certain sectors where marginal productivity is lowered by the high level of supply, as a possible counter-narrative to Becker's analysis of discrimination in the job market (Becker, 1957). Inspired by Taussig (1923) and Dewey

[6] The table of indexes revealed that, at that time (1966), the highest gender occupational gaps among Black and white male workers were in geographical areas located in Texas, Alabama, and Virginia (Bergmann & Lyle, 1971, p. 414).

(1952), Bergmann analyzed the effect on white incomes of a reduction in discrimination and pointed out the presence of a 'racial division of labor', which was aimed at benefitting the low-income white population. Hence, a reduction of discrimination would lead to a significant decrease in white workers' income; while keeping the *status quo* would benefit white workers.

In 1972, Bergmann coauthored a paper with William Krause, aimed at testing effective progress in the racial integration of employment, using data from the U.S. Equal Employment Opportunity Commission (Bergmann & Krause, 1972). Their results were quite frustrating: in spite of some anti-discriminatory efforts that were made, racial discrimination in the job market persisted and required accelerated efforts to promote incentives to hire Black workers. In the same year, Bergmann and Atkinson (1972) criticized Harold Guthrie's model that related changes in family income to the aggregate rate of unemployment, by showing that a stable 3.5% unemployment rate might bring equality between Black and white families in about 25 years (Guthrie, 1970).

According to Bergmann and Atkinson, Guthrie treated the individual parts of the income distribution as if they were independent of one another, overlooking that total family income is inappropriate as a dependent variable because it hides from view the presence of multiple workers and multiple job holders who enter into the calculation of family income. Equality needs to be assessed in terms of the ability of individual blacks to be considered for employment on the same footing as whites and, as well, the ability of equally qualified blacks to command identical wages to whites in the same occupations.

Bergmann's critique of Becker's explanation of discrimination became her main target in her paper published a few years later in the *Eastern Economic Journal*, when she extended her crowding hypothesis to women's employment too (Bergmann, 1974a). As mentioned earlier, according to Becker, discrimination is the effect of individual prejudices or tastes that are costly and lead to inefficient outcomes in the market. Nonetheless, Becker claimed, racial prejudice damages the discriminator employer, who faces higher costs for employers of their favorite group, as well as workers, who gain lower wages. Hence, discrimination leads to inefficiency that is incompatible with a free and competitive market which, given its competitive nature, will spontaneously reduce the effect of discrimination. Becker's analysis was firmly anchored in the neoclassical economic tradition, which presents the market as a self-correcting mechanism naturally gravitating toward efficiency. Within this framework, discrimination is treated as the outcome of individual preferences (tastes) and is expected to be eroded over time by the competitive pressures of the free market.

Bergmann's perspective directly challenged this view. For her, the market was not an impartial, self-regulating arena but an institution deeply shaped by social and cultural forces. Discrimination, in her analysis, could not be explained away as the sum of personal choices; it was the product of structural biases and entrenched power relations. Consequently, Bergmann argued that markets left to themselves would not eliminate inequality but would reproduce and even reinforce it, making deliberate intervention and corrective policies indispensable.

According to Bergmann, employment discrimination against Black workers revealed two distinct patterns.

First, people with similar qualifications were often sorted into very different kinds of jobs depending on their race, i.e., Black workers were not distributed across occupations in the same way as white workers.

Second, even within the same occupation, Black workers tended to earn less than white workers. Thus, discrimination operated both at the level of occupational segregation and the racial wage gap.

Bergmann concluded that occupational segregation and wage gap were also consistently observed between men and women.

Against the neoclassical economic analysis that treated these two dimensions of discrimination as separate problems, analyzing them as if they were independent and their effects simply additive, Bergmann proposed a unified framework that combined the pay gap between groups with the crowding model, first suggested by Edgeworth (1922), to show how restricting one group, i.e., women or Black workers, to a narrow set of occupations increases competition within those fields, depresses wages there, and simultaneously inflates wages in occupations dominated by the privileged group.

Henceforth, contrary to Becker's idea that discrimination will lead to inefficient outcomes for discriminators too, Bergmann showed that discrimination leads to economic benefits for the favored group by altering both wage structures and occupational patterns simultaneously.

As pointed out by Olson (2007), Small (2022), and Becchio (2024), Bergmann's occupational crowding hypothesis was soon relegated outside the neoclassical paradigm, in spite of her neoclassical framework, because it did not align with models of perfect competition adopted by the orthodoxy.

In 1976, 10 years after the Civil Rights Act of 1964, Bergmann wrote a report that was meant to analyze the effect of the legislation aimed at outlawing discrimination in employment on the basis of race and sex (Bergmann, 1976). She pointed out that the data revealed that significant disparities persisted into the 1970s, with white men continuing to hold a far stronger position in the labor market than Black men, white women, Black women, and other minority groups. Black women especially found themselves overrepresented in low-paying and unstable jobs, while being excluded from positions with greater prestige, income, and chances for promotion.

In fact, white men continued to have better access to stable jobs, higher wages, and better opportunities for advancement in their career compared to the above-mentioned minorities. The explanations for these disparities, Bergmann noted, included discriminatory practices, such as hiring biases, unequal pay, and barriers to promotion; differences in education, skills, motivation, and cultural factors.

Going beyond economic elements of unemployment and wages, Bergmann insisted that the position of disadvantaged groups in the labor market was a key factor in many of America's broader social problems. In fact, disadvantaged groups who were excluded from good jobs were far more likely to experience poverty, rely onwelfare, live in blighted urban neighborhoods, and be associated with higher rates of crime. Furthermore, social programs, such as those aimed at addressing poverty, urban decay, or crime directly, might be less necessary or at least less costly, if structural improvements were made in the labor market opportunities, making them available to minorities.

Bergmann sharply criticized economists' attitude, *à la* Becker, who denied the role of social and cultural factors when explaining economic phenomena, by defining their view as myopic. While sociologists and anthropologists rightly pointed out that labor market inequalities reflect broader social hierarchies: just as societies rank people on the basis of race, sex, age, or religion, so too do workplaces replicate these hierarchies, with employers internalizing these norms and therefore tending to perpetuate them in their hiring, promotion, and pay decisions. However, Bergmann insisted, economists denied that discrimination and social norms clearly shape employer behavior, assuming that employers act as rational profit-seekers and make decisions based primarily on productivity. Even when it might be profitable to hire or promote women or minorities, employers hesitate to challenge social hierarchies and avoid workplace tensions.[7]

A few years earlier, Bergmann had already pointed out that economists were unable to provide possible measures against discrimination in the job market, rather they were concerned with trying to determine how discrimination works and the general direction of its effect on wages and employment of particular groups (Bergmann, 1974b). Bergmann suggested that any realistic measurement of discrimination must take account of its long-term effects. For example, if employers routinely refuse to hire or promote Black workers, young Black students may lower their educational ambitions, guidance counselors may advise them to "be realistic", and parents may struggle to motivate their children in the face of systemic barriers.[8] A similar vicious cycle occurs for women: discrimination reduces opportunities that limit skill development and motivation, which is then used to justify further discrimination. According to Bergmann, the redistribution of opportunities in the job market should be seen as a social good. Hence, a vigorous government intervention focused on affirmative action is required to reduce the segmentation of the market into crowded sectors.

3.3 Discrimination on the Basis of Sex

As mentioned, starting from the early 1970s, Bergmann applied her analysis of discrimination in the labor market to women who faced limited access to jobs and often had full-time responsibilities as mothers.

[7] The same argumentation was adopted a few years later on the occasion of the 33rd Annual Meeting of the Industrial Relations Research Association, held September 5–7, 1980 in Denver (Bergmann and Darity, 1981).

[8] Bergmann's model was later refined by other economists who found that Black workers, men and women, were crowded into low-wage occupations and crowded out of high-wage occupations (Albelda, 1986; Gibson et al., 1998; Hamilton et al., 2011). For example, because the economy had changed since 1960, particularly with the decline in manufacturing and the introduction of informatics, Gibson et al. (1998) expanded Bergmann's study to include white-collar occupations. More recently, Bergmann's model has been discussed and complemented by Holder (2018) who pointed out that, due to demographic changes in the U.S. labor market, and consistent with Bergmann's model, African American men remain underrepresented in high-wage occupations. However, this group does not appear to be overrepresented in low-wage occupational categories when the analysis is conducted between major low-wage occupational categories rather than within them.

She grounded her investigation on the analysis of available data, which included marriage and divorce rates, the relationship between educational level and fertility and divorce, and related variables. In fact, her archive contains several datasets on these topics, mainly published by the U.S. Bureau of the Census in the early 1970s (Bergmann, 1974c; Bergmann et al., 1978).

In the 1980s, Bergmann devoted her research work almost exclusively to gender discrimination in the labor market. Data revealed that by the 1980s, full-time female workers in the United States were still earning 20%–25% less than men with comparable education and work experience.[9]

As mentioned earlier, Bergmann rejected economists' idea that widespread discrimination would contradict employers' economic self-interest, since it would mean overlooking capable women in favor of less-qualified men, as well as economists' attitude of attributing women's lower wages to their own choices, particularly their acceptance of responsibility for housework and child care. She insisted on pointing to case studies, lawsuits, and statistical analyses as evidence of pervasive and systemic discrimination that played a central role in women's economic disadvantage.

Bergmann pointed out that as women's labor force participation grew, it became common to argue that policy targets for average unemployment rates should be adjusted upward to account for the historically higher unemployment rates among women. Nonetheless, according to Bergmann, such 'target corrections' often rely on an oversimplified view of the labor market in real terms.

For a more realistic representation of women in the labor market experiences, which can better inform discussions of the potential effects of future macroeconomic and structural policies, two major factors should be taken into account: women's higher rates of turnover into and out of the labor force compared with men; and labor market segmentation by sex, where occupational segregation creates less favorable supply-demand conditions in female-dominated sectors.

According to Bergmann, during economic crises, women's higher turnover contributes little to their excess unemployment over that of men's, due to occupational segregation; when the economy nears full

[9] In Japan, the gender pay gap was even wider, while in many other developed countries it was somewhat smaller. As a matter of fact, no country had yet achieved earnings parity between men and women.

employment, voluntary turnover becomes more relevant, but its impact on a properly calculated full-employment unemployment rate is minimal. Although an increase in female participation largely reflects younger cohorts' stronger attachment to the labor force, which should reduce average turnover over time, occupational segregation worsens women's labor market position. Hence, occupational segregation, which remains the primary driver of women's higher unemployment, must be addressed through policies promoting access to male-dominated jobs.

Bergmann defined discrimination on the basis of sex, whether through social practices, restricted access to resources, or reinforced gender roles, as a consistent limit to women's economic opportunities. Women's economic disadvantage has often been linked to expectations surrounding childbirth, childrearing, and socialization into traditionally female roles, which in turn increased their dependence on men for access to economic resources and reinforced their subordination within both the family and society.

According to Bergmann, discrimination on the basis of sex was the effect of occupational segregation: women have historically been concentrated in a limited range of jobs, such as clerical work, retail sales, low-level factory work, nursing, librarianship, teachers in kindergartens and primary schools, and service occupations. By 1985, about half of all female workers in the United States were employed in occupations that were more than three-quarters female.

Research on workplace composition showed that segregation was even more extreme than broad occupational statistics suggested. Bergmann's agenda of remedies to sex discrimination combined lawsuits, affirmative action, and pay equity. As Lapidus and Figart (1998) pointed out, that combination unified the efforts of both feminist economists and civil rights activists. Bergmann devoted a significant amount of time to analyzing lawsuits, such as in the case of Lucky Stores (1993),[10]

[10] *Stender v. Lucky Stores, Inc.* was a class action brought on behalf of women employees of Lucky Stores, Inc., who were accused of systematically denied promotions, higher-paying jobs, and full-time hours to women, while assigning them to lower-level, dead-end positions, creating a 'two-workforce' system, with men dominating managerial and advancement-track roles, while women were concentrated in positions like cashier and deli-head, which had limited opportunities for promotion or higher wages.

Home Depot (1998),[11] and Wal-mart (2001),[12] concluding that most of the time, they were less effective than the affirmative action agenda. Anti-discrimination lawsuits have helped define what legally constitutes discrimination. Courts have ruled that sexual harassment is discriminatory, struck down neutral tests that disproportionately exclude women and minorities unless they are job-related, and prohibited statistical discrimination based on group averages. Occasionally, large class-action suits result in substantial damages, sending a signal to other employers to avoid similar practices. Still, lawsuits alone cannot drive workplace equality.

The Equal Employment Opportunity Commission (EEOC) can solve only a small share of complaints, and cases are difficult, slow, and often yield little change in employer practices. Most discrimination also goes undetected: job applicants rarely know how their qualifications compare to those hired, and employees in dead-end roles may not pursue complaints without alternatives. Finally, many workers are unaware that workplace segregation by race or sex is illegal.

Summing up, Bergmann noted that despite legal frameworks, enforcement had achieved only limited success in reducing gender disparities, as employers long held biases about women's capabilities. More aggressive measures, such as affirmative action plans with specific hiring goals and timetables for women, introduced in government contracting, were weakly enforced.

Affirmative action, Bergmann insisted, enforced by government agencies provides a means to break the cycle of workplace biases, by requiring firms to adopt selection procedures that override the prejudices of individual managers or employees. Because compliance is mandatory,

[11] *Butler v. Home Depot*, was a class action case filed in Southern California, challenging Home Depot's practice of gender discrimination in placing new female employees, either in sales positions or as cashiers. Sales jobs offered pathways to advancement into roles such as department supervisor or assistant store manager, whereas promotion prospects for cashiers were minimal. Approximately 77% of newly hired men were assigned to sales, compared with only about 20% of newly hired women. The women who did reach the sales floor were typically placed in home décor or gardening, i.e., areas stereotyped as "women's work." Attorneys for the plaintiffs described the situation as akin to a glass ceiling reinforced by glass walls, because women were largely excluded from the entry-level positions that led to promotion opportunities.

[12] *Duke v Wal-Mart* was a major class action lawsuit brought by nearly 1.5 million female employees who accused Walmart of gender discrimination in pay and promotions. Although the class was initially certified, the U.S. Supreme Court later reversed the certification, ruling that the plaintiffs' claims did not demonstrate sufficient commonality.

employers can tell male workers that integration is not a choice but an obligation. This reduces the ability of lower-level employees to block candidates on the basis of race or sex and redirects any hostility from the employer to the government.

Bergmann pointed out that another approach should be applied, i.e., pay equity, or 'comparable worth', aimed at raising wages in traditionally female occupations to align with those in male-dominated jobs requiring comparable skill, effort, and responsibility (Bergmann, 1985, 1986, 1987a, 1989b; Bergmann & Figart, 1989; Bergmann & Gray, 1984).

A pay act must establish the principle of equal pay for equivalent jobs by making mandatory for government contractors.[13] Nonetheless, according to Bergmann, the campaign for pay equity, or comparable worth, works only if political conditions are favorable. She wrote:

> The real impetus behind the pay equity campaign is the growing belief among women and among men that the present lineup of wage rates is unfair. It is plain to see that women are far behind men of equivalent education, skill, and intelligence in terms of pay. Economists have long derided St. Thomas Aquinas' idea of 'the just price'. But what people think is right and decent does influence their economic actions. This is especially true in matters of personnel administration, where a sense of grievance and unfairness can reduce productivity. Many of the women in the typical female occupations are single mothers, single-handedly supporting children at or close to the poverty line. Increasing fairness and reducing poverty are good reasons for pushing pay equity. (Bergmann, 1987b, p. 51)

By citing sociologists Bielby and Barron (1984), Bergmann provided evidence that in 60% of firms, men and women were segregated, disproving the idea that firms hire the best worker who applies for an opening, regardless of sex, was unrealistic. Therefore, Bergmann offered

[13] The Federal Fair Pay Act of 2003 was introduced in the 108th Congress (H.R.1695 and S.841) to prohibit wage discrimination on the basis of sex, race, or national origin by requiring equal pay for work of equal value, rather than solely for identical work. The proposed legislation sought to narrow gender and racial wage disparities by permitting pay differentials only when justified by seniority, merit, or the quantity or quality of work. It further provided for class action lawsuits in cases of violations and directed the EEOC to offer technical assistance to employers in implementing the act. Retrieved on October, 31, 2025 from: https://www.congress.gov/bill/108th-congress/house-bill/1695#:~:text=Introduced%20in%20House%20.

a case study, although economists had tended to dismiss case studies as nothing more than "anecdotal evidence", and considered them useless for forming serious views about an issue. Yet, she sarcastically claimed, it was striking that the same economists who readily embraced theories, which are built on invented stories, hesitated to give weight to true ones.

The case she presented was *Morgan v. Hertz* (1981), which occurred in Memphis. Two women who had worked as automobile rental agents brought the suit. They had applied four times for promotion to station manager when vacancies arose. Each time, they were rejected, and each time the job went to a man, sometimes one with less experience. The women claimed they had been denied promotion because of their sex. They also alleged that male supervisors had repeatedly harassed female agents with intrusive questions about their sexual behavior, which they argued constituted another form of sex discrimination. Although most Hertz rental agents were women, very few women had been promoted internally, despite rental-agent experience qualifying them for station-manager roles. When the lawsuit originated, the city manager in Memphis openly stated that a woman should not serve as station manager because she could not attend off-site training, could not follow angry male customers into restrooms, and ultimately because "a woman's place was in the kitchen".

The judge noted that Hertz had a long history of discrimination and that "a cadre of male management preferred men in management positions and disfavored promoting women". His conclusions were particularly relevant for economists persuaded by Becker's claim that discriminatory firms would be driven out of the market. Hertz, after all, had long been, and remained, the leading firm in its industry.

That case also raised questions about whether the discriminatory behavior of managers reflected official company policy or the independent actions of rogue actors within the firm. Evidence suggested the former: senior officials had pressured an employee to sign a false statement denying that the city manager made sexist remarks, and they had persuaded a woman manager, herself previously promoted, only after a struggle, to sign a statement criticizing the plaintiffs' abilities, though she actually believed both women to be qualified. These incidents indicated that the firm had mobilized its resources to support discriminatory managers rather than to ensure fair treatment of women.

Bergmann pointed out that the managers' attitude was often reinforced by male economists of the time, such as Victor Fuchs, who, quoting *Leviticus*, adopted a "half-joking Biblical Theory of Wages" that implied that the value of maidservants should be three-fifths the value of menservants (Fuchs 1986). She wrote:

> The Curse of Leviticus is slowly lifting from American women. Equity and efficiency considerations suggest that policies should be strengthened to accelerate this process. If current discrimination is an important factor in today's labor market, as a considerable body of evidence suggests, then affirmative action and pay equity policies can give considerable net benefits to women (and also to blacks), without imposing high and unfair burdens on other parties in the economy. (Bergmann, 1989b, pp. 59–60)[14]

Bergmann further emphasized the structural consequences of women's occupational segregation by analyzing the gender wage gap. Likely inspired by her 1975 research for AAUP on different salaries within her own University of Maryland (Bergmann & Maxfield, 1975), she observed that women's concentration in certain high-skill but overcrowded jobs perpetuated the gender wage gap. The imbalance between men and women in labor distribution made clear that wages were not simply the product of individual skills or productivity, but were also shaped by the relative proportion of women in a given field: the more women crowded into specific occupations, the lower the average pay became, reinforcing systemic inequality (Bergmann, 1974a).

[14] Fuchs' biblical reference had previously raised a debate between Bergmann, Berga and Sherman, and Fuchs himself (Bergmann et al., 1986). Bergmann lamented that in modern America, gender wage gap mirrored the ratio cited in the Bible, proudly quoted by Fuchs, who failed to account for the role of sex discrimination as a significant factor in the wage gap. Bergmann advocated for affirmative action and pay equity policies, citing examples from countries like Australia, the United Kingdom, and the Nordic European nations, where such measures had successfully raised women's wages without harming the economy. She wrote that among developed countries, the Curse of Leviticus appears strongest in the United States and Japan. Sarah L. Berga and Frederick S. Sherman added that achieving economic parity did not require women to behave like men; instead, they proposed that men and women share family and career responsibilities equally, through measures such as equal parental leave, allowing both parents to pursue careers while enriching children's lives and fully utilizing the talents of all workers. Fuchs responded by acknowledging that childbearing affected women's earnings but contended that the observed wage differences could not be entirely attributed to discrimination, noting that industries employing large numbers of women did not reap abnormal profits, and that uncertainty about future childbearing complicated the relationship between fertility and women's wages.

Her analysis led to the conclusion that reducing the gender wage gap required more than improving women's education or skills: it demanded access to higher-paying, male-dominated professions. Only by breaking down barriers to remunerative jobs could make women achieve wage parity and greater economic independence.

In the late 1980s, Bergmann and Figart (1989) showed that occupational sex segregation remained an issue of economic life: informal and institutional barriers persisted and included sexual harassment, coworker hostility, outdated administrative procedures, and gendered promotion systems. To ensure women not only enter but remain in non-traditional occupations, several retention policies were essential.

Organizations must widely disseminate Equal Employment Opportunity and affirmative action guidelines, clarify promotion opportunities, and establish transparent criteria for advancement. Managers should be held accountable for fostering women's career development and meeting diversity goals, while job ladders in traditionally female sectors, such as clerical work, can serve as pathways into professional and managerial roles. Strong anti-harassment policies and awareness training should be mandatory to combat both overt and subtle forms of discrimination, and seniority systems should be restructured when they restrict women's retraining or lateral mobility. Finally, independent research and longitudinal data collection by the Department of Labor are necessary to identify the key factors influencing women's attrition and retention, ensuring that policy initiatives translate into sustained and equitable participation across all sectors of the workforce.

In the same year (1989), Bergmann published an article on the appropriate policy response togender wage gap, although "some economists imply that the appropriate response is none at all" (Bergmann, 1989b, p. 43). She went back to her critique of human capital theory as the sole explanation for the gap, citing studies, such as Blau (1977) and Blau and Kahn (1981), that demonstrated that women's higher turnover results from their low wages, and women and men with similar wages were found by these researchers to have similar quit rates. Bergmann also noted that American academia was not immune from gender discrimination in promotions, citing the case of MIT female scientists who conducted a study and found that sexist attitudes and behaviors had placed them at a severe disadvantage compared to their male colleagues (1999).[15]

Since the 1970s, Bergmann never stopped working on gender-inequality in the job market.

In her last publications on the topic, published in the 2000s, she insisted on considering gender inequality not just as an obstacle to economic growth, but also as an indicator of unfairness. She was in favor of World Bank Public Expenditure Reviews (PERs). PERs presented a valuable opportunity to advance gender equality by identifying and promoting budget allocations that support women's employment, health, education, safety, and productivity in both formal and informal sectors. The specific policy changes and budgetary priorities vary by country, depending on factors such as development level, existing gender inequalities, data availability, civil society activism, and fiscal capacity. Since women constitute roughly half the population and contribute significantly through both paid and unpaid work, effective programs often require substantial investment in infrastructure and services (Bergmann, 2005).[16]

In one of her latest articles on gender inequality in the job market, she summarized the economic and moral effect of the phenomenon (Bergmann, 2007).

She opened her argumentation by going back to Becker's faults in understanding the problem (Becker, 1957, 1964): by applying human capital theory in an ideal market from which discrimination is absent,

[15] In the late 1990s, biologist Nancy Hopkins, Ph.D., spearheaded an initiative involving 16 women faculty in MIT's STEM departments to push the university to address discrimination, harassment, and unequal treatment of women faculty. They called for change and produced a report documenting these inequities. The report, which gained wide coverage in major media outlets in 1999, prompted MIT to acknowledge the presence of discrimination and ultimately positioned the university as a leader in advancing gender equity in STEM (Zernike, 2023). The report is available at: https://web.mit.edu/fnl/women/women.html.

[16] Bergmann presented a practical example coming from Israel, where a women's advocacy group (Adva Center, 1997) produced a concise, targeted gender-sensitive budget analysis. The report highlighted budget items affecting women, taking positions on those proposals: opposing cuts or policies that limited access to contraceptives, reduced support for job-holding mothers, shifted child allowances to fathers, or perpetuated gender-segregated vocational training; and supporting increased funding for battered women's centers, and reduced day-care fees. Such analyses serve as actionable tools for lobbying and influencing budget decisions to promote gender equity. Available at: dva.org/wp-content/uploads/2015/02/how-the-1998-Israel-state-budget-will-affect-women1.pdf.

or considered just a matter of preferences, Becker made three fundamental mistakes: he denied the phenomenon of occupational segregation, he exclusively focused on thegender wage gap, and he missed empirical evidence by never showing data supporting his theses.[17]

According to Bergmann, occupational segregation not only shapes the supply and demand of labor within specific occupations, but also exerts a powerful influence on wage structures, particularly in jobs dominated by women. Occupations classified as "women's work" often carry lower wages precisely because of this concentration, reinforcing economic inequality between the sexes. Yet, the consequences of occupational segregation extend well beyond financial disparities. When half the population is effectively barred, formally or informally, from a majority of occupational roles, society incurs heavy costs in terms of lost human potential, diminished freedom of self-expression, and violations of dignity. The mechanisms that sustain segregation, whether through biased hiring practices, discriminatory workplace cultures, or stereotypes about women's abilities, undermine not only women's access to economic independence but also their fundamental right to be valued as equals.

By restricting access to a broad range of careers, occupational segregation suppresses the expression of diverse talents, aptitudes, and aspirations. Many women are forced into roles that neither match their skills nor reflect their interests, while opportunities to compete for more fulfilling positions are systematically denied. This mismatch implies that individuals may spend their working lives in jobs they dislike, not because of lack of ability, but because discriminatory barriers prevent them from pursuing alternatives. Such practices waste human resources and diminish overall economic efficiency. At the same time, occupational segregation reinforces the system of female subordination that sustains it: women are seen as "belonging" in certain roles, and the persistence of this pattern both reflects and reproduces gender hierarchies.

The impact is not limited to the workplace. Women's social position more broadly is undermined by the reduced choices and constrained life paths that occupational segregation creates. Limited access to higher-paying and higher-status jobs leads to restricted financial independence, narrower opportunities for self-development, and greater reliance on

[17] She reported that 9/11 victims revealed that out of 343 firefighters who died, only 10 were African American, and not a single one was a woman (Bergmann, 2005).

men for economic security. Hence, occupational segregation not only contributes to wage inequality but also perpetuates women's marginalization in family life, social institutions, and political participation.

As Bergmann pointed out:

> The consequences of occupational segregation go beyond money, important though that is. Having a majority of the job titles effectively off limits to half the population has costs in terms of human expression and human dignity. Some of the means used to enforce occupational segregation also rob women of their dignity. (Bergmann, 2007, p. 216)

As a result, women are fenced off from a disproportionately small share of the overall labor market 'turf'. The portion of the turf allocated to them is often overcrowded, less diverse, and of lower quality compared to the broader and more advantageous turf occupied by men. This imbalance creates an artificial concentration of women in a limited set of occupations, driving down demand within that restricted space and depressing wages in traditionally female jobs. The consequences extend beyond these occupations: even in mixed or male-dominated fields, the specific jobs that women occupy are frequently devalued, with lower pay than comparable roles held by men.

The turf metaphor underscores the structural nature of this inequality. Just as in a physical space, where one group is confined to a smaller, less fertile area, while another group has access to wide and resource-rich territory, women's restricted access to labor market turf limits their opportunities for advancement, recognition, and fair compensation. This segregation does not reflect differences in talent or capability but rather entrenched social and institutional barriers. The result is a self-reinforcing cycle: low pay in the women's turf discourages broader entry, reinforces stereotypes about women's work, and perpetuates the undervaluation of female labor across the entire labor market. Besides occupational segregation, Bergmann pointed out that surveys reveal that a large proportion of women workers experience sexual harassment.

In her latest works on gender inequality in the job market, Bergmann introducedexperimental methods, which inspired some economists of the time, such as Riach and Rich (2002, 2006)[18] (see Chapter 5).

[18] Riach and Rich's (2002) experiment showed that in Australia, Europe, and North America, employment discrimination rates against non-whites applicants have been

Finally, in 2010, Bergmann debated with Paula England about the actual effect of gender egalitarianism. According to England, the devaluation of activities performed by women has not changed: although incentives for women to enter male jobs have increased, incentives for men to enter the female-dominated jobs have stalled. Most people continue to follow gender-biased fields of studies and occupations, except when upward mobility is impossible to achieve. This implies that lower-class women tend to choose segregated female jobs, which remain less remunerative, especially because in those jobs they can express both their ambition as workers and their femininity (England, 2010).

Bergmann criticized England's attitude to attribute sex-segregation in blue-collar sectors to either women's lack of motivation or their perceived lack of ability in performing some jobs. As Bergmann wrote:

> An important barrier to women's entry into any kind of male-dominated job was the restriction of access to training which never occurred in blue-collar trades, usually controlled by unions. (Bergmann, 2010, p. 90)

Furthermore, she added:

> High schools [also] run shop training, which used to be off limits to girls, who were required to take home economics. These classes are still highly sex segregated (ibid).

In addition to training barriers, the resistance of coworkers can harm the morale of newly hired workers who do not fit the traditional image of the employee.

At this point, Bergmann reported an episode that occurred in the early 1970s at the economics department of the University of Maryland. A Black woman was about to fill a vacant position in the administrative

measured at over 25%. A smaller set of experiments has also examined discrimination in hiring against people with disabilities in Britain and the Netherlands, as well as against older applicants in the United States. Riach and Rich's (2006) experiment involved carefully matched written applications submitted to advertised job vacancies in England to test for sexual discrimination in hiring. For each occupation, two standardized résumés were prepared to control for supply-side factors such as qualifications, experience, and age. This ensured that any differences in employers' responses could be attributed to demand-side discrimination. The results revealed statistically significant discrimination against men in the traditionally 'female' occupation of secretary, and against women in the traditionally 'male' occupation of engineer.

staff, but her potential colleagues requested her rejection because they thought she would not be suitable. When she was hired, she initially faced disrespect from her coworkers, who gradually softened their attitude. This attitude tends to be much stronger in male-dominated jobs, such as blue-collar jobs, where employers anticipate employees' attitude and avoid hiring an outsider, i.e., a woman.

Hence, England's thesis can be tested only when discrimination will be drastically reduced. Summing up, the reduction of sex discrimination in blue-collar sectors, according to Bergmann, requires enforced government measures that imply a more inclusive program of apprenticeship by unions; a revision of high school curricula to include girls in shop classes; and affirmative action plans to defend jobs for African Americans. Unfortunately, she concluded:

> President Obama needs to present himself as having equal affection for us all and is not in a position to advocate a policy that would in truth disadvantage white males. (Bergmann, 2010, p. 92)

Bergmann's work on discrimination on the basis of race and sex challenged both economic orthodoxy and cultural assumptions, situating racial and gender discrimination not as an anomaly that markets would correct, but as a persistent and functional feature of the job market.

References

Adva Center. (1997). *How the proposed 1998 Israel state budget will affect women*. Tel Aviv. Retrieved October 3, 2025 from https://adva.org/wp-content/uploads/2015/02/how-the-1998-Israel-state-budget-will-affect-women1.pdf.

Albelda, R. (1986). Occupational segregation by race and gender 1958–1981. *Industrial and Labor Relations Review, 39*(3), 404–411.

Becchio, G. (2024). Pioneering feminist economics: Barbara Bergmann's contributions to gender issues. *Eastern Economic Journal, 50*(4), 472–495.

Becker, G. (1957). *The economics of discrimination*. University of Chicago Press.

Becker, G. (1964). *Human capital: a theoretical and empirical analysis with special reference to education*. NBER.

Bergmann, B. (1968). Investment in the human resources of Negroes. In *Federal Programs for the Development of Human Resources* (pp. 263–266). Joint Economic Committee. Congress of the United States.

Bergmann, B. (1969a). Investment in the human resources of Negroes. In J. Kain (Ed.), *Race and poverty: The economics of discrimination* (pp. 52–57). Prentice Hall.

Bergmann, B. (1969b). The urban economy and the urban crisis. *American Economic Review, 59*(4), 639–645.

Bergmann, B. (1971). The effect on white incomes of discrimination in employment. *Journal of Political Economy, 79*(2), 294–313.

Bergmann, B. (1974a). Occupational segregation, wages and profits when employers discriminate by race or sex. *Eastern Economic Journal, 1*(2), 103–110.

Bergmann, B. (1974b). Towards more useful modes of research on discrimination in employment and pay. *Sloan Management Review, 14*(1), 43–45.

Bergmann, B. (1974c). Empirical work on the labor market: Is there any alternative to regression running? In *Proceedings of the 27th Annual Meeting Industrial Relations Research Association* (243–251).

Bergmann, B. (1976). Reducing the pervasiveness of discrimination. In E. Ginzberg (Ed.), *Jobs for Americans* (pp. 120–141). Columbia University Press.

Bergmann, B. (1979). Labor market data needs relating to antidiscriminatory activity. *National Commission on Employment and Unemployment Statistics, 26*, 1–30.

Bergmann, B. (1980). Discrimination and unemployment. In E. Malinvaud & J. Fitoussi (Eds.), *Unemployment in western countries. Proceedings of a conference held by the International Economic Association at Bischenberg, France* (pp. 420–431). Macmillan.

Bergmann, B. (1981a). The economic risks of being a housewife. *American Economic Review, 71*(2), 81–86.

Bergmann, B. (1981b). The Shibboleth of the shrinking pie. *Perspectives, 13*(2), 30–33.

Bergmann, B. (1985). The economic case for comparable worth. In H. Hartmann (Ed.), *Comparable worth: New directions for research* (pp. 71–85). National Academy Press.

Bergmann, B. (1986). *The economic emergence of women*. Basic Books.

Bergmann, B. (1987a). The task of a feminist economics: A more equitable future. In C. Farnham (Ed.), *The impact of feminist research in the academy* (pp. 131–147). Indiana University Press.

Bergmann, B. (1987b). Pay equity–surprising answers to hard questions. *Challenge*, May/June, 45–51.

Bergmann, B. (1989a). What the common economic arguments against comparable worth are worth. *Journal of Social Issues, 45*(4), 67–80.

Bergmann, B. (1989b). Does the market for women's labor need fixing? *Journal of Economic Perspectives, 3*(1), 43–60.

Bergmann, B. (1996). The corporation faces issues of race and gender. In C. Kaysen (Ed.), *The American corporation today* (pp. 269–291). Oxford University Press.

Bergmann, B. (2005). Gender in public expenditure review. In A. Shaikh (Ed.), *Public expenditure analysis* (pp. 135–152). The International Bank for Reconstruction and Development/The World Bank.

Bergmann, B. (2007). Discrimination through the economist's eye. In F. J. Crosby, M. Stockdale, & S. A. Ropp (Eds.), *Sex discrimination in the workplace: Multidisciplinary perspectives* (pp. 213–234). Blackwell Publishing.

Bergmann, B. (2010). Sex segregation in the blue-collar occupations: Women's choices or unremedied discrimination? Comment on England. *Gender & Society, 25*(1), 88–93.

Bergmann, B., & Atkinson, L. (1972). The prospect of equality of incomes between White and Black families under varying rates of unemployment: A comment. *The Journal of Human Resources, 7*(4), 545–547.

Bergmann, B., Berga, S., Sherman, F., & Fuchs, V. (1986). The economic well-being of women. *Science, 233*(4763), 510.

Bergmann, B. & Darity, W. (1981). Social Relations in the Workplace and Employer Discrimination. *Monthly Labor Review, 104*(4), 155–158.

Bergmann, B. & Figart, D. (1989). *Facilitating women's occupational integration for the department of labor, commission on workforce quality and labor market efficiency*. Retrieved September 30, 2025, from http://eric.ed.gov/?id=ED317693.

Bergmann, B., & Gray, M. (1984). Economic models as a means of calculating legal compensation claims. In H. Remick (Ed.), *Comparable worth and wage discrimination: Technical possibilities and political realities* (pp. 155–172). Temple University Press.

Bergmann, B., & Kaun, D. (1967). *Structural unemployment in the United States*. The Brookings Institution.

Bergmann, B., & Krause, W. (1972). Evaluating and forecasting progress in racial integration of employment. *Industrial and Labor Relations Review, 25*(3), 399–409.

Bergmann, B., & Lyle, J. (1971). The occupational standing of Negroes by areas and industries. *The Journal of Human Resources, 6*(4), 411–433.

Bergmann, B., & Maxfield, M. (1975). How to analyze the fairness of faculty women's salaries on our own campus. *AAUP Bulletin, 61*(3), 262–265.

Bergmann, B., Vickery, C., & Schwartz, K. (1978). Unemployment rate targets and anti-inflation policy as more women enter the workforce. *American Economic Review, 68*(2), 90–94.

Berman, B. (1965). *Alternative measures of structural unemployment*. The Brookings Institution.

Bielby, W., & Barron, J. (1984). A woman's place is with the women: segregation within organizations. In B. Reskin (Ed.), *Sex segregation in the workplace* (pp. 27–55). National Academy Press.

Blau, F. (1977). *Equal pay in the office*. Heath & Company.

Blau, F., Ferber, M., & Winkler, A. (1998). *The economics of women, men, and work* (3rd ed.). Prentice-Hall.

Blau, F., & Kahn, L. (1981). Race and sex differences in quits by young workers. *Industrial and Labor Relations Review, 34*(4), 563–577.

Dewey, D. (1952). Negro employment in Southern industry. *Journal of Political Economy, 60*(4), 279–294.

Edgeworth, F. Y. (1922). Equal pay to men and women for equal work. *Economic Journal, 32*(128), 431–457.

England, P. (2010). The gender revolution: Uneven and stalled. *Gender & Society, 24*(2), 149–166.

Fuchs, V. (1986). Sex differences in economic well-being. *Science, 235*(4749), 459–464.

Gibson, K., Darity, W., & Myer, S. (1998). Revisiting occupational crowding in the United States: a preliminary study. *Feminist Economics, 4*(3), 73–95.

Guthrie, H. (1970). The prospect of equality of incomes between White and Black families under varying rates of unemployment. *The Journal of Human Resources, 5*(4), 431–446.

Hamilton, D., Algernon A., & Darity, W. (2011). *Whiter jobs, higher wages: Occupational segregation and the lower wages of black men*. Economic Policy Institute Briefing Paper #268. Economic Policy Institute.

Holder, M. (2018). Revisiting Bergmann's occupational crowding model. *Review of Radical Political Economics, 50*(4), 683–690.

Lapidus, J., & Figart, D. (1998). Remedying 'unfair acts': U.S. pay equity by race and gender. *Feminist Economics, 4*(3), 7–28.

Mincer, J. (1963). Market prices, opportunity costs, and income effects. In C. Christ (Ed.), *Measurement in economics* (pp. 66–82). Stanford University Press.

Myrdal, G. (1944). *An American dilemma: The Negro problem and modern democracy*. Harper & Bros.

Olson, P. (2007). On the contributions of Barbara Bergmann to economics. *Review of Political Economy, 19*(4), 475–496.

Riach, P., & Rich, J. (2002). Field experiments of discrimination in the market place. *Economic Journal, 112*(483), 480–518.

Riach, P. A., & Rich, J. (2006). An experimental investigation of sexual discrimination in hiring in the English labor market. *The B.E. Journal of Economic Analysis and Policy, 6*(2), 1–22.

Small, S. (2022). Tracing Barbara Bergmann's occupational crowding hypothesis: a recent history. *History of Political Economy, 54*(S1), 193–220.

Taussig, F. (1923). *Principles of economics*. Macmillan.
Zernike, K. (2023). *The exceptions: Nancy Hopkins, MIT, and the fight for women in science*. Scribner.

CHAPTER 4

Marriage and Family

In the 1970s, Bergmann gradually focused her research towards the economic role of women and their contribution to the labor force, further developing her analysis of gender discrimination in the job market, which led her to extend her research from women's place in the economy to the economics of the family and the economic analysis of marriage. In addition to examining the economic circumstances of women who had limited employment opportunities and full-time responsibilities as mothers, she maintained a continuous interest in the study of child-rearing. As always, she grounded her investigation in the analysis of available data. In fact, her archive contains several datasets on marriage and divorce rates, the relationship between educational level and fertility and divorce, and so forth, mainly published by the U.S. Bureau of the Census, starting from the early 1970s (Becchio, 2024a, 2024b).

Bergmann's decision to go deeper into the study of the economic conditions of married women, as well as to directly analyze the traditional division of labor between partners within the household, was made urgent by two decisive factors. First, the evidence that gender-based segregation was even more extreme than racial segregation, as shown by Victor Fuchs' study (Fuchs, 1971),[1] often quoted by Bergmann in her writings. Second,

[1] Fuchs's (1971) article measured the gender wage gap at 0.6 in hourly wages, by using 1960 U.S. Census data and argued that it was not physical strength but social attitudes and discrimination that were major factors in this pay difference.

G. Becchio, *Barbara Bergmann*, Great Thinkers in Economics,
https://doi.org/10.1007/978-3-032-18696-6_4

the emergence of the economics of the family in standard economics, which occurred in the 1970s.

At that time, the economics of the family was a relatively new research field[2] intended to elucidate the decisions surrounding marriage and divorce as well as all choices related to the division of labor between spouses and other decisions associated with child-rearing.

Standard economics, as developed by Jacob Mincer's (1962, 1963) and Gary Becker's labor economics, explained women's participation in the labor market and the gender wage gap as effects of differing levels of human capital accumulation between genders, while Becker's New Home Economics (NHE) emphasized the centrality of the household production function as a potential substitute for the market, considering the household as a single decision-making unit and applying maximization and equilibrium to family decisions (Becker, 1974a, 1974b).

Bergmann's archive holds project files, research materials, teaching syllabi, and three (unpublished or partially unpublished) research projects that reveal her commitment to developing an economic theory of marriage that would replace the standard economic analysis of marriage and provide an 'affirmative action' to sustain child rearing and single parents (Bergmann, 2003a, 2003b, 2005a, n.d. undated, presumably between 2005 and 2008, 2008). Bergmann's works, published and unpublished, reveal her commitment to developing an economic theory of the family aimed at replacing NHE by providing a more realistic analysis of family decision-making process. While criticizing New Home Economics, Bergmann was also determined to formulate policies that would improve the conditions of the family (Bergmann, 1986, 1995a, 2005b; Bergmann & Adelman, 1973). In fact, she constantly carried out efforts to provide affirmative action policies to support welfare measures for child-rearing and single parenthood (Bergmann, 1974a, 1974b, 1986, 2003a, 2003b, 2005a, 2005b).

[2] Previously, the economics of the family had been partially introduced in early twentieth century in American academia by Chicago economists Hazel Kyrk, Margaret Reid, and Elizabeth Hoyt who were the founders of household economics (Bankovsky, 2020, 2025; Becchio, 2020, 2024a; Folbre, 1998a; Forget, 2001; Grossbard, 2001).

4.1 The Economic Emergence of Women

In the early 1970s, Bergmann was interested in the effects of feminist movements on women's lives, especially on their economic emancipation. In her paper, "The Economics of Women's Liberation" (Bergmann, 1973a), she defined gender inequality in the labor market as the consequence of entrenched social norms and psychological comfort with occupational segregation. She also pointed out that her idea of a 'postliberation economy', her term to define feminist economic stances aimed at women's empowerment, "would mean a radical reduction in the division of labor by sex, both inside and outside the home without a revolution that overthrows capitalism" (Bergmann, 1973a, p. 158).

According to Bergmann, the economic and social barriers preventing women, especially married women, from achieving equal participation in the American economy were four: employment discrimination rooted in employer prejudice and societal norms about women's work; perceptions of inferior job performance due to women's family responsibilities; women's self-sabotage that leads them to avoid traditionally male occupations; and economic interests that benefit from keeping women in low-paying roles. These four elements are reinforced by weak economic incentives to reduce discrimination that, if introduced, would raise competition in the job market. As a matter of fact, women's higher quit rates are often tied to job types rather than lack of commitment and employers actually lose profits by excluding qualified women. Furthermore, the entry of women into the workforce would help grow markets by increasing consumption of goods and services.

Bergmann's article prompted a response from Andrew Weintraub, to which she then replied (Weintraub & Bergmann, 1973). Weintraub challenged Bergmann's argument, claiming she overlooked important macroeconomic consequences and fell into the fallacy of composition. While he accepted that lowering discrimination could raise women's wages individually, he contended that the overall effects of women's liberation would actually widen the gap between rich and poor. Weintraub argued that highly competent men tend to marry equally competent women, and that these women, often from upper-income households, are traditionally less likely to work. If the women's liberation movement encouraged more such women to enter the labor force, he predicted they would outcompete lower-income men, pushing these men into lower-paying jobs and worsening poverty. He concluded by making a glib etymological remark that 'lib' in Old English meant 'to castrate', implying that men from lower-income groups will be harmed.

Bergmann responded that Weintraub's fears were misplaced: if upper-income women possess above-average skills, as he claimed, they would compete not with low-income men but with high-income men in similar professions. Hence, their entry in the job market would place downward pressure on wages in fields like engineering, business, medicine, or dentistry, not in low-wage occupations, such as factory work or driving. Moreover, she dismissed Weintraub's comment about the medieval meaning of "lib" as irrelevant and absurd, questioning whether he truly believed that a fairer treatment of women may threaten men's reproductive functions. Drawing on her own experience with male relatives, friends, and colleagues, many of whom had working wives, she remarked sarcastically that such fears appear unfounded.

In the same year, 1973, Bergmann co-authored with Irma Adelman a paper on the economic role of married women, inspired by the *1973 Report of the President's Council of Economic Advisers*, which recognized the existence of economic discrimination against women in the form of job segregation, labor force gap, and wage gap. They wrote:

> As economists, we are particularly pleased to have the official imprimatur of an Economic Report on the view that discrimination does indeed exist. Some economists have been reluctant to admit the possibility of discrimination unrelated to real or perceived productivity differences. We believe that a proper analysis of discrimination is yet to come; such an analysis will have to fuse elements of economics, sociology, psychology, and history. (Bergmann & Adelman, 1973, p. 509)

Nonetheless, the Economic Report, based on the old concept of the family wage, according to which a married woman would work only out of necessity to get the minimum income for the family, failed to recognize that women, like men, work "for greater personal autonomy, for status inside and outside the family, to reduce their own financial instability" (Bergmann & Adelman, 1973, p. 512).

One year later, in 1974, Barbara attended a Summer School organized by the UN youth of Sweden in Kungälv, Sweden. On that occasion, she gave a speech on the economic conditions of American women of the time, which is held in her archive (Bergmann, 1974b). For Bergmann, the popular view, according to which American middle-class married women were achieving fulfillment through their full-time roles as wives and mothers, was a stereotype that did not correspond to the real situation of many American housewives, who were dissatisfied with their current position. She started by quoting Betty Friedan's *The Feminine Mystique* (1963) to describe the boredom experienced by the typical American housewife.

As Bergmann wrote:

> Friedan's book raised the consciousness of many women to the insults they had suffered, to the doors that were closed to them, to the low esteem in which they were held by society. (Bergmann, 1974b, p. 2)

Bergmann also emphasized that women's concentration in high-skilled jobs and their overcrowding in certain occupations highlighted the gender wage gap's dependence on women's share of the labor market. She argued that this gap could be reduced only by allowing women to enter more remunerative jobs.

She added:

> The demand for women's labor is kept artificially low because of their virtual exclusion from many fields, and the supply of women to the few fields where they are welcomed is artificially increased thereby. (ibid, p. 5)

She also underlined that analyzing the data provided by the Bureau of Labor Statistics revealed that women's occupational segregation and overcrowding were more severe than those caused by race.

The final part of the paper explicitly challenged the common opinion mentioned above, which suggested that women's discrimination in the market was compensated by the fact that their husbands took care of them, providing a good standard of living. Bergmann rightly pointed out that the dramatic rise in divorce rates showed the opposite: women wanted to leave their marriages, even though their economic situation was likely to worsen without their soon-to-be ex-husbands' income.[3] Hence, according to Bergmann, affirmative action policies, such as legal procedures against women's employment segregation that might

[3] Between 1960 and 1972, the analysis of the data revealed a 56% increase in households that depended solely on women, who were often forced to go on welfare, given the employment segregation they faced.

include quotas, were needed, along with mechanisms that encouraged separated/divorced fathers to consistently support their children, by providing payments that cover child care to avoid any form of women's self-segregation at home.

In the same period, Bergmann was involved in setting up a specific welfare agenda that took account of women's economic conditions. In a memorandum for the *Civil Rights Digest* (Bergmann & Gray, 1975), she argued that anti-discrimination laws had established that employers can no longer make assumptions about individuals based on averages for their sex. Treating a woman as if she were the average woman, in terms of physical strength, job tenure, or productivity is unlawful discrimination. Employment decisions must be based on individual ability, not on generalized traits linked to sex: while average differences may exist between men and women in certain characteristics, such as strength or life expectancy, the distributions of these traits overlap considerably.[4] Therefore, practices such as offering different pension benefits to men and women, based on average life expectancy, wrongly assume that all men and women conform to their respective averages.

A few years later, she proposed a social security reform that involved housewives, by exploring two major strands of feminist thought: role-avoidance and solidarity-with-housewives.

The former viewed the housewife role as inherently oppressive and seeks to discourage dependence on it by prioritizing working wives through several measures such as: advocating to eliminate the 50% spouse benefit, which currently gives nonworking spouses (mostly women) larger benefits through their husbands; opposing policies that make the housewife role too comfortable by reinforcing traditional gender roles; and splitting social security credits between spouses over homemaker credits or large non-work-based benefits.

The latter emphasizes sisterhood and support for all women, including housewives, by recognizing their productive contribution to family and society. It advocates measures such as: financial security and independence for housewives, especially in cases of widowhood or divorce; social security recognition for unpaid domestic labor; earnings sharing so that each spouse accumulates benefits under their own name; and double-decker

[4] For example, in life expectancy, there is an 84% overlap between men and women, meaning that most individuals of each sex have comparable lifespans.

systems, which guarantee basic benefits for all elderly people regardless of their work history, thus enhancing the dignity of non-working spouses.

According to Bergmann, both models attempt to modernize the system, but the first favors independence and equality through labor participation, while the second emphasizes protection and dignity regardless of involvement in the labor market. Both require analysts to consider women's economic independence, unpaid labor, and life circumstances in policy design and are essential correctives to sexist assumptions in social policy especially against the rise of the antifeminist New Home Economics which, according to Bergmann, was for the most part a fatally oversimplified theory of the traditional form of family life.

She wrote:

> It is the passing away of this traditional form which is occasioning the need for the very reforms we are studying. (Bergmann, 1980, p. 233)

As Bergmann later emphasized, the U.S. feminist legislative agenda should advocate for: a federal health insurance system based on the elimination of employer tax deductions for fringe benefits; equal pay and benefits for part-time and full-time workers; the expansion of anti-discrimination laws; publicly funded child care; strict enforcement of child-support payments; and a reduction in standard working hours (Bergmann, 1985).

In the early 1980s, Bergmann intensified her focus on the economic consequences of married women's participation in the labor market (see paragraph 4.2).[5]

Bergmann's long-standing effort to merge economic theory with feminist analysis and to critique the inadequacies of mainstream economics in explaining gender inequality was codified in her book *The Economic Emergence of Women* (1986). She introduced the book by characterizing the traditional division of roles between men and women within families and society as a 'sex-role caste system'. This system, devoid of considerations

[5] A study published in 1980, using data from the 1968 and 1975 Current Population Surveys, revealed that wives' earnings continued to have a modest equalizing effect on family income between 1967 and 1974, although this impact remained relatively stable despite rising labor participation among wives of higher-earning husbands (Danzinger, 1980).

for women's employment discrimination, was reinforced by the "much cited 'theory' propounded by Becker" (ibid, p. 48).

As Hartmann rightly pointed out, Bergmann's book was shaped around six commitments: a willingness to incorporate values into her analysis; the intention of adopting applied economics; the necessity of using empirical economics and collecting data; continuous efforts to advance change in public policies through organizing public education; challenging convenient orthodoxy; and the belief that academics have the moral responsibility to move beyond critique and work for a better future (Hartmann, 1998).

In her book, Bergmann explored the causes, consequences, and policy implications of women's expanding role in the labor market, combining empirical evidence, economic reasoning, and social critique. Her aim was to show how women's entry into paid employment reshaped both the economy and the family, while revealing the persistent structural barriers that hinder full equality. Bergmann emphasized that women's economic emergence was transforming not only the workplace but also family life, gender relations, and social expectations, including marriage patterns, fertility rates, and family structures. She considered these shifts neither purely economic nor purely cultural, but deeply interconnected.

By the late twentieth century, Bergmann observed, millions of women had emerged economically by entering professions once reserved for men. Technological advances, higher education levels, and evolving attitudes toward marriage and family all supported this transformation. The women's movement of the 1960s and the 1970s also played a crucial role in challenging the cultural and institutional barriers that had kept women confined to the home.

However, Bergmann warned that the term 'emergence' should not be confused with 'emancipation'. She emphasized that although women's entry into paid work improved family incomes and reduced poverty, the structure of the labor market remained deeply gendered, shaped by historical inequalities and cultural expectations about women's natural roles. The economy still operated according to norms and policies designed for a male breadwinner and a female homemaker. As a result, systemic gender inequalities in pay and job opportunities persisted, since women's employment was often concentrated in part-time, low-paid, or service-sector jobs.

According to Bergmann, the core of economic inequality in the labor market lay in occupational segregation by sex. Women were clustered in certain occupations, such as teaching, nursing, clerical work, and social services, that paid less and offered fewer opportunities for advancement. In contrast, men dominated technical, managerial, and scientific fields with higher wages and prestige. Bergmann divided the causes of segregation into two categories. The first was demand-side factors, such as employers' discriminatory hiring practices, biased evaluations, and stereotypes that assumed women were less capable or less committed workers. The second was supply-side factors, including women's own choices, shaped by social pressures, family responsibilities, and a lack of supportive institutions such as affordable childcare and flexible work arrangements. These phenomena reinforced each other: discrimination narrowed women's options, while social norms made certain female jobs seem more acceptable, thus perpetuating segregation.

Furthermore, Bergmann noticed, women's wages continued to lag behind men's. Part of the gap reflected occupational segregation, but even within the same occupations, women often earned less. Bergmann attributed gender wage gap to biased promotion systems, the undervaluation of women's work, and weaker bargaining power due to limited alternative opportunities. She also challenged the notion that women's lower pay resulted from personal choice, such as prioritizing family over career, arguing that such explanations ignored the structural constraints that limited women's options and forced many into low-paid or part-time employment.

As always, Bergmann's personal life experience and research interests were intertwined. In a memorandum dated January 27, 1986, held in her archive, Barbara wrote that in the mid-1970s her salary was significantly lower than that of comparable colleagues in her Economics Department. After requesting a raise from the department chair, Dr. Dillard, she received only a modest increase. Upon seeing the disparities, Bergmann conducted a systematic study, published in the *AAUP Bulletin*, showing that women were generally underpaid (see Chapter 2). When she brought her findings to university administrators, including the Chancellor, her concerns were dismissed. Later, under a new chair, Dr. Marris, she was told her salary was low because her research field (discrimination in the labor market) was not important, and she was subsequently harassed for raising the issue. Despite major professional achievements, her salary remained below that of most male colleagues with less distinction. After repeated complaints, she received small equity adjustments in 1984 and 1985.

Occupational segregation and the gender wage gap, Bergmann argued, were reinforced by the limitations of neoclassical economics, which treated the labor market as fair and efficient, assuming that wages simply reflected productivity and that discrimination could not persist in a competitive market. This view ignored the fact that discrimination does persist, because social institutions, power relations, and historical inequalities continuously shape the market. Far from being neutral mechanisms, markets are socially embedded systems that reproduce traditional biases, such as the exclusion of women from certain professions and the systematic undervaluation of their work. Standard economists, by insisting on the neutrality of the market, ended up legitimizing inequality rather than analyzing and correcting it.

A significant part of Bergmann's book was devoted to the economic consequences of women's unpaid labor at home, which she argued subsidized men's paid work and the wider economy. Tasks such as childrearing, cooking, and housework, albeit essential to social reproduction, were unpaid and undervalued in standard economic models. This traditional division of labor created a double burden: even if women entered the paid workforce, they remained primarily responsible for domestic duties, leading to chronic overwork, stress, and limited career advancement. According to Bergmann, true equality required not only parity in the labor market but also a fairer division of responsibilities within the household. Achieving this goal, she insisted, demanded dismantling the ideological belief that caregiving and homemaking are inherently women's roles.

Bergmann's insistence on the equal division of household responsibilities between partners was later tested by Strober and Chan (1998) who compared household task arrangements among married 1981 graduates of Stanford University and of the University of Todai (Tokyo) roughly 10 years after graduation.[6] As they wrote:

[6] Their study found that 43% of Stanford graduates shared household tasks equally with their spouses, a rate much higher than the U.S. average, while only 12% of women and 8% of men reported such egalitarian arrangements, figures comparable to Japan's national average. Controlling for other factors, Stanford men who performed at least half of household tasks experienced an earnings penalty of about 10%, whereas women's earnings were unaffected by their share of housework.

> We agree with Bergmann's view that gender equity requires not only that women and men play similar economic roles in the workplace, but also in the home. There are important negative effects of a 'double shift' for women. In the short run, it breeds marital discontent among many wives, as witnessed by the high rates of dissatisfaction in our samples among full-time employed women with traditional household task arrangements. Moreover, in the long run, it may well have a chilling effect on younger women who would like the opportunity to combine career and family without an extremely heavy total workload. (Strober & Chan, 1998, p. 121)

Bergmann did not limit her effort to theory, she devoted a major section of her book to an economic policy agenda aimed at reducing gender inequality. Her main proposals included measures she had already outlined in earlier writings: universal health insurance, the elimination of employer tax deductions for fringe benefits, anti-discrimination legislation and quota systems, government-provided child care, and the reduction of standard working hours.

Summing up, throughout the book, Bergmann redefined key economic concepts through a feminist lens. Efficiency, she argued, should not simply mean maximizing output at the lowest cost, but ensuring that all individuals, regardless of gender, can realize their potential and contribute fully to society. Likewise, fairness cannot be achieved by pretending that the market is neutral, but rather by actively correcting the distortions created by historical patterns of discrimination and exclusion.

Bergmann concluded that the economic emergence of women was an ongoing and incomplete process. Women's participation in the labor market has transformed economies and expanded human freedom, yet the structure of work, family, and policy continues to reflect outdated gender hierarchies. Her book thus challenged the supposed neutrality of standard economic theory, becoming a cornerstone of the emerging field of feminist economics (see Chapter 6), particularly in opposition to Becker's NHE approach to the family.

4.2 Bergmann Versus Becker

Bergmann's analysis of sex segregation in the marketplace served as an open critique of Becker's approach to economics of the family. She emphasized that any economic theory dealing with marriage and divorce, family dynamics, and child-raising must begin with an inquiry into the effects of women entering the labor force, a transformative cultural shift that changed the economic dynamics of goods and services provided to family members.

As mentioned earlier, Becker's NHE dealt with marriage, fertility, the division of labor between spouses, and children's education by modelling family behaviors solely as rational responses to economic elements (prices, incomes and technologies of production), while excluding social and cultural factors from the economic model.

Becker introduced the 'price theory of marriage' in two papers devoted to the economics of marriage. In the first, Becker used human capital theory to explain how households sort breadwinners from homemakers (Becker, 1973); in the second, he applied the theory of comparative advantage to explain the division of labor between couples (Becker, 1974a, 1974b). More generally, Becker considered marriage as a long-term commitment to assure protection for women, an arrangement between individuals whose "utility expected from marriage exceeds the utility expected from remaining single". Similarly, according to Becker, the choice to divorce was explained by constructing a total utility function of a couple and by considering bargaining costs: divorce occurs "when the utility expected from remaining married falls below the utility expected from divorcing and possibly remarrying" (Becker et al., 1977, p. 1147). Finally, he regarded market-oriented investments for boys and household-oriented investments for girls as optimal strategies, by arguing that the highest returns are reached in a society where roles are specialized on the basis of gender differences.

The clash between Bergmann and Becker started in the 1970s, though the year 1981 marked a crucial turning point. On one side, Becker published *A Treatise on the Family* (1981) considered the comprehensive systematization of his NHE.[7] On the other side, Bergmann published "The Economic Risk of Being a Housewife" in the *American Economic Review* (Bergmann, 1981a) and other papers (Bergmann, 1981a, 1981b, 1981c) that represented a direct attack on Becker's approach to marriage

[7] An enlarged edition was published 10 years later, in 1991, just one year before he received the Nobel Prize. Becker's book took account of some developments of marriage theory that had been meanwhile published by other new home economists, not only colleagues, but also "students who wrote dissertations on the family, or relevant to the family, during their participation in our Workshop on Applications of Economics [at the University of Chicago]" (Becker, 1991, p. xi).

theory from any possible perspective: theoretical, methodological, and cultural.

In his *Treatise*, Becker explained the sexual division of labor as a consequence of women's "heavy biological commitment" to the production, feeding, and caring of children (Becker, 1981, 1991, p. 38), which leads to the conclusion that the men's and women's time are not perfect substitutes, but complementary: "households with only men or only women are less efficient because they are unable to profit from the sexual difference in comparative advantage" (Becker, 1991, p. 39).

Becker posed a benevolent head of the family (the husband/father) by assuming that he fairly considers the preferences of all household members and that he is able to adjust allocations in response to family members' behavior. Moreover, he reinforced the application of human capital theory to the division of labor between partners by stressing that specialized investments in comparative advantages reinforce the division of labor between men in the market and women in the household.

Bergmann's paper "The Economic Risk of Being a Housewife" (Bergmann, 1981a) represented her feminist counterpoint to Becker's approach to marriage theory. Contrary to Becker, who rationalized the *status quo* in terms of marriage and divorce as well as the division of labor between spouses and children's gender-oriented education, Bergmann emphasized that any theory of marriage and divorce should start by examining the effects of women entering the labor force that changed the economic contributions of both men and women to the family. She targeted "Becker's encomium to the advantages of the division of labor among spouses" by defining it biased by "its perspective of a male member of a traditional family" (Bergmann, 1981a, p. 81).

According to Bergmann, being a housewife was much riskier than working in many occupations. The risks and downsides of the role of a housewife included unpaid duties like housekeeping and child care, exposure to physical hazards in domestic accidents, a higher likelihood of domestic violence compared to physical assaults in the workplace, and non-cash, untaxed benefits instead of a regular salary. Furthermore, being a housewife was one of the riskiest occupations, given its high variability in payoff resulting from the possibility of marriage ending in divorce; being the financial and emotional trauma of divorcing much higher than the trauma of being fired. Moreover, while a former employer has no power over former employees after firing them, an ex-husband usually remains responsible for alimony and child support, both of which are often unpaid or provided irregularly, as Census reports reveal.

Hence, Bergmann concluded by considering that being a housewife, i.e. devoting women's time and skills to the domestic sphere, was not properly a choice, otherwise it should have been chosen equally by men, rather it can be regarded as a 'caste'. Like in any other caste system, traditional roles are reinforced by social pressure and by specific education, namely, the traditional education for girls, which included the 'Prince Charming legend' and lack of preparation for the labor market. Exiting this caste is challenging due to factors such as 'employment discrimination', the 'social stigma' attached to divorced women, and the 'social pressure on wives not to seek paid employment' (ibid, p. 84).[8]

Bergmann wanted to develop her *AER* article and started to work on a research proposal that is held in her archive (Bergmann, 1981b). Her proposal was focused on the development of an appropriate and fair economic support system for children whose divorced fathers did not consistently provide regular financial help. Organized into three parts, it encompassed a description of the situation of 'fatherless' children, an equitable model for mandated payments, and a proposal for integrating paternal payments with welfare measures. The model aimed to determine the economic cost of raising a child, exploring both a 'cost-sharing' principle, where parents share the estimated weekly or monthly costs, potentially assisted by welfare measures, and an 'income-sharing' principle, wherein ex-partners pool their income as if still married and allocate shares to their children. A concluding chapter addressed welfare provisions for children in single-parent households.

Another crucial publication on marriage theory, published by Bergmann, appeared in 1983 (later reprinted in Bergmann, 1990a). Bergmann specifically targeted Becker and his fellows as a group of 'mainline economists (…) a group of conservative economists centered in the University of Chicago (…) the NHE group', who introduced women's work and marriage theory into economics by invoking the theory of comparative advantage to reinforce the traditional division of labor between the sexes. Bergmann shared other feminist economists'

[8] In another article dated 1981, mainly focused on the decrease in the flow of financial support from separated fathers to children, she portrayed marriage as an obsolete institution intended "to limit the number of 'fatherless' children" (Bergmann, 1981c, p. 106).

concerns and critiques about the new home economics' marriage theory, such as 'the unfailing benevolence of the head of household' and 'that biological motherhood necessarily entails more responsibility for child rearing than does fatherhood', as heavily gender stereotyped and based on unrealistic assumptions unable to seriously analyze the motivations to marry, the evolution of the contribution of partners at home and in the market, and the distribution of family resources among spouses and children (Bergmann, 1990a, p. 72).

As mentioned earlier, three years later, in 1986, Bergmann systematized her contribution to marriage theory in her book, *The Economic Emergence of Women* (second and enlarged edition dated 2005), where she defined the traditional division of roles between men and women within families and society as a 'sex-role caste system' based on what has traditionally been denoted as the doctrine of the separate spheres that was reinforced by the "much cited 'theory' propounded by Becker" (Bergmann, 1986, p. 48).

Bergmann added that Becker's human capital theory applied to gender labor gap and gender wage gap "does not work well either (…) a far better explanation is that men and women are not competing (i.e. selling their human capital) in the same market, [but] in segregating markets" (ibid, p. 88). Bergmann clearly pointed out that Becker's theory of marriage based on the comparative advantage of having a husband in the job market and a full-time housewife was no longer acceptable: since the advent of the industrial revolution, women had gradually entered the job market and consequently had acquired a different role in society as well as within the family. This social transformation radically challenged the doctrine of the separate spheres. According to Bergmann, when Becker adopted the theory of comparative advantage to explain women's specialization in housework, he emphasized the rationality of employment discrimination against women as well as men's evasion of domestic responsibilities. She asserted that it was employment discrimination that made the theory of comparative advantage seem appropriate rather than the other way around.

Furthermore, Bergmann insisted that Becker's approach was detrimental to a correct explanation of both racial and sex discrimination in the job market. Such discrimination largely depended on complex social structures that influenced the choices of individuals, especially the men's choice to neglect housework and child care.

Finally, according to Bergmann, against Becker, feminist economists had clearly shown that the gender division of household labor persists and that women in dual-earner households almost entirely bear the double burden of being workers in both the job market and in the household. As Bergmann wrote later: "Becker's view of marriage as a trading relationship downplays the social side of marriage" (Bergmann 1990b, p. 12).[9]

Bergmann's critique of Becker's NHE made her one of the first feminist economists of the time, although feminist economics was not institutionalized yet (see Chapter 6). After Becker received the Nobel Prize in 1992, Bergmann felt the urgency of pointing out that his way of dealing with marriage theory and the division of labor was a huge step backward.[10] According to Bergmann, Becker's work "failed badly" in providing "a realistic appreciation of actual problems that are being encountered and the policies that might be applied to them", and assumed factors such as the distribution of resources (including material provisions, leisure time, and investments in education in favor of boys) as *ceteris paribus* conditions, regardless of any extra-economic factors that heavily influence family dynamics (Bergmann, 1995b).

Bergmann criticized "the paucity of factors" that Becker considered as "proofs of his diagrammatic and algebraic modes of characterization and persuasion" as well as his "tendency to idealize the phenomenon under examination as optimal", subjected to being undermined by any specific policy. In her view, Becker's work on the family "concentrates most of his attention on the Victorian ideal of the family, although it appears he would judge the harem, a still more retrograde version of the family, to be even more praiseworthy" (Bergmann 1996a, 1996b, p. 10).[11]

[9] As some feminist economists have underlined, Bergmann's emphasis on equal access to the labor market allowed her to explore public policies aimed at ensuring equal opportunity for men and women in the labor market (Folbre, 1998b; Olson, 2007). The only review of her book kept by Bergmann in her personal archive, written by economist David Henderson (1987), claimed that Bergmann was biased in favor of affirmative action due to her political preferences, without considering the possibility that government intervention might harm women by imposing excessive control over them.

[10] The split between feminist economists and Becker and his followers especially increased after 1992, when Becker won the Nobel Prize: many women economists felt the urgency to present an alternative approach based on a feminist point of view. Hence, in 1992, feminist economists founded the International Association for Feminist Economics (IAFFE) (Becchio, 2020; Orozco Espinel & Gomez Betancourt, 2022).

[11] Bergmann insisted on the fact that Becker's analysis of the family was misleading and unable to understand especially three topics: polygamy versus monogamy, altruism, and

Bergmann's archive reveals two more research projects specifically related to the economics of the family: *The Challenge of Single Motherhood* (Bergmann, 2003a, 2003b) and *The Decline of Marriage and What To Do About It* (undated).

The Challenge of Single Motherhood (Bergmann, 2003a, 2003b), was a research focused on policy measures for single mothers. It remained unpublished, mainly because Bergmann was unable to find a publisher, as letters in her archive indicate. As a paper, Bergmann submitted it with the title "Policy Toward Lone Mothers in the United States" to *Feminist Economics*. Two out of three referees rejected the paper because "there [wa]s little really novel here" (Referee 1), and because "this [wa]s obviously not an academic journal article, but a policy proposal with a strong American bias" (Referee 3), while the third referee required minor revisions.[12] Nonetheless, part of her rejected paper was later embedded into an article, written in the form of dialogue (Himmelwelt et al., 2004) published 1 year later on *Feminist Economics* (see Chapter 6).

Meanwhile, Barbara decided to extend her paper into a book and to propose it to a publisher. She wrote to Cheryl Fish, an associate professor of Women's Studies at CUNY and one of the most influential members of the association 'Single Mother by Choice', to help her to find a publisher for her book (email dated May 14, 2003). Fish declined her support and replied that the proposal "seems to reinforce a number of the negative stereotypes, such as disadvantaged children, pathological mothers, abject poverty, about single motherhood".[13]

In her manuscript, Bergmann stated that the increase in the number of single mothers in the United States was due to several reasons: the

fertility. In Becker's work, women fare better under polygamy than under monogamy, as their price for selling themselves into marriage under polygamy is higher. Becker thought that an altruistic individual derives positive utility from the increase in another's consumption and, given the state of the labor market, in which men have access to better jobs than women do, the benevolent member is the male breadwinner. Becker explained fertility by pointing out that people have children according to their standard of living, which are influenced by the inheritance of capital they get and the rate of return on that capital (see Chapter 5).

[12] Referee Reports and Editorial Revisions. Barbara Bergmann's papers, box 7. David M. Rubenstein Rare Book & Manuscript Library, Duke University.

[13] Letter held in Barbara Bergmann's papers, box 7. David M. Rubenstein Rare Book & Manuscript Library, Duke University.

sexual revolution; the emergence of new opportunities for women's earnings; the increase in the divorce rate; the fact that some women never married at all; relevant changes in men's behavior; and the reduction of the stigma against unmarried mothers. Thus, she explored what policies should be adopted to better support lone mothers and their children, focusing on living standards, the balance between paid work and caregiving, and the ideal mix of cash benefits and government-provided services. Bergmann noted that single mothers in the United States experience much lower living standards than married couples. A reasonable standard, she argued, would bring lone mothers at least up to the poverty line, by ensuring access to safe housing, health care, along with programs aimed at finding stable jobs for them and funding a return to school for women who dropped out when they became pregnant.

The manuscript then examined whether lone mothers should receive support to stay home full-time with their children or incentives to find a job in the market. According to Bergmann, reinstating large welfare stipends or long parental leaves would harm gender equality by encouraging women to withdraw from the labor market for extended periods, thereby undermining progress in women's employment and professional advancement. She cited Sweden as an example, where long parental leave had contributed to occupational segregation by gender.

On the question of what form government help should take, Bergmann insisted that services, not just cash, are essential. Health insurance and child care are described as "merit goods" that every family should have access to, as they are fundamental to well-being and cannot reliably be purchased privately. Providing these services universally would raise living standards, even for families with modest incomes. Additional supports such as housing assistance, educational opportunities, and improved unemployment insurance would further help lone mothers achieve stability and independence.

Finally, Bergmann emphasized that these services should ideally be universal, not restricted to lone mothers, and should include improved child support enforcement and stronger measures against job discrimination. Though expanding such programs would be politically and financially challenging, the paper concluded that the groundwork already existed in U.S. programs of the time, and that a more comprehensive welfare system was both possible and necessary to promote gender equality and family well-being.

The Decline of Marriage and What To Do About It (undated) was a book proposal on the decline of marriage rates, parts of which became a working paper presented at the University of Linz (Bergmann, 2008). The text presents a comprehensive analysis of marriage as a foundational economic institution historically responsible for channeling resources toward the reproduction and maintenance of human life. Bergmann argued that marriage has never been merely a private or romantic arrangement but, rather, a system for organizing the economic contributions of men and women in ways that ensure the survival and care of children. In this sense, the stability of marriage has historically underpinned the transmission of wealth, labor, and social norms between generations. However, this system has been undergoing a profound transformation across advanced industrial societies. The decline of marriage rates, the growth of cohabitation, and the rise of single-parent families reflect a broader social shift that challenges the capacity of traditional family structures to fulfill their historical economic and reproductive roles. These developments, while associated with gains in personal freedom and gender equality, have simultaneously exposed new forms of vulnerability, particularly for women and children.

Bergmann's central argument was that the weaking of marriage as a universal social institution is not merely a cultural phenomenon but a structural economic change that has left societies struggling to find new mechanisms capable of securing the welfare of children and redistributing resources across genders and generations.

Historically, marriage served as a contract that organized production and reproduction within households. Men's economic roles as providers and women's roles as caregivers were mutually reinforcing; through marriage, men effectively transferred part of their income to women and children. This transfer was not based solely on affection but on the institutional and legal structure that made husbands financially responsible for their families.

In pre-industrial and early industrial societies, such arrangements ensured that children were materially supported and socialized within stable family units. Marriage thus functioned as a micro-level welfare system. The husband's income covered the consumption and upbringing costs of dependents, while the wife's unpaid domestic labor sustained household production. Bergmann pointed out that this gendered economic division, although unequal, served a functional purpose: it enabled human reproduction under conditions of limited public welfare provision. This model, however, relied on rigid gender norms and legal frameworks that constrained women's autonomy. Women's dependency on male income was enforced by both cultural expectations and the scarcity of alternatives. In that sense, marriage fulfilled an economic need at the cost of individual freedom and equality. The modern crisis of marriage, therefore, represents not only a decline in family formation but also a disruption of this long-standing economic arrangement.

Across developed countries, marriage rates have fallen dramatically since the mid-twentieth century, while divorce and cohabitation have increased. Fewer adults view marriage as an essential life goal, and more children are born outside of it. Bergmann linked these trends primarily to technological change, most notably the invention of reliable contraception and the expansion of women's paid employment. Contraception allowed women to decouple sexual relations from reproduction, undermining one of the key social pressures that had historically compelled marriage. At the same time, women's participation in the labor market gave them access to independent sources of income. These phenomena altered the cost–benefit structure of marriage for both sexes. For women, economic independence reduced the need to rely on a husband for material support. For men, the expectation of lifetime financial responsibility for dependents became less appealing when women could support themselves. Bergmann argued that these changes produced a structural decline in marriage by eroding its economic rationale. While love, companionship, and emotional connection continue to motivate many unions, these factors alone have proven insufficient to sustain marriage as a near-universal institution. Instead, cohabitation and serial relationships have become increasingly common substitutes, offering more flexibility while reducing the legal and economic stability that marriage once provided.

The decline of marriage, according to Bergmann, has far-reaching implications for the distribution of resources and opportunities in society. One of the most visible outcomes has been the rise of single-parent households, predominantly headed by women. Despite progress in gender equality and labor participation, women continue to assume the majority of caregiving responsibilities, often with limited financial support from male partners or the state. Children in single-parent families face elevated risks of poverty and time deprivation. While these outcomes are not inevitable, statistical evidence shows that single mothers are disproportionately represented among the economically disadvantaged. Bergmann interpreted this not as a moral failing but as a structural effect of the breakdown of an institution that once transferred male income to children through marriage. Without alternative mechanisms for redistribution, the burden of reproduction falls increasingly on women. Bergmann also warned that the weakening of marriage exacerbates broader inequalities. Wealthier families can compensate for the absence of a second parent through private resources such as paid child care and educational support, whereas poorer families cannot. Thus, the decline of marriage may reinforce class divides, perpetuating cycles of disadvantage. In this way, the erosion of the marital system has consequences that extend beyond private life to the overall cohesion and fairness of society.

In response to these trends, Bergmann noticed, conservative and religious movements have sought to revive marriage through policy initiatives such as marriage promotion, abstinence education, restrictions on divorce, and campaigns against cohabitation. These measures rest on the assumption that moral decay and individual irresponsibility are the main causes of marital decline. Bergmann criticized these approaches as ineffective and unjust, arguing that they fail to address the structural economic causes of the phenomenon. Encouraging early marriage or discouraging divorce cannot reverse the technological and social changes that have made the traditional marriage model obsolete. Moreover, such measures often reinforce gender inequality by pressuring women to sacrifice independence and personal fulfillment for the sake of social conformity. Attempts to 'tighten' marriage norms also overlook the diversity of modern family arrangements. Many couples cohabit for long periods, raise children together, and share resources without formalizing their union. Others may prefer open or non-exclusive relationships. Bergmann claimed that these variations reflect new social realities rather than moral decline. Therefore, the goal should not be to restore a vanished model but to ensure that all forms of family life are compatible with social justice and child well-being.

Although cohabitation and other alternative family arrangements have grown in popularity, they have not succeeded in replicating the redistributive function of marriage. Cohabiting unions tend to be less stable than marriages, particularly when children are involved, and legal protections for partners are often weaker. As a result, when such relationships dissolve, women and children bear disproportionate economic costs. Some thinkers have proposed open marriage or non-monogamous models as more honest and adaptable alternatives to the traditional institution of marriage. However, Bergmann insisted, these approaches overlook the core economic dimension of marriage. The problem is not sexual exclusivity but the need for a reliable mechanism to allocate resources and caregiving labor: romantic flexibility alone cannot substitute for the financial and social security that marriage once provided.

According to Bergmann, neither cultural innovations nor changes in moral norms can restore the distributive and protective functions of marriage. Instead, new policy frameworks are required to replace the economic role that marriage historically played in supporting children and balancing gendered responsibilities. Recognizing that the traditional marital system is unlikely to be revived, Bergmann advocated for a comprehensive expansion of public welfare provisions to ensure that children receive adequate support regardless of family structure. The state, rather than the marital bond, must become the primary mechanism for transferring resources to the next generation. This would involve guaranteeing universal access to high-quality child care, health care, education, and housing, as well as publicly funded university education. Such programs would reduce the dependence of children's well-being on their parents' marital status or income level. Bergmann envisioned a social system where the costs of reproduction are shared collectively rather than borne privately by women or individual households.

However, Bergmann admitted, this policy orientation is not without challenges: while redistributive policies are essential, they should not reproduce the economic dependency that characterized traditional marriage. Supporting lone mothers and families generously might conflict with other goals of gender equality. For example, providing high allowances to stay-at-home parents could unintentionally discourage women from participating in the labor force, reinforcing traditional gender roles. Hence, instead of paying women to remain at home, governments should invest in services that enable both parents to combine work and family life, such as affordable childcare, flexible work arrangements, and parental leave for both mothers and fathers.

This approach would preserve women's economic autonomy while ensuring that children receive the care they need. It would also acknowledge that the costs of raising the next generation are a collective responsibility, not a private burden. Therefore, policy design must carefully balance the objectives of child welfare and gender equity. In this vision, the state partially replaces the economic functions once performed by marriage, but without reinstating gender inequality. As private family-based welfare systems weaken, public institutions must step in to prevent social fragmentation. If governments fail to adapt, societies risk widening inequality and perpetuating cycles of disadvantage for children born into less stable or less affluent families. Conversely, if states successfully develop inclusive welfare systems, the decline of marriage could coexist with greater freedom and equality. The text thus invites a reconsideration of how societies distribute the costs of reproduction and care—a question that lies at the heart of both economic and moral life.

Summing up, Bergmann's last writing on marriage presented a compelling analysis of the transformation of marriage from a central economic institution into a more fragile, individualized, and voluntary relationship. Bergmann considered the decline of marriage and the rise of diverse family forms not as moral decline but as the effect of profound structural changes, technological, economic, and social, that have altered the incentives and capacities of men and women alike. While this transformation has expanded individual autonomy, it has also undermined the traditional mechanisms that ensured the economic support of children and the redistribution of resources between genders. Efforts to restore marriage through moral persuasion or restrictive laws have proven ineffective because they ignore the underlying economic realities. The only viable path forward, according to Bergmann, is to build a new social contract that recognizes children as a collective responsibility and provides public support for their care and development. Such a system would replace the economic function once performed by marriage with a broader, more equitable network of social protection. The challenge lies in achieving this transition without reintroducing dependency or reinforcing old hierarchies.

Bergmann envisioned a society where both men and women share equally in paid work and caregiving, supported by state policies that guarantee security and opportunity for all families, regardless of form. In this way, the decline of marriage, far from signaling social decay, could mark the beginning of a new stage in the evolution of human cooperation, one based on fairness, autonomy, and shared responsibility.

As mentioned earlier, Bergmann's unpublished *The Decline of Marriage and What To Do About It* was transformed in part into her working paper "The Economic Consequences of the Decline of Marriage" (Bergmann, 2008). The contents of the two documents were basically the same. In the appendix to the working paper, Bergmann added some data about the decline of marriage in European countries as well as in the United States, along with some tables on the economic situation of American households with children under 12 in the case of two-earner married couples, one-earner married couples, job-holding single mothers, and single mothers on 'welfare'. In the first part of the working paper, Bergmann directly attacked Becker's *Treatise* and his followers (especially Greenwood & Guner, 2008), who attributed the decline of marriage to the introduction of new technologies that facilitated women's work at home and pushed them into the labor force by reducing the efficient specialization within marriages. As Bergmann wrote, displaying her usual sarcasm: "on this account, the invention of the vacuum cleaner and the refrigerator and the development of takeout food has made an important contribution to the decline of marriage" (Bergmann, 2008, p. 3). In the second part of the working paper, Bergmann pointed out the difficulties of transforming social welfare measures for single mothers into fully funded programs, which usually require the government to raise taxes in a politically unpopular way.

4.3 Affirmative Action for Child Care

Bergmann's research on the economics of the family was never limited to the condition of women, rather it was always extended to affordable child care, the role of the government in providing it, and its quality standards. As Bergmann explained, child care may be considered affordable if "it costs parents no more than 30 percent of the amount by which their income exceeds the poverty line" (Bergmann, 1999, p. 208).

Bergmann's archival material reveals that, in the early 1980s, Bergmann was developing a research proposal for a fair and equitable economic support system for children whose divorced fathers did not provide regular financial support: *Proposal for a Study: The Provision of Adequate, Equitable, and Assured Economic Support for Children.* Initially conceived as a book with eleven chapters, the proposal materialized only partially in an article published in 1981 (Bergmann, 1981b). Later, it was revised and included in her book *The Economic Emergence of Women* (Bergmann, 1986, 2005b), again in partial form. In 1981, Bergmann published two more papers related to child care (Bergmann, 1981c, 1981d) which substantially summarized the *Proposal.*

Bergmann's *Proposal* highlighted the growing demographic significance of children who live apart from their fathers. By 1977, one in six American children fell into this category, compared to one in ten in 1970. This trend, she observed, was largely attributable to the increasing prevalence of divorce rather than to nonmarital births, which accounted for only about 20% of the increase. Despite these changes, institutional mechanisms for ensuring paternal contributions to child-rearing had failed to evolve. Bergmann reported that only about one in five children living apart from their fathers received regular support payments, leaving mothers and taxpayers to shoulder the economic burden of child rearing. The result was a growing incidence of child poverty and increasing resentment among taxpayers toward welfare-dependent households.

The existing child support enforcement apparatus was, in her words, "archaic" and largely ineffective, dependent on private legal action rather than systematic state enforcement. The welfare system, though expanded in response to growing need, remained stigmatized and often insufficient, failing to lift many single-mother families out of poverty. Consequently, Bergmann argued for a fundamental reconsideration of how economic support for children is structured in the United States. She insisted that piecemeal reforms, such as improved enforcement measures or modest welfare adjustments, were inadequate without a broader theoretical and empirical understanding of how to coordinate the responsibilities of absent parents, the rules of custodial parents, and the role of the state.

Bergmann's *Proposal*, which situated itself within a modest but growing body of research of the time on child support,[14] was organized around three core themes: a comprehensive assessment of the current

[14] The pioneering work of Isabel Sawhill and her colleagues at The Urban Institute beginning in 1974 marked a turning point. Their analyses, compiled in *Child Support Payments in the United States* (Jones et al., 1976), provided the first systematic documentation of widespread delinquencies in support payments. Sawhill's subsequent paper, *Developing Normative Standards for Child Support and Alimony Payments* (1977), advanced an "income-sharing" formula for setting payment levels, based on the premise that former spouses should continue to share income after separation in proportion to their pre-divorce living standards. Judith Cassetty's doctoral research, published as *Child Support and Public Policy* (1978), expanded on Sawhill's conceptual model. Using data from the Michigan Panel Survey, Cassetty investigated the dimensions and determinants of payment delinquency, and, like Sawhill, advocated a federal takeover of enforcement responsibilities from local courts. Though she did not elaborate the administrative details, her argument underscored the inadequacy of the decentralized, litigation-based model. Meanwhile, David Chambers's *Making Fathers Pay* (1979) provided an important legal and institutional perspective through a case study of Michigan's county-level enforcement practices. Chambers demonstrated wide disparities in enforcement vigor (some counties jailing delinquents and others neglecting to pursue cases altogether) and found that prompt and firm enforcement produced better outcomes, though at the cost of questionable due process. Together, these studies revealed the multidimensional nature of

state of child support payments; the development and evaluation of methodologies for determining equitable payment levels; and an analysis of alternative systems for delivering child support payments and coordinating them with welfare programs. The unifying goal of the *Proposal* was to explore the feasibility and desirability of a coherent and unified system that would protect children from poverty, promote self-sufficiency among custodial parents, and reduce the long-term welfare burden on taxpayers.

Bergmann proposed to analyze the 1979 Child Support Supplement to the U.S. Census Bureau's Current Population Survey (CPS)[15] to quantify the extent of payment delinquencies, the adequacy of payments relative to household needs, and the correlation between payment patterns and child poverty. Supplementary case studies of court enforcement processes, including legal costs, delays, and payment records, would provide qualitative depth to the statistical findings.

Bergmann also envisioned a comparative analysis of alternative formulas for setting child support levels. As mentioned earlier, she identified two broad conceptual approaches: cost-sharing and income-sharing. The cost-sharing approach estimates the actual expenses of raising a child and distributes those costs between parents (and possibly the state) according to some principle of fairness. The income-sharing approach, by contrast, assumes a continued pooling of parental resources even after separation, maintaining the child's standard of living at a level commensurate with the parents' combined income.

A key challenge for the cost-sharing model, Bergmann observed, lies in defining the cost of a child. She suggested using data from the 1972–73 Consumer Expenditure Survey to compare expenditure patterns of single adults with and without children at similar income levels. The difference in expenditures necessary to equalize living standards could serve as an empirical estimate of the marginal cost of a child. This analysis could also inform adjustments for varying parental incomes, the presence of multiple children, or changes in household composition. Bergmann's methodological plan thus combined macro-level survey analysis with micro-level

the problem: legal inconsistency, administrative weakness, and the lack of an empirically grounded standard for determining equitable support levels.

[15] This nationally representative dataset included responses from 41,000 women with children whose fathers were absent, providing information on child support awards, the amounts received, other sources of household income, marital status, labor force participation, and related variables (U.S. Bureau of the Census, 1980).

expenditure data to derive realistic and equitable benchmarks for child support.

Beyond the mechanics of calculating payment levels, Bergmann's *Proposal* engaged with the broader social and policy implications of child support reform. She planned to investigate the relationship between financial contributions and paternal involvement, hypothesizing that reliable payment mechanisms may strengthen non-custodial fathers' emotional and social connection to their children. A small-sample survey would collect data on visitation frequency, communication, and the custodial parent's attitudes toward the absent parent's payment record. Bergmann underscored the importance of this inquiry: while stricter enforcement might encourage financial compliance, it could also provoke conflict or even custody disputes.

The *Proposal* also addressed ongoing efforts by the federal Office of Support Enforcement within the Department of Health and Human Services, which was implementing Title IV-D of the Social Security Act.[16] In later sections of the *Proposal*, Bergmann compared how different societies organize childrearing support systems. In industrialized nations like the United States, the intact nuclear family serves as the 'standard' system, while welfare programs and court-ordered child support function as 'second-line' systems for children outside traditional family arrangements. The weaknesses of these second-line systems, such as poverty, dependency, and social stigma, reflect broader structural inequities in how society values caregiving and distributes economic responsibility.

A particularly innovative element of Bergmann's plan was her consideration of whether single mothers should be 'expected' to work. She framed this question as both ethical and economic. On one hand, the traditional right of mothers to care for their children full-time remains socially valued; on the other, the economic realities of single parenthood often make employment necessary. Bergmann argued that in the case of single-parent households, the decision is no longer purely private: the government must either enforce private transfers from absent parents or

[16] The agency collected and reported data on amounts recovered from absent parents, often highlighting "success stories" without fully accounting for potentially collectible amounts. Bergmann suggested using the 1979 Current Population Survey (CPS) data to estimate the gap between actual and potential child support revenues, offering a more rigorous assessment of program effectiveness. A detailed case study, possibly of Maryland's IV-D program, would explore administrative practices and assess cost-effectiveness at the state level.

supply welfare funds to cover both the child's and the caregiver's needs. Thus, the issue of maternal employment becomes a matter of public policy, requiring a cost-benefit analysis of labor force participation versus full-time caregiving.

Bergmann also situated child support reform within the larger context of family dynamics and visitation rights. She observed that financial and emotional dimensions of post-separation parenting are deeply intertwined. Better enforcement and standardized payment systems could normalize paternal contributions and thereby facilitate more stable relationships between fathers and children. Conversely, she noted that some mothers resist accepting child support to avoid continued contact with the father, particularly when relationships are fraught or when abuse has occurred. Improved enforcement could also have unintended consequences, such as incentivizing more fathers to seek custody or discouraging remarriage. As always, Bergmann called for careful empirical attention to these complex interactions.

The final chapters of Bergmann's *Proposal* focused on possible policy options. These included replacing the court-based system with administrative procedures, federalizing both payments and transfers through agencies such as the Internal Revenue Service or the Social Security Administration, and integrating child support with welfare programs to guarantee a minimum income floor for all children. Each alternative, she argued, carries potential benefits and risks: administrative efficiency may come at the cost of individualized justice; federalization may enhance uniformity but intrude on family privacy; and integration with welfare could ensure universal coverage but weaken parental responsibility incentives.[17]

The overarching vision of Bergmann's proposal is to move toward a rational, empirically grounded, and ethically defensible system of child support that aligns the interests of children, custodial parents, absent parents, and taxpayers. By integrating statistical analysis with institutional case studies and theoretical modeling, the study provided the first comprehensive assessment of the economic support of children in single-parent households in the United States. Furthermore, Bergmann's approach anticipated the later development of what would become the

[17] Bergmann also discussed a proposal by Watts to levy a tax on absent parents, using the proceeds to fund benefits for children in single-parent households. Using the CPS data, she intended to simulate the fiscal and distributive effects of each proposed reform.

modern child support enforcement system, combining data-driven policy design with a concern for gender equity and child welfare.

Ultimately, Bergmann's proposal was both a critique and a blueprint. At the same time, she criticized the inefficiency, inequity, and moral inconsistency of a system that leaves millions of children economically insecure while placing disproportionate burdens on mothers, and she offered a constructive vision for reform grounded in rigorous empirical research and normative clarity. Her insistence that children's economic well-being should not depend on the marital status of their parents anticipates later debates about universal child allowances and state-guaranteed family support.

In 1987, Bergmann embedded the main ideas of her *Proposal*, into the concept of 'parental responsibility', that would require all absent parents to pay child support and would put single parents with custody in a position where they were able to take substantial jobs (Bergmann, 1987). She stressed that child support differed from welfare in crucial ways. Welfare was paid entirely by taxpayers and was reduced or eliminated when mothers worked, creating perverse disincentives. Child support, by contrast, would come largely from absent parents and could continue regardless of the custodial parent's earnings. A mother's wages combined with dependable child-support payments would lift many families above the poverty line. Bergmann acknowledged the familiar objections: many fathers were poor, unemployed, young, or simply missing. But research showed that in most cases fathers could pay something. The more difficult issue, she noted, was race. Because discrimination had constrained Black men's employment opportunities and marriage rates, single-mother families were far more common among Black Americans. Critics on the left feared that shifting from welfare to child support would extract money from already-struggling Black communities and unfairly penalize Black men. Bergmann recognized the ethical concerns but argued that welfare, even with higher benefits, simply could not lift families to a decent standard of living. Only earnings could do that.

Bergmann criticized both liberals and conservatives on this issue. On one side, some liberals remained committed to the idea that mothers, especially poor ones, should stay home with their children. According to Bergmann, this view no longer matched social reality. On the other side, she rejected conservatives who disliked dependency and paying for welfare, but also tended to judge the behaviors that led women to welfare in the first place. Bergmann emphasized that single parents needed access to well-paying jobs, and that this would require affirmative action policies and training for occupations which were traditionally excluded for women. Finally, she dismissed the objection that there simply were not enough jobs for millions of single mothers. Historically, she noted, the labor force had grown continuously and had been absorbed. There was no reason to believe that single mothers entering the workforce would create unemployment rather than be absorbed like previous entrants.

In the 1990s, Bergmann continuously worked on setting up an economic agenda aimed at supporting child care and eliminating child poverty (Bergmann, 1994a, 1994b, 1994c, 1995a, 1996a, 1996b, 1997; Bergmann & Wetchler, 1995; Renwick & Bergmann, 1993). Overall, she argued that the U.S. welfare debate had been dominated by inadequate ideas that failed to confront the basic reality: many single mothers simply could not earn enough to support their families once child care and health care were accounted for. However dysfunctional the existing welfare system was, it addressed a real and unavoidable problem. Sooner or later, she said, the nation would have to abandon the fantasy that a 'government-free' America could somehow avoid social problems. Any serious attempt to reduce child poverty requires a national program that helps parents meet the expenses of raising children. A workable alternative to the current system would have to pursue three goals simultaneously: helping single parents into jobs, reducing unplanned births, and lowering child poverty rates.

In an article published in 1996 on *Challenge*, she dismissed the Republican flirtation with abolishing welfare as politically impossible and morally unacceptable: Americans would not tolerate a system that drove mothers to relinquish their children out of sheer desperation. The other Republican idea, returning responsibility to the states with severe limitations, was merely a less generous version of the *status quo*. It would leave the same families on welfare, only poorer, and intensify a race-to-the-bottom dynamic in which states cut benefits to attract wealthier residents and industry. She also rejected the Republican 'self-reliance' model, which imagined that single mothers could support their children solely through decent jobs with benefits. In reality, a mother with two preschoolers would have needed wages far above what most single mothers earned, especially if she had to pay for child care herself. Without substantial public support, self-reliance was a myth for the majority (Bergmann, 1996a).

Bergmann often compared the situation in the U.S. with the situation in some European countries, such as Sweden, France, and the Netherlands. She was firmly convinced that child care outside the home will continue to increase, although problems with quality will require remedial regulatory action. Hence, a cogent case can be made for a large government role in the financing of child care, the only possible way to make progress against the problem of child poverty in America. She underlined that while in Sweden and France child care is provided with ample cash help to working parents, which promotes high work participation by single mothers, in the Netherlands it is provided through high cash help to mothers who stay home. According to Bergmann, a serious effort to lower child poverty in the United States would have to be modeled on the Swedish/French solution, which would involve extensive government support of child care.

In 1996, Bergmann published *Saving Our Children from Poverty: What the United States Can Learn from France* (Bergmann, 1996b) which was summarized in a paper published by the Foundation for Child Development (Bergmann, 1997). Bergmann noted that, in recent decades, there had been a growing willingness on the part of the U.S. government to provide large-scale assistance for high-cost items such as health insurance and child care to low-income working parents, particularly those transitioning off welfare, but also to other groups. This emerging willingness created a significant opportunity to combat child poverty, a persistent and pressing social problem.

The welfare legislation, enacted in 1996, responded to widespread public frustration over funding nonworking single mothers with taxpayer money. Paradoxically, this welfare reform highlighted the practical challenges faced by working single mothers, as most available jobs offered low wages, often without access to affordable health insurance or child care. Without public assistance to cover these essential services, parents leaving welfare would be effectively forced to neglect the needs of their children. Even more notably, legislative initiatives at the federal level and in several state governments have moved toward extending child care and health benefits to all lower-income parents, not just those moving off welfare. Judged by both rhetoric and appropriations, there is far less hostility toward spending public money on services that directly benefit children than toward cash transfers to nonworking mothers. This shift in political and public attitude opens the possibility of a broad-based attack on child poverty.

Bergmann introduced the Basic Needs Budget (BNB) approach to examine what families with children realistically need for a decent standard of living. She demonstrated that a single mother with two preschool children working full-time at a minimum wage could meet a minimally decent standard of living if government assistance covered child care and health insurance, alongside housing support in high-rent areas. The BNB, unlike the official U.S. poverty measure, accounts for essential living expenses, including non-dilapidated housing, public transportation, food, clothing, and basic services, while also providing for health insurance and child care for working parents.[18]

Hence, BNB served Bergmann to propose a Help For Working Parents (HWP) program that extended assistance to all low-wage parents, not only those leaving welfare, would have the potential to significantly reduce child poverty in the United States (see Chapter 6).

The proposed HWP program would provide guaranteed health insurance for all children and their parents, and for families not receiving coverage through employers, the government would pay the full cost for the least affluent families and partial support for others. Child care for preschool-aged children and after-school programs for elementary-aged children would be fully subsidized for lower-income families and partially subsidized for middle-income families, using a voucher system applicable at licensed public and private care facilities meeting quality standards. The establishment and enforcement of child support measures would be federalized and administered by the Internal Revenue Service, ensuring minimum monthly payments.

According to Bergmann, by providing services instead of cash, the HWP program addresses a central challenge of child poverty: ensuring that aid directly benefits children rather than being used for other purposes. Economists typically argue that cash benefits maximize family utility, but health care and high-quality child care are merit goods, where direct provision ensures that children receive necessary care. Furthermore,

[18] For example, a single mother with two preschool-aged children living in an area with average housing costs would require approximately $26,000 annually, exclusive of direct taxes, to meet the basic needs standard. This sum includes $12,000 for food, clothing, shelter, and transportation; $4000 for services; $10,000 for health insurance; and additional funds for licensed child care. Even a modest job could allow a life at a decent standard if government support covered child care and health costs.

high-quality child care not only protects children from unsafe environments but also enhances cognitive and social development, improving readiness for school and potentially breaking cycles of disadvantage. In contrast, tax credits and cash-based interventions, while politically popular, offer less targeted support for low-income families with young children.[19]

Alternative approaches, such as refundable tax credits, labor market interventions, or radical welfare cuts, are less effective. Tax credits fail to concentrate benefits on families with young children in low-wage jobs. Labor market programs improving employability and wages may not directly transfer resources to children. In contrast, the HWP program delivers targeted resources to families most in need, emphasizing services directly beneficial to children.

Bergmann concluded by maintaining that in the long run, a serious attack on child poverty requires a substantial increase in public resources devoted to children, particularly those in low-wage households. Health insurance and child care services provide a floor for children's well-being, supporting parents as they enter the workforce. Political and ideological resistance may challenge publicly funded child care, but evidence suggests that Americans broadly support health coverage for children, and careful program design can mitigate concerns about fairness or unintended labor market incentives. The central obstacle is not the technical feasibility of such programs but political will.[20]

As she wrote:

> Claims that the United States could not afford to provide government-financed care to children are based on obfuscatory rhetoric. Whether one favors government providing child care to the upper two-thirds of families

[19] Cost analyses suggest that transitioning a family from AFDC to a full-time minimum wage job with HWP benefits would increase public expenditure by approximately $8250 per year relative to Aid to Families with Dependent Children (AFDC), Food Stamps, and Medicaid. This investment would yield higher standards of living, access to high-quality developmental day care, and employment opportunities for the parent. Extending child care and health care benefits to low-wage families outside the welfare system would further increase costs, with estimates around $90 billion per year, representing a 71% increase over current spending for families with children.

[20] With approximately $90 billion annually, the U.S. could implement an HWP program capable of drastically reducing child poverty, representing a pragmatic and morally compelling option for a wealthy society (Bergmann, 1981a, 1981b, 1981c, 1981d, p. 23).

> with children depends mostly on one's view of women's roles in society and one's view of how the economic burden of bringing up the next generation ought to be distributed. Setting quality standards in an informed way requires that we research the tradeoffs of cost for quality. (Bergmann, 1993, p. 1083)

In the 2000s, Bergmann maintained her interest for child-care very high. In 2002, she co-authored a book with Suzanne Helburn (Helburn & Bergmann, 2002). They identified two major issues of the structural and economic challenges facing child care in the United States: the high cost of child care, given the largely inanequate current financial support mechanisms for families, and its inconsistent, and sometimes unsafe, quality, given that subsidies aimed at low-income families reached only a minority of eligible households, leaving many children without access to quality care. Similarly, tax credits for middle-class families covered only a small portion of actual child care expenses. The inadequacy of these supports often forces families with limited financial resources to rely on low-cost, low-quality, and frequently unlicensed care, which can compromise children's safety, well-being, and developmental prospects.

To address these deficiencies, the authors proposed a dual approach involving robust federal regulation and significant federal funding. They advocated for a system of vouchers for low- and middle-income families, alongside cash to care providers. Again, comparative models from other developed countries were adopted, highlighting the Swedish/French solution, which combines government-subsidized child care with cash support for working parents, resulting in high labor-force participation among single mothers. The book also addressed the political and cultural barriers to reform, such as the enduring cultural preference for mother-only care, which makes proposals for state-supported child care politically contentious. From an economic perspective, Helburn and Bergmann examined the costs and potential benefits of reform by analyzing child care expenditures relative to household income and inflation, as well as wage structures for child care workers, noting that underpaid staff can compromise service quality. By introducing targeted subsidies, vouchers, and cash support, the government could reduce financial strain on families, raise quality standards, and ensure that children, particularly those from lower-income households, receive appropriate developmental support. The authors defended government-funded child care as a 'merit good', emphasizing its positive social externalities, such as increased labor-force stability among parents and enhanced long-term outcomes for children.

Bergmann's entire work on the economics of the family revealed some fundamental points in her economic perspective. First, the complex dynamics of marriage as a social institution were often rooted in an unequal division of labor between spouses. Second, the intra-household dynamics of care-giving were primarily imposed on women. Third, the role of the legal framework greatly affected the dynamics of marriage and divorce. Fourth, economic policies aimed at improving the condition of women and children, especially after separation/divorce, should be promoted. Furthermore, Bergmann's economic analysis of marriage is pivotal for understanding the creation of feminist economics (see Chapter 6), aimed at reacting to Becker's NHE and calling for an urgent and crucial revision of the discipline as a whole.

References

Bankovsky, M. (2020). A history of early household economics: Improving the family's contribution to industrial production and rationalising family consumption. *Oxford Economic Papers, 72*(4), 985–1005.

Bankovsky, M. (2025). *Economics and the family*. Cambridge University Press.

Becchio, G. (2020). *A history of feminist and gender economics*. Routledge.

Becchio, G. (2024a). *The doctrine of the separate spheres in political economy and economics*. Palgrave Macmillan.

Becchio, G. (2024b). Pioneering feminist economics: Barbara Bergmann's contributions to gender issues. *Eastern Economic Journal, 50*(4), 472–495.

Becker, G. (1973). A theory of marriage: Part I. *Journal of Political Economy, 81*(4), 813–846.

Becker, G. (1974a). A theory of social interactions. *Journal of Political Economy, 82*(6), 1063–1094.

Becker, G. (1974b). A theory of marriage: Part II. *Journal of Political Economy, 82*(2), 11–26.

Becker, G. (1981). *A treatise on the family*. Harvard University Press.

Becker, G. (1991). *A treatise on the family* (Enlarged ed.). Harvard University Press.

Becker, G., Landes, E., & Michael, R. (1977). An economic analysis of marital instability. *Journal of Political Economy, 85*(6), 1147–1187.

Bergmann, B. (1973a). The economics of women's liberations. *Annals of the New York Academy of Sciences, 208*, 154–160.

Bergmann, B. (1973b). *The struggle of women in the United States*. Paper prepared for the WFUNA/ISMUN Summer School, Kungalv, Sweden. Barbara R. Bergmann papers, box 4, David M. Rubenstein Rare Book & Manuscript Library, Duke University.

Bergmann, B. (1974a). Occupational segregation, wages and profits when employers discriminate by race and sex. *Eastern Economic Journal, 2*(3): 103–110.

Bergmann, B. (1974b). The struggle of women in the United States. Barbara Bergmann's archive. Barbara R. Bergmann papers, box 4, David M. Rubenstein Rare Book & Manuscript Library, Duke University.

Bergmann, B. (1979). Women's interests in pension reform. Testimony delivered to the president's commission on pension policy on behalf of the women's equity action league. Barbara R. Bergmann papers, David M. Rubenstein Rare Book & Manuscript Library, Duke University.

Bergmann, B. (1980). The housewife and social security reform: A feminist perspective. In R. Burkhauser & K. Holden (Eds.), *A challenge to social security* (pp. 229–233). Academic Press.

Bergmann, B. (1981a). The economic risks of being a housewife. *American Economic Review, 71*(2), 81–86.

Bergmann, B. (1981b). Proposal for a study: The provision of adequate, equitable, and assured economic support for children. Unpublished. Barbara Bergmann papers, box 3, David M. Rubenstein Rare Book & Manuscript Library, Duke University.

Bergmann, B. (1981c). The share of women and men in the economic support of children. *Human Rights Quarterly, 3*(2), 103–112.

Bergmann, B. (1981d). The economic support of fatherless children. In P. Brown, C. Johnson, & P. Vernier (Eds.), *Income support. Concept and policy issues* (pp. 195–210). Rowman and Littlefield.

Bergmann, B. (1985). The United States of America. In J. Farley (Ed.), *Women workers in fifteen countries. Essays in Honor of Alice Hanson Cook* (pp. 170–176). Cornell University Press.

Bergmann, B. (1986). *The economic emergence of women*. Basic Books.

Bergmann, B. (1987). A fresh start on welfare reform. *Challenge, 30*(5), 44–50.

Bergmann, B. (1990a). Feminism and economics. *Women's Studies Quarterly, 18*(3/4), 68–74. Reprinted from *Academe: Bulletin of the American Association of University Professors*. 1983, *69*(5), 22–25.

Bergmann, B. (1990b). Women's role in the economy: Teaching the issue. *Women's Studies Quarterly, 18*(3/4), 6–22.

Bergmann, B. (1994a). Can we afford to save our children? Cost and structure of government programs for children in the US and France. *Feminist Economics, 3*(1), 85–94.

Bergmann, B. (1994b). The economic support of child-raising. Curing poverty in the United States. *American Economic Review, 84*(2), 76–80.

Bergmann, B. (1994c). Economic issues in child care policy. *Pediatrics, 94*(6), 1083–1084.

Bergmann, B. (1995a). *The future of child care.* Prepared for presentation at the meeting of the American Sociological Association. Barbara Bergmann's papers, box 2. David M. Rubenstein Rare Book & Manuscript Library, Duke University.

Bergmann, B. (1995b). Becker's theory of the family: preposterous conclusions. *Feminist Economics, 1*(1), 141–150. Reprinted in *Challenge* (1996), *39*(1), 9–12.

Bergmann, B. (1996a). Real welfare reform: Help for working parents. *Challenge, 39*(5), 34–37.

Bergmann, B. (1996b). *Saving our children from poverty: what the United States can learn from France.* Russell Sage Foundation.

Bergmann, B. (1997). Reducing poverty among American children through a "help for working parents" program. *Working paper series. Foundation for Child Development*, pp. 3–24.

Bergmann, B. (1999). Making child care "affordable" in the United States. *The Annals of the American Academy of Political and Social, 563*(1), 208–219.

Bergmann, B. (2003a). The challenge of single motherhood. (Unpublished). Barbara Bergmann's papers, box 7. David M. Rubenstein Rare Book & Manuscript Library, Duke University.

Bergmann, B. (2003b). What policies toward lone mothers should we aim for? (Unpublished). Barbara Bergmann's Papers, box 7. David M. Rubenstein Rare Book & Manuscript Library, Duke University.

Bergmann, B. (2005a). Pushing for a more humane society. *American Economist, 49*(2), 11–15.

Bergmann, B. (2005b). *The economic emergence of women* (2nd ed.). Palgrave Macmillan.

Bergmann, B. (n.d.). (Undated. Presumably Between 2005 and 2008). *The decline of marriage and what to do about it.* (Unpublished). Barbara Bergmann's Papers, box 7. David M. Rubenstein Rare Book & Manuscript Library, Duke University.

Bergmann, B. (2008). *The economic consequences of the decline of marriage* (Working Paper No. 0818). Department of Economics, Johannes Kepler University of Linz.

Bergmann, B., & Adelman, I. (1973). The 1973 report of the President's council of economic advisers: the economic role of women. *American Economic Review, 63*(4), 509–514.

Bergmann, B., & Gray, M. (1975). Equality in retirement benefits. The need for pension reform. *Civil Rights Digest, 8*, 25–27.

Bergmann, B., & Wetchler, S. (1995). Child support awards: State guidelines vs public opinion. *Family Law Quarterly, 29*(3), 483–493.

Cassetty, J. (1978). *Child support and public policy.* Lexington Books.

Chambers, D. (1979). *Making fathers pay.* University of Chicago Press.

Danzinger, S. (1980). Do working wives increase family income inequality? *The Journal of Human Resources, 15*(3), 444–451.

Folbre, N. (1998a). The sphere of women in early twentieth century economics. In H. Silverberg (Ed.), *Gender and American social science: The formative years* (pp. 35–60). Princeton University Press.

Folbre, N. (1998b). Barbara, the market, and the state. *Feminist Economics, 4*(3), 159–168.

Forget, E. (2011). American women and the economics profession in the twentieth century. *Oeconomica, 1*(1): 19–30.

Friedan, B. (1963). *The feminine mystique.* W. W. Norton and Co.

Fuchs, V. (1971). Differences in hourly earnings between men and women. *Monthly Labor Review, 94*(5), 9–15.

Garfinkel, I. (1978). Testimony on welfare reform to state Senate Human Services Committee, August 15–16.

Greenwood, J. & Guner N. (2008). Marriage and divorce since World War II: analyzing the role of technological progress on the formation of households. NBER Working Paper 10772, *NBER Macroeconomics Annual, 23*: 231–276.

Grossbard, S. (2001). The new home economics at Columbia and Chicago. *Feminist Economics, 7*(3), 103–130.

Hartmann, H. (1998). The economic emergence of women: Bergmann's six commitments. *Feminist Economics, 4*(3), 169–180.

Helburn, S., & Bergmann, B. (2002). *America's child care problem: The way out.* Palgrave Macmillan.

Henderson, D. (1987). The Economics of feminism. Online available at: https://www.econlib.org/archives/2015/04/my_review_of_ba.html; https://www.econlib.org/archives/2015/04/my_review_of_ba_1.html; and https://www.econlib.org/archives/2015/04/my_review_of_ba_2.html

Himmelweit, S., Bergmann, B., Green, K., Albelda, R., The Women's Committee of One Hundred, & Koren, C. (2004). Dialogue lone mother: What is to be done? *Feminist Economics, 10*(2), 237–264.

Jones, C., Gordon, N., & Sawhill, I. (1976). *Child support payments in the United States* (Urban Institute Working Paper 992-03). The Urban Institute.

Mincer, J. (1962). Labor force participation of married women: A study of labor supply. In H. Gregg Lewis (Ed.), *Aspects of labor economics* (pp. 63–105). Princeton University Press.

Mincer, J. (1963). Market prices, opportunity costs, and income effects. In C. Christ (Ed.), *Measurement in economics* (pp. 66–82). Stanford University Press.

Olson, P. (2007). On the contributions of Barbara Bergmann to economics. *Review of Political Economy, 19*(4), 475–496.

Orozco Espinel, C., & Gomez Betancourt, R. (2022). A history of the institutionalization of feminist economics through its tensions and founders. *History of Political Economy, 54*(S1), 159–192.

Renwick, T., & Bergmann, B. (1993). Expenditure budgets for single-parent families: A basic-needs approach. *Journal of Family and Economic Issues, 14*(3), 235–256.

Sawhill, I. (1977). *Developing normative standards for child support and alimony payments.* (Urban Institute Working Paper 992–04). The Urban Institute.

Strober, M., & Chan, A. (1998). Husbands, wives, and housework: Graduates of Stanford and Tokyo Universities. *Feminist Economics, 4*(3), 97–127.

U.S. Bureau of the Census. (1980). *Child support and alimony: 1978 (advance report)* (Current population Reports, Series P-23, No. 106). Government Printing Office.

Weintraub, A., & Bergmann, B. (1973). Women's lib: Who gets what? [with responds]. *Challenge, 16*(3), 69.

CHAPTER 5

Advocating New Methods for Economics

Interviewed by Liz Strober, about what being an economist means to her, Bergmann replied:

> The worst part is having to listen to other economists make fools of themselves, although sometimes it has amusement value. When you read that recessions occur because workers simultaneously decide it is not worthwhile to work for the going wage (Lucas and Rapping), or that women get lower wages than men because they happen to be in lines of work that require a greater degree of supervision (Goldin), or that Social Security has ruined the American economy by killing the savings rate (Feldstein), you don't know whether to laugh or cry for our profession. However, being an optimist, I have hope that the profession will someday get into a scientific mode, based on anthropological observation of behavior, and computer simulation of interactions. (Strober 1998, p. 5)

In another interview, she observed: "We [economists] have a certain methodology, namely the theoretical: we sit in a room and we think. It is not really too connected to the real world. It doesn't in any way take account of the complexity of the real world" (Saunders & King 2000, p. 305).

She continued with an episode that occurred on January 3, 1998, when she was chairing a session whose speakers were Deirdre McCloskey, Kenneth Arrow, Edward Leamer, and Rich van der Ploeg, at the ASSA

G. Becchio, *Barbara Bergmann*, Great Thinkers in Economics,
https://doi.org/10.1007/978-3-032-18696-6_5

meeting in Chicago. McCloskey presented a paper attacking theory, specifically the proof of the existence theorem and its empirical applications. When Arrow replied that economists get input from our lives, Bergmann said:

> Well you know we may know about household behavior but we don't know anything about business (…) You can advance mathematics by that mathematical models, or some sorts of logical structures. But you can't really say that you are observing something that is out there. (ibid, p. 307)

Then she concluded that:

> We need a more anthropological way of gathering information about what is out there" and suggested that "a better way to investigate [economic phenomena] would be some sort of detective work, talking to people. You never get it from data. (ibid, p. 309)

In these interviews, Bergmann well summarized her contribution to economic methodology that was centered on three interconnected aspects.

First, she urged a more empirical approach to the scrutiny of economic phenomena, based on the real dynamics behind decision-making. Bergmann's commitment to an empirical approach began before her academic career, during her work at the Bureau of Labor Statistics (see Chapter 2). Throughout her academic life, she continued to insist on the importance of moving away from abstraction in economics and becoming more connected with the real dynamics behind individual level decision-making processes, which are the starting point for a proper scrutiny of macroeconomic phenomena.

Second, she profoundly criticized mainstream economics, particularly its reliance on rational-choice theory and formalized equilibrium models based on maximization, which failed to describe economic realities concretely. Bergmann shared with feminist economists the urgency of rejecting the neoclassical model of the rational economic man, constructed as a self-sufficient adult, and regarded Becker's New Home Economics as a primary target. However, she did not devote her efforts to developing an alternative model of rationality designed to overcome the masculine notions of objectivity, logic, and abstraction. Instead, she preferred to conduct empirical research, collect data, and propose practical solutions aimed at understanding and reducing social inequalities, particularly those affecting women and children.

Third, she constantly worked on computer microsimulation as an alternative, empirically grounded method in economics. Influenced by Guy Orcutt, Bergmann began working on microsimulation in the early 1970s. She pursued two main goals: first, to provide a stronger microfoundation for macroeconomics based on real dynamics rather than regressions biased by theoretical assumptions; and second, to identify effective policies capable of reducing inequality and poverty. Her research on microsimulation continued into the early 1990s, though it had little immediate influence on the subsequent development of dynamic or agent-based simulation literature, which has only recently begun to recognize her pioneering contributions.

In the late 1980s, Bergmann became increasingly interested in behavioral and experimental economics, inspired in part by the emergence of prospect theory, which demonstrated that the standard model of the fully rational economic agent was not merely flawed but actively harmful to sound economic analysis. Though she never worked on those fields, she admired Tversky and Kahneman, as well as Vernon Smith.

As always, beyond her academic work, Bergmann remained deeply committed to public engagement. She tirelessly sought to explain to a broader audience the necessity of a fundamental reform of standard economic methodology, as evidenced by her numerous articles on the subject in newspapers and magazines.

5.1 Finding Things Out in Economics: Empirical Methods

Bergmann advocated the necessity of revising methodological assumptions of neoclassical economics by adopting more realistic hypotheses, based on empirical research and direct observations of economic phenomena rather than on standard sets of assumptions about human rationality, reinforced by regressions that tend to confirm theoretical scenarios without taking reality into account (Bergmann 1987). Bergmann's quest for an empirical approach to economics emerged very early in her studies. In her article on urban crisis, she proposed a systematic way to trace the connections between an urban economy and the social, environmental, and governmental (SEG) problems that confronted it, such as racial inequality, poverty, crime, failing schools, decaying housing, inadequate transportation, and fiscal strain, which stemmed more from racial hostility and the widespread preference for single-family suburban living (Bergmann 1969).

Rather than offering a theoretical model, Bergmann proposed an accounting system able to organize existing knowledge, reveal gaps, and allow policymakers to see how different kinds of economic activity contributed to metropolitan well-being or distress. This system rested on two main components: a 'behavior matrix', which recorded the actions of firms, households, and government agencies that affected SEG outcomes (such as whom businesses hired, where they located, how much they polluted, and to which jurisdiction they paid taxes), and an 'impact matrix', which translated these behaviors into effects three specific SEG indices: the economic well-being of Black residents,[1] air pollution,[2] and the fiscal sufficiency of the urban core.[3] In fact, a firm's location could affect Black employment, air pollution from commuting, and the distribution of tax revenues. Hence, a unified accounting scheme could reduce duplicated effort and expose cross-cutting consequences. By multiplying the behavior matrix, the impact matrix, and, where available, the regional input-output matrix, Bergmann's system offered an 'industry-effect matrix' that showed each industry's estimated contribution, per dollar of final demand, to each SEG index, making visible the ways business activities influenced racial equity, environmental quality, and fiscal system. Moreover, by revealing these connections, the accounting

[1] The index of Blacks' economic well-being combined unemployment, wage income, and difficulties accessing housing and credit, as well as the burdens of traveling from segregated core neighborhoods to jobs in suburban rings. The behavior matrix included detailed information on Black employment by industry and occupation, the location of jobs, and discriminatory barriers in housing and in finance. The impact matrix assigned weights that translated these factors into losses of well-being, sometimes requiring the use of subjective judgment.

[2] Air pollution was estimated from two major sources: industrial emissions and automobile exhaust generated by commuting. The system accounted for pollutants produced per dollar of output in each industry, as well as for cross-commuting patterns between core and ring areas, and it weighted their health and aesthetic impacts accordingly.

[3] Fiscal sufficiency reflected the balance between a city's tax capacity and the demand for public services. While many service needs were largely independent of economic behavior, welfare expenditures tended to rise with unemployment. Revenue capacity depended on income, employment within the core, and taxable transactions, all of which could be captured by the behavior matrix.

system could be used to pressure industries to improve their performance and to guide coordinated efforts addressing the challenges facing metropolitan America.

Later, Bergmann urged to apply new empirical techniques in her early work on occupational segregation. She insisted on the importance of measuring the degree of occupational segregation by dismissing the theoretical realm of the simple two-occupation model. Against the usual 'analysis of the occupational and wage aspects of discrimination as if they were logically separate and their effects additive', Bergmann pointed out that things are more complex in the real world: there are many occupations rigidly restricted to one race-sex group; there is more than one integrated occupation in a typical local labor market; and workers may be forced out or fitted into a specific market by education (Bergmann 1974a).[4]

Hence, against theoretical models of standard economics, which actually do not measure gender inequality, in the early 1970s, supported by a grant from the U.S. Office of Equal Opportunity, Bergmann proposed the introduction of a new input-output model to analyze externalities, including gender discrimination in the job market and in the marketplace (Bergmann 1972).

As she pointed out, in the United States, it has become widely recognized that economic activity generates significant social and environmental side effects that cannot be ignored by policymakers. These externalities include pollution from industrial and household waste, such as garbage, sewage, smoke, noise, and heat, as well as unequal regional development, labor market discrimination against women and minorities, workplace hazards, environmental degradation, and the psychological effects of monotonous or alienating work.

To address these interconnected issues, Bergmann proposed expanding traditional input–output models, which are used in economic forecasting and planning, typically to several task such as: to estimate the relationships among industries; to forecast production, resource use, and employment; to incorporate externalities; to enable planners to consider social and environmental outcomes alongside economic outputs. Her key innovation

[4] She combined the wage differential approach *à la* Becker with the approach that emphasizes the crowding effects of occupational segregation, as originally noted by Edgeworth (1922).

was the introduction of a 'social impact matrix (M)', designed to complement the standard input–output model.[5] By incorporating this matrix into economic analysis, planners could routinely generate forecasts not only of production and income, but also of pollution levels, workplace safety, gender employment patterns, and other social indicators.[6]

The urgency to apply empirical methods in economics was explained in details by Bergmann on the occasion of the inaugural meetings of the Eastern Economic Association, held in Albany on October 27, 1974, when she delivered her *Presidential Address* (later published in Bergmann 1978a), focused on the methodology of standard economics. She questioned how it was possible that the reputation of economists remained so high when they systematically failed to understand real-world phenomena. In fact, she noted, economists had recently lost public esteem in light of the prevailing economic situation. She wrote:

> The founding of the Eastern Economic Association and the publishing of its new Journal are not merely an act of entrepreneurship; it is entrepreneurship pro bono publico. That part of the public which consists of economists in the eastern United States and Canada will surely gain. How about the rest of the public? They will gain little if our Association merely contributes to the current severe overstock of regression coefficients. They will gain much if the work our Association encourages, especially in young economists, work that is broad in perspective *à la* Galbraith and Heilbroner, based on personal observation and close study of institutions *à la* Hirschmann, attentive to the threats to our freedom *à la* Friedman, and informed by a humane understanding of human needs *à la* Boulding. (Bergmann 1974b, p. 1)

According to Bergmann, the central problem of economics lies in its excessively theoretical orientation, whereas it should aim to provide pratical solutions to governments, such as 'something reliable about the probable effect on investment of a change in the tax law'. Unfortunately,

[5] This matrix contained rows representing different types of side effects and columns representing various industries. Each element (m_{ij}) measured the per-unit impact of a given economic activity (j) on a specific side effect (i).

[6] A practical example is drawn from the 93-sector Maryland Inter-Industry Forecasting Model, which uses a simplified version of the social impact matrix. This version includes four categories of side effects: solid waste disposal, workplace safety (industrial accidents), the number of women's labor-years per unit of output, and the ratio of women to men in professional or managerial positions.

she argued, economists had not advanced in any direction conducive to the development of 'useful knowledge'. The principal reason for this failure, she suggested, was economists' incapacity to properly collect empirical data, as other social scientists routinely do. She wrote: "I believe one reason for our divorce from direct observation has to do with the nature of our subject matter". (Bergmann 1978a, p. 5)

Bergmann maintained that economists should study the real dynamics of decision-making processes, which are always path-dependent. Instead, economists tend to formulate assumptions that reinforce their own theoretical models. Another reason for the neglect of direct observation, she observed, is that it frequently fails to confirm their assumptions. Furthermore, economists quit empirical inquiry and confine themselves to statistical regressions based on 'statistical significance', which often remains superficial, covering large numbers of cases, usually designed to reinforce existing theoretical frameworks.

For example, in the economics of discrimination, economists have rarely engaged in empirical research on workplace practices that discriminate against Black people and women. Rather, they have used data to reinforce human capital theory. Bergmann wrote:

> What is still the leading theory in the field of discrimination—that employers would hire Blacks and women for any job, provided they offered to work at a low enough wage—could not have survived ten minutes in a field where theoretical formulations are seriously tested by empirical observation. (Bergmann 1978a, p. 10)

Hence, Bergmann concluded, contemporary economic practice may be described as 'mousepainting', i.e., a form of research fraud.[7] In the physical sciences, such practices are swiftly corrected because physical scientists routinely replicate one another's experiments. Economists, by contrast, do not:

[7] Dr. William Summerlin, a dermatologist at the Memorial Sloan Kettering Cancer Center, claimed to have achieved successful skin transplantation without immunosuppression by grafting black skin from black mice onto white mice. However, a laboratory assistant later noticed that one of the white mice, which was supposed to have a dark patch of transplanted skin, actually had fur that had been colored with ink from a felt-tip pen.

> The former collect their own data, and the latter do not. When economists attempt to replicate a statistical procedure and obtain a different result, the bland answer will be, 'but you didn't run it my way'. (Bergmann 1978a, p. 15)

Bergmann concluded by claiming that economic methodology must adopt an approach that integrates both quantitative and qualitative elements, as institutionalists attempt to do, although even they have not yet succeeded in producing 'useful knowledge'.

In the same year, 1978, she insisted on explaining that, unlike psychologists and anthropologists, an important barrier to the formation of useful economic knowledge was:

> The unwillingness and inability of economists to collect for themselves information about behavior which should be of professional interest to them- the behavior of men and women when they act as economic agents. (Bergmann 1978b, p. 9)

Bergmann's methodological concerns consistently centered on the lack of realism in neoclassical economics, as summarized in two essays, published respectively in 1987 and 1989.

In her 1987 essay, Bergmann pointed out that in most scientific disciplines, introductory textbooks not only present what scientists know but also explain how they came to know it. Students of biology learn not just about cells but also about 'looking through microscopes'. Physics students study gravitational formulas and read about 'throwing balls off the Leaning Tower of Pisa'. Similarly, anthropologists recount their field trips to the Trobriand Islands, and psychologists describe experiments with rats and mazes. By contrast, economics stands apart. As she wrote, economists tell the students nothing about economists' methods of finding things out (Bergmann 1987).

Even when attempts are made to include methodological content, such as in the Joint Council on Economic Education's *A Framework for Teaching the Basic Concepts*, the section on "Measurement Concepts and Methods" only covers 'tables, charts, graphs, means, medians, modes, indexes, and distributions'.[8] The absence of any real description of discovery in economics is no oversight. As Bergmann noted:

> The absence in teaching materials of a portrayal of our methods of advancing knowledge in our discipline points to a fundamental difficulty with these methods, one that is unlikely to be remedied soon. (Bergmann 1987, p. 191)

Bergmann wondered why economics textbooks are so different from those of other sciences in this respect. One possible explanation is that economists seem to find things out "by running regressions on economic data based on large samples collected by highly specialized agencies with multimillion-dollar budgets" (ibid, p. 192). Yet, even if such techniques could be explained to beginners, she continued: "very little of what economists will tell you they know, and almost none of the content of the elementary text, has been discovered by running regressions". Regressions are mainly used "to bolster one theoretical argument over another", but the support they provide is "weak, inconclusive, and easily countered by someone else's regressions" (ibid).

Most economic knowledge has been derived through the method used by Ricardo: introspection and reasoning from a few known facts. Ricardo's own life, Bergmann noted, was far richer in hands-on experience than that of most modern economists. But today, she wrote:

> The impoverished factual content of our thought doesn't embarrass us economists; we are used to it. Still, it would be somewhat embarrassing to say explicitly to noneconomists that we find things out by sitting and thinking and mulling over a few factual crumbs, and that the systematic, first-hand observation of economic functioning has no place whatever in economic science. (ibid)

According to Bergmann, if economics is to advance as a science, it must gather genuine empirical knowledge:

[8] The National Council on Economic Education, now the Council for Economic Education (CEE), was a U.S.-based organization dedicated to promoting economic and financial literacy among K-12 students, teaching young students real-world knowledge of economics and personal finance and running a campaign for economic literacy. Retrieved October 22, 2025, from https://www.councilforeconed.org/.

> We need first of all to gather knowledge about actual decision making. Second, we need to gather information about the conventions that are observed when the economic agents interact. Third, we need a rigorous way of computing the progression from micro decision systems to micro interactions, and then from the interactions to the macro results. (ibid, p. 193)

Bergmann illustrated the shortcomings of current methods through the case of expectations in neoclassical economics:

> The methodological problems of economics are well illustrated by the way the subject of expectations has been introduced into economic thinking, in a garbage way by neoclassical economics (…) the paradoxical assertion of this school that their more serious preoccupation with expectations implies that it is useless for us to study how expectations might be formed is very funny. They must be afraid of what such studies might reveal. (ibid, p. 198)

Bergmann clearly stated that improving economic methodology means grounding it in empirical reality: behavioral economics might be an option as well as computer simulation: "they might serve as a 'court' for settling disagreement among economists" (ibid, p. 200). Yet neoclassical economics remains averse to direct empirical evidence for two reasons: the suspicion that we cannot handle it and the difficulty of incorporating new facts in the models. Ultimately, the lesson for teaching and for practice is clear. Meanwhile, a genuine methodological reform in economics is needed, and what we need to teach students is that economists may disagree, and that it is difficult, but necessary, to measure economic dynamics.

In her 1989 essay, published in a volume honoring John Kenneth Galbraith, she criticized the "faulty investigative technique" of mainstream economists, who run regressions on government-collected economic data primarily to reinforce their theoretical assumptions rather than to illuminate real economic phenomena (Bergmann 1989).[9] According to Bergmann, mainstream economists, instead of studying real dynamics of people's behavior, focus their attention on abstract,

[9] As an example of the idiosyncrasy between economic modeling and real life, Bergmann illustrates Lucas and Rapping's paper (1969) on real wages, employment, and inflation. The authors, through regression analyses, contend that unemployed workers opt for leisure over work.

idealized agents, i.e., figures who operate solely in perfectly competitive markets, whose preferences remain unaffected by advertising, and who act without political motives. This approach reflects a deliberate and significant disconnection from reality, resulting in an inability to deepen our understanding of how economies actually function.

Bergmann recounted that she became aware of the weak empirical foundations of economic analysis when, during a court case, a lawyer asked her to explain how an unbiased, well-functioning competitive labor market was supposed to operate. She answered by explaining human capital theory, which underlies explanations of labor supply and demand, and she realized that that theory was not properly grounded in reality. As she candidly admitted:

> My encounter with the lawyer made me realize that everything I am supposed to 'know' about the labor market comes from nowhere but the private musings of economists, a product of introspection, like mathematics. (ibid, p. 31)

She concluded by observing:

> Unfortunately, only a very limited idea of how the actual economy works can be derived logically from first principles. When the day comes that we abandon musing and regression-running on secondhand data, I predict we will be amazed at the doctrines that collapse. The cross-point on the supply-demand diagram may even have to go (…) If we are talking about the real world, as opposed to the fictional worlds that Gary Becker, Robert Lucas, and Paul Samuelson conjure up when they write their articles, the subject matter of economics is far closer to anthropology than to mathematics. That fact should inform our methodological practice. (ibid, pp. 32–33)

Computer simulations and surveys designed to understand the decision-making process may, she suggested, offer a path forward for economics to avoid failure.

5.2 Measuring Gender Inequality: The NHE's Methodological Flaws

Bergmann's critique of standard economic methodology was widely shared by feminist economists in the 1980s and 1990s, who sought to challenge the *malestream* approach of conventional economics. In several publications, feminist economists argued that neoclassical economics was grounded in a masculine set of values such as autonomy, separation, and abstraction, values that contrast with those culturally associated with femininity, such as interdependence, connection, and concreteness. This way of dealing with the complexity of economic relations, they argued, weakened the discipline's ability to understand real economic phenomena (Ferber & Nelson 1993; Kuiper & Sap 1995; Nelson 1993).[10]

As Julie Nelson pointed out, neoclassical economics "has been constructed in a heavily gendered way because of the predominance of male economists in academia and the relegation of women's and gender issues to specific niches like home economics, household economics, and the new home economics" (Nelson 1993, p. 294).[11] Similarly, Strassmann wrote: "Feminist economists call for a broadening of economic methods, with tools chosen for their usefulness in providing insight,

[10] The debate around the maleness of a representative agent, whose behavior had been used as a model to describe the economic decision-making process, was not an exclusive prerequisite of standard economics. Masculinity and male values have been considered universal standards to assess paradigms upon which arts and sciences were grounded. The founder of this supposed masculine notion of rationality, which soon became dominant, was the French philosopher René Descartes, who was able to construct a paradigm that was commonly shared by scholars in both natural and social sciences. Many feminist philosophers considered Descartes' dualism between mind (male) and body (female), which implied a supremacy of the former over the latter, as a primary source of patriarchy (Bordo 1987; Jaggar 2002; Lloyd 1984). Descartes' notion of rationality appeared masculine, or male-oriented, because it overemphasized the role of pure speculation and detachment, in contrast to a 'sympathetic thinking', which is much closer to a feminine approach. In fact, Descartes' notion of rationality was based on the purification from everything derived from sensitive perception (including feelings and emotions), in order to achieve the theoretical purity of logical inference (Bordo 1987; Nelson 1996).

[11] She added: "Many feminist economists were finding that traditional formal choice-theoretic modeling and a narrow focus on mathematical and econometric methods were a Procrustean bed when it came to analyzing phenomena fraught with connections to others, tradition, and relations of domination. Feminists began to raise questions about the mainstream definition of economics, its central image of 'economic man,' and the exclusive use of a particular set of methodological tools" (Nelson 1996, p. 67).

rather than for their coherence with a specific methodological definition of economics" (Strassmann 1999, p. 369).[12]

Bergmann shared feminist economics' critique and specifically complained that standard economists fail to properly understand discrimination because in their model both direct evidence and experimental evidence are missing (Bergmann 2008). According to Bergmann, neoclassical economics exhibits two main methodological flaws: a lack of realism in describing individual behavior, and the reduction of economic phenomena and dynamics, such as discrimination in the marketplace and the division of labor within the household, to mere individual preferences. These methodological flaws are closely intertwined. The neoclassical approach fails to properly account for empirical data, relying instead on abstract models based on a rational economic agent, without considering real phenomena that play a decisive role in the decision-making process. Data show that minorities (including women) often face situations in which prejudices or habits generate preferences that favor the dominant group (white men). Furthermore, the neoclassical view is unfair: by assuming that the market will eventually eliminate discrimination, it reinforces the *status quo* of those who discriminate and prevents improvement in the condition of those who are actually discriminated.

Again, Gary Becker's approach served Bergmann as a main target in both his analysis of discrimination in the job market, based on race and gender, and in his economics of the family, based on the traditional division of roles which assigns women to caregiving and men to breadwinning (Becchio 2024a, 2024b) (see Chapter 4). Bergmann explicitly criticized NHE by pointing out the lack of realism in its key methodological assumptions, such as "the unfailing benevolence of the head of household" and "that biological motherhood necessarily entails more

[12] The genesis and development of modern science reinforced a male sociability model which originated and perpetuated the mechanism of women's subjection. More specifically, metaphors of masculinity had been able to build up the ideals of rationality and objectivity in modern philosophy. The critique of a masculine notion of rationality was introduced by psychologists and philosophers. They underlined that the notion of rationality as the logical and objective faculty of thinking was gender-biased and was related to the stereotype of masculinity as opposed to the feminine stereotype based on emotions, feelings, and instincts. This procedure had generated a gendered notion of rationality that had systematically ignored that gender differentiation is part of a learning process, and it had ignored that both objectivity and emotionality are acquired, and not innate (Becchio 2020).

responsibility for child rearing than does fatherhood" (Bergmann 1990a, p. 72). Another methodological flaw of Becker's neoclassical approach is that it assumes factors such as the distribution of resources, including material provisions, leisure time, and investments in education, as *ceteris paribus* conditions (Bergmann 1995).

According to Bergmann, the NHE failed to deepen our understanding of the forces that shape family formation and behavior and it failed to offer insights that could guide public policy. The theoretical and methodological framework of the NHE, developed by Becker's *Treatise* (Becker, 1991), is the main cause of this failure. While Becker's work displays technical sophistication, Bergmann contends that its assumptions strip family life of its social and emotional complexity, leading to conclusions that are both misleading and dangerous for policymaking.

In Bergmann's 1995 paper, she observed that across the developed world rising rates of divorce and single parenthood have weakened the traditional two-parent household, while in many developing nations unchecked population growth threatens economic stability. A sound theory of the family should help diagnose these problems and guide effective policy responses. Yet, rather than providing such guidance, the NHE has instead entrenched a sterile formalism. Its models, designed to yield neat algebraic proofs, rely on extreme simplifications that ignore the empirical realities of family life.

Becker's analysis, she argued, exemplifies these flaws. Like traditional market economics, it treats human relationships as if they were transactions among self-interested, rational agents. The family is conceptualized as a market in which individuals "exchange" goods and services, and marital arrangements are analyzed through supply-and-demand curves. Such models may be mathematically elegant, but they fail to account for the moral, emotional, and institutional dimensions of family life. Moreover, Becker's conclusions consistently idealize the *status quo* and cast government intervention as harmful, which is an ideological bias disguised as neutral analysis.

Bergmann's critique was structured around three examples from Becker's *Treatise*: his analyses of polygamy, altruism, and fertility. In Becker's model of marriage, women offer themselves into marriage if the utility they expect from married life exceeds what they could achieve alone. Men, in turn, demand wives to enhance their own consumption. Becker argued that, under certain conditions, women might fare better under polygamy than monogamy because increased demand for wives would raise the price they receive, that is, their share of family resources. For Bergmann, this claim bordered on absurdity. She pointed out that the advantages of polygamy for women are false as "in societies that allow polygamy, the status of women is abysmal". Becker's argument ignored all historical and sociological evidence showing that polygamous societies systematically oppress women, restricting their freedom, education, and personal development. Becker's methodological framework also failed to consider why men, who historically control legal and political institutions, would voluntarily adopt a system that, according to his logic, disadvantages them. By abstracting from questions of power and rights, Becker's model trivialized the lived realities of gender inequality. Bergmann suggested that his willingness to accept such conclusions stems from an uncritical faith in the efficiency of markets and a reluctance to confront empirical evidence that contradicts theoretical proofs.

Then, Becker extended his market framework to the inner dynamics of the family through his concept of altruism. He defined an altruist as someone who derives satisfaction from another person's consumption. In this scheme, the husband, who is typically the higher earner, is labeled the altruist because he contributes more financial resources to the household. The wife, who performs most of the domestic labor, receives no comparable recognition. Becker's altruist thus became a paternalistic figure whose generosity ensures the family's harmony.

Bergmann dismantled this notion by exposing its underlying asymmetry. In Becker's definition, even a husband who consumes 90 percent of the couple's joint income and allows his wife only 10 percent still qualifies as an altruist, as long as he could have taken more but chooses not to. Such logic justifies inequality and erases the agency of women. By portraying the family as a unit governed by a single 'altruistic' will, implicitly male, Becker eliminated the need to consider conflicts of interest, coercion, or emotional abuse. Bergmann likens this vision to the 'wife locked in the power of a petty tyrant'. Far from depicting a happy, cooperative household, Becker's theory rationalized domination under the guise of benevolence.

Finally, in Becker's model of fertility, couples decide how many children to have based on their altruistic enjoyment of their descendants' future happiness. The rate of interest, by affecting the return on inherited capital, becomes a key variable in determining fertility. From this framework, Becker concluded that the number of children families have depends solely on altruism and interest rates, not on income levels, social norms, religion, or access to contraception. Bergmann called this conclusion 'plainly ridiculous': by reducing fertility to a mathematical function, Becker ignored the most crucial determinants of reproductive behavior, such as economic conditions of women and men, cultural expectations, social relations between partners, availability of contraception and abortion, religion, and state policies.

Moreover, Becker's reliance on equilibrium logic led him to claim that the government cannot meaningfully influence fertility, except perhaps by educating citizens about overpopulation. Such reasoning, Bergmann argued, reveals the emptiness of a model that prioritizes internal consistency over empirical validity.[13]

In Bergmann's view, Becker's argumentation on these three topics was biased by:

> a naive, not to say boyish, faith in the ability of pared-down models with as few as two variables to produce truth, even where the situation being analyzed has many variables, most of which cannot be represented handily on a supply-and-demand curve diagram. (Bergmann 1995, p. 11)

The core of Bergmann's critique is a rejection of the neoclassical methodology itself: by relying on simplified assumptions that abstract from real social relations, Becker's models generated elegant but irrelevant conclusions. Worse, they consistently depicted existing institutions as optimal and government action as harmful, reinforcing conservative policy biases. Bergmann warned that this kind of 'recreational mathematics' diverts intellectual energy from genuine social inquiry and risks misleading policymakers. When applied to issues like family breakdown or overpopulation, such models offer no guidance and may even justify inaction. While she doubted that Becker's most extreme claims will directly shape policy, she saw his approach as symptomatic of a broader problem in economics: the elevation of mathematical elegance over realism. The prestige accorded to such work, as symbolized by Becker's Nobel Prize,

[13] Though, she did not emphasize Becker's methodological flaws when he implicitly assumed that partners can compare their utility to maximize family utility, especially when presenting the Rotten Kid Theorem, which states that it is not worth any member going against the father's wishes, because he will subsequently reallocate, relying on the father having sufficient knowledge of other members' utility to operate in that way. Neither did Bergmann specifically note that Stigler and Becker's notion of stable preferences (1977) creates problems in explaining divorce and rising divorce rates.

demonstrates how deeply entrenched this bias has become. According to Bergmann, rather than illuminating the realities of family life, NHE reproduced a narrow and patriarchal vision under the guise of scientific objectivity. By treating families as markets and love as utility, Becker's framework strips human relationships of empathy and complexity.

In her view, until economists abandon the fantasy of universal rationality and the worship of formal proof, the study of the family will remain, not a tool for understanding and reform, but a monument to misplaced intellectual confidence. As she wrote:

> Economic theory as applied to the family should increase our understanding of the phenomena we are studying, and allow us to implement fruitful intervention in cases where we are not satisfied with what is occurring. Much if not all of the theory of the family fails to achieve these aims. Examples are given from the most recent edition of Gary Becker's *Treatise on the Family*, where the analysis leads to conclusions that are, on their face, preposterous. (Bergmann 1995, p. 141)

A decade later, Bergmann insisted on considering the way NHE economists were dealing with the theory of marriage as "an example of their foolishly imperialistic attitude toward the other social and behavioral sciences" (Bergmann 2006, p. 32).

5.3 From Micro to Macro: Computer Microsimulation and Experiments

Bergmann never limited herself to criticizing mainstream economics' methodology, and specifically, Becker's work. As mentioned earlier, two further aspects characterize Bergmann's methodological approach to understanding individual behavior and economic dynamics within a more complex and realistic social framework: her work on computer simulation (1970s–1990s), which made her a forerunner of agent-based modeling,[14] and her genuine interest in experimental economics. Both were intended to ground economic theory in empirical evidence, free from the biases of theoretical models formulated *ex ante* (Becchio 2024a).

[14] Her work on computer microsimulation inspired authors who contributed to the Symposium on Agent-based Computational Economics, published in 2011 in the *Eastern Economic Journal*.

Bergmann's own methodology began to attract attention outside academia as well. In 1970, an article by Israel Shenker, "Professor of Jargon Finds That Yesterday's 'Ins' Are Out and 'Outs' Are, Too", appeared in *The New York Times*. By adopting a humorous rather than hostile tone, the author lampooned the changing fashions of academic jargon; Bergmann was singled out among prominent social scientists for her distinctive linguistic creativity. Shenker cited her references to 'impact matrix', 'behavior matrix', and 'inverse input–output matrix', placing her within a constellation of academics whose technical terminology exemplified what sociologist Robert K. Merton called "verbal coin whose value has been depreciated by excessive and indiscriminate use" (Shenker 1970).

Influenced by Guy Orcutt's work on microsimulation,[15] who pioneered the construction of models of the household sector and families as if they were following certain postulated behavioral rules (Orcutt 1957; Orcutt et al. 1961), Bergmann became interested in introducing microsimulation into economics in order to better suggest proper policies to solve economic inequalities.[16] As she clearly wrote in presenting her model of the U.S. economy aimed at forecasting macroeconomic variables:

> That macroeconomics should be anchored in descriptions of microeconomic behavior is a principle well understood and universally agreed to, although often only loosely honored in practice (…) The major inspiration for the present model is the pioneering thought of Guy Orcutt (1960), although this model differs from the work of him and his associates considerably in terms of subject-matter focus, disaggregation of time periods, and econometric methodology. It is hoped that the model can eventually be used in short-term and medium-term forecasting, much as

[15] Microsimulation, broadly defined, is a methodology applied across many scientific disciplines to model the states and behaviors of individual units, such as people, households, or firms, as they interact and evolve within specific environments like markets, governments, or institutions. Orcutt criticized the macroeconomic models of his time for their inability to assess the effects of government policies on issues such as income distribution or poverty. These models relied on highly aggregated data, overlooking the detailed micro-level interactions and decision-making processes that drive economic outcomes.

[16] As rightly pointed out by Chassonnery-Zaïgouche and Goutsmedt (2024), Bergmann's focus on the distributional effects of policies was central to her criticism of macroeconomic modeling, though both her epistemological and political positions were marginalised in the 1980s.

> a conventional model based on simultaneous linear macroeconomic equations is used. However, the major contribution of the model is expected to be in uses which exploit the features of the model which sets it apart from other macroeconomic models-its delineation of the behavior of micro-units. (Bergmann 1974c, p. 475)

Bergmann applied microsimulation to the labor market (Bergmann 1974d, 1990b) by shifting attention from simple supply-and-demand models toward the role of job search processes in shaping wages and unemployment, against the traditional econometric approaches, such as linear regression, which cannot easily capture the complexity of labor market dynamics. Bergmann proposed an alternative microsimulation model tracking simulated individuals and employers over time, incorporating their histories, decisions, and interactions to replicate real labor market behavior. By mimicking Bureau of Labor Statistics surveys, the model generates macro-level outcomes, such as unemployment rates and durations, that can be compared with real data for validation. The model, implemented using U.S. data from 1969 to 1973, allows researchers to analyze how turnover, labor-force participation, market segmentation, and wage-setting mechanisms affect unemployment.

Between 1973 and 1975, *Econometrica* hosted a debate on Bergmann's article that combined regression and microsimulation to measure the poverty incidence on unemployment and growth (Bergmann 1973, 1975; Mirer & Peck 1975). Following Orcutt, Bergmann worked to propose a new type of model based on representative micro-level distributions of individuals, households, or firms, emphasizing their heterogeneous decision-making, as occurs in reality. In her 1973 article, she criticized the overreliance of empirical economics on regression analysis, which often reflects little real understanding of economic processes. Traditional regressions tended to impose a rigid form on data, 'the Procrustean bed', and focused mainly on maximizing statistical fit (R^2) rather than modeling underlying mechanisms.

As an alternative, she proposed combining small-scale microsimulation models with regression analysis to better capture the structure and nonlinearities of economic phenomena. In this hybrid method, the simulation prepared the data by incorporating theoretical insights and modeling the complex interactions among variables, while the regression scaled the simulated results to observed real-world magnitudes. This approach can also help mitigate issues like multicollinearity.[17] After running multiple simulations under different conditions, the resulting data were used in a regression model where simulated poverty served as an explanatory variable for actual U.S. poverty rates (1959–1970). The findings suggested that combining microsimulation with regression provides a more realistic and theoretically grounded understanding of economic processes, enabling richer insights into complex phenomena like poverty dynamics than regression alone can offer.

Bergmann's article was commented on by Mirer and Peck, who argued that simulation cannot replace the analytical theoretical methodology adopted by standard economics and whenever both are possible, the theoretical approach should be preferred, being more 'compact, elegant, and less risk of errors'. Bergmann's reply admitted that "the science of validating simulations is admittedly in its infancy", but she suggested "to use the output of the simulation as a proxy variable in a regression and observe the fit" (Bergmann 1975, p. 531).

In a following article on microsimulation of the U.S. economy, Bergmann explicitly considered the interaction between the supply and demand for labor, and she modeled the behavior of firms and workers by providing a complete and structural, although relatively simple, model of the economy, which was calibrated to replicate many features of the U.S. economy, albeit her approach remained mainly unnoticed in the dynamic microsimulation literature (Bergmann 1974c).[18] Bergmann herself acknowledged that the model was a "work in progress", further developed in an article co-authored with Robert Bennett (Bergmann

[17] To illustrate the method, Bergmann developed a simplified microsimulation of poverty incidence among the working poor, by tracking a population of 1000 identical workers whose annual income depends on employment, unemployment, and job turnover rates. Each worker earns a fixed weekly wage, and their family is classified as poor if annual income falls below the poverty threshold. The simulation repeatedly randomized employment and unemployment transitions over 52 weeks to estimate how changes in wages, unemployment, and turnover affect poverty levels. By varying these parameters, the study demonstrates that poverty incidence was shaped by strong nonlinearities and interactions among variables, features often missed in standard regression models.

[18] The dynamic microsimulation literature can be identified as an earlier antecedent of agent-based modeling. The main differences are that microsimulations are more policy-oriented and rely on a partial equilibrium approach, while agent-based models are more theory-oriented and most often closed-system models. Bergmann questioned the second tenet, and she could be interpreted as a bridge between the older dynamic microsimulation literature and the more recent agent-based modeling literature (Delli Gatti et al. 2018).

& Bennett 1977), that reached completion only several years later (Bennett & Bergmann 1986).

Meanwhile, in 1977, Bergmann edited a book along with Eliasson and Orcutt (Bergmann et al. 1977).[19] In the foreword, they clearly stated the necessity to revise standard economics' methodology that pretended to adequately capture the complexity of economic reality. As a result, economists naturally developed multiple models to interpret similar phenomena, each emphasizing aspects that are important to the specific question at hand. Yet, the authors insisted, any theoretical approach must ultimately withstand empirical scrutiny: in a scientific discipline such as economics, theories that fail to align with observation should be replaced by better-grounded ones. Progress therefore depends on a continual process of discarding outdated doctrines and integrating new, empirically valid insights.

The core of the authors' point was that a central challenge for economics is the integration of theory and measurement. Theories must not only explain behavior but also provide clear guidance on how to measure key variables. In this sense, the division between theoretical and empirical work is artificial; the two should be inseparable. The authors claimed that microsimulation offers a particularly promising framework for achieving this integration. The term microsimulation itself has been used in many ways, sometimes leading to confusion. Properly understood, it refers to a numerical method for analyzing complex versions of conventional economic theories. It enables the coordination of large volumes of micro-level data and focuses on testing behavioral assumptions rather than relying solely on aggregate 'goodness of fit'. In this way, it frees economics from the constraints of the traditional analytical paradigm and offers a new, richer language for theoretical and empirical work. By combining theoretical modeling with empirical observation at the micro level, microsimulation enables a more coherent and testable understanding of economic systems. Furthermore, microsimulation is valuable because it allows researchers to organize scattered theoretical ideas within

[19] The volume's main goal was to explore large-scale, economy-wide microsimulation modeling, building on the pioneering work of Guy Orcutt at Yale, Barbara Bergmann's transactions model applied to the U.S. economy, and Gunnar Eliasson's IUI-IBM project in Sweden. These three model systems demonstrate the diversity of methodological approaches and the flexibility of microsimulation in addressing various economic problems.

a consistent empirical framework. It provides direct access to detailed micro-level data, on individuals, firms, and households, and thereby facilitates more precise estimation and analysis. This makes it possible to apply empirical inference more effectively than in traditional macroeconomic models, which often rely on aggregate data and simplifying assumptions. This blending of theory and empiricism is one of the most significant advantages of the microsimulation approach.

While some microsimulation models may appear 'theoretical' in the conventional sense, they differ from standard theoretical constructs as they are built upon rich empirical foundations. A sound economic theory, the authors insist, must be grounded in relevant data. Historically, economists have used macroeconomic models to study large-scale phenomena such as business cycles and national income determination. The Keynesian revolution was a major step forward, providing a systematic framework for analyzing aggregate demand and output. Two important classes of models emerged from this approach: demand-driven, national income–based business cycle models, and demand-driven input–output models of the Leontief–Keynesian type. Both have achieved significant empirical success in explaining macroeconomic dynamics and guiding policy. However, these traditional models have critical limitations. First, they omit the market process, i.e., the very mechanism through which prices and quantities adjust. Second, they fail to exploit detailed micro-level data, relying instead on aggregated information that obscures individual behavior. Third, they struggle to model genuine economic dynamics, since macro-level equilibrium conditions conceal the underlying micro-level interactions that drive change over time.

According to Bergmann, the advantage of adopting microsimulation is threefold.

First, microsimulation addresses all three problems simultaneously. By constructing models that explicitly represent individual decision-making units (such as households, firms, and workers) and allowing them to interact within a simulated economy, microsimulation provides a richer and more realistic picture of how macroeconomic outcomes emerge. It avoids the need for "deliberate misspecification" that often characterizes macro models and replaces abstract equilibrium constructs with dynamic, behavior-based processes. Although the resulting models can appear complex and less immediately transparent, this complexity reflects the richness of real economic systems.

Second, microsimulation serves as a powerful educational tool. Because it represents economic dynamics explicitly, it allows researchers to describe assumptions clearly and trace the consequences of individual actions through time. Unlike traditional macroeconomic theory, which often depends on highly abstract equilibrium concepts, microsimulation can model dynamic adjustments one process at a time in accessible and concrete terms. While it may be difficult to grasp the full workings of an entire microsimulation model at once, familiarity with its structure and behavior allows economists to gain deep insights into the functioning of real economies.

Third, microsimulation represents an important methodological advance, comparable to the introduction of new mathematical tools in other sciences. It allows for the integration of market price theory and income determination in an empirically relevant manner—something that older modeling traditions struggled to achieve. In essence, microsimulation provides a means of unifying theory and measurement, ensuring that economic models remain grounded in observable reality. According to the authors, this synthesis of micro behavior and macro outcome represents a fundamental step toward a more integrated, empirically informed, and dynamic economic science.

In conclusion, microsimulation stands as a bridge between economic theory and empirical measurement, enabling economists to construct detailed, realistic, and testable models of complex systems. It resolves key limitations of traditional macroeconomic modeling by incorporating individual decision-making, dynamic adjustment, and the market process itself. Though it demands new computational tools and ways of thinking, microsimulation offers a powerful approach for advancing both the analytical rigor and empirical relevance of modern economics.

In 1986, Bergmann co-authored a book with Robert Bennett, *A Microsimulated Transactions Model of the United States Economy*. They aimed to present macro models that were "consistent with the action on the microeconomic level, since the macro derives exactly from the micro" (Bennett & Bergmann 1986, p. 1). Their transaction model was constructed using microdata collected by the Bureau of Labor Statistics 1972/73, in the United States, which included information on consumer expenditure, financial assets, labor participation, marital status, car ownership, home ownership, and occupation.

According to them, microsimulations were able to formally incorporate qualitative descriptions of individual and institutional behavior.

Bennett and Bergmann extended that methodological approach to firms and government to study the effects of fiscal and monetary policies. In their model, economic agents included ten firms, a bank, a financial intermediary, a federal government, a state government, a monetary authority, and 700 members (employed and unemployed) of households that consume and hold assets.[20] Regarding the economics of the household, Bennett and Bergmann explained that the people who populate the households in their model come in two sexes and four occupations. At all times, they know their current situation, including whether they are employed, by whom and at what wage, whether they have a spouse and whether the spouse is working, and what the value and character of their assets and debts are, along with the age of their car. They also have access to knowledge about the economy, such as the rate of inflation and the rate of unemployment. Many elements of the household's situation at any moment in time are the result of actions taken previously. The value of assets reflects past saving decisions, and the current composition of the portfolio results from past decisions concerning which assets to acquire. Furthermore, people in their model have a repertoire of decision-making processes and activities, which they follow in each round of the action. They share the same tastes in consumer goods, using the same linear expenditure system; differences in each person's situation and history result in differences in their actions. In their microsimulation example, agents did not maximize, but used simple rule of thumb in deciding what to do.

Computer simulations might be applied to policy-relevant methodological issues, such as the 'basic needs budget approach' (BNB), a way to analyze poverty based on seven budget categories that might be adjusted for different family sizes, the employment status of parents, the age of children, the different cost of living, and so forth (Renwick & Bergmann 1993).

As summed up by Bergmann:

[20] Any transaction, intended as a monetary exchange, is registered. Any decision is made once a week, with no simultaneity. Any macro event is consistent with action on the micro-level. They explained that their microsimulated model "would seem to be an ideal vehicle for the incorporation of the virtues of microeconomic theory into macroeconomics" (Bennett & Bergmann 1986, pp. 6–7).

> Microsimulation models have a number of advantages over conventional methods used by economists. One advantage is the explicitness with which the interactions on the micro level can be depicted. Conventional methods of economic analysis often provide cogent derivations of individuals' contingency plans, but tend to be weak in describing the process that allows all the contingency plans to mesh together. (Bergmann 1990b, p. 100)

In a later interview, she added:

> [In computer simulation], you are depicting decisions, you are depicting individuals, you are depicting what they are doing and how they are interacting much more realistically than in a line of algebra (...) computer simulation is a good methodology for going from the micro to the macro. (Saunders & King 2010, pp. 313–315)

As mentioned earlier, in the late 1980s, Bergmann became interested in experimental economics. More specifically, she merged her research on microsimulation with her interest in experiments in an article published on *JEBO* (Bergmann 1988) focused on how individuals interpret and forecast from economic time-series charts, similar to those frequently published on the front page of the *Wall Street Journal*. These charts, intended to inform readers about historical trends, also implicitly invite them to speculate about future movements. The experiment explored how people form expectations about the future direction of a series when presented with graphical data alone, stripped of any identifying context or economic meaning.[21] The results revealed several consistent findings.

First, respondents demonstrated generally poor forecasting ability, with predictions deviating substantially from the true underlying trends. Despite the regularity of the data, forecasts showed a strong upward bias: participants tended to expect future increases more frequently than decreases. This optimism persisted across variations in the data and suggests a systematic cognitive bias in interpreting time series patterns.

[21] Participants were shown a series of computer-generated time series that mimicked cyclical economic data. Each series was constructed to resemble a sine curve with random errors added, ensuring that the patterns appeared realistic but controlled. The characteristics of the series, such as amplitude, frequency, and degree of randomness, were systematically varied so that the effects of these features on forecasting behavior could be analyzed. Respondents were asked to predict the future direction of each series based solely on its visual pattern.

Second, while overall accuracy was low, respondents did appear to recognize the cyclical nature of the series. Their forecasts reflected an attempt to identify and anticipate turning points, i.e., the peaks and troughs of the cycles. This indicates that individuals intuitively perceive cyclicality in data and seek to use it as a forecasting cue, even when the precise timing or magnitude of the next shift is unclear. However, their ability to predict these turning points was limited: small changes in the data, such as the addition of one more observation, frequently altered their forecasts drastically. This instability suggests that people's interpretations are highly sensitive to recent information and prone to overreaction.

Third, the study tested whether respondents' behavior could be captured by a fixed-lag forecasting model, in which only the most recent few observations influence the forecast. The findings indicated otherwise. Instead of focusing solely on recent data, participants appeared to give substantial attention to past turning points, suggesting that they tried to construct an implicit narrative of cyclical behavior rather than relying on short-term momentum.

The findings confirm that even when presented with relatively regular, sinusoidal data, far simpler than real-world economic series, people struggle to discern underlying trends accurately.[22] These results have implications for understanding how both experts and laypersons interpret economic information. The inability to perceive trends and turning points accurately is not limited to professional forecasters but appears to be a general human trait. This calls into question the common economic assumption that aggregating individual expectations yields collectively rational forecasts. If individuals are systematically biased and inconsistent in interpreting even simple time series, then the notion that the market or 'collective intelligence' produces accurate predictions warrants careful empirical re-evaluation.[23]

[22] The experimental results align with and extend earlier studies by Schmalensee (1976), who found similarly low forecasting accuracy when individuals predicted from a single irregular time series. However, unlike those earlier studies, the present research employed a large number of respondents and systematically varied the properties of the series, enabling more robust inferences about how chart features influence forecasting behavior.

[23] It is acknowledged that the experimental setting differs from real-world forecasting. Unlike in the laboratory, a reader of the *Wall Street Journal* typically knows what the chart represents (e.g., stock prices, industrial output) and may supplement the graphical information with extraneous knowledge about economic events, policies, or market

According to Bergmann, from a methodological standpoint, the study highlights the importance of understanding how individuals visually process economic information. Economists typically model expectation formation using formal, mathematical approaches such as macroeconometric models. However, most real-world decision-makers do not rely on such tools. The majority of economic agents form expectations through intuitive, visual, and heuristic reasoning. The findings suggest that these informal methods are prone to systematic bias and instability.

In summary, Bergmann pointed out that this research provides experimental evidence that individuals' forecasts based on graphical time series are inaccurate, biased, and unstable. While respondents recognized the cyclical nature of the data and attempted to predict turning points, their forecasts were overly optimistic and highly sensitive to small changes in information. These tendencies indicate fundamental limitations in human ability to infer trends and reversals from visual patterns alone. The results challenge assumptions about rational expectation formation and underscore the need for further empirical study of how people interpret and act upon economic data presented in graphical form.

She concluded:

> Rationality apart, if prediction is so chaotic and difficult, perhaps most people have an incentive to avoid it. In economic life, people can avoid depending on their expectations by keeping flexible, responding rapidly to realized changes, and hedging or avoiding situations where they can be severely hurt by a bad prediction. If this is the case, then perhaps the role of expectations of the future as an ingredient in the decision making of economic actors has been exaggerated by economic theorists. (Bergmann 1988, p. 151)

Two years later, inspired by Tversky and Kahneman's empirical research (1988) on decision-making process which results in non-optimal outcome, Bergmann presented simulations as "non optimal but empirically true behavior patterns [that] should yield more realistic predictions

conditions. The relative weight given to visual information versus contextual knowledge depends on the individual's understanding of how these sources of information interact. Nevertheless, the mental process of examining a chart, i.e., identifying past turning points, estimating amplitudes, judging current trends, and anticipating reversals, is an activity that occurs independently of additional information and is therefore of theoretical interest.

than normative theories that are empirically false" (Bergmann 1990b, p. 102).

The aim of Bergmann's simulation method applied to labor was not, in her words:

> How will utility-maximizing individual behave, rather what will the mechanical result of their interactions be. Even though the actors are not depicted as fervid optimizers, the simulation does shed light on the pattern of spell durations over the cycle and on the effect of unemployment insurance on unemployment rates, which were goals of the analysis. Of course, one could construct a model in which the simulated actors behaved with greater rationality (...) The analyst might assume that a mathematical derivation of the optimal malingering rule is within the workers' capabilities. Unfortunately, it is not within the present author's. But it is unlikely that a simulation model with actors more inclined toward finding and following optimal rules of behavior would give answers that differ qualitatively from those given by this model. The non-optimizing actors of this model were serviceable for the analysis we aimed at. The reader should remember, moreover, that the simulation model with nonoptimizing actors provided better insights about how unemployment is generated than the conventional models depicting allegedly optimizing actors. (ibid, p. 115)

Bergmann's ideas inspired Riach and Rich in testing racial discrimination in the job market as well as in developing an experiment to investigate whether firms discriminate in granting interviews to men and women for various job types (Riach & Rich 1991, 1995, 1998).[24] Years later, writing Bergmann's obituary, Peter Riach remembered that Bergmann was very pleased by Riach and Rich's paper on experiments of sexual discrimination in the Melbourne labor market. They sent their paper to Barbara who replied: "I think it is a contribution to knowledge to a degree rare in economic research ... (W)e should do a great deal more of this kind of work than we do, and maybe yours will inspire some" (Riach 2015).

Bergmann's suggestion to adopt experimental economics also implicitly inspired Bewley (1999) who, through interviews with over 300 businesspeople, concluded that wage rigidity arises from a desire to foster loyalty, which is incompatible with layoffs. This finding contrasts with the

[24] Their experiment effectively demonstrated that women face discrimination in male-dominated jobs.

unrealistic psychological assumptions of the existing economic theories of wage rigidity.[25]

Throughout her career, Bergmann called for reforming economic methodology by expanding the direct observation of human behavior, as made possible by experimental economics and computer simulation. As mentioned several times, for Bergmann, the main obstacle preventing progress in economics was its persistent lack of realism.[26] She expressed these convictions not only in her academic writings but also in numerous articles for the general press.

In 1999, she wrote a popular article advocating for the abolition of the Nobel Prize in Economics, arguing that:

> Having a Nobel prize for economics is making the economics profession look ridiculous, since recipients typically receive it for producing a totally made-up simplified representation of some process we all know takes place. (Bergmann 1999, p. 52)

As she pointed out:

> People snickered when they heard that James Buchanan's prize was for telling us that politicians and bureaucrats act in their own interests, Robert Lucas's was for telling us that people do the best they can in doing out what to do, and Franco Modigliani's was for telling us that people save and spend their savings at different times in their lives. (ibid, p. 53)

Moreover, she criticized the Nobel Committee for awarding prizes to economic models she considered ethically questionable, such as:

> Robert Fogel's demonstration that slavery was a jolly good business, at least to those with the whip hand [and] Gary Becker's paean to a form of the family frequently oppressive to women. (ibid, p. 55)

As she noted:

[25] Keynesians attribute unemployment to "a grave misfortune forced on people, most of whom want to work, even at wages lower than those earned previously", while neoclassicals consider wage rigidity an illusion, asserting that wages and salaries are flexible and labor markets can always clear (Bewley 1999, p. 2).

[26] On this point, see also Polkington and Thompson (1998).

> Those prizes honored work that distilled complicated and sometimes painful phenomena into simplistic representations of cheerily optimal processes—in one case by regression running, in the other by representing affairs of the heart through supply and demand curves, in both cases throwing a lot of vital issues out the window in the process. (ibid, p. 56)

At the end of that article, she expressed the hope that Vernon Smith would eventually receive the prize, a prediction that came true in 2002, when he shared the Nobel Prize with Daniel Kahneman.

A few years later, in an article published in *The Economists' Voice*, Bergmann proposed a 'new empiricism' in economics, grounded in experimental research as exemplified by Herbert Simon, Daniel Kahneman, and Vernon Smith. She noted that experiments on racial and gender discrimination in the labor market "disproved Gary Becker's oft-quoted theory, based solely on conjecture and the usual assumptions, that markets are free of discrimination" (Bergmann 2007, pp. 2–3).

Nonetheless, in an expanded version of that paper, published two years later in 2009, Bergmann adopted a more critical stance toward both behavioral and experimental economics. She expressed disappointment with recent behavioral economists, who remained preoccupied with testing the rationality of individuals. She regarded experimental economics, first initiated by Edward Chamberlin's experiments with Harvard students in the 1940s and later advanced by Vernon Smith, as more promising, since it focused on the real dynamics of human decision-making rather than on abstract theorizing by economists "sitting in their chairs at home or in the office" (Bergmann 2009, p. 6). Nevertheless, she admitted:

> You may think that the micro problem in economics is being solved by the rising popularity of behavioral and experimental economics, or even possibly by the coming of neuroeconomics. I do not think so. (ibid, p. 4)

According to her, behavioral and experimental economists still failed to devote sufficient attention to understanding the behavior of managers and businesspeople. However, for Bergmann, the most promising recent development in economics might be neuroeconomics. In her view, real progress in economic methodology would occur only when the job market for economists became genuinely open to these innovative perspectives. Meanwhile, as it is reported in an interview, Bergmann encouraged women economists to publish in top journals, such as *Journal of Political Economy*, "by pointing out anomalies in economic theory and trying to understand them" (Emami & Olson 2002, p. 67).

References

Becchio, G. (2020). *A history of feminist and gender economics*. Routledge.

Becchio, G. (2024a). Pioneering feminist economics: Barbara Bergmann's contributions to gender issues. *Eastern Economic Journal, 50*(4), 472–495.

Becchio, G. (2024b). *The doctrine of the separate spheres in political economy and economics. Gender equality and classical liberalism*. Palgrave Springer.

Becker, G. (1991). *A Treatise on the family*. Harvard University Press. (Original work published 1981).

Becker, G., & Stigler, G. (1977). De Gustibus non Est Disputandum. *The American Economic Review, 67*(2), 76–90.

Bennett, R., & Bergmann, B. (1986). *A microsimulated transactions model of the United States economy*. Johns Hopkins University Press.

Bergmann, B. (1969). The urban economy and the "urban crisis". *The American Economic Review, 59*(4), 639–645.

Bergmann, B. (1972). Assessing the impact of alternative economic outcomes on social objectives. In A. Brody & A. Carter (Eds.), *Input-output techniques* (pp. 31–43). North Holland Publishing Company.

Bergmann, B. (1973). Combining microsimulation and regression: A "prepared" regression of poverty incidence on unemployment and growth. *Econometrica, 41*(5), 955–963.

Bergmann, B. (1974a). Occupational segregation, wages and profits when employers discriminate by race and sex. *Eastern Economic Journal, 2*(3), 103–110.

Bergmann, B. (1974b). Inaugural message. *Eastern Economic Journal, 1*(1), 1.

Bergmann, B. (1974c). A microsimulation of the macroeconomy with explicitly represented money flows. *Annals of Economic and Social Measurement, 3*(3), 475–489.

Bergmann, B. (1974d). Empirical work on the labor market: Is there any alternative to regression running? In *Proceedings of the 27th Annual Meeting of the Industrial Relations Research Association* (pp. 243–251).

Bergmann, B. (1975). Combining microsimulation and regression: A reply. *Econometrica, 43*(3), 529–531.

Bergmann, B. (1978a). Have economists failed? *Studies in Economics and Finance, 2*(2), 3–18.

Bergmann, B. (1978b). Economists and the real world. *Challenge, 21*(1), 9–10.

Bergmann, B. (1987). Measurement, or finding things in economics. *Journal of Economic Education, 18*(2), 191–201.

Bergmann, B. (1988). An experiment on the formation of expectations. *Journal of Economic Behavior and Organization, 9*, 137–151.
Bergmann, B. (1989). Why do most economists know so little about the economy? In S. Bowles, R. Edwards, & W. Shepard (Eds.), *Unconventional wisdom: Essays on economics in honor of John Kenneth Galbraith* (pp. 29–37). Houghton Mifflin Company.
Bergmann, B. (1990a). Feminism and economics. *Women's Studies Quarterly, 18*(3/4), 68–74. (Reprinted from *Academe: Bulletin of the American Association of University Professors.* 1983, *69*(5), 22–25. (Original work published 1983).
Bergmann, B. (1990b). Micro-to-macro simulation: A primer with a labor market example. *Journal of Economic Perspective, 4*(1), 99–116.
Bergmann, B. (1995). Becker's theory of the family: Preposterous conclusions. *Feminist Economics, 1*(1), 141–150.
Bergmann, B. (1999). Abolish the Nobel Prize for economics. *Challenge, 42*(2), 52–57.
Bergmann, B. (2006). On wives and prostitutes. *Women's Review of Books, 25*(6), 32–33.
Bergmann, B. (2007). Even after. *Times Supplement Magazine*, 10–12.
Bergmann, B. (2008). Discrimination through the economist's eyes. In F. Crosby, M. Stockdale, & S. Ropp (Eds.), *Sex discrimination on the workplace* (pp. 213–234). Blackwell Publishing.
Bergmann, B. (2009). The economy and the economics profession: Both need work. *Eastern Economic Journal, 35*(1), 2–9.
Bergmann, B., & Bennett, R. (1977). Macroeconomic effects of a Humphrey-Hawkins type program. *American Economic Review, 67*(1), 265–270.
Bergmann, B., Eliasson, G., & Orcutt, G. H. (Eds.). (1977). Micro simulation: Models, methods and applications. In *Proceedings of a Symposium on Micro Simulation Methods in Stockholm*, September 19–22, 1977. IUI Conference Reports.
Bewley, T. (1999). *Why wages don't fall during a recession.* Harvard University Press.
Bordo, S. (1987). *The flight to objectivity: Essays on cartesianism and culture.* Albany State University of New York Press.
Chassonnery-Zaïgouche, C., & Goutsmedt, A. (2024). Modelling intervention: Barbara Bergmann's micro-to-macro simulation projects. *The European Journal of the History of Economic Thought, 32*(3), 342–362.
Delli Gatti, D., Fagiolo, G., Gallegati, M., & Richiardi, M. (2018). *Agent-based models in economics: A toolkit.* Cambridge University Press.
Edgeworth, F. (1922). Equal pay to men and women for equal work. *The Economic Journal, 32*(128), 431–457.

Emami, Z., & Olson, P. (Eds.). (2002). Barbara Berman Bergmann. In *Engendering economics: Conversations with women economists in the United States* (pp. 53–72). Routledge.

Ferber, M., & Nelson, J. (Eds.). (1993). *Beyond economic man: Feminist theory and economics*. The University of Chicago Press.

Jaggar, A. M. (2002). Challenging women's global inequalities: Some priorities for western philosophers. *Philosophical Topics, 30*(82), 229–252.

Kuiper, E., & Sap, J. (Eds.). (1995). *Out of the margin: Feminist perspectives on economics*. Routledge.

Lloyd, G. (1984). *The man of reason: "Male" and "female" in western philosophy*. University of Minnesota Press.

Lucas, R., Jr., & Rapping, L. A. (1969). Real wages, employment, and inflation. *Journal of Political Economy, 77*(5), 721–754.

Mirer, T., & Peck, J. (1975). Combining microsimulation and regression: Comment. *Econometrica, 4*(3), 523–528.

Nelson, J. (1993). Gender and economic ideologies. *Review of Social Economy, 51*(3), 287–301.

Nelson, J. (1996). *Feminism, objectivity and economics*. Routledge.

Orcutt, G. H. (1957). A new type of socio-economic system. *The Review of Economics and Statistics, 39*(2), 116–123.

Orcutt, G. (1960). Simulation of Economic Systems. *American Economic Review, 50*(5), 893–907.

Orcutt, G. H., Greenberger, M., Korbel, J., & Rivlin, A. M. (1961). *Microanalysis of socioeconomic systems: A simulation study*. Harper & Row.

Polkington, B., & Thompson, D. (1998). *Adam Smith's daughters*. Edward Elgar Publishing.

Renwick, T., & Bergmann, B. (1993). A budget-based definition of poverty: With an application to single-parent families. *Journal of Human Resources, 28*(1), 1–24.

Riach, P. (2015). Barbara Bergmann (20 July 1927 – 5 April 2015). *The Economic and Labour Relations Review, 26*(3), 493–495.

Riach, P., & Rich, J. (1987). Testing for sexual discrimination in the labour market. *Australian Economic Papers, 26*, 165–178.

Riach, P., & Rich, J. (1991). Testing for racial discrimination in the labour market. *Cambridge Journal of Economics, 15*(3), 239–256.

Riach, P., & Rich, J. (1995). An investigation of gender discrimination in labor hiring. *Eastern Economic Journal, 21*(3), 343–356.

Riach, P., & Rich, J. (1998). Of chicken entrails, anthropology, and a realistic social science. *Feminist Economics, 4*(3), 187–191.

Saunders, L. & King, M. (2000). An Interview with Barbara Bergmann: leading feminist economics. *Review of Political Economy, 12*(3), 305–316.

Saunders, L., & King, M. (2010). An interview with Barbara Bergmann: Leading feminist economics. *Feminist Economics, 12*(3), 305–316.

Schmalensee, R. (1976). An experimental study of expectation formation. *Econometrica, 44*(1), 17–41.

Shenker, I. (1970, January 10). Professor of jargon finds that yesterday's 'ins' are out and 'outs' are, too. *The New York Times.*

Stigler, G., & Becker, G. (1977). De Gustibus Non Est Disputandum. *American Economic Review, 67*(2), 76–90.

Strassmann, D. (1999). Feminist economics. In J. Peterson & M. Lewis (Eds.), *The Elgar companion to feminist economics* (pp. 360–370). Edward Elgar.

Strober, E. (1998). Interview with Barbara Bergmann. *Feminist Economics, 4*(3), 5–6.

Tversky, A., & Kahneman, D. (1988). Rational choice and the framing of decision. In D. Bell, H. Raiffa, & A. Tversky (Eds.), *Decision making: Descriptive, normative, and prescriptive interactions* (pp. 167–192). Cambridge University Press.

CHAPTER 6

Between Feminist Economics and Institutionalism

Barbara, do you consider yourself a feminist economist?

When Bergmann was asked this question in 2002, she replied:

> Of course, I am a feminist. However, I don't know that everyone would agree that I'm an economist. I work on social issues; maybe that's not economics. But I've been a feminist since I was perhaps three years old. I remember sitting on my stoop in the Bronx and thinking that you had to earn your own money or you were nobody. (Emami & Olson 2002, p. 66)

This is the essence of feminism in Barbara Bergmann's view: women's freedom to choose their own lives within a society that allows them to pursue their own individual aims in both the private and public spheres, without structural discrimination preventing their personal fulfillment.

How did Bergmann combine her personal vision of feminism with feminist economics, a multifaceted field encompassing a range of political orientations? What kind of feminist economist was Barbara?

Considering her incisive critique of Becker's New Home Economics, her explicit rejection of Marxism, her firm conviction that gender inequality is rooted in traditional stereotypes, cultural barriers, and persistent discrimination that collectively sustain patriarchal structures, as well as her rejection of the doctrine of the separate spheres, which legitimizes

G. Becchio, *Barbara Bergmann*, Great Thinkers in Economics,
https://doi.org/10.1007/978-3-032-18696-6_6

the gendered division of labor between the public (male) and private (female) domains, Bergmann may be best characterized as a post-liberal feminist.[1]

Post-liberal feminism seeks to integrate feminist insights on gender and power into a progressive framework, while preserving classical liberalism's fundamental commitments to individual rights (Pateman 1988; Young 1990). More precisely, Barbara's stance aligns with egalitarian liberalism, a strand of egalitarian liberal feminism that, while grounded in individual freedom, acknowledges the social constraints and gender stereotypes that curtail women's autonomy. Drawing inspiration from John Rawls (1971), who proposed a theoretical reconciliation between liberty and distributive justice, egalitarian feminist liberals advanced policies aimed at strengthening women's autonomy and empowerment. These include anti-discrimination legislation, affirmative action, and welfare state programs aimed at reducing not only inequality but also poverty. Bergmann's analysis of the institutional origin of both inequality and poverty led her to adopt an institutionalist approach which she integrated in her feminist agenda.

6.1 From CSWEP to IAFFE

As mentioned in Chapter 2, Bergmann was actively involved in the foundation of the Committee on the Status of Women in the Economics Profession (CSWEP), which took place in 1971 during the meetings of the American Economic Association (AEA). Barbara chaired a session on "What economic equality for women requires" and was part of the *Women's Caucus*, a group aimed at formally inviting the Executive Committee of the American Economic Association to recognize that the economics profession should be more open to women and to monitor the status of women within the profession (Becchio 2020).[2]

Many years later, Bergmann recalled the CSWEP experience and lamented the slow progress in gender reforms in economics, by comparing economics with other social sciences (Bergmann 1998a). She

[1] Prominent scholars in this tradition include Susan Moller Okin and Martha Nussbaum, and among economists, besides Bergmann, Amartya Sen.

[2] The Caucus also requested a formal commitment to promote equal opportunities, from early career encouragement to tenured positions, which led to the formation of 'Job Openings for Economists' (JOE) in 1974.

noted that over the past quarter century, the economics profession had shown a striking resistance to feminist reform. Despite widespread transformations in other social sciences, such as psychology, sociology, and history, economics remained largely unaltered in its treatment of gender. Ideas and practices once deemed "outrageous and laughable" remained so, and few feminist initiatives had become institutionalized within the discipline. This stagnation was mainly due, according to Barbara, to the limitations of CSWEP.[3] While in psychology, sociology, and history, feminist scholars and professional women's committees have not only secured a stronger role for women within their respective disciplines but have also challenged and transformed the theoretical frameworks underpinning gender inequality, economics persisted in retaining misogynistic assumptions, systemic barriers, and in ignoring the real origins of discrimination and power relations affecting women's lives.

Bergmann provided some examples. In sociology, the once-dominant paradigm of Talcott Parsons's functionalism justified the doctrine of the separate spheres, i.e., the confinement of women to domestic roles and men to the public roles, as necessary for social stability. However, feminist sociology fundamentally reshaped this view by exposing the economic and social costs of these arrangements for women and revealing that occupational segregation and wage inequality were not the result of voluntary choices but of entrenched discrimination (Bielby & Barron 1984; England 1982; Tomaskovic-Devey 1993).

In psychology, traditional conceptions of mental health equated well-being with traits associated with masculinity, such as assertiveness, rationality, and independence, while pathologizing women who exhibited them. Feminist psychologists and therapists redefined psychological health as the capacity for personal agency and self-realization, irrespective of gender, by dismantling Freudian doctrines such as "penis envy" and the notion that women's fulfillment lay in maternity and subordination.

In history, women's contributions were long omitted from narratives of human development. Feminist historians founded the field of women's

[3] One year later, she wrote a marginal follow up of her article, pointing out that she was too confident when she included NBER among those institutions with no gender gap. Martin Feldstein, President of NBER at that time, wrote to Bergmann that this was not, unfortunately, the situation (Bergmann 1999).

studies, ensuring that women's experiences, achievements, and struggles became legitimate subjects of scholarly inquiry.[4]

Sociologists, psychologists, and historians institutionalized feminism through structural initiatives: dedicated research projects on gender, paid staff, and public advocacy. Women's committees in those fields pushed for increased representation of women in academia, publishing data on faculty gender composition, and even securing an affirmative action target. For instance, sociologists stipulated that, by 1990, one in four tenured sociology professors in the American academia should be women.

By contrast, according to Bergmann, economics has remained largely impervious to such feminist transformation, mainly because of CSWEP's inertia, which refrained from controversial or confrontational strategies: it never proposed affirmative action quotas, publicized departments with low female representation, or challenged the gender blindness of mainstream economic thought. Efforts to address sexism in economics education were similarly muted. In the early 1980s, Susan Feiner documented pervasive gender bias in economics textbooks, which portrayed women as passive, intellectually inferior, or absent altogether. Yet CSWEP declined to endorse her call for textbook reform. Instead, CSWEP initiatives focused on technical skill-building workshops for women economists and the publication of newsletters, activities that, though supportive, did not question the discipline's core assumptions or its exclusionary structures.

According to Bergmann, the ongoing presence of overtly sexist assumptions in economic theory and practice not only persists but sometimes receives prestigious recognition, including Nobel Prizes. She provided three examples as emblematic of economics' non-inclusive attitude.

First, Becker's model of the family (Becker 1981), which portrays patriarchal authority as economically efficient and beneficial to women, even suggesting that more regressive arrangements, such as harems, could improve their welfare under certain legal conditions.

Second, Becker's conjecture that women's lower wages stem from fatigue due to domestic responsibilities (Becker 1985) ignoring empirical evidence that a double burden reduces productivity regardless of gender,

[4] The American Historical Association (AHA) institutionalized this shift by creating a Women's Committee, supporting conferences, and integrating women's history into the educational curricula.

which led him to justify men's avoidance of housework as economically rational, reinforcing gender asymmetry.

Third, gender wage gap analysis provided by mainstream economics attributes unexplained differences to "unobserved productivity" rather than to discrimination, thereby reaffirming the free market's presumed efficiency to spontaneously eliminate gender inequality.

According to Bergmann, even World Bank publications, meant to advance gender equality, adopted these assumptions (Birdsall and Sabot 1991). Such examples revealed a disciplinary orthodoxy that continued to interpret gender inequality as the natural outcome of women's preferences or incapacities, rather than as a product of structural injustice. Hence, mainstream economics continued to frame gender disparities as individual choices rather than systemic discrimination, perpetuating patriarchal assumptions under the guise of economic rationality.

Bergmann called for more assertive strategies by feminist economists and their organizations. Potential initiatives may include: publicly naming institutions with disproportionately low numbers of women economists; urging associations, such as the National Science Foundation, to reconsider their support for such institutions; campaigning for a paid AEA staff position dedicated to women's participation and gender equity; establishing 'Economics of Gender' as a major subject classification within the American Economic Association; encouraging the introduction of letters-to-the-editor sections in academic journals to challenge unsupported conjectures about gender; considering theories that portray women's economic subordination as voluntary and ridicule; supporting outreach and recruitment efforts to increase the number of women entering graduate programs in economics; and stimulating research and policy debates on the economic dimensions of child-rearing and care work.

Bergmann concluded that even the foundation of the International Association for Feminist Economics (IAFFE) and its journal *Feminist Economics* had been relatively cautious in challenging the mainstream. This was a kind of self-criticism. In fact, she was directly involved in IAFFE foundation (1992); in setting up the journal *Feminist Economics* in 1995 (she was an associate editor, and for a while she ran the Exploration part of the journal); and in constantly getting involved in IAFFE's network and initiatives. Finally, she served as IAFFE's president in 1998/1999.

From her archive, as well as from IAFFE's archive, it is possible to follow Barbara's direct involvement in the project of the institutionalization of feminist economics step by step. In 1990, at the ASSA annual meetings, held in Washington, DC, a session entitled "Can Feminism Find a Home in Economics?" attracted an overflow crowd. On that occasion, many women economists discussed the difficulties they faced when doing feminist work within the discipline. A follow-up survey of that discussion was published in February 1991. Meanwhile, in a newsletter dated January 27, 1991, Diana Strassmann announced the official foundation of IAFFE to the group of feminist economists who were planning to attend the ASSA meetings, to be held in New Orleans, in January 1992. Strassmann proudly wrote: "after brainstorming and discussion, the Founding Members came up with a name for the group, so we are no longer nameless. We are the International Association for Feminist Economics (IAFFE)".[5] On that message, Bergmann appeared as a volunteer in organizing a two-day follow-up conference for the summer of 1991.

A few months later, in May 1991, Barbara joined the Committee for Race and Gender Balance in the Economics Curriculum and presented a memorandum that emphasized the need for vigilance against gender and race bias in economics teaching and research.[6] The memorandum identified three interconnected areas where bias commonly occurs: defining economic problems, which can exclude or distort the experiences of women and minorities; reviewing previous research, which may overlook contributions by or about underrepresented groups; and using examples and discussions that marginalize or stereotype women, African Americans, and Hispanics.

In August 1991, the first 'Feminist Economists Network Update' newsletter began to be printed. In its first issue, April Aerni and Jean Shakelford announced that an organizational meeting of IAFFE would be held during the ASSA meetings the following January 1992, after the CSWEP meeting, probably on January 2nd. The first point was to decide whether or not to formalize IAFFE and if IAFFE should become

[5] IAFFE archive, David M. Rubenstein Rare Book & Manuscript Library, Duke University.

[6] Other members of the group included: Robin Bartlett, William Baumol, Robert Cherry, William Darity Jr., Robert Eisner, Marianne Ferber, Donald McCloskey, Paul Samuelson, Robert Solow, Lester Thurow, and Rhonda Williams.

part of AEA. Therefore, the authors presented the results of a survey (circa 50 economists have been involved) about what feminist economics should address: over half of those who responded were interested in economic issues relating to race or gender; 34% in labor economics; 27% in economic development or trade; and 14% in economics of families or households.

Between September and November 1991, Bergmann, along with Iona Thraen, April Aerni, and Jean Shackelford channeled their energy into establishing an official e-mail network, *femecon-l*, aimed at giving instant communication of any initiative or working paper to feminist economists worldwide.[7] In December 1991, the newsletter announced the names of the founding members of the "(yet to be named) feminist economist group": among them, Barbara Bergmann, who co-signed, along with Aerni, Shackelford, Strassmann, and Thraen, the welcome letter to other founders of the group, dated December 17, 1991: "Welcome and thank you for becoming a founding member of the as yet unnamed organization of feminist economists! As of this date, we count twenty-nine!".[8]

Although the foundation of the International Association of Feminist Economics (IAFFE) officially occurred in 1992, the official recognition of feminist economics within the general scheme of the American Economic Association happened in 2006, when feminist economics got JEL code B54.[9]

[7] The first IAFFE newsletter was edited by Nancy Folbre. In July 1992, over one hundred participants gathered and elected Jean Shackelford as President of IAFFE.

[8] Other founding members were: April Aerni, Randy Albelda, Amott Teresa, David Andrews, Rose Amrie Alvin, Drucilla Barker, Robin Barlett, Barbara Brown, Marian Chamberlain, Marianne Ferber, Deborah Figart, Nancy Folbre, Sushila Gidwani, Barbara Hopkins, Joyce Jacobsen, Maggie Levenstein, Elaine McCrate, Donald McCloskey, Majorie McElroy, Julie Nelson, Pamela Nickless, Paulette Olson, Janice Petersen, Janet Seiz, Jean Shackelford, Diana, Strassmann, Janet Tanski, and Iona Thraen.

[9] B54 is a subcategory of B that stands for "History of Economic Thought, Methodology, and Heterodox Approaches". The American Economic Association website specified that: "the categories for B5 were created to accommodate the recent substantial developments in non-mainstream (non-neoclassical) economic approaches to contemporary economic problems. Studies about an economic subject (or subjects) adopting a given heterodox approach should be cross-classified under the appropriate B5 category and also under the appropriate subject category (or categories)". Hence, feminist economics was officially labeled as a heterodox approach, with the following formulation: "Feminist economics studies issues related to feminist approaches to economics, as well as studies about economic subjects, using these approaches. Studies may deal with either (applied)

In 1994, Bergmann served on the Board of Directors of IAFFE. On March 1, 1994, IAFFE promoted a member survey aimed at "knowing more about members of the organization, particularly in relation to assembling panels for conferences and perhaps in finding referees for papers". Bergmann's reply is particularly interesting, as she described her main research interests (gender, child care, and social policy) and her main courses (economics of gender with feminist content). She also pointed out that the most important activity of IAFFE was its annual meeting. Finally, she stated that her main research interests were public goods and economic demography, and concluded by lamenting the obsolete nature of those JEL codes that "need reform!".

As Ferber later specified in an interview, while the CSWEP was performing well in its function of promoting women economists, founding members of IAFFE believed that an independent and institutionalized group in the field of feminist economics was necessary in order to promote the progress of women in the profession and an expansion of feminist theory within the discipline (Saunders & King, 2000).

As mentioned earlier, Bergmann had an opposite opinion about CSWEP's performance, and she was also critical about IAFFE. This was mainly due to the fact that feminism, feminist economics, and IAFFE itself are not monolithic. In fact, the radical tradition as well as classical liberal tradition, along with other nuances between them, were represented in IAFFE. As Shackelford wrote: "IAFFE faces the challenge of making up considerable ground if economics is to achieve the integral feminist traditions found in other social science disciplines" (Shackelford 1999, p. 487).

Although feminist economists may differ in their vision and economic analysis, they share some common fundamental aims, scopes, and contents of the discipline. First and foremost, they shared the urgency to revise, and eventually to reject, Becker's NHE methodology and results. This urgency was fully endorsed by Bergmann (see Chapter 5). As reported in Chapter 5, according to Bergmann, the predominance

microeconomics or (applied) macroeconomics or both, and may be either theoretical or empirical".

of neoclassical economics has constrained alternative approaches, and the NHE has retarded the development of feminist economics.[10]

In a paper published in 1983, Bergmann described the neoclassical aura of the new home economists in her famous sentence:

> To say that the 'new home economists' are not feminist in their orientation would be as much of an understatement as to say that Bengal tigers are not vegetarians. (Bergmann 1990, p. 72)

Bergmann summarized her consistency with feminist economics' agenda in her article mentioned above (Bergmann 1990). According to Bergmann, the emergence of feminist economics was determined by women's relative exclusion from high-status and well-compensated economic activity that constrained their capacity to exercise influence, develop talents, and escape deprivation. For much of the discipline's history, economists, despite recognizing such disparities, did not regard them as topics of professional importance. Only in recent decades, with the rise of women's participation in paid labor, the growth of single motherhood, and the resurgence of feminist ideology, have questions of gender and economic justice entered the mainstream of economic inquiry. The central determinant of social status in modern economies is an individual's position in the labor market. Women's weaker performance in this sphere is universally acknowledged: even college-educated women earn less, on average, than men who never completed high school.

The disagreement among economists lies not in the existence of inequality, but in its causes and its meaning. As a result, the economics profession has been divided into two main camps. Feminist economists, of both sexes, sought to document women's economic disadvantages, develop theoretical frameworks for greater equity, and propose policy reforms to correct systemic bias. Non-feminist economists, by contrast, have defended existing structures, portraying gender differences as natural, economically efficient, and even beneficial. They have rejected feminist analyses as ideologically driven and economically irrational.

Bergmann pointed out that mainline economists tend to dismiss claims of unfairness, attributing disparities to differences in individual choice

[10] Bergmann anticipated the discussion around economic imperialism of neoclassical economics, i.e., its capacity to become mainstream and to colonize other social sciences (Fine 2000).

rather than structural bias. Their skepticism reflects both the profession's ideological commitment to free-market principles and its overwhelmingly male, conservative composition. According to conventional economic theory, labor markets reflect the rational interaction of self-interested agents seeking to maximize material gain. Within this model, discrimination on the basis of gender appears irrational unless it confers a measurable economic advantage. By assuming that markets are inherently efficient, many economists conclude that gender inequalities must arise from productivity differences or personal preferences, not from prejudice. If women are underrepresented in an occupation, the reasoning goes, it must be because they voluntarily avoided it due to domestic obligations or because their performance is lower than men's. According to Bergmann, this model of the economic agent, as a rational and unbiased decision-maker, leaves little room for the influence of stereotypes, cultural norms, and institutional barriers, which are central in feminist economics

Bergmann also shared with the majority of feminist economists the analysis of marriage, seen as a social institution that responds to social norms that had traditionally relegated women to be housewives and segregated them specific occupations. For Bergmann, marriage is a social institution whose complex dynamics have been too often rooted in gender inequality which persists in the intra-house dynamics as well as in the dynamics of divorce and break-ups. In contrast to Becker's theory, a feminist economic theory of marriage seriously analyzes the motivations to marry, the evolution of the contribution of partners at home and in the market, and the distribution of family resources among spouses and children, adopting more realistic assumptions (see Chapter 4).

Another common point between Bergmann and many feminist economists was the focus on the social organization of care, emphasizing how economic systems fail to provide adequate support for childrearing, child care, and family responsibilities. A fundamental goal of the feminist agenda, shared by Bergmann, was in fact the equal participation of men and women in both paid work and unpaid household and caregiving duties. Bergmann's article concluded with a historical anecdote and a final remark on the nature and scope of feminist economics: when at a conference on equity, a scholar remarked that the integration of women into professional life in the Soviet Union had occurred only because wars and purges had decimated the male population, she replied that she hoped such catastrophic events would not be required to achieve gender equality in the United States. Feminist economists, she emphasized, are dedicated precisely to envisioning and pursuing pathways toward fairness that rely not on tragedy, but on deliberate, informed, and humane transformation.

In a revised version of Bergmann's article that appeared one year later (Bergmann 1984) on *Challenge*, she emphasized that her feminism was based on the notion of equality of individuals, not on the supremacy of the female sphere, as endorsed by some feminist scholars and activists. She wrote:

> The major preoccupation of feminist economists is precisely to try to sketch visions of a system of work and family relations which will be fair to men, women, and children, and to try to devise methods, short of mayhem, to get us from here [New Home Economics] to there. (Bergmann 1984, p. 49)

As a matter of fact, only a small number of her articles appeared in *Feminist Economics*, albeit she was a highly prolific writer, publishing extensively both in academic journals and in the popular press (see Chapter 7). These included her critique of Becker's New Home Economics (Bergmann 1995) (see Chapter 5); two additional papers, both published in 1995 and co-authored with Heidi Hartmann (Bergmann & Hartmann 1995; Hartmann & Bergmann 1995); another one on child care (Bergmann 2000a); and a final article, on lone mothers, presented as a dialogue among economists from different countries (Himmelweit et al. 2004, as mentioned in Chapter 4). As we see, all of them, with the only exception of the article that dealt with Becker's methodological and theoretical faults, were about policy.

Bergmann and Hartmann (1995) advocated for a reform promoting employment, family stability, and dignity through the Help for Working Parents (HWP) program, a welfare model designed to help low-income families achieve economic independence without sacrificing decency or security by providing a full-time minimum-wage job, supplemented by the Earned Income Tax Credit (EITC), Food Stamps, and housing assistance, which could enable families to live decently. The authors noted that empirical data show that most women on welfare possess high school diplomas and work experience, but inadequate support systems trap them in dependency. They also pointed out that working mothers tend to have fewer children than those who stay home, meaning access to jobs and child care would reduce long-term welfare dependency and child poverty simultaneously.

The Help for Working Parents (HWP) plan included: universal health insurance; accessible child care; expanded housing assistance; and voucher-based safety nets for unemployed parents. Finally, the authors proposed to finance the reform through cuts to excessive defense spending, CIA operations, and agricultural subsidies to wealthy farmers, or alternatively through higher taxes on affluent households. As Hartmann and Bergmann (1995) wrote:

> While the HWP plan moves in a universalistic direction by including working parents as well as nonworking parents, married parents as well as single parents, it remains focused on the poor where the need is greatest. (Hartmann & Bergmann 1995, p. 117)

In her article on child care (Bergmann 2000a), Bergmann argued that parental child care subsidized by governments created serious problems of equity, gender equality, efficiency, and administrative feasibility. In fact, it risked reinforcing traditional gender roles and undermining women's participation in the labor force (See Chapter 3 and Chapter 4). Bergmann compared Sweden, where the government heavily subsidized both public child care and parental leaves, and France, where major resources were devoted to public facilities and preschools but far less support to at-home parents. On a third row, Germany and the Netherlands traditionally granted generous benefits to parents who stayed home, usually mothers, while offering little for nonparental care. The United States, by contrast, modestly subsidized paid care through tax credits for middle-class families and vouchers for a small proportion of low-income households, while parents who cared for their own children at home received no compensation. Furthermore, welfare reform in 1996 cut subsidized at-home care for single mothers, signaling a shift toward encouraging employment and nonparental care.

At the core of Bergmann's analysis lay the issue of equity. Was it fair to subsidize families who purchased child care while denying equivalent aid to those who provided care themselves? On the surface, both groups faced similar financial burdens in raising young children, yet Bergmann argued that at-home parents were often better off than dual-earner or single-parent families once nonmonetary factors were considered.[11] The

[11] She illustrated this with a hypothetical scheme in which nonparental care cost $9000 per year, and subsidies cover most of the expense for low- and middle-income families.

stay-at-home parent contributed valuable unpaid labor that enhanced the family's living standard. Extending subsidies to such families would therefore have created inequity by rewarding those already advantaged in time and nonmarket resources. Bergmann acknowledged that subsidizing lower-income, one-earner families might have seemed compassionate, but it would have produced new inequities relative to single working parents who faced heavier time constraints.

Beyond financial fairness, Bergmann emphasized the gendered implications of subsidizing at-home care: policies rewarding stay-at-home care threatened to reverse this progress by reestablishing the norm that mothers, not fathers, should withdraw from the labor market. Even when programs were formally gender-neutral, women overwhelmingly took the leave, as seen in Sweden, where mothers used the vast majority of parental leave despite its availability to fathers. This trend, Bergmann observed, reinforced traditional gender roles and discouraged employers from hiring or promoting women. Hence, such dynamics entrenched gender inequality in the labor market.

Bergmann also questioned the quality and efficiency of subsidizing at-home care: providing cash incentives for home care could have led parents, especially low-income ones, to prioritize income over children's developmental needs, thereby depriving them of the benefits of early education and socialization. Empirical studies, she noted, found no significant behavioral differences between children cared for by their mothers and those in quality nonmaternal care once family background was controlled, while children from disadvantaged families often benefited more from professional early education.

From an efficiency standpoint, paying a full-time parent to care for one or two children was far more costly per child than funding group-based care, where a trained caregiver could attend to several children. Monitoring care provided at home is not easy. Bergmann next claimed that paid parental leave, common in Europe, raised the same equity and efficiency issues as direct subsidies for at-home care: short leaves caused few problems, but extended ones often undermined women's labor market continuity and imposed heavy fiscal costs. Because benefits were tied to prior wages, higher earners received larger payments, making the system

Comparing several family types—two-earner, one-earner, and single-parent households—she showed that even without subsidies, one-earner families that provided their own care remained better off once household production and leisure were taken into account.

regressive. Moreover, when fathers were not required to take part of the leave, mothers overwhelmingly withdrew from the workforce, again reinforcing traditional gender division of labor.

Finally, in the article written in the form of a dialogue on lone mothers (Himmelweit et al. 2004), Bergmann pointed out that single mothers are especially vulnerable to material hardship and poverty, especially when mothers must also pay for healthcare and child care. Studies show that many such mothers remain thousands of dollars below the poverty line, revealing a deep structural problem rather than a personal failing. Bergmann did not support caregiving stipends, as they might discourage women's labor force participation, undermine gender equality, and reduce women's job opportunities and promotion prospects. Furthermore, evidence from Sweden's paid parental leave system suggests that long leaves contribute to occupational sex segregation, as men rarely take equal leave. Hence, Bergmann proposed providing two to three months of paid parental leave to each of up to two adults per household, while avoiding long-term stipends for stay-at-home mothers.

6.2 Against the Separate Spheres: The Notion of Care

A crucial aspect of feminism, which is also central to feminist economics, is the treatment of care. Economists define care as unpaid work performed within the private sphere, typically by women, in contrast to paid work carried out in the public sphere by both men and women (Becchio 2024). The traditional model of the male breadwinner and female caregiver has been regarded by the New Home Economics as rational and efficient. Feminist economists, however, reacted against this justification of the status quo, viewing it instead as a manifestation of patriarchy. Nonetheless, some feminist approaches aimed at revaluing care work through remuneration may inadvertently reinforce the doctrine of separate spheres. From a cultural standpoint, feminists have responded to this doctrine in three main ways.

First, following the classical liberal tradition, some feminist philosophers denied any essential differences between men and women, the very premise underlying the doctrine of separate spheres. They emphasized that gender stereotypes, which assign women to the domestic sphere and men to the public sphere, are culturally and socially constructed rather than the result of natural differences (Haslanger 2000; Scott 1988).

Consequently, care provided within the household by any family member, regardless of gender, should not be remunerated. Only jobs in the marketplace can be quantified economically, and gender equality should instead be pursued by eliminating gender labor gaps, the gender wage gap, the glass ceiling, occupational segregation, and all other economic phenomena that reinforce gender inequality and women's subordination.

Second, some feminists acknowledged that women may be naturally more inclined to provide care than men, and, therefore, a sex-based division of labor can be acceptable, provided it is voluntary and not imposed by social pressure. Nonetheless, they stressed that care work has never been properly valued and its importance has long been underestimated. Hence, any form of compensation for care work performed by women is acceptable (Gilligan 1982; Noddings 1986).

Third, some feminists argued that even if biological and cultural differences between men and women exist, social structures have historically been shaped in a masculine way, harming women by making them victims of poverty, injustice, domestic violence, and other forms of inequality (MacKinnon 1989; Rhode 1997).

Between the 1970s and 1980s, while feminist economists largely converged in rejecting Becker's theory of marriage, many proposed models that included care work, love, power, and obligation, as well as the role of cultural and social norms, all of which mainstream economics had either misrepresented or ignored. Feminist economists explicitly identified the influence of the doctrine of separate spheres in several New Home Economics assumptions, such as: optimal decisions depending on the different skills of household members; the division of labor within families reflecting biological and cultural differences between men and women; the allocation of women's time to the household and men's time to the market as rational; marriage as a long-term commitment ensuring women's protection; and the view that market-oriented investments in boys and household-oriented investments in girls constituted optimal strategies (Barker & Feiner 2004; Bergmann 1995; Lamanna et al., 2014; Paterson & Lewis 1999; Schultz 1974).

By rejecting Becker's standard approach to gender issues, many feminist economists instead advocated transforming the male world into a female one, conceived as more emotional and less competitive. This perspective was common among feminist philosophers of the time and strongly influenced some feminist economists (Fricker & Hornsby 2000). However, Bergmann was not among them. Rather she shared the first position, according to which transitioning toward a feminine world may inadvertently reinforce the doctrine of separate spheres, which is the primary obstacle to women's emancipation.

Bergmann rejected the justification for it offered by standard economics, which failed to acknowledge discrimination and segregation and insisted that women's traditional role in the domestic sphere was an efficient allocation of their labor and a free choice. She specifically argued that Becker's new home economics was inadequate in understanding the dynamics of families. Bergmann outlined her own policy proposals to enhance family conditions.

Hence, Bergmann proposed a threefold approach: first, the full commodification of care work; second, the promotion of an education system focused on equal job opportunities for both genders and on shared domestic responsibilities between partners; and third, a robust program of affirmative action aimed at protecting families from poverty, particularly single-parent households, which are predominantly headed by mothers.

Almost unique in her position among feminist economists, she integrated a feminist perspective, which called for affirmative action to diminish market discrimination and eliminate gender stereotypes concerning women's domestic roles, with a classical liberal vision, focused on the role of markets and political institutions in providing the means necessary to facilitate women's emancipation as active participants in the public sphere.

Bergmann's vision of feminist economics in relation to the doctrine of the separate spheres is well summarized in two articles and in a review (Bergmann 1987b, 1998b, 2005a).

In her 1987 paper, Bergmann viewed marriage as an institution that responded to social norms, which had traditionally segregated women into the domestic sphere, thus discriminating them in the public sphere. According to her, standard economists defended and justified 'the old regime'. As she wrote: "Becker explained, justified, and even glorified role differentiation by sex" (Bergmann 1987b, p. 132). Influenced by Becker, standard economists opposed women's calls for affirmative action, as they held "a stereotypical attitude about women", and carried a "sexist baggage". They applied the theory of comparative advantages to explain the division of labor between the sexes and the specialization of women in the domestic sphere without acknowledging the discrimination and segregation of women in the private sphere. Bergmann argued that women's traditional roles in the domestic sphere, which resulted in their accumulation of less human capital, should be seen as a form of discrimination rather than a free and rational choice. On the opposite side of the ideological spectrum, Marxist economists, focused on building up a system able to destroy inequalities of all kinds, do not spend energies on "fighting inequalities here and now" (ibid). According to Bergmann, both neoclassical economics and Marxist economics are wrong when they deal with gender inequality.

Bergmann's feminism is well summarized by a letter she wrote to *The Women's Review of Books*, aimed at defending the central ideas of her book *The Economic Emergence of Women* (Bergmann 1986), namely practical ways to reduce the persistent inequality between men and women in both the workplace and the family.

Bergmann's letter was a reply to M. Hart, who perceived Bergmann's focus as limited to social reforms, without attacking capitalism itself, and for Bergmann's failing to engage with the so-called 'New International Division of Labor', preferring instead to discuss possible reforms within the 'illusory' goal of inequality with privileged men. Bergmann addressed Hart's 'wild impatience' to solve gender inequality by overthrowing the capitalist system as a typical attitude of those women who, while claiming to be ardently feminist, substitute ideological rhetoric for real action. Bergmann criticized those who prioritize abstract Marxist theory over tangible progress toward gender equality, arguing that such attitudes ultimately align them with male supremacists on both extremes of the political spectrum. Just as women like Phyllis Schlafly on the right resist feminist advances, Bergmann contended that certain leftist feminists also obstruct progress by rejecting achievable reforms (Bergmann 1987a). For Bergmann, the true feminist struggle lies not in trading ideological slogans, but in ensuring women's fair access to employment, wages, and opportunities, i.e., goals that bring measurable improvements to women's lives.

In her 1998(b) paper, Bergmann's central thesis was that true gender equality requires that men and women live economically and socially similar lives, participating equally in all spheres of public and private activity. Moreover, such equality can initially only be achieved through women's integration into what has historically been the "male world" of paid labor, competition, and public achievement. Hence, her position diverges from much feminist thought, which often seeks to revalue or preserve a distinctive 'female world' rather than transcend it.

According to Bergmann, women's exclusion was not simply differentiation but subordination. The tasks assigned to them, such as care for the very young and very old, maintenance of cleanliness, and repetitive household labor, were essential but devalued. Though vital to human survival, they were monotonous, unremunerated, and lacking in honor or autonomy. In many societies, women's domestic labor was coupled with exposure to physical danger, economic dependency, and male violence, with few means of escape or protection. Cultural enforcement has perpetuated this view of the separate spheres.[12] Thus, gender inequality is a deliberate structure of power maintained through cultural and institutional reinforcement.

Since the boundaries between the male and female worlds have loosened, women have entered paid employment in increasing numbers, and some men have become more involved in family life. Yet, integration remains incomplete and asymmetrical, as empirical data reveal. The result is a society still divided along gendered lines, one where women have entered the public sphere more readily than men have entered the private one.

Therefore, Bergmann presented three possible ways for achieving gender equality and evaluated their feasibility and desirability.

First, the integration of both worlds: men and women would both participate equally in paid employment and unpaid domestic labor. "Family-friendly" workplace policies would enable shared responsibilities, and the gendered division of labor would disappear.

Second, high commodification: women would join the male-dominated money economy fully, while household and caregiving tasks would be largely commodified, performed by paid workers or publicly funded services. In this system, domestic work becomes part of the formal economy, shared between both sexes as wage labor rather than unpaid obligation. Governments would provide or subsidize child care, eldercare, and domestic services through programs, vouchers, or tax incentives.

Third, a separate but more equal system: women would remain primarily within the domestic sphere, but their work would be accorded greater respect, security, and reward. Advocates of this model envision an elevation of 'women's work' through policies such as paid parental leave,

[12] Bergmann cited Felix Mendelssohn's discouragement of his sister Fanny's musical composition as emblematic of how women's participation in creative or intellectual work was deemed improper.

pension reforms, or symbolic recognition (e.g., incorporating unpaid domestic labor into national income accounts).

Bergmann clearly dismissed the third model as both impractical and inherently unfair. Women's mass entry into the paid labor force suggests a clear preference for the freedoms and rewards of the public sphere. Efforts to improve the honor or compensation of domestic labor, while morally appealing, would entrench a caste system based on sex. Even policies such as paid parental leave, though valuable, cannot substitute for economic integration, especially if they exclude single parents or reinforce women's disproportionate responsibility for child care.

Between the remaining two models, Bergmann concluded that high commodification is the more plausible route toward gender equality. Yet even this path requires deliberate intervention: ending workplace discrimination, supporting family income through public policy, and encouraging women to engage competitively in professional and political arenas. Without these efforts, commodification alone will merely replicate existing inequalities within new economic forms.

A key challenge to Bergmann's thesis arose from a strand of feminist thought that rejects the goal of assimilation into the 'male world'. This kind of feminism, labeled as 'cultural feminism', values women's distinctive traits, such as empathy, cooperation, and emotional intelligence, and envisions a transformed social order that celebrates these qualities rather than adapting women to male norms. It does not seek androgyny but the affirmation of 'women's ways' of knowing, reasoning, and caring.

Bergmann strongly criticized this position as politically ineffective and psychologically comforting rather than emancipatory. Characteristics often celebrated as 'women's ways' evolved under conditions of subjugation, serving to placate male dominance rather than challenge it. Traits like gentleness and patience may be virtues worth universalizing, but others, such as submissiveness or childlike behavior, are adaptive responses to oppression. Loyalty to these behavioral repertoires hinders women's ability to compete and claim power within existing institutions.[13]

[13] Bergmann drew analogies between cultural feminism and other identity-based resistance movements that valorize distinctiveness rather than integration. Examples of African American youth who accused high-achieving peers of "acting white", or disabled activists who rejected the desire to be "cured", illustrated similar dynamics of defensive separatism. Such attitudes can serve psychological or communal purposes, preserving pride in marginalized identities, but they also perpetuate exclusion and disadvantage.

Against cultural feminism, Bergmann proposed 'equality feminism' that requires participation in the dominant world's institutions of power, even if this means adopting its norms: women must engage the existing structures of economic and political life to transform them from within. Integration does not guarantee acceptance, yet withdrawal guarantees continued subordination. According to Bergmann, the "high commodification" model, where household tasks become marketized and both sexes participate in the paid economy, will continue to expand. Government support for child care, healthcare, and family subsidies can accelerate this process, as can broader cultural acceptance of men's participation in domestic work. The gradual transformation of unpaid care into waged labor represents both an economic and symbolic revaluation of traditionally female work.

However, Bergmann specified, equality will not emerge automatically from market participation. It requires three additional conditions.

First, the elimination of discrimination in employment and pay, ensuring equal access to opportunities. Second, women's full competitiveness, both in professional advancement and in political struggle for institutional reform. Third, public investment to offset the economic burdens of childrearing, so that parental responsibilities do not penalize women disproportionately.

Bergmann acknowledged that many feminists imagine an alternative world of exchange, less competitive, more cooperative, and emotionally warmer. While sympathetic to this vision, she warned that such transformation cannot precede women's acquisition of power within the existing order. The 'male world' may be hierarchical and cold, but its methods have proven effective in organizing large-scale production and governance. Only when women attain positions of influence can they begin to humanize these systems from within. Summing up, Bergmann envisioned a society in which gender distinctions no longer determine life paths, i.e., a world modeled less on complementarity than on equivalence. Such a world will initially resemble the male sphere as it exists, not because male norms are ideal, but because equality requires first mastering the dominant system before reforming it. Bergmann's position thus presents a peculiar feminism that calls for strategic assimilation as the path to transformation, insisting that androgyny, not cultural difference, is the foundation of equality.

In Bergmann's words: "when women [are] incorporated into the 'male world' of money exchange, with a distribution of jobs similar to that of men" (Bergmann 1998b, p. 76), they share equally the responsibilities between spouses when it comes to housework. These measures and commitments would actually render the doctrine of the separate spheres obsolete. She explained that this transition toward gender equality will be completed neither through mere integration of the male and female worlds nor simply by making the separate spheres more equal, but mainly through a significant program of government support aimed at "high commodification". Against many feminists, who advocated transforming the male world into the female world, more emotional and less competitive, Bergmann claimed that "[women] must play the male game, at least until a gentler and warmer way of human interactions evolves and becomes standard" (ibid., p. 82).[14]

In an interview with Liz Strober (1998) when Bergmann was asked for her definition of feminist economics, she replied:

> Feminism is a movement to achieve equality for women and men. I would hope that feminist economics, whatever else it may do, will be useful in showing the path to equality, in terms of appropriate policies. I don't see too many people who think they engage in feminist economics working in the field of policy. (Strober 1998, p. 6)[15]

In another interview (Emami & Olson 2002), when she was asked to say more about her being a feminist economist, she replied:

> I am an economist, and I am also a feminist. If feminist economics is postmodernist blathering, then I am not a feminist economist. I have a very different idea of what feminist economics should be compared to what I see at the meetings of IAFFE, at the ASSA, and in the journal, *Feminist Economics*. (Emami & Olson, 2002, p. 66)

Again, she lamented that feminist economists were diverging toward models without paying attention to social policy, while many papers on social reforms were written by non-feminists who tried to demonstrate that it is useless and harmful for the society as a whole.[16] Bergmann

[14] On this specific aspect of Bergmann's feminist agenda, see Folbre (1998).

[15] The interview was conducted on August 20, 1997.

[16] Bergmann cited Blau and Hagy (1998) who presented subsidized child care as inefficient since the quantity and quality of child care are substitutes. Hence, if you lower the price of child care, parents will demand more of it, and its quality will decline.

insisted on complaining that the main practical interest of feminist economists was to include unpaid work in the GNP, "which is not wrong, it's useless, of no practical importance. Yet that is what fires them up". In other words, according to Bergmann feminist economics was on the wrong track, "except me, of course[!]", she concluded and insisted that she was not interested in feminist theory "because too much attention has been given to the French trash, which is purposely murky", with very abstract content and far from concrete problems that must be actually solved (ibid).

Another point that made Bergmann's feminist economics peculiar was her view of feminist macroeconomics, which she did not "have a lot of sympathy for (…) When I see a session labeled 'feminist macroeconomics', I tend to go in the other direction" (ibid, p. 67).

In a previous interview (Saunders & King 2000), she was asked what type of feminism she advocates, Bergmann replied that she supported 'the total commodification of family work where we dismantle the female sphere, the unpaid family work', in contrast to the other two possible feminist options: family-friendly policies that allow the integration of men into family work and the integration of women into the market; and the maintenance of the traditional female spheres by adopting some form of rewards. She firmly believed that the only possible 'ticket to gender equality' was a 'totally androgynous model' that eliminates gender stereotypes and barriers, making it possible for women to inhabit the same world as men currently do.

In the same interview, Bergmann expressed her disappointment with IAFFE's agenda for lacking engagement in practical policy work, especially compared to male economists, who often address issues like child care or divorce. She criticized feminist economists for focusing on debates, like including household work in GDP, rather than on concrete policy challenges such as child care, welfare reform, and child support that directly affect women's lives. Regarding counting housework in GDP, she said:

> I'm not against it. What strikes me as peculiar is that you can get people on Femecon [an IAFFE listserv] excited about that, but you can't get them excited about child care, or child support. (Saunders & King 2000, p. 311)

Furthermore, she argued that welfare reform could help women enter the labor market, provided they receive adequate support for child care and healthcare. Her feminist stance favors commodifying family work, i.e., integrating women into paid labor and replacing unpaid domestic work with market-based services, over promoting traditional gender roles or simply making family policies more friendly. When answering the question about what kind of feminism should be advocating, she replied:

> I come out very radically. Among the three possibilities, namely: family-friendly policies to ensure gender equality in the marketplace and in the household; the total commodification of family work where we dismantle the female sphere; the unpaid family work; and the maintenance of separate spheres with more kudos to the female sphere and more rewards perhaps, I'm advocating the second one. And that's the way I've led my life. (ibid, p. 312)

As some feminist economists have emphasized, Bergmann's emphasis on equal access to the labor market allowed her to explore public policies aimed at ensuring equal opportunity for men and women in the labor market (Emami & Olson 2002; Folbre 1998; Olson 2007).

Bergmann's attitude in favor of the commodification of the unpaid labor within the domestic sphere was well expressed in her review of *The Purchase of Intimacy* by Viviana A. Zelizer (Bergmann 2005a; Zelizer 2005). Bergmann took on one of the most provocative and enduring questions about intimate life: where did love and money meet? The book dismantled the long-standing divide between the 'separate spheres' of the market and the home, showing that intimate relationships, such as marriages, partnerships, caregiving, and even sexual arrangements, were deeply entangled with economic exchanges. Zelizer's argument challenged both the economists who saw intimacy as nothing more than a marketplace transaction and the idealists who imagined love and money as existing in entirely different realms.

Bergmann opened her review by referencing a striking claim made by a pair of economists, reported by Forbes, who equated wives and prostitutes as similar types of 'business deals'. To economists steeped in rational-choice models, a wife 'traded' sex and domestic labor for room, board, and financial support, while a prostitute offered the same services on a shorter-term, cash-for-service basis. This view, Bergmann noted, represented a kind of economic imperialism, i.e., the tendency of economists to interpret all human activity as a form of market exchange. Against this, there existed the opposite ideal: that everything within the household, i.e., sex, care, budgeting, and labor, was performed for love alone, untouched by the cold logic of money. In this sentimental vision, the home and the marketplace were distinct moral universes. But Zelizer's central argument was that both pictures were incomplete. Care and money, she insisted, coexisted in complicated, negotiated, and socially meaningful ways. Marriages and families involved economic exchanges, but they were not reducible to mere transactions. The ways money circulated within intimate life, whether in shared bank accounts, allowances, gifts, or 'treats', carried moral and emotional significance that could not be understood through purely economic models.

Bergmann summarized Zelizer's main point: although housewives did not explicitly consider sex or domestic work as paid labor, they knew their access to economic resources depended on maintaining the relationship. If sex and housework were to cease, the household might collapse, and with it, financial support. In this sense, an exchange was implicit, though rarely acknowledged. Yet, to describe marriage as prostitution was equally misleading. Marriage differed in duration, emotional depth, legal recognition, and often, in the presence of children. Reducing it to a business contract missed the complexity of the emotional, legal, and moral dimensions that shaped it. Zelizer showed that societies actively concealed or blurred the economic dimensions of intimacy in order to protect relationships from stigma. Her historical examples of early twentieth-century working-class women were revealing. Many young women earned meager wages that barely supported their families, leaving them dependent on boyfriends for gifts, such as clothes, meals, and entertainment. Sexual relations were common, but women were careful to ensure that these gifts were not seen as direct payment for sex. Timing and form mattered too: a gift of a dress was acceptable, but a cash payment following an encounter would have marked them as prostitutes. This delicate choreography of exchange allowed couples to preserve moral distinctions between 'love' and 'commerce'. As Zelizer argued, the ways in which people named their relationships, and the ways they gave and received money within them served to define and defend moral boundaries.

Bergmann expanded on Zelizer's insight that certain forms of mixing intimacy and money were inevitable, while others were unacceptable. Doing business with family or friends could destroy relationships if conflicts arose. Conversely, bringing intimacy into professional contexts, such as sexual involvement between therapists, professors, or employers and their subordinates, could create exploitation and resentment. These examples underscored Zelizer's central theme: society constantly negotiated where and how intimacy and economic exchange might overlap.

Zelizer was sympathetic to feminist arguments that unpaid domestic labor devalued women's work. She acknowledged that paying wages for housework could, in principle, have enhanced women's economic standing. Yet, Bergmann challenged this idea, arguing that formal 'wages for housework' would have had little real effect. If the husband paid the wife, the funds would have circulated within the same household economy, changing nothing. If the government paid, taxpayers, including single people and dual-income couples, would have subsidized traditional gender arrangements, reinforcing rather than dismantling domestic inequality. The true path to equality, Bergmann insisted, lay not in compensating housewives but in ensuring equal pay in the workplace and reducing women's economic dependence on men.

A particularly rich portion of Zelizer's study, as Bergmann noted, lay in her examination of court cases of separations and divorces, which represent moments when relationships broke down and the implicit economic terms of intimacy are revealed. When engagements ended, for example, disputes often arose over who kept the diamond ring. Courts typically treated such gifts as 'conditional', returning them to the giver if the marriage never took place. In cases involving caregiving, the law's assumptions about family and gender became especially visible. A non-relative who provided long-term care to an elderly person was often compensated, while a family member performing the same labor was denied payment, on the grounds that familial love precluded economic exchange. Zelizer observed that such rulings lagged behind social change and often reflected anti-female bias, reinforcing the notion that women's domestic labor should remain outside the economy's reach. Bergmann highlighted the social harm of this 'separate spheres' ideology. It sustained the belief that buying services from outsiders, such as child care, elder care, or domestic help, was inferior to receiving them from family members, usually women. When such work was outsourced, it was often devalued and underpaid, justified by the assumption that any woman could provide care. This moral undervaluation translated directly into economic inequality. In Zelizer's account, dismantling this bias required acknowledging that care and intimacy could coexist with fair compensation without corrupting the emotional core of the relationship.

As Bergmann reflected, most unmarried women and many wives earned their own income, giving them more direct control over money.

This shift reduced the flow of material 'treats' and allowances from men to women, though inequalities persisted. The lingering expectation that women performed a disproportionate share of housework, even when employed full time, revealed how economic and emotional labor remained unequally distributed. Meanwhile, the old courtship rituals in which men 'treated' women to meals or gifts had faded, casualties of changing gender norms and the sexual revolution. As sexual relationships became more openly pursued outside marriage, the economic 'price' of intimacy, once mediated through gifts and promises of commitment, had arguably fallen. Bergmann even speculated that this change might have contributed to the declining marriage rate: if sex was more freely available, fewer men felt compelled to 'pay' for it through marriage.

Finally, Bergmann praised Zelizer's work for having compelled readers to confront the uncomfortable truth that intimacy was never free of economic meaning and for showing that boundaries between love and money are not fixed but socially constructed (Bergmann 2005b).

In Bergmann's last work on marriage theory, *The Decline of Marriage and What To Do About It* (see Chapter 4), Bergmann claimed again the necessity of a ticket to androgyny by directly attacking those who attributed the decline of marriage to the introduction of new technologies that facilitated women's work at home and pushed them into the labor force, by reducing the efficient specialization within marriages. As Bergmann wrote, displaying her usual sarcasm:

> On this account, the invention of the vacuum cleaner and the refrigerator and the development of takeout food have made an important contribution to the decline of marriage. (Bergmann 2008, p. 3)

Summing up, unlike many feminists, including some feminist economists, who promoted the adoption of a female style of behavior (grounded in cooperation, emotions, and feelings as distinct from a male style grounded in competition, rationality, and efficiency) in order to reshape society, Bergmann insisted on a more realistic solution: gender equality for men and women in our society as it is. This objective encompasses a two-part approach: equal job-market opportunities for both genders and an equal distribution of household responsibilities between spouses. As she wrote:

> Marriage can become a loving alliance between two economically and socially equal people. For this to happen, attitudes toward housework will have to be reformed. (Bergmann 2005b, p. 9)

Bergmann regarded gender discrimination in the labor force and in the family as two sides of the same coin, namely the 'sex-role caste system', that has penalized women and, consequently, society as a whole. Bergmann's feminist agenda involved implementing affirmative action measures to balance the division of labor in both work and family between men and women. She saw this as the only path to achieving gender equality. Bergmann's assertion that gender relations have wide-ranging economic impacts does not mean that feminist economics should be limited to 'economics for women'. Instead, it should be seen as an improved economic theory in general. Her theoretical work aimed to challenge the position of 'mainline' economics.

Bergmann's feminism advocated a combination of specific policies to reduce gender inequality and to promote an educational system that provides equal opportunities in the job market and equal sharing of responsibilities between spouses in household. This combination of short-term policy measures and long-term educational commitments would make the doctrine of the separate spheres finally obsolete (Bergmann 2005b).

6.3 The Institutionalist Approach to Poverty

In an interview (Saunders & King 2000), Bergmann recalled that her interest in social issues was inspired for the first time during her college years, when she read Myrdal's *American Dilemma* (1944) (see Chapter 2). It was at that time that she realized that racial discrimination, and shortly thereafter, gender discrimination, would be her main research interests. As it is well known, Galbraith and institutionalists rejected neoclassical economics and focused their research on the crucial role of social institutions in the economy. In doing so, institutionalism embedded politics, sociology, and history within economics in order to capture the complexity of economic phenomena. This was Bergmann's perspective too. Nonetheless, when she was asked whether she considered herself an institutionalist, she replied that, on one side, her approach to social issues was definitely 'institutional', but on the other side, she admitted that she never conducted first-hand studies of institutions. However, her work on poverty and her commitment to affirmative action in some ways made her close to institutionalism in a broader sense. As Pressman pointed out (2007), Bergmann, along with Myrdal, Galbraith, and Sen, was one of the American economists of the second half of the twentieth century who were influenced by institutionalism. In fact, besides racial and gender inequality in the job market due to discrimination, Bergmann was constantly focused on poverty as the main social problem that, on one side, represents the worst effect of badly managed institutions, and, on the other side, requires an active role for benign political institutions.

Inspired by a combination of Myrdal's (1944) and Galbraith's (1958, 1973) ideas, Bergmann struggled to propose economic policies aimed at reducing poverty, especially related to single parenthood, which usually affected women (Bergmann 1986, 1994, 1996, 1997, 2000b; Renwick & Bergmann 1993). In her review of Galbraith's book (1973), she emphasized the duality of the economy, as described by Galbraith, who portrayed the economy as an overdeveloped 'planning system' dominated by large corporations run by a powerful 'technostructure' and as an underdeveloped 'market system' made up of smaller firms lacking technological and political power. The former excels at shaping consumer demand, securing government contracts, and conducting research, while the latter struggles with inefficient sectors such as housing and healthcare. This dichotomy leads to poor distribution, which is bound to make the former richer and the latter poorer. As Galbraith explained, big corporations overproduce, contribute to inflation, maintain rigid prices during recessions, and perpetuate income inequality through hierarchical pay structures. Among the worst social consequences of corporate-driven consumption, women appeared as 'crypto-servants' to the lifestyles shaped by large firms (Bergmann 1974).

Hence, Bergmann's commitment to understanding the causes of poverty started very soon. In her archive, an essay, dated 1978, on poverty prepared for the Committee on Evaluation of Poverty Research of the National Academy of Sciences, revealed her opinion, according to which there is a direct relation between poverty and the lack of public health system. Thus, she advocated a sustained welfare plan against economists "*à la* Milton Friedman", who are hostile toward government intervention into social system. According to Bergmann, single parenthood, old age, high population growth, discrimination in the job market, poor education, any form of disability, involuntary unemployment, regional economic decline are the main phenomena of the origin and persistence of poverty. Bergmann concluded by applying her methodological pluralism to the analysis of poverty, which is not only an economic issue, but rather a broader problem that must be treated by a joint effort of economists, sociologists, anthropologists, and psychologists (Bergmann 1978).

As explained later, in Bergmann 1983, in the early 1980s, millions of women in the United States were in poverty or on the edge, mainly due to occupational segregation, which kept women concentrated in lower-paying jobs and largely excluded them from managerial, professional, and technical positions. Over decades, the median income of full-time working women had stagnated at roughly 60 percent of men's earnings, reflecting the structural barriers they faced in the labor market. Another significant challenge was the rising number of single-parent households, the vast majority of which were headed by women. In fact, single mothers faced extraordinary economic pressures: they had to balance full-time work with sole responsibility for child care, often with inadequate support from absent fathers. Finally, limited access to affordable child care exacerbated the difficulty of maintaining employment, particularly in well-paying positions.

Bergmann also noted that older women used to experience heightened economic vulnerability. By 1980, nearly 43 percent of widows and single women over 65 were living below the poverty line, with median incomes barely above $4000 per year. Social Security and other federal support systems represented their main sources of economic stability, and any erosion of social security benefits threatened to increase the already high rates of poverty among elderly women. The Reagan administration's policies actively worsened women's economic position. Budget cuts in human services, dismantling of federal programs supporting single parents, termination of training programs for women in non-traditional occupations, and attempts to weaken enforcement of pay equity and back-pay claims all undermined progress made in previous decades. These policies disproportionately affected women who were single, divorced, widowed, or otherwise without an employed male partner, making an already difficult situation more precarious.

According to Bergmann, such policy directions reflected an ideological emphasis on reinforcing traditional family structures, yet they neglected the reality that millions of American women lived and worked outside these norms, facing systemic barriers to economic security. She wrote:

> Perhaps it is no accident that this policy is in accord with the "family policy of the extreme right, with its belief in strengthening the subordination of women to men within the traditional family (...) The present administration's dismantling of federal programs is going to make [poor women's] already bad position more hopeless. (Bergmann 1983, p. 26)

As Bergmann hypothesized in *The Economic Emergence of Women* (1986), the U.S. government's poverty statistics understate the extent of poverty among single-parent families. For example, in 1995, the poverty rate for single-parent families whose head of household was employed full-time outside the home would have nearly doubled if the Basic Needs Budget (BNB) approach was substituted for the official U.S. government methodology (see Chapter 4).

The Basic Needs Budget (BNB) was presented by Renwick and Bergmann as an alternative and more comprehensive method for defining and measuring poverty in the United States (Renwick, 1991; Renwick & Bergmann 1993). It defined poverty not by a fixed, outdated food-cost multiplier, but by the real costs of meeting families' essential needs in contemporary society.[17]

In their paper, Bergmann and Renwick maintained that a new measure of poverty was much needed, as the U.S. official poverty line, established, in the 1960s, by Mollie Orshansky, was obsolete and failed to reflect changes in family structures, labor participation, and living expenses, particularly for single-parent households.[18] In fact, it disregarded crucial components of modern household budgets, such as child care, transportation, housing variation, taxes, and healthcare, and counted only pre-tax cash income, ignoring both noncash benefits and private supports (for example, employer health insurance or child care provided by relatives). Consequently, it underestimated both the true costs of living and the extent of poverty, particularly among working single parents who face high work-related expenses.

[17] Later, Renwick (1998) adopted the BNB to examine whether or not changes in the overall consumer price index, the tool most commonly used in the United States to measure inflation at the retail level, accurately reflect changes in the cost of living for low-income families.

[18] It was based on the cost of a minimal food plan multiplied by three, under the assumption that food expenditures represented one-third of household income. While simple, this formula has remained largely unchanged since its creation, aside from annual inflation adjustments through the Consumer Price Index (CPI).

Conversely, the BNB approach established a poverty line by calculating the minimum amount needed for a family to maintain a basic but decent standard of living. Instead of relying solely on food costs, the BNB includes a broad set of goods and services such as housing, food, clothing, transportation, child care, medical care, and taxes. Importantly, the model allows these components to vary by family characteristics and region, recognizing that not all families face identical needs or prices.[19] Another major innovation of the BNB framework was its comprehensive treatment of noncash benefits not only for governmental programs like food stamps, Medicaid, and public housing, but also for private or informal supports, such as employer-provided health insurance or child care assistance from relatives. These were valued not at their cost to the provider, but at their monetary value to the recipient. By integrating these resources into the calculation of a family's total available income, the BNB produced a cash-flow-based poverty assessment that was more accurate and equitable than the traditional model.

Applied to single-parent families in 1989, BNB revealed a striking difference between the poverty rates measured by official methods, mainly based on the status of unemployment, and by BNB. Under the BNB method, 47 percent of single parents in 1989 were classified as poor, compared to 39 percent according to the official measure. These results highlight that employment alone does not guarantee economic security for single parents. The additional expenses of child care and health-care, combined with limited access to noncash benefits compared to nonworking parents, place even full-time workers at risk of poverty. Hence, BNB restored realism to poverty measurement by showing that poverty is not merely a question of income level but of the relationship between available resources and the real cost of meeting essential needs.

As mentioned in Chapter 4, in 1997, Bergmann wrote an article by considering the effect of the 1996 welfare reform in the United States, driven by public frustration over supporting nonworking single mothers: millions of women were expected to move from welfare into paid employment; yet the jobs available to them generally paid low wages and offered little to no benefits such as health insurance or child care coverage. This

[19] For instance, the BNB distinguishes between households that require nonparental child care (for working parents) and those that do not. It also adjusts for regional differences in housing costs, acknowledging that the expenses faced by a family in New York City differ substantially from those in rural areas.

transition forced policymakers to confront the uncomfortable truth that full-time work, without adequate public support, could still leave families in poverty. According to Bergmann, while the welfare reform ended the federal guarantee of income support for single mothers, it also prompted widespread acknowledgment of the necessity for child care and health care assistance for parents entering the workforce.

Both Democrats and Republicans recognized that without help covering these essential services, many working mothers would be unable to adequately care for their children. This new political consensus led to the emergence of programs at both federal and state levels designed to subsidize child care and health insurance for families leaving welfare. Surprisingly, the public showed little resistance to funding such services, even though it had long opposed cash welfare. Furthermore, some state governments began expanding such support to all low-income working parents, not only those transitioning off welfare.

This shift represented a crucial political and moral turning point: it was now broadly acceptable for the government to pay for services, such as child care and health insurance, that directly benefit children, even if there remained hostility to providing cash assistance to parents. Such service-based assistance could form the foundation of a new and more effective 'war on poverty'. Bergmann argued that if government support were provided to help working parents cover the costs of child care, health care, and, in some cases, housing, the majority of single working mothers could achieve a decent standard of living.

The previous Aid to Families with Dependent Children (AFDC) merely prevented destitution among nonworking single mothers and their children. Its limited goals, combined with widespread public perceptions that it rewarded irresponsibility and discouraged work, made it politically toxic. The fact that most AFDC recipients were African American also deepened racial resentment and opposition to welfare spending. On the opposite side, the Kennedy-Johnson War on Poverty focused on job creation and training but ignored the needs of single mothers and the structural costs they faced, especially child care. These policies failed to reduce welfare rolls; indeed, as single parenthood rose, AFDC caseloads grew. Conservatives later mocked the campaign's futility, declaring, "We declared war on poverty, and poverty won". The political legacy of that failure was deep cynicism toward government anti-poverty efforts.

According to Bergmann, a truly effective anti-poverty strategy would require major public investment. Hence she proposed the Help for

Working Parents (HWP) program based on the BNB approach. As mentioned earlier, the HWP program included: universal health insurance, subsidized child care, income support, food stamps, and housing assistance. This was against what economists often argue that aid should come in cash so families can allocate resources according to their preferences. Bergmann rejected this logic for child poverty policy: certain goods, especially health care and child care, are essential social goods, whether or not families would purchase them voluntarily. Providing high-quality child care not only protects children while parents work but also promotes school readiness, cognitive development, and socialization. Moreover, delivering benefits in service form is politically more acceptable: taxpayers trust that funds for child care and health care will benefit children, whereas cash transfers provoke moral outrage and fears of dependency.

Bergmann concluded by asserting that the United States cannot return to a mythical past of universal stable marriages with female caregivers and male breadwinners. Instead, it is necessary to build a modern social contract that ensures all working parents can provide their children with decency and opportunity: the path to reducing child poverty lies not in punitive welfare cuts or marginal tax breaks, but in a national commitment to support working parents, which represents both a moral and practical social goal.

In her 2000b article, Bergmann discussed alternative approaches that better capture the meaning of being poor in a changing society, stressing that poverty definitions are ultimately moral and political judgments to be corrected, and this new mindset requires public opinion to play a major role.

For instance, according to Bergmann, the polling method, used by some European economists, allows the poverty line to evolve as living standards rise, rather than being frozen in obsolete assumptions. A simpler version of this is the 'half-the-median' method, which defines poverty as income below 50 percent of the nation's median family income. This method reflects a relative view of poverty: people are poor if they have far less than what is typical in their society, echoing Adam Smith's observation that necessities include not only life's essentials but also what society deems respectable to possess. However, these measures fail to capture variations in family circumstances and regional costs. Hence Bergmann re-proposed the BNB approach that incorporated major modern expenses that the 1960s formula ignored, by assuming that married mothers stayed home and that unmarried mothers received welfare, so families supposedly spent nothing on child care. Similarly, hospitals once provided free or low-cost care to the poor. Today, both assumptions are outdated: most mothers work, and unpaid medical care for the poor has largely disappeared.

Bergmann recalled that, in 1995, the National Academy of Sciences (NAS) recommended that the Census Bureau would adopt a method similar to the BNB, accounting for both modern expenses and noncash benefits.[20] Some economists, such as Sheldon Danziger and Gary Burtless, worried that adopting a measure showing higher poverty would create political controversy. Thus, they suggested using the new method only to track changes over time, not to replace the official rate. Bergmann strongly rejected this compromise, arguing that the point of measuring poverty is not only to track trends but to inform moral and political judgment. If a better method reveals that more Americans are struggling than previously thought, the proper response is to confront that reality and craft stronger policies, not to hide behind outdated numbers: recognizing the real, modern cost of living, through a fair and comprehensive poverty measure, is the first step toward meaningful action to lift families out of poverty and fulfill America's moral obligation to its children.

References

Barker, D., & Feiner, S. (2004). *Liberating economics: Feminist perspectives on families, work and globalization*. The University of Michigan Press.

Becchio, G. (2020). *A history of feminist and gender economics*. Routledge.

Becchio, G. (2024). *The doctrine of the separate spheres in political economy and economics: Gender equality and classical liberalism*. Palgrave Springer.

Becker, G. (1981). *A treatise on the family*. Harvard University Press.

Becker, G. (1985). Human capital, effort, and the sexual division of labor. *Journal of Labor Economics, 3*(1), S33–S58.

Bergmann, B. (1974). Economics and the public purpose by John Galbraith. *Journal of Economic Literature, 12*(3), 899–901.

Bergmann, B. (1978). *New direction of poverty research*. Committee on evaluation of poverty research of the National Academy of Sciences. Barbara Bergmann's papers, box 3. David M. Rubenstein Rare Book & Manuscript Library. Duke University.

[20] When the Bureau tested this approach for 1998 data, the official poverty rate rose from 12.7% to 15.7%, with a 24% increase for families with young children.

Bergmann, B. (1983). Women's plight: Bad and getting worse. *Challenge, 26*(1), 22–26.

Bergmann, B. (1984). The growlery: Feminism and economics. *Challenge, 27*(3), 46–49.

Bergmann, B. (1986). *The economic emergence of women*. Basic Books.

Bergmann, B. (1987a). Letter to the editor. *The Women's Review of Books, 5*(2), 4.

Bergmann, B. (1987b). The task of a feminist economics. In C. Farnham (Ed.), *The impact of feminist research in the academy* (pp. 131–147). Indiana University Press.

Bergmann, B. (1990). Feminism and economics. *Women's Studies Quarterly, 18*(3/4), 68–74. Reprinted from *Academe: Bulletin of the American Association of University Professors, 69*(5), 22–25. (Original work published 1983).

Bergmann, B. (1994). Curing child poverty in the United States. *American Economic Review, 84*(2), 76–80.

Bergmann, B. (1995). Becker's theory of the family: Preposterous conclusions. *Feminist Economics, 1*(1), 141–150.

Bergmann, B. (1996). Child care: the key to ending child poverty. In I. Garfinkel, J. Hochschild, & S. McLanahan (Eds.), *Social policies for children*, (pp. 112-135). The Brookings Institution.

Bergmann, B. (1997). Helping working parents is key to reducing child poverty in America. *NCCP News and Issues*, pp. 6–24. Reprinted and enlarged in Reducing Poverty Among American Children Through a "Help for Working Parents" Program. *Working Papers Series*. Foundation for Child Development, pp. 3–24.

Bergmann, B. (1998a). Two cheers for CSWEP? *The Journal of Economic Perspectives, 12*(4), 185–189.

Bergmann, B. (1998b). The only ticket to equality: Total androgyny, male style. *Journal of Contemporary Legal Issues, 9*, 75–86.

Bergmann, B. (1999). Women at NBER: A correction. *Journal of Economic Perspectives, 13*(3), 240.

Bergmann, B. (2000a). Subsidizing child care by mothers at home. *Feminist Economics, 6*(1), 77–88.

Bergmann, B. (2000b). Deciding who's poor. *Dollars and Sense, 228*, 36–45.

Bergmann, B. (2005a). On wives and prostitution. *Women's Review of Books, 23*(6), 32–33.

Bergmann, B. (2005b). *The economic emergence of women* (2nd ed.). Palgrave Macmillan.

Bergmann, B. (2008). *The economic consequences of the decline of marriage* (Working Paper No. 0818). Department of Economics. Johannes Kepler University of Linz.

Bergmann, B., & Hartmann, H. (1995). A welfare reform based on help for working parents. *Feminist Economics, 1*(2), 85–89.

Bielby, W., & Barron, J. (1984). A woman's place is with other women: Sex segregation within organizations. In B. Reskin (Ed.), *Sex segregation in the workplace* (pp. 27–55). National Academy Press.

Birdsall, N., & Sabot, R. (Eds.). (1991). *Unfair advantage: Labor market discrimination in developing countries*. World Bank.

Blau, D., & Hagy, A. (1998). The demand for quality in child care. *Journal of Political Economy, 106*(1), 104–146.

Emami, Z., & Olson, P. (2002). Barbara Berman Bergmann. In *Engendering economics: Conversations with women economists in the United States* (pp. 53–72). Routledge.

England, P. (1982). The failure of human capital theory to explain occupational sex segregation. *Journal of Human Resources, 17*(3), 358–370.

Fine, B. (2000). Economics imperialism and intellectual progress: The present as history of economic thought. *History of Economics Review, 32*(2), 10–35.

Folbre, N. (1998). Barbara, the market, and the state. *Feminist Economics, 4*(3), 159–168.

Fricker, M., & Hornsby, J. (Eds.). (2000). *The Cambridge companion to feminism in philosophy*. Cambridge University Press.

Galbraith, J. (1958). *The affluent society*. Houghton Mifflin Harcourt.

Galbraith, J. (1973). *Economics and the public purpose*. Houghton Mifflin.

Gilligan, C. (1982). *In a different voice: Psychological theory and women's development*. Harvard University.

Hartmann, H., & Bergmann, B. (1995). Get real! Look to the future, not the past. *Feminist Economics, 1*(2), 109–119.

Haslanger, S. (2000). Gender and race: [What] are they? [What] do we want them to be? *Noûs, 34*(1), 31–55.

Himmelweit, S., Bergmann, B., Green, K., Abelda, R., & the Women's Committee of One Hundred & Charlotte Koren. (2004). Dialogue lone mother: What is to be done? *Feminist Economics, 10*(2), 237–264.

Lamanna, M. A., Riedmann, A., & Stewart, S. (2014). *Marriages, families, and relationships: Making choices in a diverse society* (12th ed.). Cengage Learning.

MacKinnon, C. (1989). *Toward a feminist theory of the state*. Harvard University Press.

Myrdal, G. (1944). *An American dilemma: The Negro problem and modern democracy*. Harper and Brothers.

Noddings, N. (1986). *Caring: A feminine approach to ethics and moral education*. University of California Press.

Olson, P. (2007). On the contributions of Barbara Bergmann to economics. *Review of Political Economy, 19*(4), 475–496.

Pateman, C. (1988). *The sexual contract*. Stanford University Press.

Paterson, J., & Lewis, M. (Eds.). (1999). *The Elgar companion to feminist economics*. Edward Elgar.

Pressman, S. (2007). *Fifty major economists*. Routledge.

Rawls, J. (1971). *A theory of justice*. Harvard University Press.

Renwick, T. (1991). *Poverty among single parent families*. (Ph.D. dissertation). The American University.

Renwick, T. (1998). Basic needs budgets revisited: Does the U.S. consumer price index overestimate the changes in the cost of living for low-income families? *Feminist Economics, 4*(3), 129–142.

Renwick, T., & Bergmann, B. (1993). A budget-based definition of poverty with an application to single-parent families. *Journal of Human Resources, 28*(1), 10–24.

Rhode, D. (1997). *Speaking of sex: The denial of gender inequality*. Harvard University Press.

Saunders, L., & King, M. (2000). An interview with Barbara Bergmann: Leading feminist economics. *Review of Political Economy, 12*(3), 305–316.

Schultz, T. (Ed.). (1974). *Economics of the family, marriage, children, and human capital*. The University of Chicago Press.

Scott, J. W. (1988). *Gender and the politics of history*. Columbia University Press.

Shackelford, J. (1999). International association for feminist economics (IAFFE). In J. Peterson & M. Lewis (Eds.), *The Elgar companion to feminist economics* (pp. 486–489). Edward Elgar.

Strober, E. (1998). Interview with Barbara Bergmann. *Feminist Economics, 4*(3), 5–6.

Tomaskovic-Devey, D. (1993). *Gender and racial inequality at work: The sources and consequences of job segregation*. ILR Press.

Young, I. (1990). *Justice and the politics of difference*. Princeton University Press.

Zelizer, V. (2005). *The purchase of intimacy*. Princeton University Press.

CHAPTER 7

Changing Peoples' Life

Barbara Bergmann considered her work in economics at the service of an actual commitment to changing people's lives. Whether discussing affirmative action, child care, welfare reforms, or social security, she consistently challenged the assumption that markets alone can provide fairness or efficiency in areas fundamental to human well-being. For her, issues like caregiving, retirement security, and family support were moral and social imperatives. Her approach reflected her broader intellectual philosophy: economic policy must be understandable, equitable, and grounded in social responsibility. She consistently resisted efforts to reduce social welfare debates to technical or ideological extremes, advocating instead for clarity and moral purpose.

Across her projects, Bergmann advanced a coherent and compassionate vision of public policy: one that recognizes care, equity, and social stability as pillars of a healthy society that requires robust public funding and regulation, aiming to support both working parents and professional caregivers. She constantly emphasized the collective responsibility of society to support people in need, by arguing that effective economic policy requires substantial public investment and regulation. She applied the same logic to child care as well as to aging and retirement, defending the principle of intergenerational solidarity.

She believed that social policy should protect the vulnerable, empower women, and strengthen community bonds. Through her research,

G. Becchio, *Barbara Bergmann*, Great Thinkers in Economics,
https://doi.org/10.1007/978-3-032-18696-6_7

teaching, and writing, whether in technical reports or illustrated books, she insisted that economics is not just about numbers but about people, justice, and the shared responsibilities of a democratic society. Hence, Bergmann's work tied her to a larger feminist and egalitarian economic vision that is able to bridge rigorous economic analysis with accessible and clear communication.

7.1 Affirmative Action for Social Reforms

Bergmann's writings on affirmative action collectively form a rigorous, unapologetic defense of policies designed to correct systemic racial and gender inequities in employment and education. Across her works (Bergmann 1995, 1996a, 1996b, 1996c 1997a, 1997b), she investigated not only how such policies are perceived and resisted but also why they remain necessary despite decades of formal legal equality. Her approach combined empirical research, moral reasoning, and pragmatic policy analysis, all guided by the conviction that fairness in labor markets cannot emerge from good intentions alone. Bergmann challenged the myths surrounding affirmative action, exposed the inadequacy of proposed alternatives, and insisted on the moral legitimacy and practical necessity of using quotas to dismantle entrenched exclusion.

Bergmann's essay (1995) offered an empirical foundation for her defense. Conducted in the 1990s, at a time when affirmative action faced increasing political hostility, her study sought to test whether public opposition was as widespread as commentators claimed. She surveyed 173 mostly white college students, asking them to respond to two hypothetical scenarios: one involving a company that had never hired Black workers for well-paying blue-collar jobs, and another involving a company that had never hired women for those same positions. Both cases featured seemingly neutral hiring practices that, in practice, perpetuated exclusion through subjective judgments and informal bias. By structuring the scenarios this way, Bergmann forced respondents to confront a realistic instance of systemic discrimination, one that could not be justified by differences in skill, education, or interest.

The results of her survey challenged the prevailing narrative of universal opposition to affirmative action. About half of the respondents supported at least one form of active hiring intervention, such as increased recruitment or pressure to hire from underrepresented groups. A strong majority rejected the idea that women or Black workers were excluded because they lacked ability or motivation, revealing widespread recognition that discrimination, not merit, explains persistent exclusion. Yet, support was not uniform. Respondents favored moderate, non-coercive measures, especially active recruitment, while showing less enthusiasm for strong remedies like numerical hiring goals or timetables. Still, nearly 40 percent endorsed at least one of these stronger measures, demonstrating a willingness among many to go beyond symbolic fairness. Only a small minority, around 11 to 16 percent, rejected all forms of action beyond mere exhortations to be fair.

Perhaps the most striking finding concerned differences in how respondents viewed racial versus gender exclusion. Both men and women tended to recognize racial exclusion as unjustified, but opinions diverged when the scenario involved women being barred from traditionally male occupations. Many male respondents, and even some women, did not regard this as a serious problem. The result highlights how gender bias in blue-collar fields, such as construction or machinery work, remained normalized even among young, educated individuals who otherwise condemned racial discrimination. Bergmann interpreted this as evidence of a cultural double standard: while overt racism is widely stigmatized, gendered assumptions about capability and job fit continue to shape people's judgments about fairness.

From these results, Bergmann concluded that public attitudes toward affirmative action are far more ambivalent and nuanced than political discourse suggests. Rather than being divided into clear camps of supporters and opponents, most people fall somewhere in between, acknowledging the need for fairness and even modest corrective measures, while hesitating to embrace policies perceived as coercive or quota-like. This ambivalence, she argued, reflects the tension between two competing ideals: the belief in individual merit and the recognition of structural inequality. Her study thus exposed not a wholesale rejection of affirmative action, but a lack of clarity about what justice demands in practice.

In her book *In Defense of Affirmative Action* (Bergmann 1996a), Bergmann shifted from empirical investigation to normative argument, addressing the growing political campaign to dismantle affirmative action programs in the name of 'color-blindness'. As courts and legislators began restricting race-conscious policies, some former supporters sought compromise by proposing class-based or disadvantage-based alternatives. They argued that society should just help the disadvantaged rather than explicitly addressing race or gender. Such programs, in theory, would assist the poor regardless of identity and might thus benefit many African Americans and women indirectly, while also including poor white men, making them more politically palatable.

Bergmann recognized that these class-based proposals have moral and social value but insisted they are insufficient as substitutes for affirmative action, being poverty and race correlated but not interchangeable. While a disproportionate number of African Americans were economically disadvantaged, racial discrimination cuts across class lines, affecting middle-class and even affluent Black individuals who encountered barriers unrelated to income. Similarly, gender bias affected women of all economic backgrounds. By focusing exclusively on economic disadvantage, society risks addressing symptoms of inequality while ignoring its structural causes.

She further argued that such 'help-the-poor' programs fail to challenge the social and institutional mechanisms that perpetuate exclusion. A policy that happens to aid some Black workers because they are poor does not acknowledge, much less rectify, the fact that race itself has been used as a basis for exclusion. Substituting class for race allows opponents of affirmative action to maintain a veneer of moral concern while sidestepping uncomfortable truths about racism and sexism. In practice, Bergmann observed, such approaches would often replicate the same patterns of exclusion but under the politically neutral banner of 'helping the disadvantaged'. A white applicant might lose a job to a Black applicant, but the rationale would shift from racial equity to class assistance, concealing the racial dimension of the issue and depoliticizing systemic injustice.

Bergmann concluded that while society should certainly expand efforts to assist the poor, those initiatives cannot replace the explicit, race-conscious, and gender-conscious components of affirmative action. She also dismissed another common proposal advanced by opponents: simply enforcing existing anti-discrimination laws. Such enforcement, she noted, depends on individuals filing complaints and proving intentional bias, a process that is burdensome, reactive, and inadequate for addressing the subtle, cumulative forms of exclusion that shape modern employment. Affirmative action, by contrast, is proactive. It compels institutions to examine their outcomes, not merely their intentions, and to take deliberate steps toward inclusion. Without such proactive measures, Bergmann warned, the labor market will revert to its 'natural' tendency toward homogeneity and exclusion.

A selection of excerpts from Bergmann's book appeared in 1997b in the AAUP newsletter, mainly aimed at responding to African Americans, who oppose affirmative action out of fear that the program may undermine respect for them as privileged. Bergmann pointed out that this kind of concern about fairness is usually applied only to women and Blacks, while in many institutions, such as prestigious colleges, there are already quotas based on geographical provenance of candidates as well as on their skills in performing sports.[1]

On the occasion of Bergmann's book publication, a significant debate arose among supporters and detractors of affirmative action. In the *New York Times*, an article by Paul Berman, appeared on April 14, 1996, compared Bergmann's book with Terry Eastland's *Ending Affirmative Action* (1996), and Clint Bolick's *The Affirmative Action Fraud* (1996). The author pointed out their three sharply contrasting perspectives on the merits and problems of affirmative action in the United States. Bergmann, defined as "a liberal economist", argued that affirmative action is essential and should be expanded to address structural inequalities: she viewed affirmative action as economically advantageous, socially necessary, and a tool to improve opportunities for historically marginalized groups, particularly African Americans and women. Eastland and Bolick, by contrast, offer a conservative critique. They saw affirmative action as

[1] Bergmann used to be against quotas for athletes in American Colleges. According to her, the belief that college sports brought millions to universities proved false. Athletics might deliver entertainment, excitement, and attention, but these came at the cost of money, academic values, and institutional integrity. Universities seemed unable to reform athletics because doing so supposedly meant giving up large sums of money. That money was largely an illusion, because much of the spending on athletics was hidden in academic budgets. Because only a few teams could be major winners, fierce competition pushed institutions toward rule-breaking, special admissions, academic short-cuts, and the creation of fake courses for athletes. When revenue exceeded expectations, spending simply expanded; when deficits emerged, universities filled the gap by diverting funds from other sources such as dining services or summer programs. Scholarships were sometimes diverted from academically talented students to athletes focused primarily on sports. Although athletic programs were often portrayed as opportunities for disadvantaged minority students, they could instead diminish educational outcomes by shifting students' focus from academics to unlikely professional sports careers. A clear example emerged from the University of Maryland's 1986 athletic budget. Although Maryland expected \$6.5 million in revenue during a successful sports year, it planned to spend the entire amount. In fact, after postseason appearances boosted revenues to over \$8 million, expenses still exceeded income. Even during winning seasons, Maryland lost money, an outcome far from unique (Bergmann 1991).

coercive, economically harmful, and morally problematic: it undermines meritocracy, demoralizes its intended beneficiaries, and perpetuates racial consciousness at the expense of individual liberty. They argued that affirmative action betrays America's civil rights vision, which they interpret as a long-standing tradition of color-blind natural rights dating back to the Founding Fathers. In their view, the policy subverts universal competition and undermines the principles of fairness and liberty enshrined in the U.S. Constitution.

Nonetheless, all three authors recognized that African Americans are at the center of the affirmative action debate, reflecting the policy's original purpose of addressing the legacy of slavery and systemic discrimination. Bergmann situated affirmative action historically as an evolution from civil rights initiatives: from Johnson's limited 1965 justification addressing Blacks' structural disadvantages, to a broader inclusion of women and other marginalized groups, and eventually to the modern 'diversity' argument, which seeks proportional representation of various identities in institutions. Furthermore, Bergmann distinguished herself in her practical approach. She acknowledged potential overreach in some applications of affirmative action, noting, for example, exaggerated claims for universal beneficiaries, but insisted the policy remains necessary to address ongoing inequalities. She highlighted the persistence of job segregation by race and sex, noting that litigation alone is insufficient to correct systemic biases due to its limited reach and long timelines. Affirmative action, she argued, mitigates discrimination and expands opportunities for under-represented groups in education and employment while avoiding the stigmatization that might arise if minorities were entirely absent from high-status positions.

Eastland and Bolick, meanwhile, employed historical and philosophical arguments to frame affirmative action as a betrayal of long-standing American ideals. They invoked color-blind antiracism as the original civil rights vision and depicted affirmative action as a novel, coercive intrusion into a society that should have functioned on meritocratic principles. Bolick, in particular, framed the issue dramatically, presenting it as a moral and civic crisis that threatened liberty itself. These appeals, though rhetorically forceful, often hinged on selective interpretations of history, portraying America's past as a near-continuous realization of color-blind justice.

From an economic point of view, Bergmann challenged the claim that affirmative action harmed business or productivity. She observed that major corporations favor such policies, likely because they broadened the talent pool and created a more integrated, competitive workforce. Eastland and Bolick, by contrast, emphasized anecdotal cases of perceived unfairness to individuals displaced by affirmative action, framing the policy as both morally and economically misguided. Bergmann acknowledged that affirmative action had been imperfect and sometimes misapplied, but she stressed its proven value in expanding middle-class opportunities for Blacks and women. While not solving poverty for the very poor, affirmative action had been critical in integrating historically excluded groups into the workforce and advancing social mobility. The need for ongoing policy adjustment was clear, but Bergmann argued that the program remained defensible and necessary as a temporary, targeted measure.

The reviewer summarized that the debate on affirmative action reflected a clash between two visions of justice and equality in America. Bergmann advocated a pragmatic, historically grounded defense of affirmative action as a corrective for structural discrimination, while Eastland and Bolick argued from a principled liberty-focused perspective that saw any race-conscious policy as a betrayal of universal rights. The tension between these perspectives continued to shape the discourse on race, opportunity, and fairness in contemporary American society.

In a paper, published by Bergmann in 1997, she extended her defense of affirmative action into the most controversial terrain of all: the role of quotas within affirmative action. Rather than denying the charge, Bergmann provocatively embraced it. She argued that affirmative action did, and must, involve numerical goals that some might call quotas, because counting was the only way to measure and correct persistent exclusion. The widespread insistence that affirmative action had nothing to do with quotas, she contended, was politically expedient but intellectually dishonest. Without counting, institutions had no mechanism to know whether progress was being made. She wrote:

> If you want to desegregate, it is indispensable to count by race and sex, or you end up hiring thirty white men in a row. (Bergmann 1997a, p. 228)

Bergmann situated her argument within the political debates of her time, particularly President George W. Bush's criticism of the Civil Rights Restoration Act. Bush warned that allowing courts to consider statistical evidence of racial or gender disparities would amount to 'forcing quotas'. Many liberals responded defensively, insisting that affirmative action merely set 'goals and timetables'. Bergmann rejected this rhetorical evasion, arguing that progress depends on transparency and accountability. Calling a quota a 'goal' did not change its function. What mattered was not the label but the purpose: to ensure that patterns of exclusion are visible and corrected.

She supported her argument by invoking psychological research, particularly Faye Crosby's studies on how people perceived discrimination. When individuals evaluate one case at a time, a man and a woman doing similar work, they rarely detect unfairness. But when shown an overall pattern, men consistently earning more or being hired more frequently, biases become undeniable. Counting, in this sense, is not an exercise in bureaucracy but a moral and cognitive necessity. It reveals systemic inequities that individual cases conceal. Quotas, therefore, are not about preferring one group over another but about identifying and rectifying patterns that would otherwise go unnoticed.

Bergmann's defense of quotas was both pragmatic and moral. She pointed out that many workplaces remained racially and sexually segregated not because of overt hostility but because of self-reinforcing networks. Hiring often occurred through informal referrals, and workers tended to recommend others like themselves. A white workforce, left to its own devices, reproduced whiteness through everyday familiarity and convenience. Affirmative action interrupts this cycle. By setting numerical targets, it forces managers to look beyond their habitual networks and actively include those historically excluded.

Bergmann recounted everyday examples, such as a luncheon where all the servers are white; a hotel where management insists 'those people don't want to work'; a supermarket chain fined for sex discrimination, to illustrate how systemic bias persists beneath the surface of normalcy. In each case, she argued, quotas are not punitive but corrective: they prevent complacency and compel institutions to examine whether their practices truly aligned with their stated values of equality.

While Bergmann acknowledged that quotas can provoke resentment or fears of reverse discrimination, she insisted these reactions were based on misunderstanding. The claim that quotas stigmatized beneficiaries, by implying they were hired only to fill numerical targets, mirrored old sexist and racist arguments that women and minorities were inherently less capable. The stigma, she argued, did not arise from the policy but from prejudiced attitudes the policy sought to change. Moreover, she warned against letting such fears paralyze reform: avoiding quotas to protect the feelings of potential beneficiaries only preserved the *status quo* of exclusion.

She did, however, recognize limits. Quotas should be applied judiciously, focused on groups with well-documented histories of discrimination, such as women, racial minorities, people with disabilities, and possibly gay individuals. Expanding them indiscriminately to every conceivable category would have diluted their effectiveness and provoked legitimate concerns about fragmentation. Yet this risk, she maintained, was minor compared to the moral and social cost of abandoning active intervention altogether.

Bergmann also criticized the way opponents of affirmative action framed public debate. They often reduced the issue to a single, misleading scenario: a white man and a Black man apply for the same job, and the Black man is hired despite the white man being 'better qualified'. This framing obscures the structural context, as it assumes that past exclusion never occurred and that judgments of merit are objective and unbiased. Bergmann proposed an alternative framing: imagine a company that had never hired a Black worker for a particular job. What should it have done to change that pattern? When presented this way, the fairness of affirmative action becomes far clearer. Yet, this version of the story, she lamented, rarely appears in public discourse, leaving the impression that affirmative action imposes unfair preferences rather than redresses systemic exclusion.

Across these writings, Bergmann developed a coherent vision of justice grounded in both empirical reality and moral clarity. She rejected the illusion that neutrality or 'color-blindness' could produce equality in a society still shaped by centuries of exclusion. Her research shows that even well-intentioned individuals harbor blind spots and contradictions, and that only structured, measurable interventions can counteract these biases. The belief that fairness will emerge naturally once laws are in place, she argued, ignores the evidence of persistent disparity. For Bergmann, affirmative action, complete with its goals, timetables, and quotas, was not a deviation from fairness but its practical expression.

Her work also underscored an enduring psychological and political truth: people tend to support equality in the abstract but resist it when it demands tangible changes in distribution, privilege, or comfort. Many of her survey respondents endorsed 'fairness' yet balked at specific corrective measures; politicians claimed to oppose discrimination while dismantling the only policies proven to reduce it. Bergmann's response to such contradictions was straightforward: justice requires not only good will but also accountability. Counting, measuring, and setting goals are the means by which society can ensure that opportunity is not merely promised but delivered.

Taken together, Bergmann's writings formed a powerful argument for intellectual honesty and moral courage in debates about affirmative action. She refused to sanitize her claims to make them more palatable, acknowledging that equality was neither costless nor easily achieved. Her insistence that quotas were necessary challenged the evasions of policy-makers and the discomfort of liberals who wished to appear progressive without confronting structural privilege. In her view, fairness cannot survive on rhetoric alone; it should be institutionalized through mechanisms that ensure change actually occurs.

Ultimately, Bergmann's legacy lies in her ability to connect empirical observation, policy analysis, and moral philosophy into a single coherent defense of affirmative action. She showed that opposition to these programs was often less about principles of fairness than about fear of redistribution and discomfort with the exposure of privilege. By revealing the persistence of bias, the inadequacy of class-based remedies, and the indispensability of quotas, Bergmann built a compelling case for affirmative action as both a moral obligation and a practical necessity. Her message remains strikingly relevant: equality does not happen by accident, it must be measured, enforced, and continually defended against complacency and denial.

The most important social problem to be fixed by affirmative action in Bergmann's last years work was subsidizing child care (Bergmann 1997c, 2000a, 2001; Bergmann & Helburn 2002).

In 1997, Bergmann compared child poverty rates between France and the United States: 6% in France versus 22% in the United States (Bergmann 1997c). These disparities largely resulted from differences in the scope, generosity, and structure of family support programs in the two countries. French programs aimed to ensure children's well-being and social integration across all income levels, whereas U.S. programs primarily targeted the prevention of destitution among jobless families, particularly single mothers.

French policies historically emerged from pronatalist goals, aiming to increase the country's birth rate. While these efforts did not significantly boost fertility, public support persists due to a widely shared view of children as central to the nation's future. French programs were therefore broadly inclusive, providing support to families at all income levels, with extra benefits for low-income and single-parent households. Anti-immigrant sentiment has not substantially diminished support for these child-focused policies. In contrast, U.S. policy has been narrowly focused on preventing extreme deprivation among poor or jobless mothers and their children. Assistance was limited primarily to families without substantial earnings, discouraging employment by reducing benefits if recipients work. Public attitudes toward welfare recipients were often negative, portraying them as undeserving, idle, or morally lax, which had fueled political support for benefit reductions. Furthermore, the 1996 U.S. welfare reform cut benefits and decentralized administration but left the basic structure largely intact, potentially increasing child poverty by over a million children.

Regarding child care, France provided extensive child care and early education services, including nearly universal public nursery schools (ages 3–6), partially subsidized nurseries for younger children, compensated maternity leave, and government subsidies for child care expenses. These programs supported parental employment while promoting child development. The U.S. equivalents focused mainly on child development, offering limited hours, primarily for children in poverty, and providing minimal help for working parents. Welfare programs in the United States often acted as *de facto* child care support by allowing mothers to remain home, but at low living standards and without incentives for employment. Subsidized care for working parents exists but is limited and often targeted to reduce welfare dependency rather than to broadly support low-income families.

Regarding income supplements, French family benefits included universal family allowances, cash payments to pregnant women, and income-tested housing or support for children under three. U.S. income support primarily benefited "welfare" recipients, such as mothers with little or no income, through AFDC and Food Stamps. Benefits were often insufficient to lift families above the poverty line, declined as recipients worked, and were only partially supplemented by the Earned Income Tax Credit. Couples or working low-income families received minimal support, limiting incentives for employment.

Finally, a low-income, single mother in the United States faced stark choices: remain on welfare with minimal income but guaranteed health coverage, or work at low wages while losing benefits and paying for child care, often leaving her barely better off. The incentives to move from welfare to work were weak, and the 1996 welfare reforms failed to substantially improve this situation. In France, a single mother of a child under three could remain on welfare-like support, or take a minimum-wage job while receiving substantial benefits, including affordable child care and uninterrupted health coverage. Employment improved her standard of living and quality of life, providing a clear incentive to work. Consequently, fewer French single mothers depended on welfare, and those who work are better supported. Despite generous benefits, the overall cost to the French government was manageable due to lower reliance on welfare and broader distribution of support.

In 1998, Bergmann received a fellowship granted by the Rockefeller Foundation to work with Suzanne Helburn, on the failure of U.S. social policy to adequately serve ordinary citizens, especially those most economically vulnerable, and the urgent need for government-led reforms that were both fair and comprehensible to the public.[2] The manuscript was later published as a book titled *America's Child Care Problem: The Way Out* (Bergmann & Helburn 2002).[3]

Bergmann and Helburn analyzed the deep inefficiencies, inequities, and inadequacies of the American child care system. They described a fragmented, underfunded industry that provided care of generally poor to mediocre quality, while imposing high costs on parents, particularly single mothers. Many low-income families spent up to a quarter of their income on child care, yet the care available often failed to meet even basic developmental and safety standards. This mismatch between cost and quality reflected what Bergmann saw as a market failure rooted in the absence of a coherent national policy.

Bergmann and Helburn's project sought to design a new child care policy framework that could deliver affordable, high-quality care while addressing the political challenges of implementation. Their approach recognized child care not as a private family matter but as a public good essential to economic productivity, gender equality, and child development. They argued that child care should be treated with the same

[2] Bergmann was a scholar in Residence at Bellagio Study and Conference Center at the Villa Serbelloni, Lake Como, Italy. Barbara Bergmann's papers, box 6. David M. Rubenstein Rare Book & Manuscript Library, Duke University.

[3] The book was initially planned to be published as *What Should We Do About Child Care?* by St. Martin's Press in 2001, as specified in Bergmann's interview (Saunders & King, 2000).

seriousness as public education, as something society must collectively fund and regulate rather than leaving it to the vagaries of the market.

To this end, their proposed a major federal subsidy program far more ambitious than the incremental measures proposed by President Clinton in the 1990s. The plan envisioned substantial public investment to make child care universally affordable and to raise professional standards within the industry. In addition to subsidies, Bergmann and Helburn emphasized the need for stronger government oversight and quality assurance mechanisms, such as higher training standards for caregivers, improved wages, and national accreditation systems. Their goal was not only to make child care more accessible but also to elevate its quality and status, ensuring that caregivers, most of whom are women, receive fair compensation for their labor.

At the heart of this project was a conviction that the United States had long neglected the infrastructure of care, leaving women to shoulder the burden in ways that perpetuate gender inequality and economic instability. Affordable, reliable child care, Bergmann insisted, was not merely a family issue; it was an economic necessity that enables women to work, supports children's development, and strengthens the labor force. Without systemic reform, she argued, both children and working parents, especially low-income mothers, remained trapped in a cycle of stress, limited opportunity, and inadequate support.

Between her 1998 manuscript and the publication of its revised and enlarged version in the co-authored book in 2002, Bergmann published a further defense of subsidizing child care in two more writings (Bergmann 2000a, 2001).

In her 2000 article, Bergmann analyzed two primary approaches for government-subsidized child care: direct provision of care in public or private facilities funded by public money, or by vouchers given to parents to purchase care from qualified providers.[4] She pointed out that child

[4] These subsidies are often scaled according to family income, with parents covering any additional costs. A table illustrates the impact of a $9000-per-child child care subsidy on five hypothetical families: Family A: Two-earner couple; Family B: One-earner couple with the same income as A; Family C: One-earner low-income family; Family D: Low-income single-parent family; Family E: Low-income two-earner couple. Families without a full-time adult at home (A, D, E) receive subsidies, while families B and C, where a parent provides care at home, receive none. If subsidies were extended to B and C, inequities would arise because B is already financially better off than A in terms of cash resources, household services, and leisure time. In essence, the value of at-home parental

care policy is closely tied to gender roles: since women's workforce participation has advanced gender equality, through career continuity, independence, and better job opportunities, a policy favoring at-home maternal care could risk undermining these gains.

Subsidies or long paid parental leave programs may exert social pressure on mothers to stay home, reinforcing traditional gender norms and limiting women's career prospects. International examples, such as Sweden, show that extended parental leave taken almost exclusively by mothers can reinforce occupational gender segregation, with women clustered in caregiving roles and underrepresented in prestigious professions. Hence, attitudes toward gender equality heavily influence opinions on subsidies: those favoring male-dominated social structures support at-home maternal care, while advocates for gender parity prioritize non-parental child care. Thus, the policy choice between maternal home care subsidies and non-parental child care subsidies is not only an economic question but also a social one, with significant consequences for women's status in the labor market.

Beyond equity and gender, quality and efficiency are key considerations. Non-parental child care is generally considered superior after age three, and for infants and toddlers, high-quality care can be delivered efficiently at ratios of 3–4 children per adult. Paying a parent full time for one or two children is inefficient, especially compared to providing care through regulated centers. Long-term paid parental leave, while temporarily maintaining income for at-home parents, poses problems similar to unconditional subsidies. High pay encourages extended leave, which is costly and regressive, disproportionately benefiting higher-income families. Additionally, long leave further pressures mothers to stay home, reducing labor market participation and reinforcing gender inequality. Short leaves (1–2 months) are less problematic, maintaining income continuity without the adverse effects of long-term absence.

Administrative challenges also arise if cash payments are made to at-home parents while vouchers are provided for paid care. Verifying that

work, though unreimbursed in cash, contributes to family well-being and should not automatically be subsidized like paid care. Family C may appear deserving of subsidies due to low income, but providing them would create inequities with similarly low-income families D and E, turning child care subsidies into general income supplements. Thus, subsidies for at-home parental care blurred the distinction between child care support and income supplementation.

parents are not working while receiving subsidies can be difficult, and unrestricted cash payments may fail to improve the quality of child care, unlike targeted vouchers for licensed care.

Finally, according to Bergmann, unrestricted cash payments ('unearmarked benefits') for child care aim to give parents freedom, but they are inefficient in improving care quality. Families may spend funds on non-child care needs, particularly low-income families with many competing demands. In contrast, vouchers tied to licensed care ensure that resources directly enhance child care quality, similar to targeted health insurance subsidies.

In conclusion, Bergmann's proposal for an affordable child care policy should prioritize equity, quality, efficiency, and gender equality, focusing on non-parental care while providing separate, targeted income support where needed.

The same arguments were adopted by Bergmann in her following article. She wrote:

> [I] believe that only a large, active, and expensive federal program, providing both financing and a national framework for quality improvement, will serve the nation's purpose adequately. (Bergmann 2001, p. 47)

Furthermore, Bergmann later insisted that government programs that provide or subsidize nonparental child care can play a crucial role in advancing gender equality. By reducing the burden of unpaid care-giving work that disproportionately falls on women, such programs allow mothers to participate more fully in the workforce and pursue long-term career advancement on a more equal footing with men. In fact, accessible child care helps normalize dual-earner households and challenges traditional gender norms that tie women's identity and social role to domestic labor. However, policies that emphasize lengthy paid parental leaves of six months for both parents, or that encourage part-time employment, risk undermining these gains. In practice, women are more likely than men to take advantage of extended leave or reduced working hours, leading to an unequal division of domestic responsibilities. This could reinforce the traditional model in which women shoulder the majority of child care, cleaning, cooking, and laundry, while men remain more fully engaged in paid employment. Moreover, in professional settings, employers might anticipate these gendered patterns and become more hesitant to assign women to demanding or nonroutine positions that require continuity and commitment. As a result, well-intentioned family policies could inadvertently re-entrench gender inequalities in both household labor and career opportunities, slowing or even reversing progress toward true gender parity (Bergmann 2008a).

7.2 Welfare Measures *Versus* Basic Income

Bergmann intensively worked on proposing reforms aimed at making life easier for people in need.

Her initial interest in welfare was focused on the need for pension reform. In an article co-authored by Bergmann and Gray (1975), they pointed out that employers can no longer treat any woman as though she were the average woman. In fact, employment law now rejects the practice of grouping individuals by sex to make decisions about hiring, promotion, pay, or benefits. Instead, each person must be judged by their actual abilities and circumstances, not by statistical assumptions tied to gender. The law recognizes that individual differences within each sex are far greater than the differences between the averages of men and women. While the average man might, for example, have greater upper-body strength or a shorter life expectancy than the average woman, these averages conceal a large overlap. Many women are as strong as many men, and many men live as long as many women. To treat all women as weaker or longer-lived than men is to ignore this overlap and to replace individual assessment with gender stereotypes.

Bergmann and Gray illustrated this principle with data on life expectancy. Although women, on average, live longer than men, the overlap between male and female life spans is about 84 percent.[5] Nevertheless, many pension systems use sex as a determining factor when calculating benefits. Under these systems, men receive higher monthly pension payments than women who have made the same contributions, on the assumption that women, on average, will collect benefits for a longer period. This approach wrongly allocates all the savings from early-dying men to men as a group, while shifting the financial burden of

[5] This means that if 1000 men and 1000 women aged sixty-five were tracked until death, 84 percent of them could be paired with someone of the opposite sex who dies in the same year. Only 8 percent of men die unusually early and 8 percent of women live unusually long.

longer-living individuals entirely onto women, even though the majority of both sexes fall into the overlapping group.

According to Bergmann and Gray, this practice effectively denied equal pay for equal work. Women in the overlap group, those who live roughly as long as men, receive lower monthly pensions even though they cost the system less than their male counterparts. They are penalized solely because of their sex, not because of any individual characteristic. The supposed justification for women's higher average longevity rests on group averages that fail to describe most individuals and therefore cannot serve as a lawful basis for unequal treatment.

Anti-discrimination law, the authors insisted, requires that both sexes share the financial consequences of longevity differences. Just as society pools risk in health insurance or social security, the extra costs of supporting the small fraction of long-lived individuals should be distributed across the whole population, not assigned only to women. Some employers claim that women receive equal total benefits in the long run, since they collect smaller payments over a longer period. But this reasoning is misleading. Even if every woman lived precisely to the statistical average and every man died exactly at the male average age, unequal monthly payments would still create unequal benefits. Life is lived day to day, not in actuarial averages; bills must be paid monthly, and no one purchases groceries with expected years of life. Moreover, life expectancy is not a guarantee. Some women die young, and some men live long past their statistical life span. If the risks and costs of longevity are not shared equally, women as a class are disadvantaged. The issue is not actuarial prediction but equal treatment under the law.

The discriminatory effect is compounded by the way many employers buy annuities from private insurance companies. Instead of paying pension benefits directly, employers often buy group annuity contracts. Insurers typically offer a lower price per employee if the employer accepts lower monthly benefits for women. This arrangement benefits both employer and insurer: the employer saves money, and the insurer profits from sex-based pricing. But, as the authors emphasized, this practice simply shifts the responsibility for discrimination. The employer passes the 'dirty work' to the insurance company, which uses the excuse of "higher costs" for women, based on their longer average life spans, to justify paying them less. Such reasoning would never be acceptable in other employment contexts. An employer cannot justify paying women lower salaries, hiring them less often, or promoting them less frequently on the grounds that women, on average, leave the workforce earlier or take more family leave. There is no legitimate reason to allow this logic in pensions or other fringe benefits.

The inconsistency becomes even clearer when comparing retirement and death benefits. Many universities, for example, ignore the higher mortality rates of men when calculating life-insurance or death benefits, offering equal payouts to both sexes. Yet, the same institutions cite women's longer life expectancy to justify smaller pension payments. If costs were truly the driving concern, such institutions would adjust both benefits symmetrically. Their selective use of statistics exposes an underlying bias: taking advantage of women's weaker bargaining position to reduce benefits under the guise of actuarial fairness.

Supporters of sex-based pension rates often defend them as "actuarially sound", implying that equal benefits would violate principles of financial stability. The authors dismantled this argument by noting that actuarial soundness was compatible with many different ways of grouping a population. A pension system can be sound whether it divides people by sex, race, geography, smoking habits, or any other trait or whether it treats everyone as one large group and calculates the costs.

What matters for soundness is that the total discounted value of benefits equals the total discounted value of contributions, plus administrative margins. Financial equilibrium can be achieved under numerous classification schemes. Thus, the choice to use sex as a dividing criterion is not a technical necessity but a social and legal decision. The law can, and should, require unisex tables, mandating that all employees contribute and benefit equally, regardless of sex.

Many existing retirement systems already operate successfully under unisex rules. The federal and most state retirement systems, as well as social security, pay equal benefits to men and women with identical work histories. Their continued solvency demonstrates that sex-neutral systems are both practical and fair.

Critics of reform warn that if unisex rates are imposed, male-dominated institutions might withdraw from mixed insurance plans and form single-sex groups to secure lower premiums. The authors find this scenario unlikely. First, it would be illegal for insurance companies to sell coverage exclusively to predominantly single-sex groups. Second, as more workplaces become gender-balanced, opportunities for such segregation will disappear. Finally, in certain sectors, such as higher education, one insurer, like the Teachers Insurance and Annuity Association (TIAA), holds such a dominant position that few institutions would switch providers for small short-term savings.

In short, according to the authors, fears of mass withdrawal were exaggerated. The real obstacle is not financial but ideological: employers' and insurers' reluctance to abandon entrenched practices that advantage men and preserve outdated stereotypes.

By the mid-1970s, the federal government's stance on sex discrimination in pensions was inconsistent and confusing. Although some commentators claimed that these agencies' interpretations conflicted, the authors note that this is largely a misunderstanding. A plan that meets the strictest standard, i.e., equal benefits and equal contributions, automatically satisfies all lesser standards. Therefore, adopting the strongest possible interpretation would simplify compliance and strengthen protections against discrimination. Two main policy alternatives were under discussion among federal agencies: equal benefits regardless of sex and allowing employers to choose between equal benefits or equal contributions.

The authors preferred the first option but went further, advocating that both equal benefits and equal contributions be mandated through unisex actuarial tables. If only equal benefits are required while contributions remain sex-differentiated, the cost of employing women will appear higher, discouraging their hiring and perpetuating inequality. Requiring both equal contributions and benefits removes any financial incentive to discriminate by sex. The authors also address the issue of optional benefit structures within retirement plans, such as single-life or joint-life annuities. Under the current sex-segregated system, significant differences in payouts exist mainly under the single-life option. If men and women were grouped together for risk-sharing, these differences would vanish, since employees would no longer even be identified by sex. Equal benefits would naturally follow from the unified risk pool.

The authors concluded that the principle at stake is simple but profound: in employment, individuals must be treated as individuals, not as representatives of a gender average. To assume that all women resemble the 'average woman' or all men the 'average man' is to violate both logic and law. In the context of pensions, such assumptions translate directly into unequal pay for equal work and into systematic economic disadvantage for women.

The overlapping nature of male and female traits, whether in strength, skill, or longevity, renders group-based distinctions unjustifiable. Public policy must ensure that the small percentage of long-lived individuals is supported by society as a whole, not by penalizing women as a class. Employers and insurers who claim that unequal pensions are merely "actuarially fair" misrepresent the issue. Actuarial fairness cannot override the legal and moral imperative of equality. Financial systems can remain sound under unisex rules, as shown by existing state and federal programs.

Ultimately, the authors called for comprehensive reform: the abolition of sex-based actuarial tables, the establishment of equal benefits and contributions, and consistent enforcement across all federal agencies. Such measures would bring pension policy into alignment with the larger principle of anti-discrimination law, that sex must never serve as a proxy for individual capacity, performance, or worth. Only when pension systems treat men and women as fully equal participants in the workforce will the promise of equal pay for equal work be realized in both employment and retirement.

In the following years, Bergmann's commitment to welfare reform was much more focused on family welfare.

In 1987, Bergmann promoted a major shift in U.S. welfare reform centered on Senator Daniel Patrick Moynihan's idea of 'parental responsibility'. After decades of frustration, this approach promised to reduce poverty among single mothers, help them join the workforce, and lessen the burden on taxpayers. The reform envisions replacing traditional welfare payments with a new system based on child support, where both parents, especially the noncustodial one, share financial responsibility for their children. Under this plan, absent parents would be required to contribute a portion of their income to child support, while single parents with custody would have the opportunity and incentive to work and support themselves. Unlike welfare, which discourages employment by reducing benefits when recipients earn income, child-support payments would continue regardless of the custodial parent's job status. This combination of wages and reliable child-support payments could lift many single mothers above the poverty line.

A pilot version of this system was developed in Wisconsin, led by Professor Irwin Garfinkel and his colleagues at the University of Wisconsin's Institute for Research on Poverty.[6] Their plan replaces the cumbersome court-based process with a simple, tax-like system: employers would automatically withhold child-support payments from paychecks and forward them to the state, which would then send regular payments to the custodial parent.

Bergmann was particularly in favor of parental responsibility because it advocated jobs for single mothers by introducing incentives to employers for hiring them, contrary to "some old-fashioned liberals who are attached to the idea that the best place for mothers is home full-time with their children" (Bergmann 1987, p. 48).

In a paper published on *Dissent*, Bergmann explained that millions of American families struggle to raise children amid economic and social pressures, and that their problems deserve central attention in national politics (Bergmann 1988). Issues like child care, welfare reform, and single parenthood should be major topics in election debates: while conservatives already have a 'family policy' focused on banning abortion, promoting school prayer, and enforcing traditional gender roles, a progressive agenda should focus on social changes such as women's widespread participation in the workforce, rising divorce rates, and increasing numbers of single-parent households, which are irreversible and have expanded women's independence while creating new challenges, particularly the loss of many functions once performed by traditional two-parent families.

Hence, reliable child care and stable financial support within families can no longer be taken for granted. Many parents struggle to find affordable, trustworthy care for their children, while millions of men have abandoned financial responsibility for their offspring. As a result, many children are placed in unsafe or poor-quality care, and many single mothers live in poverty or depend on welfare.

[6] The Wisconsin model also introduces a guaranteed minimum child-support payment from the state, ensuring that children receive basic financial support even if the absent parent earns too little or cannot be located. Payments would be calculated as a fixed percentage of the absent parent's income, i.e., about 17 percent for each child, and would rise automatically with earnings and inflation. This reform marks a significant departure from the traditional welfare system, promoting shared parental responsibility and steady income support rather than dependence on taxpayer-funded assistance.

According to Bergmann, the failures of the Reagan era's neglectful approach have created an opportunity for well-designed, activist programs that could be both socially beneficial and politically popular. Liberals need to develop a coherent family policy grounded in government action to find practical solutions: high-quality, affordable child care, stronger child-support enforcement, and targeted welfare reforms that lift families out of poverty.

In 1990, Bergmann presented a paper at the 85th Annual Meeting of the American Sociological Association, later published in 1993, where she proposed to adapt the French Child Welfare System (Bergmann 1993). Despite being one of the richest nations in the world, the United States fails to provide many preschool children with essential needs such as health care, protection from abuse, safe and nurturing day care, and early education. The system, meant to protect children from abuse, is described as chaotic and ineffective, with alarming levels of neglect and violence. France, by contrast, with a lower per capita income, has successfully created a comprehensive system that ensures children receive proper care, health services, and protection.

In France, welfare system for child care is valued primarily for how they benefit the children, not just for how they help parents. These programs are universal, available to all social classes, but are especially beneficial for children from poor or minority backgrounds. French child welfare policies mitigate the harmful effects of poverty, neglect, and abuse more effectively than those in the United States.

When Americans learn about the French system, they often admire it but dismiss it as unaffordable. However, Bergmann argued that financial constraints are not the main barrier, rather, ideological and cultural attitudes prevent similar progress in the U.S. France views child welfare as a national priority, grounded in the belief that children represent the nation's future and deserve collective investment. According to Bergmann, this cultural commitment to children's well-being could serve as an important example for the United States in building a more humane society.

A few years later, Bergmann published a book on her ideas about the comparison between the United States and France (Bergmann 1996b) where she proposed adopting her Help for Working Parents (see Chapters 4 and 6). She compared the systems of child welfare and family support in France and the United States, using the situation of a single mother as a lens through which to examine the broader social and economic differences between the two nations. Her analysis revealed that while both countries share similar demographics and labor patterns, their governmental priorities and welfare structures lead to dramatically different outcomes for low-income families, especially for single mothers and their children.

In the United States, a single mother who leaves welfare for a low-wage job receives limited financial help.[7] Once she begins working, she loses free health insurance and must pay for child care, which typically consumes about a quarter of her income. The result is that her financial situation may worsen when she moves from welfare to work. Despite welfare reform policies that push single mothers into employment, many remain below the poverty line because of inadequate support for child care and health care. The American system effectively penalizes work, trapping many single mothers in poverty rather than helping them achieve economic independence.

By contrast, a single mother in France who transitions from welfare to employment continues to enjoy free health insurance and pays only minimal fees for child care. Because these benefits extend to middle- and upper-class families as well as two-parent households, there is no stigma attached to receiving assistance. This universality strengthens social cohesion and normalizes government support as an integral part of citizenship rather than as a form of charity. As a result, fewer single mothers in France rely on welfare, only about 23 percent compared to 67 percent in the United States, and they are better able to sustain employment and raise their children above the poverty line. Although France spends more overall on social welfare, the efficiency of its programs and the broad participation of its citizens reduce long-term dependency and improve outcomes for children.

Government expenditures further illustrate these differences.[8] France spends a much larger share of its budget on programs that support families and children, even outspending its defense budget by 66 percent. The United States, on the other hand, devotes less than half as much to child welfare as it spends on defense. This contrast underscores a difference in

[7] A single mother may qualify for the Earned Income Tax Credit (EITC) and food stamps, totaling roughly $3600 annually for two children.

[8] To match France's level of investment in children's well-being, U.S. federal, state, and local governments would need to increase spending by 59 percent, roughly $85 billion more than the amount spent in 1991.

priorities: where France views investment in children as a form of national security, the United States continues to allocate far greater resources to military power than to the protection and development of its youngest citizens.

The two countries are similar in many respects: both have comparable rates of female labor force participation (around 72–73 percent), similar rates of births outside marriage (about 28–30 percent), and similar rates of economic growth and investment. Yet, France has higher taxes and higher unemployment. Despite this, it has managed to build a system that effectively reduces child poverty and enables single mothers to work. The success of French policies suggests that comparable results could be achieved in the United States if cultural attitudes and fiscal priorities shifted toward collective responsibility for children's welfare.

France's system for child well-being is built on three main pillars: child care and development, income supplementation, and medical care. Every French child between two and a half and six years old is guaranteed a place in a free, high-quality public nursery school. These nursery schools prepare children for elementary education while enabling parents, particularly mothers, to work full time. Beyond regular school hours, before- and after-school programs are widely available at very low cost. The closest U.S. equivalents, Head Start and public kindergarten, are limited to one year and often operate only part of the day, making them insufficient to support working parents.

French policies also ensure care for infants and toddlers through public day-care centers, paid maternity leave, and subsidies for private child care. In addition to child care, France supplements family income through child allowances, housing aid, and cash benefits for pregnant women and parents of newborns. These benefits are not limited to the poor; most families, regardless of income, qualify for at least some support. Only about 10 percent of income supplements are restricted to families without earnings. This approach, which blends universal and targeted aid, reduces stigma, broadens political support for welfare programs, and strengthens the social fabric.

On the health care front, France provides universal national health insurance to all legal citizens. This coverage remains intact regardless of employment status, meaning that individuals do not lose their health care when they change jobs, go from welfare to work, or face costly illnesses. In contrast, the American system ties insurance primarily to employment, with 72 percent of U.S. citizens relying on private employer-based insurance, 11 percent on government programs like Medicare and Medicaid, and 18 percent of the population, including 12 percent of children, being uninsured. This gap in coverage leaves many low-wage workers and their children vulnerable to both financial and medical crises.

The French government also employs a specialized corps of public health nurses dedicated to children's welfare. These nurses monitor child development, visit homes to ensure children's safety, and supervise day-care facilities to maintain standards. The existence of such a professional infrastructure ensures that health and welfare services are proactive rather than reactive, identifying risks early and preventing abuse or neglect before they escalate into crises.

Overall, France's higher level of public spending and its integrated, universal approach to child welfare result in significantly better outcomes for children. Fewer live in poverty, more receive quality education and health care, and working parents, especially single mothers, face fewer barriers to employment. The United States, by contrast, spends less on child well-being and delivers its aid through fragmented, means-tested programs that often stigmatize recipients and fail to lift families out of poverty.

Finally, Bergmann argued that the United States could afford to adopt similar policies if it restructured its budget priorities. When politicians claim that the government "cannot afford" new child welfare programs, this often reflects not a financial impossibility but a lack of political will. The United States is an extraordinarily wealthy nation, with one of the lowest tax burdens among developed countries. Redirecting a portion of existing expenditures, such as those devoted to defense, could make possible an expansion of child care, health care, and family support systems that would benefit millions of children and working parents. Bergmann's Help for Working Parent program would provide child care vouchers to all families, with full support for the poorest 20 percent and partial support for middle-income families. It would also guarantee medical insurance for all families with children who lack employer-provided coverage. The estimated cost of such a program would be about $80 billion annually, less than the cost of many existing federal expenditures.

Bergmann's central argument was that investing in children's well-being is not merely a moral imperative but an economically sound strategy, one that builds a stronger and more equitable society for future generations.

In early 2000s, Bergmann started to consider the possibility of Basic Income versus the welfare system (Bergmann 2004, 2006). She contrasted two progressive visions for achieving greater economic equality and social security: a Swedish-style welfare state, emphasizing state provision of "merit goods" and targeted benefits, and universal cash payments like a Basic Income or stakeholder grant, which distribute unconditional funds to all citizens. While both seek to reduce inequality and dependency on the labor market, Bergmann argued that state-provided welfare services should take priority. Her central claim was that advanced economies lack the fiscal capacity to finance both a generous welfare state and universal cash grants simultaneously. At current income and taxation levels, governments must choose, and a well-funded welfare state better serves human needs and social equity. Bergmann situated her argument within a broader debate about the future of social policy in advanced economies, warning that prioritizing Basic Income over welfare provision would be "putting the cart before the horse".

Using Sweden as a case study, Bergmann examined the budgetary realities of advanced welfare states. Sweden, one of the most comprehensive welfare states in the world, allocates about 60% of its GDP to public revenue and spending, including cash transfers (pensions, unemployment benefits, child allowances, and public goods and services, including education, health care, and child care). If Sweden were to add a basic income equivalent to a poverty-level income for every adult, this would require an additional 15% of GDP, a massive expansion that would push taxation rates to unsustainable levels. Thus, Bergmann concluded that countries cannot simultaneously sustain a robust welfare state and large universal cash payments.

Bergmann introduced the concept of merit goods, i.e., goods and services that society deems essential for all citizens to have access to, regardless of income. These include education at any level, health care, child care, housing, public transportation, and mental health services. She defined merit goods by two criteria: universality and market failure. Furthermore, she justified their provision both as humanitarian and economic: individual welfare and social cohesion depend on universal access to these goods. Hence, she argued that direct state provision ensures equitable quality and distribution, while cash grants do not.

Bergmann concluded that without a comprehensive welfare infrastructure, basic income would leave many core needs unmet: people might spend cash grants on other priorities, leaving them still without health insurance, adequate child care, or quality housing.

Bergmann emphasized that even Sweden, with its already high taxation levels, could not easily add a basic income without severe economic trade-offs. This leads to a key dilemma: to fund Basic Income, taxes on earned income must rise, but higher taxes reduce the incentive to work, thereby shrinking the tax base. She warned of a vicious cycle: fewer people working for pay lead to lower tax revenues that leads to higher tax rates, resulting in even fewer workers. This dynamic makes large-scale Basic Income unviable under current economic conditions.

Bergmann also highlighted political feasibility. In the United States, she contended, it is far more realistic to expand welfare programs (e.g., healthcare, child care, and housing subsidies) than to introduce a nationwide Basic Income. Universal cash payments risk being perceived as wasteful or unearned, undermining public support.

Moreover, unlike merit goods, Basic Income lacks a clear moral or humanitarian justification in voters' eyes, especially when pressing needs like health care remain unmet. Bergmann advised progressives to focus their political energy on defending and expanding the welfare state before advocating for Basic Income.

Beyond fiscal concerns, Bergmann identified three social drawbacks of Basic Income.

First, work disincentives: guaranteed income may encourage some to withdraw from the labor market, reducing overall productivity and shrinking the tax base, which would lower per capita consumption and income, making society poorer overall.

Second, gender equality: a Basic Income might unintentionally reinforce traditional gender roles, because women, given the option, may leave the workforce to care for children, reversing decades of progress in employment equality, and employers might again view women as less committed workers, undermining wage parity and career advancement.

Third, youth and family relations: if teenagers receive substantial Basic Income payments, they might choose to live independently, weakening parental authority and reducing motivation for education or work, which could create new social problems rather than alleviating existing ones.

Bergmann acknowledged that welfare states are not perfect: bureaucracy, inefficiency, political favoritism, and uneven quality are persistent challenges. However, the experience of Scandinavian and Western European countries demonstrates that these problems can be mitigated through democratic oversight, professional public administration, and citizen engagement. In contrast, a Basic Income system may be administratively simple, but it fails to guarantee equitable outcomes. The welfare state, despite its flaws, remains the most effective mechanism for ensuring that essential human needs are met.

Bergmann concluded that giving everyone the same cash grant cannot equalize conditions between people with vastly different needs, such as those requiring expensive medical treatment versus those who do not. Only direct provision of merit goods can address such disparities effectively. In the long term, as productivity rises and fewer workers are needed, Basic Income might become both desirable and feasible. At that stage, society could begin gradually introducing universal cash payments, financed by growing national wealth. But in the present, when many countries (especially the United States) still lack universal access to basic welfare goods, Basic Income's appeal must yield to the more urgent project of building and sustaining the welfare state.

A few years later, Bergmann joined a debate about whether feminist economists should endorse Basic Income Grants (BIG) or promote welfare reforms (Bergmann 2008b). In her contribution, Barbara compared the effects of Basic Income Grants (BIG), Low Provision, and the welfare state on gender equality. A Basic Income Grant would use a large share of national income, raised through progressive taxation, to provide equal cash payments to all citizens. By contrast, the Low Provision model, favored by conservatives, limits redistribution and public services, allowing individuals to spend or save their income freely, as in the current U.S. system. The welfare state preferred by those on the Left, uses similar or higher tax revenues to fund government-provided goods and services, such as health care, child care, housing subsidies, education, and social services, alongside targeted cash benefits for the elderly, disabled, unemployed, and families with children.

Bergmann argued that, in promoting gender equality, a welfare state with generous in-kind benefits but without long paid parental leaves is far superior to both BIG and Low Provision. Long parental leaves can discourage women's participation and advancement in the labor market, reinforcing gender inequality. A Basic Income Grant however, is seen as the worst option for gender equality. It could encourage women, especially mothers, to withdraw from paid employment, increasing economic dependence and occupational segregation. Moreover, BIG is fiscally unrealistic alongside a robust welfare system: in high-tax countries like Sweden, where welfare spending already equals about 60% of national income, adding a substantial BIG would raise taxes on workers to unsustainable levels.

Before evaluating these regimes, the author clarifies the meaning of gender equality: it entails the elimination of traditional gender arrangements that exclude women from leadership and well-paid, prestigious jobs, and that assign them disproportionate responsibility for domestic work and child care. True gender equality would dismantle this "caste system" of gendered labor, ensuring that social and economic opportunities are not determined by sex. From this perspective, the welfare state, by publicly providing essential services that support women's employment, is the system most conducive to achieving genuine equality between men and women.

Again, in this argumentation, Bergmann provided a strong attack on supporters of the doctrine of the separate spheres. She wrote:

> Some would argue that a move toward gender equality should include giving women a choice as to whether to maintain their traditional household activities, perhaps with higher prestige, better pension arrangements, and even pay for housework. On this view, making it easier to combine household activities with paid work, and making it easier to move into the labor force after a spell at home would also lead toward greater gender equality. Without question, that would accommodate arrangements that some women would prefer. However, measures that lead in that direction would likely reduce opportunities for women in the workplace, and would reinforce the cultural habits of assigning housework and child care to women. In other words, implementing such measures would most likely lead, not to greater gender equality, but to its opposite. (Bergmann 2008b, p. 3)

Other advantages of welfare versus BIG are that the former provides benefits, while the latter provides cash that can be wrongly directed. Moreover, BIG provides cash to everyone, while welfare provides support to those who really are in need, such as lone mothers, whose number has been dramatically increased.

7.3 Social Security Reform

One of Bergmann's first essays on social security reform (Bergmann 1980) explored how the system's structure reflects outdated gender assumptions and how feminist thought offers crucial insights for change. She argued that nearly all current criticisms of social security, whether about inequities between one- and two-earner couples, unfair treatment of divorced spouses, or the so-called wasted taxes of working wives, ultimately revolve around the system's handling of the housewife. The core issue, she maintained, lies in how the system defines and values women's roles within marriage and work.

Historically, the social security system was designed around a traditional family model in which men were breadwinners and women were full-time homemakers. Under this model, the system's 'spouse benefit' allowed a retired married man to receive 50 percent more than an unmarried retiree with the same earnings record, an arrangement that appeared equitable when most women were housewives. However, as societal patterns changed, with more women entering the labor force, marriage rates declining, and divorce rates increasing, the inequities embedded in this system became increasingly visible. The system's reliance on spousal dependency and its disregard for women's independent economic contributions no longer reflected social reality.

Bergmann situated the debate within the broader context of feminist thought. The rise of feminism, she explains, has brought attention to how institutional structures, including social security, perpetuate gender inequality. Feminists have challenged not only discriminatory practices but also the deeper cultural assumptions that devalue women's unpaid labor and tie their financial security to men. Feminist movements have thus been essential not just in providing a framework for critique, but in mobilizing political action to place reform on the national agenda. Without feminist insights, Bergmann insisted, discussions of social security reform risk overlooking the lived realities of women whose economic roles differ from traditional norms.

As mentioned in Chapter 4, within feminist discourse, she identified two main strands of thought concerning the housewife.

The first was the role-avoidance strand, which focused on liberating women from domestic confinement and promoting their economic independence. This view saw the traditional housewife role as inherently disadvantageous, limiting women's opportunities and autonomy. Feminists in this camp, echoing thinkers like Betty Friedan, argued that women should be encouraged to participate fully in the paid labor force rather than rely on spousal support. Many even contended that society should phase out the notion of full-time homemaking as a viable or desirable life path for women.

The second was the solidarity-with-housewives strand, which emphasized empathy and shared identity among women regardless of employment status. From this perspective, reform should aim to protect and dignify housewives, recognizing the social and economic value of their unpaid labor. Feminists in this camp advocated for policies that reduce the financial vulnerability of homemakers, such as social security credits for housework, pension entitlements under their own names, and protections in cases of divorce or widowhood. This approach tried to ensure that women who choose or are compelled to remain at home do not suffer economic marginalization.

Bergmann noted that these two strands are not logically incompatible. One can oppose the social structures that confine women to housework while still advocating protection for those who occupy that role. The tension lies in emphasis: the role-avoidance strand pushes for independence from the role itself, while the solidarity strand seeks justice and respect for women within it.

From these differing feminist frameworks two sets of critiques of the current social security system emerged. Some feminists argued that housewives are treated too well, receiving disproportionate benefits through their husbands' entitlements compared to working wives from two-earner families who contribute similar amounts. Others contended that housewives are treated not well enough, forced into dependency, and stripped of rights to benefits when marriages dissolve.

Bergmann emphasized that both critiques are valid, as the system simultaneously reinforces dependency and produces inequality among women themselves.

The solidarity approach has inspired several reform proposals aimed at granting housewives more autonomy and security. One idea is to award homemaker credits, recognizing domestic labor as economically valuable and thus deserving of pension benefits. These credits could be funded either through household contributions or publicly financed as recognition of unpaid labor's societal worth. Supporters of this approach argue that it would elevate the status of housework, provide economic independence in cases of divorce, and make women's economic contributions more visible.

The role-avoidance strand of feminism called for prioritizing the concerns of working wives over those of homemakers. Advocates of this view argued that it is unfair for one-earner households to receive higher benefits than dual-earner households contributing the same total amount. From this perspective, the 50 percent spousal benefit should be abolished, as it perpetuates dependency and penalizes women who work outside the home. Role-avoidance feminists also warn that making the housewife's position too comfortable might discourage women from seeking employment and hinder progress toward equality in the labor market.

Bergmann synthesized these feminist positions into two principal reform programs that most feminists would likely support. The first involved sharing earnings credits between spouses and eliminating the spousal benefit. This would ensure that homemakers gain benefits under their own names and are not left destitute after divorce or widowhood. While easier to implement than homemaker credits, earnings sharing does not fully equalize the standing of housewives and working wives, since it still ties benefits to the husband's employment record rather than directly valuing domestic work. The second, the two-tier or double-decker system, combined those measures with a universal basic pension tier, reducing the extent to which benefits depend on lifetime earnings and would grant all individuals of retirement age a basic benefit regardless of work history, supplementing it with an earnings-based component. This model, by detaching pension entitlement from employment records, would particularly help those, such as long-term homemakers, who lack formal work experience. Though not explicitly framed around recognizing the value of housework, this system enhances the dignity of the housewife by ensuring a universal safety net and reducing the stigma of dependency. The first approach was more aligned with role-avoidance feminism, as it discourages the traditional housewife role; the second leans toward solidarity feminism by providing a broader safety net for those without wage income. Together, these approaches represented efforts to balance fairness, independence, and protection within a changing social structure.

In her conclusion, Bergmann stressed that feminist analysis was indispensable for developing just and realistic reforms. Historically, social scientists and policymakers have overlooked women's experiences, even when policies directly affected them. For instance, in debates about welfare reform, researchers often ignored that most adult recipients were women caring for children, focusing instead on "work incentives" and treating motherhood as an afterthought. Similar oversights threaten to distort discussions of social security reform unless feminist perspectives are actively incorporated.

As pointed out earlier, Bergmann criticized the dominance of the New Home Economics that idealizes the traditional family and assumes rational, harmonious gender roles (see Chapters 4, 5, and 6). This economic model, she argued, was fundamentally inadequate for understanding the realities of modern households, where dual-earner and single-parent families are common and gender roles are fluid. As traditional family structures change, reforming systems like social security becomes essential to reflect new social and economic realities.

Ultimately, Bergmann's analysis revealed that debates over social security reform are inseparable from broader struggles over gender equality and the valuation of women's work. Feminist thought offers both a critique of entrenched inequities and a guide to constructing fairer institutions. Whether by recognizing the economic value of domestic labor, ensuring equitable benefit distribution, or redefining the social meaning of dependency, feminist insights remain vital to designing a system that serves all citizens with dignity. Without such perspectives, any reform might perpetuate the very inequalities it seeks to correct.

In 2000, Bergmann published a cartoon book, *Is Social Security Broke? A Cartoon Guide to the Issues*, which extended her lifelong mission to make economic debates accessible to non-specialists (Bergmann 2000b). Written in collaboration with illustrator Jim Bush, the book was aimed at explaining how the U.S. Social Security system works, what problems it faces, and how they can be solved without dismantling the system's fundamental purpose. The book was also aimed at responding to widespread public anxiety about the future of social security especially among retirees, baby boomers approaching retirement, and younger generations skeptical about whether the system will still exist when they need it. Bergmann's answer to the central question, i.e., whether social security will run out of money, was clear and confident negative. She explained that social security operates on a 'pay-as-you-go' basis, meaning that current workers' payroll taxes fund current retirees' benefits. As long as people are working and paying taxes, she argued, the system will continue to receive income.

The real issue, she acknowledged, lies not in the system's survival but in its balance between income and obligations. As the baby boom generation retires, the number of beneficiaries will increase faster than the number of workers contributing to the system, creating a funding shortfall. Yet, Bergmann insisted, this problem is manageable through relatively modest adjustments, such as small increases in payroll taxes, gradual benefit reforms, or raising the wage ceiling on taxable income. These measures, she argued, are far less risky and more equitable than the drastic proposals to privatize the system.

A central theme of Bergmann's book was her opposition to social security privatization, a policy idea that gained traction in the 1990s and early 2000s. Privatization advocates claimed that allowing individuals to invest their social security contributions in private financial markets would yield higher returns. Bergmann dismantled this argument by emphasizing that social security is not an investment scheme but a social insurance program designed to provide economic security across generations. Each working generation supports retirees, the disabled, and survivors, ensuring that no one is left destitute due to age or misfortune.

She highlighted that comparing social security to private investments was misleading because it ignores the element of risk. Private investments fluctuate dramatically, as stocks can fall by 40% in a year, and are subject to market volatility. In contrast, social security offers guaranteed benefits, indexed to inflation, and operates with minimal administrative costs. To replace this stability with individual risk-taking, Bergmann argued, would undermine the system's moral and practical foundation. Social security's purpose, after all, is not to maximize returns but to guarantee security.

In 2005, Bergmann wrote in *The Economists' Voice*, a defense of social security (Bergmann 2005), pointing out, against all detractors worried that the social security system will run out of money in 2024, that going bankrupt implies that a subject cannot make required payments. However, government programs get the money from taxes, and any form of deficit may be adjusted through a democratic process.

As mentioned, to communicate these complex issues clearly, Bergmann used humor and visual storytelling. Every other page of the book features cartoons, transforming abstract policy concepts into accessible, memorable scenes. Inspired by earlier illustrated guides to Marx, Freud, and statistics, Bergmann saw the cartoon format as a tool for democratic education. By blending plain language with visual explanation, she sought to empower readers to engage critically with political rhetoric and media myths. Her use of accessible formats, including cartoons and straightforward prose, reflects a deep belief that public understanding is a precondition for democratic reform. Economic systems, she argued, should not be the exclusive domain of experts or politicians; citizens must understand how policies affect their lives to participate meaningfully in shaping them.

References

Bergmann, B. (1980). The housewife and social security reform: A feminist perspective. In R. Burkhauser & K. Holden (Eds.), *A challenge to social security* (pp. 229–233). Academic Press.

Bergmann, B. (1987). A fresh start on welfare reform. *Challenge, 30*(5), 44–50.

Bergmann, B. (1988). A workable family policy. *Dissent, 35*(1), 88–93.

Bergmann, B. (1991). Do sports really make money for the University? *Academe, 77*(1), 28–30.

Bergmann, B. (1993). The French child welfare system: An excellent system we could adapt and afford. In W. Wilson (Ed.), *Sociology and the public agenda* (pp. 341–350). Sage Publications.

Bergmann, B. (1995). Probing the opposition to affirmative action. *Gender, Work and Organization, 2*(2), 88–94.

Bergmann, B. (1996a). *In defense of affirmative action*. Basic Books.

Bergmann, B. (1996b). *Saving our children from poverty: What the United States can learn from France*. Russell Sage Foundation.

Bergmann, B. (1997a). Is affirmative action a quota system? In S. L. Myers (Ed.), *Civil rights and race relations in the post reagan-bush* (pp. 227–230). Greenwood Publishing Group.

Bergmann, B. (1997b). Selections from in defense of affirmative action. *Academe, 83*(1), 29–34.

Bergmann, B. (1997c). Government support for families with children in the United States and France. *Feminist Economics, 3*(1), 85–94.

Bergmann, B. (2000a). Subsidizing child care by mothers at home. *Feminist Economics, 6*(1), 77–88.

Bergmann, B. (2000b). *Is social security broke? Illustrated by Jim Bush*. University of Michigan Press.

Bergmann, B. (2001). What would we gain by subsidizing child care? In M. King (Ed.), *Squaring up: Policy strategies to raise women's incomes in the United States* (pp. 46–62). University of Michigan Press.

Bergmann, B. (2004). A Swedish-style welfare state or basic income: Which should have priority? *Politics and Society, 32*(1), 107–118.

Bergmann, B. (2005). Could social security go broke? *The Economists' Voice, 2*(1), 1–4.

Bergmann, B. (2006). Reducing inequality. *Dissent, 53*(1), 67–72.
Bergmann, B. (2008a). Long leaves, child well-being, and gender equality. *Politics & Society, 36*(3), 350–359.
Bergmann, B. (2008b). Basic income grants or the welfare state: Which better promotes gender equality? *Basic Income Studies, 3*(3), 1–7.
Bergmann, B., & Gray, M. (1975). Equality in retirement benefits. The need for pension reform. *Civil Rights Digest, U. S. Civil Rights Commission, 8*(1), 25–27.
Bergmann, B., & Helburn, S. (2002). *America's child care problem: The way out*. Palgrave Macmillan.
Berman, P. (1996, April 14). Redefining fairness. *The New York Times*.
Bolick, C. (1996). *The affirmative action fraud can we restore the American civil rights vision?* Cato Institute.
Eastland, T. (1996). *Ending affirmative action the case for colorblind justice*. Basic Book.
Saunders, L. & King, M. (2000). An Interview with Barbara Bergmann: Leading feminist economists. *Review of Political Economy, 12*(3), 305–316.

CHAPTER 8

Spreading a Progressive Agenda Outside Academia

Barbara Bergmann refused to view the world solely through an academic lens and was a fierce advocate for social change. She consistently devoted herself to spreading her progressive agenda through newspapers, magazines, and blogs, reaching audiences far beyond academia.

Her democratic, progressive, and feminist convictions were clearly expressed in her non-academic work. In addition to her public writings, she actively participated in congressional hearings and testimonies, where she presented data-driven analyses and proposed practical solutions to improve the lives of those in need.

Of particular significance were her columns that appeared regularly between 1981 and 1982 in the Sunday edition of *The New York Times*, along with numerous articles published in national journals and magazines. Bergmann's public interventions in the national press did not go unnoticed by her peers, journalists, or commentators: her analyses provoked both recognition and critique, situating her among the public intellectuals in the American economic debate.

The topics she addressed were wide-ranging, including gender discrimination, social security, affirmative action, quota systems, Reaganomics, the shortage of nurses, welfare reform for single parents, child-rearing, and, later in her career, environmental issues. Although not exhaustive,

G. Becchio, *Barbara Bergmann*, Great Thinkers in Economics, https://doi.org/10.1007/978-3-032-18696-6_8

this chapter brings together many of her non-academic writings and the public reactions they provoked, serving as a testament to her role as one of the most influential public proponents of a feminist agenda.

8.1 Testimonies and Hearings

The first involvement of Bergmann in the Joint Economic Committee of the Congress was in 1968. On that occasion, she examined racial inequality in the United States through an economic perspective (Bergmann 1968). She argued that the disadvantages faced by Black Americans stemmed not from a lack of natural ability but from a long history of systematic underinvestment in their human capital, the education, training, and work experience that determined productivity and earning power. She estimated that the average Black man possessed about $10,000 less human capital than the average white man, which added up to a staggering national deficiency of roughly $50 billion. Although this estimate was approximate, it reflected the cumulative economic consequences of centuries of discrimination and neglect, which had deprived generations of Black Americans of the resources needed to develop their potential.

Bergmann's central argument was that even if racial prejudice might magically disappear overnight, inequality would still persist because of the disparities in qualifications that resulted from this historical underinvestment. Employers might not discriminate explicitly on the basis of race, but they would still prefer candidates with more education and experience, advantages that Black Americans had long been denied. Therefore, she contended that achieving racial equality required not only ending discrimination but also making deliberate and large-scale investments in Black education and training to remedy the economic damage of the past.

Thus, Bergmann explained a vicious cycle created by the combination of discrimination and poverty. For generations, Black Americans had been excluded from schools, jobs, and institutions that built skills and experience. Because they had been kept poor, they lacked the means to invest in themselves, thus perpetuating their disadvantage. She distinguished between two forms of discrimination: one based purely on race, which could be eliminated by law, and another based on qualifications, which could only be corrected through investment in human capital. Ending prejudice without addressing this second form of discrimination, she argued, would still have left Black Americans at a disadvantage because they would not have had the same preparation for high-paying and high-productivity occupations.

Furthermore, according to Bergmann, there are two kinds of inequality: immediate and long-term.

The former can be corrected immediately if employers stop discriminating. In fact, there were many qualified Black workers who were excluded from good jobs solely because of their race. Bergmann pointed to examples where employers who decided to hire Black workers found no difficulty in locating capable candidates. Department stores, banks, and supermarkets, when pressured to do so, were able to employ well-spoken and competent Black clerks, tellers, and cashiers. Similarly, many Black workers could have served as foremen if given the chance. The problem, Bergmann insisted, was not a lack of qualified Black workers but rather the unwillingness of white employers to give them opportunities.

The second category included occupations that required substantial formal training and long on-the-job experience, such as medicine, law, or executive management, where equal representation could not be achieved quickly. These professions demanded years of education and development, and because Black Americans had been systematically excluded from them for generations, correcting these inequalities would require sustained investment over time. Education, Bergmann argued, lay at the core of this investment. Using 1960 census data, she showed that white men aged 25 or older had completed an average of 10 years of schooling, while nonwhite men averaged only 7.3 years, a difference of nearly three years. This educational gap represented a major component of the total human capital deficit. Moreover, because nearly 80 percent of Black Americans had been born in the Southeast, where public education spending was notoriously low, the quality of schooling was also inferior.[1]

[1] In 1963, southern states spent an average of $305 per pupil per year, compared with $473 elsewhere, and earlier decades revealed even starker disparities. In 1929–30, most southeastern states spent less than half the national average on education, and under segregation, the gap between white and Black schools widened further. In 1952, southern states spent $165 per white pupil and only $115 per Black pupil, and in 1940, the figures were $50 and $22 respectively. These decades of unequal funding meant that generations of Black children received a poorer education, leaving them ill-prepared for well-paying jobs. Bergmann estimated the value of these 'missing' years of education and the lower quality of schooling at roughly $460 per year per person. When multiplied by the 4.7 million Black men over 25 in 1960, this amounted to a total educational investment deficit of about $7 billion, a conservative estimate that excluded the costs of lost college education or vocational training.

Beyond education, Bergmann identified the lack of work experience as another major source of inequality. Even when Black workers achieved the same educational level as whites, they were often confined to low-skill jobs with little chance for advancement. Using income data by age, education, and race, she demonstrated that white college graduates typically saw their earnings rise by about $6400 between ages 25 and 54, while Black college graduates saw an increase of only about $1000 over the same span. This gap could not be explained by education alone. It reflected the limited opportunities for Black workers to gain experience that translated into higher pay. A white worker with similar education might have moved from operative to supervisor, while a Black worker might have spent his entire career in a menial position.[2]

Combining the educational and experiential gaps, Bergmann estimated a total shortfall of $50 billion in the human capital of Black Americans compared with whites. This estimate, she emphasized, was more than an abstract number: it represented a tangible economic loss to both the Black population and the nation as a whole. The underdevelopment of millions of people's skills and capacities meant lower productivity, less innovation, and slower national growth. She described this situation as a kind of debt that American society owed to Black Americans, a moral and economic obligation to repair the damage done by centuries of exclusion. To address it, Bergmann proposed a two-part approach. For younger generations, the focus needed to be on preventing further underinvestment through better schools, health care, and access to jobs that built skills and experience. For older generations, who had already been deprived of opportunities to gain education or training, the government should provide income supplements to compensate for their disadvantage.

Bergmann's approach included all areas where human capital was formed, i.e., schools, workplaces, health systems, and homes. Education provided the foundation, workplaces developed skills through experience, health services maintained productivity, and family environments shaped work habits and attitudes. Effective policy, she argued, had to act on all these fronts. The goal was providing not charity but investment aimed at

[2] Bergmann calculated the capitalized value of work experience for both groups: $13,912 for white men and $4049 for Black men, a difference of nearly $9900 per person. When applied nationally, this represented a deficiency of about $42 billion in the experience-based human capital of Black men.

building the productive potential of an entire segment of the population that had been systematically neglected.

In conclusion, Bergmann reframed racial inequality as a question of national investment and economic efficiency. The $50 billion human capital gap she identified was both a measure of the harm that had been done to Black Americans as well as an indicator of the potential gains that could be achieved, by investing in their education and training and unlocking vast reserves of human talent and productivity. Equality, in Bergmann's view, was not only a matter of justice; it was also sound economic policy. The nation's prosperity depended on developing all its citizens, and only by committing to rebuild the human capital denied to Black Americans could the United States realize its full potential.

Between the 1970s and the 1980s, Bergmann publicly emerged as a leading advocate for women's economic equality. On March 23, 1975, Isabelle Shelton reported in *The Washington Star* that Bergmann viewed women's lack of money as their main problem and suggested lobbying to give women access to money through organized systems, such as tithing, as a means to empower women economically (Shelton 1975a). Shortly thereafter, on April 16, 1975, Shelton reported Bergmann's activism in the National Commission on International Women's Year (IWY) and her efforts to prioritize the Equal Rights Amendment (ERA).[3] Within the Commission's meetings, Bergmann urged the Commission to make enforcement of existing anti-discrimination laws its top priority. She criticized current enforcement for firms holding federal contracts as "a mockery", and suggested working with Black groups to protect job rights for both women and minorities, while other delegates recommended extending protections to Spanish Americans and other minority groups.[4]

[3] At its first meeting, held at the Pan American Health Organization headquarters, the commission voted to make ERA ratification its "major commitment". Alan Alda and Rep. Margaret Heckler were appointed co-chairmen of a committee tasked with communicating the commission's work to states with upcoming ERA votes, including Florida, Illinois, Missouri, and North Carolina. The ERA, passed by Congress in 1972 and ratified by 34 states at the time, required four more ratifications to become law. Senator Birch Bayh, D-Ind., introduced the resolution and urged commission members to counter misinformation spread by opponents, including Phyllis Schlafly.

[4] Additional topics slated for discussion included federal child development programs, women's health, concerns of disadvantaged women and elderly women, and media representation of women. Alan Alda offered to facilitate meetings with directors of major television networks, and abortion was discussed as a potential position the commission might take (Shelton 1975b).

In 1973, Bergmann testified three times before the Joint Economic Committee of Congress.

The first occasion was covered in *The New York Times* article "Top Nixon Economists Say Job Bias Reduces Women's Wages by 10 to 20%", written by journalist Eileen Shanahan, who reported on congressional hearings that exposed the persistence of gender discrimination in pay. Testifying before the Joint Economic Committee, Bergmann challenged the Nixon administration's own Council of Economic Advisers, chaired by Herbert Stein and Marina Whitman, who had estimated that gender discrimination accounted for only 10 to 20 percent of the wage gap between men and women. Bergmann countered that the most recent studies showed the differential to be far greater, arguing that the administration had relied on inconsistent data drawn from mismatched surveys. She also accused the government of complacency toward women's unemployment and dismissed the claim that female labor-force reentrants were to blame for joblessness. Every woman who left a job, she observed, created a vacancy that should help another find work. Her testimony, which drew a sharp contrast with the official stance, positioned Bergmann as one of the few academic economists confronting the structural and political roots of women's economic inequality (Shanahan 1973).

The second occasion was covered by Leonard Silk's analytical report "Peers Give Nixon's Advisers Bad Reviews" (Silk, 1973), which surveyed some economists' responses to the 1973 *Economic Report of the President*. Among the harshest critics of the Nixon administration's economic advisers were Bergmann and Irma Adelman. Their critique appeared alongside those of other economists, such as Carl F. Christ of Johns Hopkins and David Meiselman of Virginia Polytechnic Institute. Although Bergmann praised the report's inclusion of women's issues, she deplored its silence on unemployment, poverty, and the economic difficulties of Black Americans. Silk's article portrayed Bergmann as a dissenting voice insisting that social and racial inequality was not peripheral but central to national economic health. Her stance aligned her with a generation of economists unwilling to accept the narrowing technocratic focus of policy analysis under Nixon.

The third occasion was summarized in Bergmann's report "A Policy Agenda for Women's Economic Problems", in which she urged a more rigorous child support enforcement by the government to ensure adequate support for children (Bergmann 1973). Bergmann identified two possible ways to improve the economic position of women: stopping discrimination in employment and improving arrangements for the financial support and physical care of children, given the rapidly growing share of families with children headed by single women and their higher incidence of poverty.

In addition to her testimonies before Congress, Bergmann was often involved in legal cases related to gender inequality. In 1976, she wrote a memorandum for the case *Wenzel v. Liberty Mutual*, a legal controversy initiated by actress Rita Wenzel, who filed a complaint alleging that the company's employee insurance benefits and maternity leave policies discriminated against women, in violation of Title VII of the Civil Rights Act of 1964. Wenzel sought injunctive relief, damages, costs, and attorneys' fees (Bergmann 1976).[5].

In her memorandum, Bergmann criticized the idea endorsed by the company's insurance plan, according to which women during pregnancy and child-rearing are usually covered by their husbands. She noted that the long-standing assumption that women would depend primarily on men's labor market income during their childbearing years was no longer valid, if it ever truly had been. She emphasized the growing economic importance of women's earnings, both for themselves and for their families. In fact, she presented data revealing that between 1950 and 1972, the proportion of married women who worked outside the home rose dramatically from 24 to 42 percent. By the 1970s, a large and increasing number of women of working age was heavily dependent on their own wages was raising children without the financial support of a

[5] Wetzel and others (Respondents), filed a complaint in district court in which they asserted that the Petitioner, Liberty Mutual Insurance Company's (Petitioner), had employee insurance benefits and maternity leave regulations that discriminated against women in violation of Title VII of the Civil Rights Act of 1964 (the Act). Respondents filed a complaint in district court in which they asserted that Petitioner's employee insurance benefits and maternity leave regulations discriminated against women in violation of the Act. After extensive discovery, Respondents moved for partial summary judgment only as to the issue of liability. Finding no issues of material fact in dispute, the district court ruled in favor of Respondents on the issue of Petitioner's liability under the Act. However, Respondents did not receive all of the relief they had prayed for, including an injunction, damages, and attorney's fees. Petitioner appealed to the Court of Appeals for the Third Circuit. That court held that it had jurisdiction over Petitioner's appeal under 28 U.S.C. Section: 1291, and affirmed the judgment of the district court on the merits. Retrieved October 24, 2025, from https://www.casebriefs.com/blog/law/civil-procedure/civil-procedure-keyed-to-yeazell/appeal/liberty-mutual-insurance-co-v-wetzel-2/

husband or alimony, whether as single, divorced, or widowed mothers, and many households, including those headed by married couples, relied substantially on women's earnings.

For these women, the continuity of income was crucial to maintaining stability and independence. Any interruption in earnings, especially due to maternity, could have devastating financial consequences. Without guaranteed paid leave or income protection during pregnancy and childbirth, many women were forced into untenable choices: turning to welfare, which often entailed loss of privacy and social stigma, or resorting to abortion, which carried potential health risks and posed deep moral or religious conflict.

According to Bergmann, the exclusion of pregnancy from insurance coverage, such as in the case of Liberty Mutual's policies, which treated pregnancy as a voluntary condition rather than a legitimate work-related risk, were discriminatory. Such policies, she argued, were inherently discriminatory practices, since they penalized women for their biological role in reproduction. Bergmann concluded that employers should not be free to treat pregnancy differently from other temporary medical conditions. Protecting women's right to income continuity during maternity was essential not only for economic fairness but also for personal dignity, health, and family stability. Her argument reflected a broader call for equal treatment of women in the workplace and for public policies that recognized their dual roles as workers and mothers. As she wrote:

> A decision to allow employers to treat pregnancy as different from other temporary disabilities will make it easier for employers to continue to pose barriers in the way of women's entry into certain job categories, using special rules relating to pregnancy as a vehicle for excluding them. Such exclusions would allow the continuation of conditions which damage women's incentives to undergo training or education for such positions and the continuance of conditions which result in women (and men) having a restricted range of occupational choice, with all this meaning, in terms of reduced productivity, reduced satisfaction on the job, as well as unequal pay and status. (Bergmann 1976, p. 19)

In 1979, Bergmann testified before the Task Force on Social Security and Women of the Select Committee on Aging in the U.S. House of Representatives. On that occasion, she presented a deeply reasoned analysis of how the social security system affects women, and how reforms to that system could better serve their interests by promoting gender equality

(Bergmann 1979). Bergmann's testimony was both an economic and feminist critique of the way social security had been structured, a system designed around the male breadwinner model, which she argued left many women economically dependent and socially disadvantaged especially in old age. Her central concern was that any reforms to social security should not only improve women's immediate financial situation, but also advance the broader feminist goals of equal opportunity and dignity for all, regardless of sex.

Bergmann began by observing that the economic and social roles of women and men were changing, and that the social security system was failing to adapt to these transformations. The system's design, rooted in mid-twentieth-century assumptions about family structure and work, still treated women primarily as dependents rather than as independent workers. Because women often experienced career interruptions due to childbearing, caregiving, or discrimination, they tended to have lower lifetime earnings than men and therefore received lower benefits. Moreover, because women live longer than men on average, they were more likely to spend many years in retirement, often widowed or living alone, and dependent on a limited or derivative income source. For these reasons, Bergmann stressed that reform was not simply a question of fairness, but of economic survival, for millions of women.

However, she warned that not all reforms benefit all women equally, and policymakers must consider the casualties of a reform as well as its beneficiaries. Women are not a homogeneous group: their life experiences, marital histories, and employment patterns vary widely, and so benefits for one group may disadvantage another. For example, a reform that increases benefits for homemakers might help those who have never worked outside the home, but could simultaneously discourage women from entering or remaining in the workforce. This, she argued, would run counter to feminist aims. Reforms that make it more "economically and psychologically comfortable" for women to remain housewives would, in her view, reinforce traditional gender roles and slow the movement toward equality.

To clarify how reforms might better serve women's interests, Bergmann examined the two competing rationales underlying social security. The first, which she called the "fringe benefit" rationale, views social security as a kind of employment-based insurance, something workers earn through their labor. Under this model, social security is a reward for paid work and is funded through payroll contributions that directly tie benefits to individual earnings. The second rationale, which she called the "universal entitlement" rationale, conceives of social security as a guarantee that all elderly people, regardless of their work histories, should have a minimum income sufficient to live with dignity.

The tension between these two perspectives, Bergmann argued, lay at the heart of many inequities in the current system. Since the Social Security Act's inception, in the 1930s, policymakers had leaned heavily toward the fringe benefit model. By framing benefits as "earned", they sought to distinguish social security from welfare programs, which were stigmatized as "handouts" for the undeserving poor. This political framing made social security more acceptable to the public but came at a cost: it institutionalized gender biases. Because women were less likely to work steadily in paid employment and more likely to earn lower wages, the system treated them as dependents, granting wives, widows, and mothers benefits only through their husbands' earnings records.

Bergmann pointed out that this structure reflected and reinforced the traditional division of labor between men and women. Men's work in the paid economy was rewarded with "earned" social security benefits, while women's unpaid labor in the home was treated as economically invisible. Even though many women contributed indirectly to the family's well-being, by raising children, managing households, or supporting their husbands' careers, they were excluded from direct recognition as earners. This dependency model, she argued, not only devalued women's contributions but also left them vulnerable to poverty in old age if they divorced, remained single, or outlived their husbands without independent benefits.

While the rhetoric of the social security system emphasized fairness and the idea that benefits were a return on contributions, Bergmann noted that, in practice, the program already contained elements of universal entitlement. Spousal and survivor benefits, minimum benefit provisions, and other redistributive features demonstrated a quiet acknowledgment that older Americans, especially women, needed some guaranteed income regardless of their work histories. Nonetheless, these protections were inconsistently applied and insufficiently robust. Bergmann urged Congress to recognize this inconsistency openly and to move more decisively toward a universal entitlement model.

She warned that maintaining the 'fringe benefit' rationale as the dominant framework produced several undesirable effects. First, it tied the financing of social security exclusively to the payroll tax, which disproportionately burdened low- and middle-income workers while exempting earnings above a certain ceiling. This made the system regressive, placing a heavier relative burden on those least able to pay. Second, the system's design excluded unpaid homemakers and part-time workers from full participation, perpetuating the notion that only paid labor deserved social protection. Third, it reinforced the ideology of dependency, granting benefits to women primarily through their husbands' earnings records rather than recognizing their independent contributions.

For Bergmann, the moral and practical solution was clear: social security should evolve into a system that guarantees universal entitlement to a minimum income in old age. Such a shift would not only address the economic vulnerability of elderly women, but also affirm the principle that all citizens deserve dignity and security as a right, not merely as a reward for labor market participation. She recognized that this would require rethinking the system's financing, potentially through general revenues rather than payroll taxes, and confronting the political resistance to expanding social security's redistributive character.

Bergmann concluded her testimony with a powerful appeal for reform, grounded in both economic justice and feminist principles. She argued that the United States could not achieve true gender equality while maintaining a system that treated women as economic appendages of men rather than independent contributors. The goal of social security reform, she maintained, should not simply be to address inequities within the existing structure, but to reorient the system toward inclusivity, fairness, and universality, by ensuring that aging women, whether they had worked for wages, cared for families, or done both, would be protected from poverty and dependence in their later years.

Summing up, Bergmann's testimony offered both a critique of the past and a vision for the future. She recognized the historical reasons why social security had evolved as it did, but insisted that it must evolve alongside social reality. Women's roles in the economy were changing, and so, she argued, must be the nation's most important social insurance program. The debate over social security, she argued, was not just about technical adjustments to funding formulas or benefit levels, it was about redefining the moral foundation of social protection in a way that affirmed equality, independence, and human dignity for all.

In 1981, she testified again before the Joint Economic Committee of Congress about the economic situation of the time when inflation and unemployment were both urgent national problems (Bergmann 1981a). On that occasion, she delivered a detailed critique of the so-called supply-side economics that was dominating Washington's economic policy debate, and urged policymakers to move beyond it to find alternative economic strategies.

Bergmann began by acknowledging the complexity of the economic problems facing the United States at the dawn of the 1980s. The nation, she noted, was afflicted by multiple problems that economists only partially understood and for which there were no quick or painless cures. The possible economic resolution, however, was being distorted by the ideological rhetoric of supply-side economists, who claimed that massive tax cuts, reduced business taxation, and deregulation would unleash productivity and growth while curbing inflation. Bergmann cautioned that these measures, though appealing in theory, require careful scrutiny because they promise much but could easily yield harmful side effects and unintended social consequences.

Bergmann placed the supply-side approach within a long intellectual tradition. Since Adam Smith's *Wealth of Nations* in 1776, the central premise of classical school of political economy had been that the economy's supply side, i.e., its capacity to produce goods and services, was the key driver of growth and employment. This tradition, she recalled, was encapsulated in Say's Law, i.e., the idea that supply creates its own demand. According to this view, the government should focus on removing obstacles to production, rather than stimulating demand. Bergmann reminded the Committee that this philosophy had dominated economic thought until the Great Depression of the 1930s exposed its limitations. In response, the Keynesian or demand-side school of thought emerged, arguing that recessions stemmed from insufficient demand and that government spending and fiscal policy could be used to restore full employment.

Bergmann explained that while Keynesians did not ignore the importance of supply, they had in practice assumed the opposite of Say's Law, believing that demand creates its own supply: if consumers and governments spent enough, production and employment would follow. Yet, by the late 1970s, confidence in demand-side policy had waned, largely because it seemed ill-equipped to deal with the new phenomenon of stagflation, i.e., a combination of high unemployment and high inflation. Policymakers were now caught in a dilemma: traditional Keynesian tools to increase spending risked worsening inflation, while opposite measures to curb inflation exacerbated unemployment. This confusion, Bergmann noted, had created fertile ground for the reemergence of supply-side thinking.

She then examined each major supply-side proposal in turn, beginning with the call for across-the-board cuts in personal income taxes. Supply-siders argued that such cuts would stimulate work effort, savings, and investment, thereby increasing output and lowering prices. Bergmann challenged this claim, pointing to the precedent of the 1964 tax cut, enacted under the Kennedy and Johnson administrations. Following that tax cut, the economy had indeed expanded, and federal revenues eventually rose. However, Bergmann argued that this growth had not resulted from an increased incentive to work, as supply-siders claimed, but rather from a boost to consumer demand at a time when the economy still had considerable slack. Businesses had responded by hiring more workers and utilizing idle capacity, not because workers were more motivated, but because consumers were buying more. The 1964 experience, she contended, was better understood through a Keynesian lens, as an instance of demand creating its own supply, rather than as proof of supply-side effectiveness.

While Bergmann acknowledged that a tax cut might help reduce unemployment, she warned that it would likely worsen the federal deficit, which in turn could fuel inflation. Given these mixed effects, she argued that a large across-the-board income tax cut should not be included in the policy package at that time.

Her second target was the proposal to cut taxes on business profits, often through accelerated depreciation allowances or investment tax credits. Promoters claimed that such measures would encourage investments, boost productivity, and thereby moderate inflation. Bergmann was skeptical. She cited empirical studies of the investment tax credit in effect between 1963 and 1969, which found little to no measurable impact on overall investment levels. Even if such tax incentives succeeded in modestly increasing productivity, she argued, the effects on inflation would be minimal and delayed.

To illustrate this point, Bergmann referred to an estimate by Lyle Gramley of the Federal Reserve Board, who projected that investment incentives costing the Treasury $25 billion per year might increase productivity growth by only 0.4 percentage points after several years. Even under optimistic assumptions, this would translate into perhaps a 1 percent reduction in the inflation rate, a negligible gain given that inflation was running at 11 to 12 percent. By this logic, she concluded, supply-side remedies would take between 12 and 30 years to bring inflation under control.

Moreover, Bergmann emphasized that the distributional effects of such policies were regressive. Tax cuts for corporations and investors would disproportionately benefit the wealthy, since dividend income and capital gains were heavily concentrated among high-income households. According to the most recent IRS data, she cited, only about 1.6 percent of taxpayers earned more than $50,000 annually, yet they received the majority of dividend income. A $25 billion annual tax reduction for businesses would thus primarily enrich a small elite while doing little to help ordinary workers or consumers.

Bergmann also criticized the third major supply-side prescription, i.e., the call for widespread deregulation of business. Promoters argued that government rules and restrictions were stifling efficiency and innovation. Bergmann acknowledged that poorly designed regulation could have negative effects, but she warned against a wholesale dismantling of protections that served important public purposes. Deregulation, she suggested, might benefit certain industries or large firms while harming consumers and workers. Furthermore, it offered no guarantee of lower prices or greater economic stability.

In conclusion, Bergmann rejected the three central claims of supply-side economics by arguing that its proposed tax and regulatory policies would not deliver the promised results of faster growth or lower inflation and would instead exacerbate inequality and fiscal imbalance.

As an alternative measure, she advocated for a more balanced program that would combine a serious effort to reduce the federal deficit with measures to preserve employment and social protection. Sound economic policy, she insisted, required recognizing the complexity of the nation's economic problems and avoiding simplistic solutions dressed up in ideological slogans. She concluded:

> I do not need to be told that President Reagan was not elected to carry out such program, but I believe that it would constitute the best and the safest attack on the economic problems on account of which the electorate rejected President Carter – inflation and unemployment. (Bergmann 1981a, p. 91)

Bergmann's remarks offered a counterpoint to the optimism of supply-side advocates and underscored the enduring importance of empirical analysis and social equity in economic policymaking. In her testimony, she acknowledged the need for policies that encouraged production and efficiency, while maintaining that these goals could not be achieved through tax cuts for the wealthy or deregulation alone. Instead, she insisted, a pragmatic mix of fiscal responsibility, employment initiatives, and social support was needed to confront the intertwined challenges of inflation, unemployment, and inequality.

Two years later, in October 1983, Bergmann was again asked to testify before the Joint Economic Committee of Congress, on the profound and ongoing changes in the roles of women and men in both the workplace and the family (Bergmann 1983a). On that occasion, she emphasized that society was living through a period of dramatic transformation in which the traditional boundaries separating male and female responsibilities were steadily eroding. As data revealed, each year, the distinctions between the roles of men and women were becoming less rigid, both in employment and in the domestic sphere. These changes, Bergmann argued, were affecting essential aspects of life, such as the work people perform, the income they earn, the structure of marriage, and the care and upbringing of children.

Drawing on data from the U.S. Bureau of the Census Publication American Women: Three Decades of Change Report, Bergmann acknowledged that the past several decades had brought significant progress for women. Their growing participation in the labor force, increased educational attainment, and expanded opportunities reflected a remarkable shift toward gender equality. Yet, she cautioned, the same data revealed persistent and serious problems, some of which were worsening. Discrimination in employment, economic insecurity among single-parent families, and the uneven distribution of domestic labor remained critical issues. Bergmann contended that these challenges required vigorous and sustained governmental intervention, not complacency.

At the heart of her testimony was the persistent problem of employment discrimination. Although women were entering careers in unprecedented numbers, Bergmann noted that they were still far from enjoying the fair and equal treatment promised under Title VII of the Civil Rights Act, which outlawed discrimination in hiring, promotion, and pay. Despite two decades of legal protection, the wage gap between men and women remained wide, and academic research consistently demonstrated that a significant portion of this disparity was attributable to discrimination rather than to differences in education or experience. Moreover, court rulings across the country had confirmed the persistence of biases, with numerous judgments finding employers guilty of discriminatory practices. Finally, occupational segregation as well as the concentration of women in certain low-paying jobs remained common and perpetuated inequality by reinforcing stereotypes about men's work and women's work.

Bergmann argued that this pattern of discrimination had become even more damaging given broader social trends, including rising divorce rates and the growing number of single-parent families. Women who supported themselves and their children without a partner were often confined to low-wage occupations, systematically denied access to better-paying jobs, and blocked from advancement opportunities. As a result, their children suffered from economic deprivation and inadequate care. The issue, therefore, was not merely one of fairness in employment but one of social justice and child welfare.

The expanding participation of women in the labor force, Bergmann explained, made the need to combat discrimination even more urgent. In her testimony, Bergmann explained her crowding hypothesis: as more women sought employment, many found themselves crowded into traditionally female occupations, such as teaching, clerical work, and nursing, because they were excluded, often illegally, from positions considered to be men's jobs (see Chapter 3). This overcrowding placed downward pressure on wages in those sectors, worsening women's economic position overall. To reverse these trends, Bergmann called for a renewed national campaign against employment discrimination based on sex, race, or national origin.

She criticized the federal government, particularly the then-current administration, for drastically reducing enforcement of anti-discrimination laws. According to Bergmann, the minimal efforts of prior administrations, whether Democratic or Republican, had already been inadequate, and the rollback of enforcement activity had rendered the situation pathetically low. What was needed, she insisted, was not a return to the weak standards of the past but a much more vigorous and sustained commitment to equity.

Bergmann outlined several elements essential to this renewed effort. She emphasized the necessity of restoring affirmative action requirements for employers, including the use of measurable goals and timetables to ensure progress. Enforcement agencies, she argued, needed to focus their resources strategically on large and influential employers whose practices set industry-wide standards. Government contractors found guilty of discrimination should face debarment, denying them access to federal contracts until they demonstrated compliance with equal opportunity laws. Finally, she urged Congress to allocate greater funding for enforcement agencies so they could fulfil their mandates effectively rather than symbolically.

Beyond employment discrimination, Bergmann addressed the issue of single parents, most of whom were women. She proposed stronger public policies to support these families, particularly through child care subsidies and effective enforcement of child support obligations. Without such measures, she warned, single mothers would continue to bear a disproportionate economic burden, limiting their ability to provide for their children and to participate fully in the labor market.

Bergmann also touched upon the need for structural reforms in the organization of work itself. She suggested that reducing the length of the workweek could help both men and women share family responsibilities more equitably. By shortening working hours and providing more flexibility, society could enable fathers and mothers alike to engage more fully in homemaking and childrearing, promoting genuine equality in both the domestic and professional spheres.

Summing up, Bergmann's testimony presented a vision of a society still struggling between the old and the new, between persistent patterns of discrimination and the promise of genuine equality. She portrayed gender equity not as a matter of individual adaptation but as a challenge to public policy and collective will. The progress women had achieved, she argued, was real and worth celebrating, but it was fragile and incomplete. Without active government intervention, through enforcement of civil rights laws, support for single parents, and policies promoting shared family responsibilities, the nation risked losing the momentum of the past decades. For Bergmann, the ongoing transformation of gender roles represented not only a social revolution but also a moral imperative, one that demanded courage, creativity, and commitment from policymakers and citizens alike. She concluded:

> There is no legislation or government commission or administration policy that could possibly be effective in sending women back into full time homemaking, or in lessening the number of divorces. On the other hand,

> there is much that the government should and can do to ease the transition to a world of gender equality. (Bergmann 1983a, p. 8)

In the same period, Bergmann was honored as Washington Woman Economist of the Year by the Washington Women Economists (see Chapter 2). As Cheryl Hogue recalled, Bergmann's primary concerns were the needs of single-parent families,[6] the unequal division of housework,[7] and the conviction that men should take a more equitable share of domestic labor, famously stating that being a housewife was "a terrible way to make a living" (Hogue 1985).

In 1993, Bergmann appeared at a House Subcommittee on Economic Development Hearing. The meeting was recorded by the C-SPAN Network.[8] It was the first in a series of hearings on short-term and long-term strategies for domestic spending aimed at boosting the national economy, given that the Bush administration was promoting the construction industry as a means to pump up the economy and reduce unemployment.

Bergmann was heard along with other economists. Her position was clear: she described the then-current state of the American economy as one of "medieval stagnation", arguing that the country was not in a vigorous recovery, despite the Bush administration's assumption that the recovery was just around the corner. According to Bergmann, the size of the deficit and the national debt were the result of the "shameless and irresponsible policies of the Reagan years". She predicted an extra year of stagnation with no vigorous signs of recovery. Therefore, she insisted that the case for more stimulus was stronger than ever: the benefit of acting now would be that people could go back to work and gain the extra output they produce, an output that would otherwise be lost. Furthermore, there was relatively little risk in providing immediate government stimulus for worthwhile projects, since private spending is very weak and

[6] Bergmann pointed out that roughly 20 percent of U.S. children lived in single-parent households, many of which experienced poverty even in affluent areas. Hence, she proposed assistance with childcare, training, employment, child support enforcement, and housing with integrated childcare facilities.

[7] Bergmann noted that more than half of American women had jobs outside the home, including 61 percent of mothers with children under age 18.

[8] Infrastructure Investment. January 15, 1993. Video available at: https://www.c-span.org/program/house-committee/infrastructure-investment/28845.

will not be crowded out as much as private investment, which is crucial for productivity growth. In fact, there will be little danger of crowding out private investment if the Federal Reserve plays its part in keeping interest rates low.

As for the downsides of stimulus, Bergmann listed two of them: in the short run, an increase in the deficit; in the long run, an increase in the national debt. As mentioned, the former should have little negative effect on the economy if the Fed restrains bond issuance. The latter is more serious, as the Treasury's increased interest payments detract from its ability to finance worthwhile projects with taxpayers' money. Higher interest costs increase the deficit, further accelerating the national debt. However, according to Bergmann, a temporary stimulus does not preclude adopting a long-term plan to reduce the deficit. Hence, she argued that it was a good time to raise income taxes on upper-income groups, which would have a minimal effect on demand.

Regarding what the stimulus package should include, Bergmann urged that the recovery program must include support for states and localities to avoid cuts in essential services, such as medical care, youth counseling, policing, assistance for the homeless, investments in public schools as well as in public housing. While past models of public housing have not been successful, the continuing need for affordable housing among low-income groups must be addressed. This approach, she insisted, would create jobs immediately.

Contrary to what the government wanted to do, long-term construction projects should be avoided. Bergmann was concerned about the construction industry's persistent exclusion of minorities and women from skilled jobs. In the construction industry, for instance, Black unemployment was around 12% at that time. A fair recovery policy must prioritize reducing minority unemployment and welfare dependency by opening job opportunities for all.

In 1996, Bergmann took part in another panel recorded by the C-SPAN Network, this time on affirmative action.[9] She pointed out that discussions of affirmative action often deal in generalities, while she preferred to talk in concrete examples. To illustrate her point, she presented the case of a business that has never hired an African American or a woman. Someone once told her such businesses do not exist,

[9] Affirmative Action Future, May 29, 1996. Video available at: https://www.c-span.org/program/public-affairs-event/affirmative-action-future/56734.

but she could prove otherwise by showing a full-page ad from *The New York Times* (published on April 9, 1996) featuring a top-rated restaurant that showed 36 waiters: not a single one was African American, and not a single one was a woman. Bergmann revealed that she had called the restaurant to ask whether, in its 60 years of operation, a Black person or a woman was hired. They said no. Bergmann strongly argued that this did not happen by chance, or by "color-blindness" or "gender-blindness". According to Bergmann, only race or gender-conscious action would be effective to solve this discrimination. In fact, lawsuits under the Civil Rights Acts of 1964 and 1991 are expensive, slow, and their outcomes uncertain. Furthermore, victims of discrimination often lack access to lawyers. So, she concluded:

> When we discuss affirmative action, we must be practical and deal with real situations. And when people talk about preferences, I ask: Who has the preferences now? Not women, not African Americans. The unfair preferences are already being given to others.

Bergmann's archive reveals that, between 1993 and 1994, she was involved in the Giant Food case, which began in 1972, when the National Organization for Women (NOW) and the Women's Legal Defense Fund (WLDF) filed a complaint with the Equal Employment Opportunity Commission (EEOC), on behalf of ten women managers in Giant's bakery department.[10] These women alleged wage discrimination, claiming they were paid less than other (male) managers, despite performing comparable managerial work. In 1993–1994, Bergmann supervised two student-led surveys examining sex segregation in four of Giant's managerial positions (Bergmann 1995). The studies found

[10] The United Food and Commercial Workers Union Local 400 was also named in the complaint, accused of complicity in the discriminatory pay practices. In 1976, after investigation, the EEOC issued a report confirming wage discrimination against bakery workers and broader sex discrimination in access to managerial positions at Giant Food. Eight years later, in 1984, a consent decree was signed, under which Giant Food agreed to pay $246,000 in compensation to affected women employees. The decree also required the company to enhance its affirmative action program, recruit female trainees for management positions, and establish measurable goals and timetables for the advancement of women into management. Francine Weiss, an attorney representing the union, was designated to oversee the enforcement of the decree's provisions. The decree appears to have expired around 1989.

that gender segregation persisted, and that women's representation in management had improved only marginally since 1972.

In May 1994, Bergmann reached out to Donna Lenhoff of the WLDF to discuss possible renewed action in this case. Lenhoff agreed and suggested scheduling a meeting that would include representatives from the union. The meeting took place on June 6, 1994, at the WLDF offices. Attendees included Barbara Bergmann, Donna Lenhoff, a WLDF staff member, C. James Lowthers (Secretary-Treasurer of Local 400), and Francine Weiss, who had been responsible for monitoring Giant's compliance with the 1984 decree.

During this meeting, Weiss and Lowthers both stated that they had received no discrimination complaints from Giant employees, implying satisfaction among women workers. Weiss emphasized her work on sexual harassment issues but acknowledged that she had known Giant was failing to meet its management goals for women; she had inquired but never pursued the matter further. Lowthers admitted that some jobs remained heavily sex-segregated; he cited, for example, the absence of women meat-cutters, and conceded that female bakery managers were still paid less than other managers. He also made racially insensitive remarks about the lack of Black employees in suburban stores, attributing it to 'blacks not liking to cross the river'.

Following this unsatisfactory meeting, Bergmann and Lenhoff corresponded to clarify the situation and plan next steps. On June 7, 1994, Bergmann wrote to Lenhoff listing data that needed to be gathered, such as the gender distribution of deli, meat, fish, and assistant managers; promotion processes; turnover rates; and reports that had been submitted under the consent decree. In this letter, Bergmann criticized the union's weak enforcement of the decree, describing its monitoring as 'derelict'. She noted that the union and Weiss had minimized the issue of sex segregation, excused Giant's lack of progress by blaming women's preferences, and failed to push for equal pay for bakery managers. Bergmann concluded that a new court order, with rigorous independent monitoring, would be necessary to make real progress.

On June 13, 1994, Bergmann wrote another letter to Donna Lenhoff and Judy Lichtman (also of the WLDF), reacting to a *Washington Post* article about a similar discrimination case at Lucky Stores. She urged the WLDF to help publicize the Giant case and involve legal organizations that could support new complainants. Bergmann expressed frustration at

WLDF's slow response, particularly its deference to the union, which she believed had failed to defend women's interests.

The correspondence continued over the summer. On July 12, 1994, Barbara Robinson, a management consultant collaborating with Bergmann, wrote to Donna Lenhoff before leaving for Europe. She emphasized the urgency of moving from the information-gathering phase to concrete legal action. Robinson proposed negotiating a new binding agreement requiring Giant to desegregate its workforce and pay for an external monitor, explicitly excluding the union from this role, which she believed had "sold the women down the river" previously. She anticipated that legal action and new plaintiffs might be required.

Subsequent efforts aimed to bring the issue to the EEOC once again. On November 4, 1994, Bergmann wrote to Ellen Vargyas at the EEOC's Office of Legal Counsel, referencing advice from Marcia Greenberger. In her letter, Bergmann summarized the history of the Giant case, the 1984 decree, and the 1993–94 survey results showing a lack of progress. She requested a meeting to discuss how the EEOC could reopen the case, and indicated she would follow up by phone.

Meanwhile, on the same date (November 4, 1994), Donna Lenhoff of WLDF wrote to Bergmann, stating that WLDF lacked the resources for a large-scale renewed effort. However, she would send a letter to the EEOC recommending a Commissioner's Charge, urging the agency to investigate Giant. Bergmann also wrote separately to the EEOC in support of this action.

By January 13, 1995, the matter had been referred to the EEOC's Baltimore District Office, where Bergmann and Robinson met with Issie Jenkins, the District Director, and her staff, including Barbara Veldhuizen, who specialized in systemic investigations. The EEOC staff expressed potential interest in investigating Giant but emphasized that they would need at least one formal complaint to proceed. Bergmann and Robinson agreed to look for a complainant.

Later, on March 13, 1995, Bergmann wrote to Avis Sanders of the Washington Lawyers' Committee for Civil Rights and Urban Affairs, enclosing the relevant documentation she had collected. Her letter explained that the project had originated as a student research assignment at American University and had evolved into an effort by the Economic Equity Group, a small informal coalition including Heidi Hartmann (Institute for Women's Policy Research), Mary Gray (American University), Sandra Tangri (Howard University), and Barbara Robinson.

The materials she sent included: the chronology of events; the 1984 consent decree; results of the 1993–94 telephone surveys; documentation showing Giant's failure to meet affirmative action goals; press clippings on Giant and similar cases; and employment data by race and sex from Giant's 1992 EEO-1 report.

In an October 18, 1995 confidential note to Barbara Robinson, another unnamed contact advised her to visit the Food Marketing Institute's library to review trade materials, annual reports, and industry coverage of the Giant and Lucky cases. The letter suggested that while the industry remained male-dominated, some departments, such as bakeries, had gained prestige over time, possibly giving Giant a defense that bakery jobs were no longer "dead-end" roles. The correspondent cautioned against circulating the note publicly, in order to protect the source.

The Giant Food case reflected the persistent failure of corporate, unions, and legal mechanisms to achieve gender equity in management and pay. Despite a formal EEOC-backed consent decree in 1984, Giant maintained significant sex segregation and wage disparities, particularly in its bakery division. Bergmann led renewed efforts, through research, correspondence, and coalition-building, to revive legal and public pressure on the company and its union. Her extensive letters to the WLDF, the EEOC, and allied advocates reveal her frustration with institutional inertia and her commitment to ensuring that women's equality in the workplace was not merely symbolic, but was enforced through concrete oversight and accountability.

As mentioned, Bergmann's interest in the Giant Food case was demonstrated by her participation in a panel on women and affirmative action, recorded at C-SPAN.[11] On that occasion she promoted affirmative action, noting that lawsuits are an expensive and often ineffective substitute, as the Giant Food case had revealed. She opened the floor by revealing that she did not know the session's title when she accepted to join it. When she found out that the title was "Sex, Lies, and Affirmative Action", she said: "I suspected I was being cast as the liar, but I'll take it as a joke". Then, she began to discuss the matter, by admitting that women made remarkable progress, thanks to talented men and women who fought not only to stop government discrimination, but also to push schools, colleges, and businesses to do the same. Nonetheless, she added, the question is not

[11] Women and Affirmative Action. December 13, 1996. Video available at: https://www.c-span.org/program/public-affairs-event/women-and-affirmative-action/60839.

whether there has been progress, but how much, and what policies we still need to solve the gender pay gap.

On that panel, a flyer was circulating among speakers. It claimed that gender pay gap was two cents. Bergmann noticed that the datum was misleading as it came from youth employment. She cited Paula England and her group, who found that the actual gender pay gap was 14–17%. Most of the gap appears in workers in their late 30s and 40s, when men begin to earn more.

Bergmann pointed out that these data were not about CEOs, who are 'rare birds', but about ordinary workers. In fact, the major problem was not the number of female CEOs, but the segregation of occupations. For example, she invited the audience to look at the New York Stock Exchange floor: all white men. She also cited a survey in North Carolina that found that 70% of workplaces lacked a colleague of the opposite sex. In craft occupations, 18% of workers were men, and only 2% were women. Many jobs, Bergmann noted, were controlled by unions which adopted exclusionary practices. For instance, apprenticeship programs, which provide good wages without requiring a college education, often discriminate against women. Bergmann continued by claiming that if we want women, especially single mothers, to raise their children decently, high-quality jobs must be accessible to them. Bergmann concluded by asserting that gender inequality in the labor market must be remedied by adopting a specific measure, she claimed "Quotas: let's be realistic!".

8.2 *The New York Times* Coverage

Across more than four decades of coverage in *The New York Times*, between mid-1970s and 2010, Bergmann's voice reflected her efforts to apply economic analysis to issues of inequality, welfare, and work, as well as the evolving national conversation on gender, labor, and public responsibility through reviews, policy commentary, published letters, and her weekly columns, written between 1981 and 1982. Bergmann's writings revealed her commitment to social justice, feminist economics, and the moral responsibilities of democratic governance. Here, they are presented in a chronological order. Published commentaries and discussions arising from Bergmann's articles are also included.

Bergmann's earliest intervention, a *Letter to the Editor*, published on July 17, 1974, came amid the Watergate scandal, when national confidence in political integrity was in crisis. Identifying herself as a Democrat who had often supported Republicans, Bergmann expressed profound disappointment at the party's willingness to defend President Richard Nixon, despite clear evidence of wrongdoing. She accused Republican members of Congress of 'buckling' under Nixon's pressure rather than upholding the rule of law, lamenting their complicity in obstruction of justice and the misuse of taxpayer funds. Her letter concluded with a declaration of moral disillusionment: unless 'decent Republicans' joined in impeaching Nixon, she could never again vote for one, no matter how deserving. For Bergmann, Watergate was not only a test of individual conscience but a test of the Republican Party's very right to survive as political integrity, she insisted, must outweigh party loyalty (Bergmann 1974a).

In her first article, "Economist, Poll Thy People" (Bergmann 1974b), Bergmann offered a sharp and self-critical reflection on the state of the economics profession that echoed her methodological writings against abstract theorizing and statistical fetishism that perpetuate unrealistic models treating people as mechanical optimizers, while ignoring how decisions are actually made (see Chapter 5). She began by noting that, judged by its own favored metric, i.e., market success, economics had flourished, and the discipline's prestige was expanding far faster than the world economy itself. Yet, paradoxically, economists' intellectual authority and public confidence were in decline. Bergmann recalled the optimism of the early 1960s, when economists such as Walter Heller, James Tobin, and Kermit Gordon, persuaded President Kennedy that macroeconomic fine-tuning could stabilize growth. Two decades later, she observed, that confidence had collapsed. The U.S. economy was suffering from chronic instability, and economists had proven unable to diagnose or cure the malaise. Their prescriptions, she suggested, resembled patent medicine, eagerly sold despite little evidence of efficacy. Competing ideological flavors of economic advice, conservative and liberal alike, ensured that politicians can always find a credentialed economist to legitimize any policy. Thus, the profession's prosperity has been perversely secured by its very failure to produce cumulative and reliable knowledge.

As mentioned, between 1981 and 1982, Bergmann regularly wrote the *Economic Affairs* columns for *The New York Times* Sunday Business Section by offering a lucid and forceful commentary on the moral, political, and structural tensions of U.S. economic life during the early Reagan years. Her columns set the tone for what would become one of the most incisive economic commentaries of the period. She challenged both conservative orthodoxy and the complacencies of mainstream economics, by insisting that public policy be judged by its impact on ordinary people rather than on abstract theories.

In "The Economics of Expectations" (Bergmann 1981b), Bergmann explored the rising fascination with expectations in economic policy-making. She criticized the Reagan administration's tendency to substitute psychological management, manipulating public moods and market confidence, for promoting its fiscal policy. For Bergmann, this faith in collective optimism risked turning the government into a 'therapist for markets rather than a steward of real resources'.

A month later, in "A Recession Could Put Reagan in a Box" (Bergmann 1981c), she anticipated the economic and political crisis that would soon define Reagan's presidency. With the administration locked into large tax cuts favoring the wealthy, a ballooning deficit, and an anti-inflationary stance that discouraged expansion, Bergmann predicted that Reagan would find himself trapped between conservative fiscal dogma and the social costs of deep unemployment. Her piece presciently framed the dilemma that would haunt Reagan's first term: how to sustain political credibility while unemployment soared past 8 percent.

In "Relax, Social Security Is Doing Its Job" (Bergmann 1981d), she countered alarmist claims from the Reagan administration that social security was nearing bankruptcy. For Bergmann, social security was not an economic liability but a moral achievement sustained by government authority and collective willingness to protect the elderly from poverty.[12] Hence, she rejected alarmism and clarified that the system was not a private pension fund but a public commitment. Furthermore, in response to economist Martin Feldstein's claim that social security discouraged private savings, she called the trade-off worthwhile, as ensuring collective security was more important than maximizing private wealth.

In response to Bergmann's article Barbara Daniel wrote a letter titled "Pro Bergmann", published on November 29 (Daniel 1981), praising Bergmann's defense of social security and emphasizing that the program's funding through payroll taxes, matched by employer contributions, protects it from the kind of political interference that has undermined other federal programs. She noted that this financing

[12] She credited social security with reducing the proportion of poor elderly Americans from 25 percent in 1970 to 16 percent in 1980, and recommended only modest reforms, such as taxing benefits for high-income recipients.

structure gives contributors a strong sense of ownership and political influence, making the system resilient to change. Daniel argued that maintaining high employment is essential for the program's continued strength since payroll contributions from active workers sustain benefits for retirees. Hence, she urged voters to support policies and representatives committed to economic stability, asserting that such measures would ensure a secure and sustainable pension program.

A few weeks later, James McNabb replied with a letter titled "Whose Security?" published on December 20 (McNabb 1981). McNabb strongly disagreed with Bergmann's ideas and Daniel's optimism, arguing that social security was not financially secure but rather operating 'hand-to-mouth'. He warned that the system is bound to face inevitable bankruptcy due to an imbalance between contributors and beneficiaries, a situation worsened by demographic and economic trends. McNabb dismissed the idea that higher employment alone could stabilize the system. Instead, he called for a deeper structural reform and policies that would encourage capital investment and personal savings, insisting that long-term viability depended on fostering productivity rather than consumption.

Together, these letters illustrate a sharp ideological divide that mirrored broader national debates during the early Reagan years: inspired by Bergmann, Daniel defended social security as a politically protected, pay-in/pay-out system sustained by collective responsibility, while McNabb saw it as an unsustainable structure requiring fundamental overhaul and a shift toward market-based incentives.

Bergmann's column "Charity Needs Coercion" (Bergmann 1981e) was focused on Reaganomics too. She challenged President Reagan's call for volunteerism to replace federal social programs that were cut under his administration. Bergmann argued that the push for private charity as a substitute for government aid implicitly acknowledges that these cuts will create real hardship, yet ignores the economic and social realities that make voluntary action insufficient. Bergmann explained that many government responsibilities, such as ensuring clean air and water, workplace safety, and equal employment, cannot be replicated by private initiative. Even in areas where volunteer work already exists, like health, education, and welfare, Bergmann maintained that private efforts lack the capacity to meet public needs.

Drawing on economic theory, she referenced Mancur Olson's argument about 'the free rider problem', noting that individuals acting in rational self-interest are unlikely to contribute enough to collective causes voluntarily. Without the coercive power of taxation, she wrote, charity inevitably falls far short of what is required. Bergmann also pointed out that the costs of raising voluntary funds are high, with many charities spending most of their income on fundraising rather than relief. Moreover, she observed that the traditional social institutions that once encouraged giving, particularly religious communities, have weakened over time.

Compounding the issue, she criticized the Reagan administration for fostering hostility toward recipients of aid, portraying them as undeserving, thereby further discouraging charitable generosity. Ultimately, Bergmann concluded that relying on volunteerism to replace government welfare is both impractical and unjust. Coercive taxation, she argued, is not a flaw but a necessary mechanism through which society translates compassion into action. While she conceded that federal programs may need reform, she insisted that expecting private charity to fill the gap is "asking for the impossible", helping neither the poor nor the volunteers who try to respond.

Summing up, Bergmann argued that private charity could never adequately replace the social programs being cut by the Reagan administration and that reliance on voluntarism masked the need for collective, tax-supported provision. Bergmann's article provoked a strong reaction from leaders of the nonprofit sector, which was published under the title "Bergmann's Coercion", in *Letters to the Business Editor*, December 27, 1981. The letter, signed collectively by representatives of major philanthropic organizations, accused her of misrepresenting "the true nature of American philanthropy". While they conceded her point that voluntarism could not fully offset federal retrenchment, they rejected her implication that private giving was inefficient or insubstantial. They noted that 31 percent of Americans volunteered at least two hours a week, and 83.7 percent of charitable contributions came from individuals, totalling nearly $40 billion in 1980. They insisted that most nonprofit institutions spent less than 15 percent of their income on fundraising, contradicting Bergmann's claim that voluntary organizations often absorbed most of their revenue in overhead costs.

Bergmann's critics framed her as dismissive of civic generosity, a charge she would continue to face whenever she emphasized structural, rather than moral, explanations for inequality.

In "An Affirmative Look at Hiring Quotas" (Bergmann 1982a), Bergmann shifted focus from macroeconomic policy to labor equity.

Responding to detractors of affirmative action, she defended hiring quotas as pragmatic tools serving both justice and business efficiency. Properly implemented, she argued, quotas could reduce discrimination suits, improve workplace morale, and better align firms with a diversifying labor market. She cited corporate leaders, like Time Inc.'s J. Richard Munro, to show that affirmative action, far from undermining merit, could enhance performance and fairness simultaneously.

Her "Here Is Why You Lost Your Jobs" (Bergmann 1982b) took the form of an open letter to a laid-off worker named Joe. Bergmann's letter condemned the administration's anti-inflationary obsession, which had deliberately induced a recession by tightening the money supply. Bergmann ridiculed the President's claim that joblessness resulted from laziness or poor motivation, contrasting official rhetoric with the lived misery of the unemployed. The letter's sharpest irony lay in her observation that those who suffered most from economic discipline were least responsible for inflation and least protected against its consequences.

In "Investment Is the Business of Business" (Bergmann 1982c), Bergmann addressed liberal proposals for a National Investment Authority designed to steer private investment. Although sympathetic to its egalitarian aims, she cautioned that centralized investment planning would likely be captured by political interests and hampered by inefficiency. True reform, she emphasized, required the government to do better what it already needed to do: fight poverty, control pollution, and improve health and safety, while leaving risk-taking and innovation to private enterprise. Her pragmatism was summed up in her line: "The motto should be more of the same, only done better".

In "Lobbying: Shakedown on Capitol Hill" (Bergmann 1982d), Bergmann denounced the explosion of lobbying and political action committees as a corruption of the democratic process. The proliferation of special interests, 'like cockroaches in dirty kitchens', was blamed for distorting fiscal priorities and driving up deficits. She concluded that only public financing of congressional campaigns could restore rational policy-making.

Bergmann's column, "It's Single Parents Who Need Help", dealt with single-parent families, particularly those headed by women (Bergmann 1982e). She argued that these families performed essential social labor, such as raising children, while bearing unfair economic burdens. One in six U.S. families with children, she noted, was led by a single parent, yet the child-support system failed them through weak enforcement and bureaucratic neglect. Proposing a federal payroll-deduction system modeled on France's, Bergmann called for guaranteed payments to custodial parents, subsidized child care, and equal employment opportunities. Here, her vision of welfare reform, not punitive but enabling, emerged: she sought a system that made work and stability possible, rather than one that punished dependency.

Just weeks later, in "A Threat Ahead from Word Processors" (Bergmann 1982f), Bergmann turned her attention to technology's gendered effects on the labor market. She warned that the spread of word processors would eliminate clerical jobs, most of them held by women, and exacerbate economic inequality unless policies were enacted to support retraining and job transitions. Though she predicted that 'keyboarding' might eventually lose its low-status stigma as managers began typing their own documents, the overall shift risked deepening poverty and dependency among displaced female workers. In Bergmann's analysis automation was not socially neutral but shaped by gender, class, and power.

In her letter published on June 13, 1982, to *The New York Times* Business Editor, Willoughby Ann Walshe, editor of *Word Processing and Information Systems* magazine, responded sharply to Bergmann's earlier column. Walshe accused Bergmann of spreading misinformation and creating an unduly pessimistic impression about the technological and occupational consequences of word processing. Rather than seeing automation as a destroyer of clerical jobs, Walshe emphasized its potential to expand opportunities for office workers by offering better pay and clearer career paths. She argued that Bergmann's focus on job loss overlooked how electronic office equipment was transforming work processes in positive ways, requiring employees merely to update their skills rather than fear displacement. Walshe also rejected Bergmann's claim that proofreading software would make skilled typists obsolete, and disputed Bergmann's data.[13] Walshe insisted that such programs cannot catch all errors, and thus spelling and grammar expertise remain

[13] She claimed that the estimated 2.5 million electronic workstations likely included non–text-editing equipment such as typewriters, microcomputers, and data terminals, and that the true number of dedicated word-processing machines is closer to 500,000. She further corrected Bergmann's pricing figures, noting that a full business setup, including a display screen, dual floppy drives, and a high-quality printer, costs between $7000 and $8000, roughly double Bergmann's estimate.

essential. Moreover, she argued that executives are unlikely to type their own correspondence, both because many lack typing skills and because social norms discourage high-status professionals from performing clerical tasks. Walshe called Bergmann's portrayal of automation as a source of 'increased poverty and dependency among women' both unfounded and contrary to lived experience. In her view, thousands of office workers have benefited from word processing, finding their work more enjoyable and better paid than before.

Bergmann's "A Vicious Cycle of High Rates" (Bergmann 1982g) examined the persistence of extraordinarily high interest rates amid recession. She dismantled fashionable theories that blamed inflationary 'expectations', arguing instead that the Federal Reserve had trapped the economy in a self-reinforcing spiral: high rates fueled deficits, which in turn sustained high rates. Bergmann insisted that only a measured expansion of credit could break the cycle.

In "Where Deregulation Makes No Sense" (Bergmann 1982h), she turned her analytical lens on the nursing home industry, one of the Reagan Administration's targets for deregulation. She warned that privatizing the sector would expose vulnerable residents to neglect, noting the industry's dependence on public funds and its record of abuse. True efficiency, she wrote, depended on 'real oversight, not deregulation with a meat ax'.

In her "The Sound and Fury Over Poverty" (Bergmann 1982i), Bergmann criticized both liberal and conservative approaches to America's persistent poverty problem. Writing amid the deep recession of the early 1980s, Bergmann underscored the moral and economic urgency of addressing poverty, which affected 29 million Americans, including 12 million children, according to official data released by the Reagan administration. Yet, she argued, national debate on the issue remained shallow and polarized. Bergmann observed that liberals and conservatives alike resort to simplistic 'throw-money-at-'em' policies. Liberals, she wrote, tend to favor increased welfare benefits and cash transfers, which offer temporary relief but do little to address the root causes of poverty. Conservatives, on the other hand, advocate tax cuts for the wealthy in the name of job creation, while simultaneously insisting that the poor should 'pull up their socks'. Both parties, in her view, misunderstood the complex structural reasons why people remain poor, ranging from illness, poor education, racial and gender discrimination, and single parenthood, to regional economic decline.

Bergmann dismissed conservative claims that welfare recipients are no longer truly poor once noncash benefits like food stamps and Medicaid are counted. Such arguments, she wrote, ignored the continuing realities of unemployment, slum housing, underfunded schools, and social alienation. While she conceded that stricter welfare policies might push some individuals toward greater self-reliance, she warned that such austerity will only deepen the suffering of millions who are genuinely unable to help themselves. As an alternative to both liberal and conservative dogmas, Bergmann called for policies that expand opportunities for decent, self-sustaining work.

Central to her argument is the need for affirmative action, which she described as the only proven mechanism to open well-paid jobs to women and to Black and Hispanic workers, groups that, along with their children, make up roughly two-thirds of the non-aged poor. She contended that broader access to higher-paying employment would not only uplift these groups but also narrow the gap between low-wage and high-wage jobs across the economy. Bergmann also advocated for strict federal enforcement of child-support payments and experimentation with on-the-job training programs, both of which could help integrate the poor into productive employment. These measures, she argued, command broad bipartisan support and hold far greater promise for lasting progress than either increased welfare spending or tax breaks for the wealthy.

Her article, "The Sound and Fury Over Poverty", elicited a response from Catherine H. Powell, assistant professor at Trinity University (Powell 1982), who gently, but firmly, responded to Bergmann's argument, which claimed that affirmative action was "the only program anyone has thought of to make decently paid work open to women and to black and Hispanic men". Powell objected that Bergmann had overlooked "the most successful remedy ever tried: a public works program". Public employment, Powell argued, had long-term benefits for the economy and the quality of life if managed 'with care and sensitivity'. She envisioned projects from low-cost housing to waste recycling plants and mass transit systems, forms of socially useful work that could, in her view, dignify labor and strengthen communities. Powell's critique was not hostile. Rather, it reflected a shared commitment to public intervention but a different sense of how government action might best create opportunity. In the wake of Reagan-era austerity, both women sought to reimagine the role of the state, and Powell's focus on infrastructure and physical reconstruction complemented Bergmann's emphasis on social and distributive justice.

Just a week later, in her columns "Why the Football Union Can Hit Hard" (Bergmann 1982l), Bergmann coped with the dispute between football players and management, contending that athletes deserved a major share of the industry's revenue since fans paid to see them, not the owners. Her argument prompted an indignant response from Lawrence Serlin, who titled his letter "Author Fumbled" (Serlin 1982). Serlin accused Bergmann of 'sophistry', insisting that she ignored the owners' capital investment and entrepreneurial risk. Bergmann, he implied, misunderstood the economic balance between labor and capital in entertainment, by comparing football management to Broadway production. However, he argued, without the financial and organizational genius of owners, even the best players would fail.

Later that year, in "Who's to Blame for the Economy?" (Bergmann 1982m), Bergmann confronted the administration's narrative that inflation had been caused by Democratic overspending. She traced its real origins to global commodity shocks and to the political choice to fight inflation by inducing recession. Citing Stanford economist Emile Despres, she likened inflation to a struggle of 'burden-shifting', where each group sought to pass higher costs to others, until policymakers decided to break the cycle by deliberately creating unemployment.

By the end of that year, Bergmann returned to the subject of social security. In "Social Security's Overblown Problems" (Bergmann 1982n), she reignited one of the most contentious debates of the decade. She rejected the Reagan administration's warnings of bankruptcy, describing social security as a pay-as-you-go moral compact rather than a savings plan. She attacked the alarmism surrounding the program's supposed insolvency. Social security, she argued, was not an investment fund but a 'resource flow' from current workers to retirees. The issue, she emphasized, was not technical viability but social choice: how generous Americans chose to be toward the elderly.

Bergmann proposed supplementing payroll taxes with general revenues, rejecting austerity-driven reforms that would weaken the program's redistributive logic. She argued that Americans misunderstood the system as individual accounts rather than a mechanism for intergenerational resource-transfer. As long as the nation remained productive and willing to share, the program could not truly go broke. The debate, she insisted, was moral rather than fiscal: attempts to save social security by cutting benefits amounted to dismantling it. She recommended modest reforms, such as taxing wealthy beneficiaries and drawing on general revenues, but urged Americans to see social security as a collective choice about the kind of society they wanted to sustain. As previously described, Bergmann would expand her theses on social security later in her book *Is Social Security Broke?* (Bergmann 2000), and in several more articles (see Chapter 7).

Three reactions appeared within weeks in response to Bergmann's article.

In "Social Security" (Bryant 1982), Jesse Bryant accused Bergmann of promoting dependence on government, arguing that affluent retirees did not need benefits and that poorer ones could simply rely on welfare.

A week later, Michael D. Hurd, a professor of economics at the State University of New York at Stony Brook, countered Bergmann in "Not Overblown" (Hurd 1982). While agreeing with her idea of taxing benefits, he warned that demographic changes would soon make the program unsustainable. Unless workers saved privately, he said, future generations would face an unbearable tax burden. These exchanges highlighted how Bergmann's moral framing, emphasizing intergenerational solidarity, clashed with emerging neoliberal concerns for fiscal restraint.[14]

Finally, in a letter to *The New York Times* published on December 5, 1982, Arthur Tufts supported Bergmann's position that taxing social security benefits for retirees would be fair and reasonable. Tufts, himself a private-sector retiree, explained that he received income from both a private pension and social security. The former is taxed under existing income tax rules, specifically, only the portion exceeding his after-tax contributions to the pension plan is taxable. Therefore, he argued, social security payments should be treated in the same equitable manner. Tufts further extended the comparison by referencing his contributions to an Individual Retirement Account (IRA) and a Keogh plan, both designed to defer taxation during working years. Payments from these accounts, he noted, are fully taxable upon receipt, since they represent deferred income. Social security, in his view, functions similarly and should therefore be subject to current income tax when benefits are paid. Finally, Tufts

[14] The public debate over gender and labor returned to the fore the following year. In "Earning Gap Is Narrowing Slightly for Women" (Pear 1983), Robert Pear reported new data on women's earnings, quoting Bergmann as rejecting the notion that working wives were responsible for family-income inequality. She dismissed such claims as a form of male defensiveness against women's increasing independence and success. Pear's inclusion of Bergmann highlighted her prominent role as an interpreter of the evolving labor landscape for women.

suggested that taxing benefits could serve a civic purpose, allowing financially capable retirees to contribute to the long-term sustainability of social security.

As the 1982 closed, Bergmann published "The Failures of a Chair-Bound Science" (Bergmann 1982o), a sharp critique of the economic profession. Drawing on Wassily Leontief's complaints about the profession's detachment and Vernon Smith's experimental innovations, she condemned academic economists as chair-bound theorists, more concerned with equations than with economic life. The field, she argued, needed fieldwork, experiments, and humility, a science closer to factories, homes, and offices than to blackboards (see Chapter 5).

Her June 1983 essay, "Beware the Industry's Logics" (Bergmann 1983b), Bergmann attacked insurance industry resistance to sex-neutral coverage. Bergmann argued that fairness required equal treatment, even if actuarial adjustments increased short-term costs. Insurance practices that penalized women for longer life expectancy or reproductive capacity, she maintained, were simply economic discrimination under another name. According to Bergmann, equity, rather than technical justification, should guide policy.

In 1985, Bergmann's testimony at the U.S. Civil Rights Commission's consultation on affirmative action appeared in *The New York Times*, titled "The Dispute Over Affirmative Action: Whose Civil Rights?". Bergmann argued that despite the discomfort affirmative action might cause, representation was essential to breaking entrenched racism and sexism. Suspicion toward protected-group hires, she said, could only be overcome through genuine integration in the workplace (Bergmann 1985a).

A few years later, Bergmann widened her critique to the realm of child policy by publishing "Why America Fails Its Children" (Bergmann 1990). Contrasting the United States' neglect of families with France's comprehensive welfare state, she argued that federal leadership, rather than scattered local efforts, was essential to tackle child poverty, inadequate health care, and the lack of universal early education. France, she noted, provided income supplements to all families with children, free medical care for pregnant women, and universal nursery schools. A comparable U.S. program, she estimated, would cost $30–50 billion annually, a sum easily within the capacity of the American economy. The real barrier was not fiscal constraint but political will. America's failure to invest in its children, Bergmann concluded, reflected moral and social blindness rather than economic necessity.

In "In France, the Grass Isn't Greener Than Ours—Low Child Poverty" (Bergmann 1997a), she presented the French model to the readers of *The New York Times,* to challenge romanticized American views of European welfare. France's low child poverty rate, 6 percent compared with 22 percent in the United States, was achieved not by moralizing, but by supporting work and caregiving through sustained benefits, housing aid, and national health care. The U.S., she suggested, could emulate such policies without sacrificing prosperity.

Later, she turned to the economics of parenting with "Day-Care Subsidy Only Benefits Employed; Government Must Pay" (Bergmann 1997b), contending that low-wage parents could not afford childcare without direct government support. A single mother, she calculated, needed about $11,000 a year merely to survive, while the minimum wage yielded only $10,300. Only public fundings could bridge that gap. When a reader claimed that the Earned Income Tax Credit was enough to cover government support for child care, she replied that the EITC helped families survive, but did not ensure access to reliable and high-quality childcare (Bergmann 1997c).

In her article, "Does It Matter Who Regulate Managed Care?", Bergmann continued her critique of anti-government rhetoric, by pointing out that Americans' supposed hostility to "government" was largely semantic. As polls reveal, overwhelming support for regulating health maintenance organizations demonstrated that people still wanted collective solutions, even if they preferred not to call them governmental (Bergmann 1998).

In the early 2000s, Bergmann's tone became more urgent in terms of social reforms. In "Notion Building" (Bergmann 2003), she called on liberals to reclaim taxation as a moral instrument of civilization. Government spending, she wrote, was 'vital to a good life for all citizens', and progressives should stop apologizing for being 'tax and spend'. Two years later, in "Paying for Social Security" (Bergmann 2005), she once again dismantled the myth of social security's impending collapse. The system, she explained, was 'a pay-as-you-go government program, like defense', dependent not on accounting gimmicks but on political will: social security endured because democracy willed it so.

In one of her later articles appeared in *The New York Times*, "How to Reduce the Trade Deficit" (Bergmann 2010a), she challenged economic orthodoxy by defending tariffs as a means to protect workers from destructive global wage competition. Globalization, she warned, had erased traditional productivity gaps, exposing American workers to downward pressure on wages and living standards. Without new economic barriers, the middle class, and democracy itself, would erode.

In the same year, she argued for slowing economic growth to save the planet (Bergmann 2010b). She wrote that although people had long believed that economic growth was the basis of the American Dream, that raised living standards, created jobs, and allowed each generation to hope for more than the one before, the world had entered a moment when wealthy countries might no longer be able to rely on endless growth. Climate change, along with the rapid rise of China and India, suggested that continued expansion of output could become dangerous, or even impossible.

She pointed out that even if nations dramatically reduced carbon emissions per unit of GDP, the planet might still not remain liveable unless rich countries held their living standards steady while poorer nations grew. In that scenario, growth in the United States and other developed countries would need to slow or stop altogether. Yet, Bergmann insisted that prosperity without growth was possible. To achieve it, however, society would have needed to make major changes. Work hours would be reduced as productivity rose, so employment could remain high even when output did not expand. New products and production methods would be regulated, possibly through a system that limited firms' total labor use. The government would take on a larger role, providing essential services, such as health care, housing, education, transportation, and child care, to ensure that everyone's basic needs were met in a more static economy. Immigration would be tightly controlled to prevent job shortages and limit emissions from movement between poorer and richer countries. In such a world, Americans would have had to let go of the expectation of ever-increasing material abundance: larger houses, more cars, more gadgets. However, Bergmann believed that if unemployment stayed low and essential needs were guaranteed, a no-growth society could still feel prosperous. Higher taxes, similar to those in Sweden, might be necessary, but they would fund widely shared public benefits. She concluded that while a no-growth future might have seemed politically daunting, it was neither unthinkable nor unpleasant.

Finally, in "Climate Change and the Environment" (Bergmann 2011), Bergmann directed her attention to the planetary crisis. She called for collective restraint, urging the United States to curb its own growth and consumption, even at economic cost. Job sharing and shorter workweeks, she suggested, could maintain employment without relying on endless expansion. 'Even the leaders of the oil industry', she reminded readers, 'have grandchildren they care about'.

Bergmann's articles reveal that she regarded economic justice, environmental stewardship, and moral courage inseparable as well as a consistent intellectual and ethical thread: the conviction that economic systems must serve human dignity and that government, far from being an obstacle, is the instrument through which a moral society fulfils its obligations. From Watergate to climate change, she insisted that the measure of a democracy lay not in its wealth but in its willingness to act collectively for the common good.

As mentioned earlier, Bergmann's ideas were often the subject of discussion in the columns of *The New York Times*. For instance, in "Books & Business; Not As Easy as It Sounds" Wendy Kaminer reviewed Bergmann's *The Economic Emergence of Women* alongside other works on gender and labor. Kaminer regarded Bergmann's book as a lucid and accessible survey of women's long struggle to enter and remain in the workforce on equal terms. She credited Bergmann for tracing women's steady exodus from the home since the nineteenth century and for emphasizing that equality remained elusive because social policies and employment practices had failed to keep pace.

Kaminer highlighted Bergmann's insistence on the structural nature of discrimination and her call for affirmative action, government intervention in the labor market, and comprehensive child-care reform. Yet, Kaminer placed Bergmann's analysis in the company of other feminist studies on dual-career couples and corporate women, and subtly suggested that even if Bergmann diagnosed systemic injustice, she represented a strand of feminism grappling with the challenge of reconciling economic rationality with the emotional and domestic realities of working women. Nonetheless, Kaminer positioned Bergmann as a sober voice within a movement that risked romanticizing its own progress (Kaminer 1986).

A few months later, in "Economic Scene; Women Gain, But at a Cost", columnist Leonard Silk invoked Bergmann's conclusions to temper the Reagan administration's optimistic portrayal of women's advances. The Council of Economic Advisers had celebrated the entry of millions of women into the labor force as proof of the free-market's flexibility. Silk, citing Bergmann's *The Economic Emergence of Women*, reminded readers that beneath the aggregate data lay deep social tensions, family instability, child care shortages, and the persistent undervaluation of female occupations. Bergmann's critique reframed the 'success story' of working women as a paradox: economic necessity had propelled their progress, but the market alone could not correct its own inequities. Hence, she called for overhauling pay scales, enforcing child-support obligations, and building a publicly funded child-care system. In Silk's piece, Bergmann was the clear-eyed economist injecting moral urgency into an administration eager to congratulate itself on structural change that it neither initiated nor fully comprehended (Silk 1987).

By 1989, Bergmann's advocacy for welfare reform had widened to international comparison. In Carol Lawson's report, "How France Is Providing Child Care to a Nation" (Lawson 1989), Bergmann appeared not as a critic of American labor policy in isolation, but as part of a cross-national dialogue on social investment. As a member of a French-American Foundation delegation, Bergmann admired France's public commitment to early-childhood care and pointedly contrasted its tax-supported system with the United States' piecemeal approach. Lawson quoted Bergmann on how France's higher taxes reflected national priorities and political will, priorities that America lacked. Here, According to Lawson, Bergmann's voice blended policy analysis with moral indictment: a society that values economic growth but not child well-being, she implied, impoverishes both. Finally, Lawson underlined that Bergmann was a rare example of an economist who consistently linked gender equity to national economic vision.

Bergmann's battles outside academia also inspired other contributions that appeared in *The New York Times*.

For instance, William Celis' article on stagnating academic salaries (Celis 1992), reflected Bergmann's idea that attributed wage erosion not to hostility toward education, but to fiscal mismanagement and declining federal aid to states.

William H. Honan's paper (1994), painted Bergmann's sharp wit and rigorous standards as intellectually fearless and unwilling to temper her critique with collegial diplomacy.

In "White House Promotes Economic Efforts for Women", Sewell Chan cited Bergmann in reporting on a 2010 White House initiative, led by the National Economic Council, to highlight how Obama administration policies had supported women's economic security amid the Great Recession.[15]

8.3 Newspapers and Magazines

Bergmann's late-career voice continued to press for public investment in welfare, anti-discrimination enforcement, and a fairer redistribution through the tax system, reflecting both continuity and frustration: she acknowledged some progress, but found them insufficiently transformative. Nonetheless, her commitment to addressing social problems through a robust agenda of progressive policy never ceased and extended across several fields. She never stopped publishing her views and proposals in newspapers and magazines to help the public understand how such problems could be confronted and solved. As previously done with her testimonies and her articles published in *The New York Times*, Bergmann's contributions are reported in chronological order.

Between 1983 and 1988, Bergmann published a series of incisive opinion pieces in *The Los Angeles Times* advocating for equality, fairness, and structural reform. Her writings, which mirrored the ones published on the same issues in *The New York Times*, reveal a consistent concern for the social costs of economic inequality and the gendered dimensions of the American labor market.

In her article on the Reagan administration's economic agenda, which appeared in 1983, Bergmann condemned Reaganomics as a policy designed to favor the wealthy at the expense of the broader public, describing its economic program, centered on large tax cuts for the rich and reductions in domestic spending, as a redistribution of resources upward. By dismantling social protections and weakening public investment, she argued, the administration's policies widened inequality and

[15] The report, strategically timed before the midterm elections, emphasized policies such as the expansion of the Earned Income Tax Credit, increased work-study funding (especially benefiting women in community colleges), and state aid that preserved teaching and nursing jobs. Senior adviser Valerie Jarrett framed these measures as essential lifelines for women disproportionately affected by the recession, arguing that Republican opposition threatened to dismantle programs crucial to women's progress. The report also acknowledged persistent gender disparities: women represented nearly half the labor force but continued to earn only 77 cents for every male dollar, a gap largely unexplained by education or work patterns.

undermined the social contract that had sustained American prosperity since the New Deal (Bergmann 1983c).

Just a few weeks later, Bergmann turned to the issue of sexual harassment and its profound effects on women's employment opportunities. She explained that harassment was not merely an individual problem but a systemic barrier that had effectively excluded women from dozens of occupations. The result, she wrote, was a labor market sharply segregated by gender, with women crowded into lower-paying, lower-status jobs, often under male supervision and subject to abuse. This reality, Bergmann argued, required not only legal remedies but also a cultural transformation in how workplaces treated women (Bergmann 1983d).

By 1984, her attention shifted to labor policy and the structure of work itself. Bergmann proposed experimenting with a shortened workweek of four and a half days as a way to promote flexibility, reduce unemployment, and create opportunities for part-time employment. Such a policy, she suggested, could better balance economic efficiency with human needs, allowing workers to share available work more equitably while maintaining productivity (Bergmann 1984a).

In a following article, Bergmann addressed the growing tensions between women and Black workers, cautioning against division among groups facing economic inequality. She argued that women and minorities shared common struggles against systemic discrimination and unequal pay, and that their energies should be directed toward fighting inequality itself rather than each other. Solidarity, not competition, was in her view the key to meaningful progress in civil and economic rights (Bergmann 1984b).

In another article published in 1984, she focused on the urgent need for welfare reform, particularly for single mothers. Bergmann criticized both major political parties, Democrats and Republicans, for their failure to advocate meaningful change. She argued that welfare policies had long ignored the realities of women raising children alone, offering insufficient support for employment, childcare, and income stability. Genuine reform, she maintained, would require a system that empowered single mothers to participate fully in the workforce while ensuring their children's well-being (Bergmann 1984c).

In "The Economics of Abortion" (Bergmann 1984d), she explored the abortion debate through a deeply personal and economic lens, arguing that the decision to end a pregnancy is often rooted not in moral indifference, but in rational concerns about women's lives, work, and autonomy.

She began by inviting readers to approach the issue differently: rather than abstractly debating the 'personhood' of the fetus, she suggested asking one's own mother whether she ever had an abortion, and why. As already mentioned (see Chapter 2), at age twenty-two, she learned that her own mother had undergone three abortions. The revelation initially shocked her; she imagined the siblings she might have had and the personal loss of their absence. Yet, as her mother explained her reasons, Bergmann came to understand that they were primarily economic. Her mother did not want to sacrifice her time, energy, and limited income to raise more children than she could comfortably support. She preferred to work, earn money, and live a fuller life on her own terms.

Bergmann noted that while the medical experience of abortion changed and it was safer and virtually painless, the motivations remain much the same. Women seek abortions because they believe doing so will improve their lives. To outlaw abortion, she argued, would force women into 'a long sentence at hard labor in the prison of poverty' simply for engaging in sexual relations, even within marriage. Her mother's life, she insisted, was made better by having that choice, and so are the lives of millions of women who choose to get an abortion.

The right to abortion, Bergmann continued, is inseparable from women's broader social and economic progress. The sexual revolution and the transformation of gender roles depend on women's ability to control their fertility. Without abortion access, women's participation in the labor force, their financial independence, and their pursuit of meaningful careers would be gravely limited. Unwanted pregnancies would push many families into poverty and make sexual life itself 'rife with hateful risk'. Low and controlled fertility, she emphasized, is what has made both women's emancipation and affordable child care possible.

Bergmann then criticized the anti-abortion movement, noting that its leaders focused on the fetus's loss of life, while simultaneously opposing birth control and women's sexual freedom. She argued that they actually wanted to reimpose 'obligatory domesticity', returning women to dependence and fear, discouraging sex outside marriage and undermining gender equality.

Although she acknowledged that political forces, especially under President Reagan and with a conservative Supreme Court, might succeed in outlawing abortion, Bergmann concluded that women would not accept such a loss of autonomy. Even if abortion were criminalized again, she insisted, women would continue to seek it, just as her own mother did decades earlier, enduring fear and danger to preserve control over her life.[16]

In 1985, Bergmann returned to her core critique of Reagan's economic policies, emphasizing that deep tax cuts combined with reductions in federal domestic spending were damaging the social fabric. By prioritizing defense spending and corporate interests, the Reagan administration, she warned, was eroding public services and the welfare of ordinary Americans. The result was a society increasingly divided between the privileged few and the struggling many (Bergmann 1985b).

Later, Bergmann criticized sharply then Vice President George Bush's economic proposals. Labeling his platform as 'voodoo economics' or even 'clown economics', she predicted that his policies, rooted in further tax reductions and unbalanced budgets, would produce massive increases in the national debt. Her critique reflected her broader view that conservative fiscal ideology consistently sacrificed long-term economic stability for short-term political gain (Bergmann 1987).

Finally, in her July 31, 1988, piece, Bergmann examined Bush's proposed child-care program, dismissing it as largely ineffective. She noted that the program was targeted toward families who did not need assistance, while the working poor, especially single mothers, were left behind. True child care reform, she argued, required substantial public investment to ensure that all families, regardless of income, had access to affordable and high-quality care (Bergmann 1988).

In her 1993 article, she analyzed President Bill Clinton's early welfare reform proposals. Bergmann believed the Clinton administration had the opportunity to create a modern safety net that upholds both economic self-sufficiency and human dignity. Nevertheless, she argued that an effective welfare reform, aimed at helping single mothers, required more than simply pushing them into jobs: it required policies that made work financially viable and family life sustainable. Nonethless, according to Bergmann, Clinton's statement that welfare recipients were 'aching for the chance to move from dependence to dignity' captured the complexity of the reform: Bergmann warned that forcing mothers into low-wage work without adequate support would only deepen their hardships. Furthermore, she pointed out that most jobs available to mothers on

[16] On June 24, 2022, the Supreme Court overturned *Roe v. Wade*, removing the federal constitutional protection for abortion rights. In the absence of a national standard, each state now determines its own policies, either restricting or safeguarding access to abortion.

welfare paid poorly and lacked health benefits, making it nearly impossible to live decently or provide properly for children. The transition from welfare to work, she wrote, often felt like moving 'from the frying pan to the fire', as mothers lost access to Medicaid and had to pay for costly child care. To make work genuinely attractive for mothers, regardless of whether they are single or in a partnership, the government must supplement wages and provide essential services, especially affordable and high-quality child care.

Drawing inspiration from France, where generous public nursery schools and subsidized child care systems have successfully reduced child poverty and welfare dependence, Bergmann suggested expanding the U.S. Head Start program into a universal, full-day, year-round system that supports working parents (see Chapter 7). She also emphasized that comprehensive health care reform is vital, since many single mothers remain on welfare solely to retain medical coverage for their families. She cited economist Irwin Garfinkel's idea of 'child-support assurance', under which all fathers would be required to contribute according to their ability to pay, and the government would guarantee a minimum payment if the father was unable to do so. This, she argued, would provide a more reliable income base for working mothers and their children, helping them escape poverty without dependence on welfare (Bergmann 1993).

Across her articles published between the 1980s and the 1990s in *The Los Angeles Times*, Bergmann proved herself to be a persuasive public advocate for the idea that economic fairness and social compassion must go hand in hand. Her voice remained consistently pragmatic, morally engaged, and deeply committed to equality.

In the early 2000s, she continued to publish in popular press, proposing an economic policy agenda not based on an abstract matter of numbers, but on a reflection of national values and on instruments that could either promote justice or entrench privilege. Under George W. Bush's presidency years, she sharply criticized both Alan Greenspan's endorsement of Bush's massive 2001 tax cut and the Democratic Party's misguided fixation on paying down the national debt instead of insisting on public funding for people in need (Bergmann 2001). Bergmann began by questioning Greenspan's abrupt reversal: after years of warning against tax cuts and supporting the use of budget surpluses to retire federal debt, Greenspan changed course just days after Bush's inauguration. His justification, that surpluses would eventually grow so large that the government might have to buy private assets, thereby creating a conflict of interest between government and business, was, in Bergmann's view, transparently false. She argued that such a scenario was decades away, if ever likely, and that Greenspan's explanation was a political smokescreen. The real reason, she suggested, was that Greenspan feared an economic downturn and hoped a tax cut would provide short-term stimulus.

To understand Greenspan's attitude, Bergmann turned her attention to the Democrats' attitude in the 1990s, arguing that Greenspan's defection exposed the weakness of their own economic position. According to Bergmann, the Democratic Party, which had once been a strong supporter of investment for welfare and economic justice, had, by the 1990s, drifted into a timid, fiscally conservative stance. Instead of fighting for expanded social programs, many Democrats, under President Bill Clinton, had embraced the rhetoric of debt reduction and fiscal restraint. By the late 1990s, as the economy boomed and surpluses appeared for the first time in decades, Democrats had made paying off the national debt their central goal, effectively abandoning the New Deal tradition of using government spending to meet the country's social and economic needs. Clinton's political calculation, Bergmann noted, was rooted in fear: after the defeat of his healthcare plan and years of right-wing attacks on big government, he declared that 'the era of big government is over'. When surpluses emerged, rather than propose large-scale investments in health care, education, and infrastructure, he pledged to use the money to "save social security first" by paying down the debt. This slogan was politically effective, as it helped Democrats fend off Republican tax cuts, but it also tied the party to an austerity-minded fiscal policy that constrained its own agenda for years to come.

Bergmann dismantled the supposed economic rationale for debt reduction, focusing on the crowding-out theory, which claimed that government borrowing reduced private investments by absorbing available capital. According to this theory, reducing the national debt would supposedly do the reverse, releasing capital that businesses could then invest in new equipment and facilities. Bergmann dismissed this argument as outdated and ideological, born out of the 1930s opposition to the New Deal, and later used against Keynesian policies of deficit spending. As a matter of fact, she argued, business investment was driven not by the availability of funds but by the prospect of profit: when companies expected strong consumer demand and high returns, they found financing easily, from retained earnings, credit markets, or foreign capital. Conversely, when demand was weak, investment dried up, regardless of how much money was theoretically available. Running government surpluses, she warned, could actually worsen recessions by reducing demand for goods and services, leading businesses to cut investment rather than expand it.

Even if the crowding-out theory were true, Bergmann insisted, paying down the debt was still a poor use of public money compared with investing in people and communities. The budget surpluses of the late 1990s and early 2000s, she argued, could have been used to fund urgent social needs, such as health care, child care, school repairs, drug treatment, and mental health services, that would have made the population healthier, more productive, and more secure. Such programs, she wrote, would have yielded far greater long-term benefits than boosting corporate profits or reducing the government's debt burden. She also emphasized the moral aspect of the argument: even if social spending did not directly increase economic growth, relieving the suffering of low-income families was a worthier national goal than producing more consumer goodies for the well-off.

Looking ahead, Bergmann proposed an alternative to Bush's regressive tax cut: a temporary reduction in the payroll tax, paid by all workers, aimed at funding social security. Unlike Bush's plan, which disproportionately benefited the rich, a payroll tax cut would have increased the paychecks of low- and middle-income workers, including those who paid no income tax. Because poorer households were more likely to spend their extra income, such a policy would have stimulated the economy more effectively. Moreover, she argued, it would have strengthened the social security system by keeping its funding within the public system and making privatization efforts more difficult.

Bergmann concluded with a call for Democrats to reclaim their progressive economic mission. By aligning themselves with Greenspan and embracing the politics of debt reduction, they had trapped themselves in a 'fiscal straitjacket' and ceded moral and political ground to Republicans. The party needed leaders who would reject the 'debt reduction canard' and fight openly for intelligent taxation and robust public spending. She cited Alice Rivlin, the former Congressional Budget Office director, as one of the few Democrats courageously arguing for renewed investment in social programs. But Rivlin, Bergmann lamented, was a lone voice in the wilderness. The Democrats, she concluded, needed to rediscover the courage of their New Deal roots, to champion not the repayment of financial debts, but the repayment of the nation's social debt to its people.

In the early 2000s, Bergmann's articles in the popular press spanned topics ranging from child care, economic issues, to the nurse shortage.

In 2002, Bergmann wrote an article endorsing a proposal by the Committee for Economic Development (CED), a group funded by major U.S. corporations such as Exxon, Ford, Merck, J.P. Morgan, and Prudential Insurance, to establish universal, publicly funded pre-kindergarten education for all American children beginning at age three. Bergmann highlighted the striking nature of this proposal, given its source: a prominent business organization advocating for a major increase in public spending, estimated at $25 to $35 billion annually, to fund early childhood education. She interpreted their proposal as evidence that many top corporate leaders recognize the long-term economic and social benefits of investing in early learning. According to Bergmann, these business leaders understand that early education strengthens the nation's economy, boosts workforce reliability and productivity, and ensures that more children enter school ready to learn. By supporting universal pre-kindergarten, big business is not acting out of pure altruism, she suggested, but out from an enlightened sense of economic self-interest, seeing social stability and educational opportunity as foundations for sustained prosperity (Bergmann 2002).

In 2006, Bergmann wrote a letter to the editor of *Foreign Affairs* criticizing Alan Blinder's optimism about the U.S. adapting to large-scale offshore outsourcing (Bergmann 2006a; Blinder 2006). Blinder believed the country could shift toward non-offshorable jobs, such as truck driving, teaching, or personal services, but Bergmann contended these kinds of jobs cannot generate the exports necessary to pay for rising imports. She criticized Blinder's reliance on classical trade theory, based on Ricardo's model, which assumed individuals can always move to more valuable activities, whereas nations may lose essential industries and fail to create better alternatives for displaced workers. Hence, Bergmann called for:

> Imposing tariffs on manufactured goods and on services imported through electronic means and prescribing criminal penalties for violators, levy heavy taxes on corporate importers and use the proceeds to increase the income of consumers, and control illegal immigration, which is just another form of job outsourcing. (Bergmann 2006a, p. 202)

Starting from 2004, Bergmann became interested in the nurse shortage in the United States. Reports of shortages have appeared repeatedly for decades, with government data predicting rising deficits in the nursing workforce. She examined why nurse shortage persisted despite the expectation that higher wages would normally eliminate such shortage in a competitive market. Typically, when demand exceeds supply, prices or wages rise until the shortage disappears, yet this has not happened for nurses.

Bergmann argued that the real issue lies in wages that fail to compensate for difficult conditions. Hospitals have managed shortages not by raising pay but through temporary fixes such as hiring bonuses, recruiting nurses from low-wage countries, employing agency nurses at higher per-hour costs, increasing workloads for existing staff, and assigning more nursing tasks to less skilled workers. These strategies ease short-term staffing pressures but worsen overall job quality and retention.

Bergmann suggested several structural reasons why wages have not risen: limits on hospital reimbursements by Medicare, the high marginal costs of hiring additional nurses, and possible collusion among hospitals to avoid competing for nurse labor by keeping pay low. Such anti-competitive behavior, she noted, has drawn the attention of the Department of Justice's antitrust division.

To resolve the shortage, she proposed identifying and investigating any hospital-run organizations engaged in wage-suppressing practices, enacting legislation to establish minimum nurse-patient ratios to improve working conditions, and creating incentives that would make hospitals more willing to raise salaries and expand hiring.

Two years later, in 2006, Bergmann published "The Nurse Shortage Is a Crime" (Bergmann 2006b) where she presented a sharp economic and moral critique of the long-standing nursing shortage in the United States, arguing that the crisis persists not because of overwork or lack of training facilities, but because of low wages deliberately held down by anti-competitive hospital practices. For more than thirty years, hospitals have faced chronic understaffing, yet instead of raising pay to attract and retain nurses, they have relied on temporary fixes and misleading narratives. Bergmann insisted that the root cause was clear: nurses are not paid enough to meet demand, and the failure to raise wages constitutes both an economic distortion and a social injustice with deadly consequences.

Bergmann began by reminding readers that nurse shortage is not merely an inconvenience, but rather a matter of life and death. Studies show that mortality rates increase by 7 percent for each additional patient assigned to an overworked nurse. Despite repeated government predictions that the shortage will worsen, reaching nearly 30 percent by 2020, the true cause of the problem is rarely addressed. Instead of applying basic economic principles, policymakers and hospital administrators continue to obscure the issue. In any other labor market, she noted, shortages are temporary: when demand exceeds supply, employers raise wages to attract more workers. But in nursing, this natural market correction has been deliberately suppressed. Hospitals prefer to maintain low wages even when this leads to dangerous understaffing, forcing nurses to shoulder overwhelming patient loads while administrators pursue profit and cost-cutting.

To avoid paying higher wages, hospitals have adopted a series of substitutes for fair compensation. They offer large hiring bonuses to new recruits, ironically paying newcomers more than experienced staff, and import nurses from low-wage countries, who are willing to accept U.S. salaries that remain low by international standards. Hospitals also rely heavily on expensive temporary agency nurses rather than raising base pay for permanent employees, and they increase workloads for the nurses already employed, often assigning nursing duties to less trained personnel. These short-term fixes only worsen the long-term problem. They fuel resentment, cause burnout, and lead to extraordinarily high turnover rates (more than 21 percent of nurses leave their jobs annually). Patients, too, suffer as staffing gaps persist, reducing the quality and safety of hospital care.

The consequences extend beyond U.S. borders. Bergmann highlighted the global injustice caused by the recruitment of nurses from poorer nations, many of which face health crises such as HIV and malaria. These countries invest scarce resources to train nurses, only to lose them to wealthier nations like the United States. This "brain drain" deepens the suffering of patients in low-income countries while allowing U.S. hospitals to maintain depressed wage levels. The familiar argument that 'foreign workers do jobs Americans won't do' is misleading, Bergmann argued. Americans would do these jobs, if wages were sufficient.

According to Bergmann, despite the clear economic logic that higher wages would attract more nurses, public discussions of the shortage continue to misidentify its causes. Instead of addressing pay, most reports emphasize non-economic factors such as stressful working conditions, a poor public image of nursing, or a lack of training opportunities.

Hospital lobbying groups even call for importing more foreign nurses rather than improving conditions domestically. Policymakers and think tanks produce vague recommendations like ‘reinventing work environments’ or ‘improving nursing’s image’, while steering clear of the salary issue altogether.

Bergmann cited an influential report by the Robert Wood Johnson Foundation that offered five recommendations to address the shortage, none of which mentioned wages. Likewise, professional associations and hospital administrators talk about marketing campaigns, ethics, or changing the public perception, but not about paying nurses fairly. Bergmann showed that economic evidence contradicts these narratives. Surveys of nurses show that half have considered leaving the profession, and more than three-quarters of those say that higher pay would help with retention and recruitment. Difficult working conditions, Bergmann pointed out, are not unique to nursing, as coal miners and construction workers, which are typically male sectors, also face hardship, danger, and long hours. Yet, these jobs do not suffer from chronic shortages, because they pay enough to compensate for their risks. If nurses were paid commensurately with their training, responsibility, and stress level, at or above the level of similarly educated male workers, the shortage would diminish rapidly.

Why, then, have wages not risen? Bergmann considered collusion among hospitals to be as the most likely cause. In many metropolitan areas, hospitals are few in number, which makes it easier for them to coordinate on wage suppression, whether through explicit agreements or informal understandings. Hospital administrators have strong incentives to avoid bidding wars for nurses; any hospital that raised wages would have to be matched by others, driving up costs across the board. This implicit cartel behavior allows hospitals to stabilize wages below the market-clearing levels.[17]

[17] Historical evidence supports this claim: in the 1970s, most hospital associations in major cities maintained “wage standardization” programs for nurses. In 1994, the U.S. Department of Justice sued the Utah Society for Healthcare Human Resources, which represented hospitals employing 75 percent of the nurses in Salt Lake County, for conspiring to exchange salary data and coordinate wage-setting. Although the case was settled without penalties, the facts revealed a long-standing pattern of anticompetitive conduct. Even after the Justice Department and the Federal Trade Commission issued formal warnings in 1996, enforcement remained weak and hospital collusion continued largely unchecked.

Bergmann argued that this situation amounts to a crime against nurses and patients alike. By conspiring to keep wages low, hospitals not only exploit their workforce but also endanger lives. Yet change may finally be coming. Nurses' unions, including the Service Employees International Union (SEIU) and the California Nurses Association (CNA), have begun taking aggressive action. In 2006, nurses filed antitrust lawsuits against hospital groups in several major cities, including Chicago, Albany, Memphis, and San Antonio, accusing them of wage-fixing. These suits, supported by the SEIU, seek triple damages under U.S. antitrust law, meaning hospitals could face penalties amounting to three times the wage losses nurses have suffered. If successful, such actions could cost hospitals billions of dollars and force a long-overdue adjustment in pay scales.

Bergmann also advocated legislative intervention, particularly through laws mandating minimum nurse-to-patient ratios.[18] Minimum staffing laws not only protect patients but also pressure hospitals to raise wages to meet staffing requirements. Failure to do so would force them to reduce patient intake, cutting revenue and increasing costs per patient, an outcome administrators would find financially untenable.

Beyond legal and legislative measures, collective action remains essential. The SEIU's Nurse Alliance, under the slogan "Value Care, Value Nurses," has focused on mobilizing nurses to demand fair compensation and safe staffing levels. While the rhetoric often emphasizes improved patient care rather than higher pay, the underlying message is clear: solving the nurse shortage requires paying nurses what they rightfully deserve.

Bergmann concluded with a pragmatic economic calculation to dispel fears that fair pay would bankrupt the health care system[19]: considering that inadequate staffing increases patient suffering, medical errors,

[18] California paved the way in 1999 to establish a 1:5 ratio in hospitals after years of lobbying by the CNA. Although the law faced fierce resistance, including an attempted suspension by Governor Arnold Schwarzenegger, it ultimately survived, setting a model for other states. By 2005, legislatures in Massachusetts, Illinois, Connecticut, Kansas, and New York were considering similar measures.

[19] In 2005, total U.S. spending on medical goods and services amounted to $1.8 trillion. Employing 1.8 million full-time nurses would cost about $84 billion, less than 5 percent of total health expenditures. Raising nurses' salaries by 10 percent and increasing the workforce by another 10 percent would add approximately $18 billion, or about 1 percent of total medical spending.

and even mortality, Bergmann argued that failing to spend this modest amount is indefensible.

Summing up, Bergmann reframed the nursing shortage as an economic crime sustained by institutional greed, gender bias, and political negligence. Nurses' wages have been held artificially low through collusion and social attitudes that undervalue women's labor. Hospitals' reliance on temporary fixes, foreign recruitment, overwork, and marketing campaigns, has masked the underlying injustice while endangering both patients and staff. The path forward, she insisted, lies in economic realism and moral courage: enforce antitrust laws, legislate safe staffing ratios, strengthen unions, and pay nurses what their vital work is worth. Only then will the United States finally end the nurse shortage and restore dignity to one of its most essential professions.

Inspired by Bergmann's work, on May 24, 2006, *The New York Times* hosted a debate on the situation of nurses in the United States, publishing six letters to the Editors.[20] In Bergmann's archive there is an email sent to the *New York Times*, dated May 24, 2006, which was not included in the printed journal.

In her email, Bergmann summed up her economic arguments on the causes and effects of the shortage of nurses in the country and provided some cases of antitrust lawsuits that recently occurred as possible legal solutions. She pointed out that the United States must rely on foreign nurses to fill domestic shortages, and argued that the so-called "nurse shortage" is not a natural or inevitable outcome, but rather a man-made crisis created by hospital administrators who have deliberately suppressed nurses' wages for decades. According to Bergmann, the same institutions now lobbying for expanded immigration quotas are the ones most responsible for the persistent shortage of qualified nurses within the United States.

Bergmann added that each additional patient assigned to a nurse increases the risk of death by seven percent. Yet, instead of raising wages to attract more domestic nurses, hospitals have chosen to import foreign labor from impoverished countries, many of which already suffer from AIDS, malaria, and a severe lack of medical professionals. She condemned this practice as both unethical and ineffective, noting that foreign recruitment cannot possibly fill the projected 29 percent shortfall in nurses by

[20] Retrieved November 1, 2025, from https://www.nytimes.com/2006/05/29/opinion/l29nurses.html.

2020. Moreover, it drains vital human resources from nations that can least afford to lose them.

Drawing on basic economic theory, Bergmann asserted that the real root of the problem lies in simple supply and demand: nurses are not paid enough to balance the labor market. Despite the difficulty, stress, and responsibility of nursing work, wages have not kept pace with the demands of the profession. Public discourse on the shortage, however, tends to obscure this fact. Policymakers and hospital representatives often point instead to 'poor working conditions', a negative public 'image of nursing', or a supposed 'shortage of faculty' in nursing schools. Bergmann found these explanations superficial. She argued that higher pay would naturally correct all of these issues, compensating for harsh conditions, attracting more students to nursing programs, and encouraging qualified faculty to teach.

The central barrier, Bergmann explained, is the anticompetitive behavior of hospitals. Because hospitals in most metropolitan areas are few and large, they can easily coordinate, formally or informally, to avoid bidding up wages. This tacit collusion keeps nurse pay artificially low and prevents the market from functioning as it should. Bergmann cited a 1975 survey by medical economist Donald Yett, who found that nearly all hospital associations in major U.S. cities operated 'wage-standardization' programs for nurses. A similar pattern continued decades later: in 1994, the Department of Justice sued a consortium of Utah hospitals for illegally sharing wage information to suppress nurse salaries. Although the case was settled without penalties, Bergmann emphasized that such behavior has persisted because enforcement of antitrust law has been weak and inconsistent.

Bergmann was encouraged, however, by emerging resistance of nurses' organizations that have begun filing new antitrust suits against hospitals in several U.S. cities, demanding accountability and fair compensation. She highlighted legislative and union initiatives such as California's landmark law mandating a minimum one-to-five nurse-to-patient ratio, an effort that was spreading to other states. The Service Employees International Union's Nurse Alliance, which seeks to unite both unionized and nonunion nurses, is another promising example of collective action aimed at raising wages and improving working conditions.

Finally, Bergmann addressed the predictable counterargument from hospitals: that raising nurses' wages will make health care too expensive. She dismissed this as exaggerated. Even a ten percent increase in nurses' pay and employment, she calculated, would raise total national health care costs by only about one percent, a modest price for improved care, reduced mortality, and a more equitable labor market. For Bergmann, the ethical and economic logic was clear: the United States must not exploit poorer countries to compensate for its own unwillingness to pay nurses fairly. The true solution to the nursing shortage was domestic investment in wages, staffing, and respect for the profession, not a global transfer of human capital from those who can least afford the loss.

Bergmann exchanged several emails about the problem of nurse shortage with Linda Aiken, Professor of Nursing at the University of Pennsylvania, provided a revealing look at the economic and institutional factors shaping the U.S. nursing shortage in the early 2000s. The correspondence, dated June and July 2004, is complemented by later contractual and legal documents that show how Bergmann's ideas about anticompetitive wage control in hospitals eventually helped inform union strategies and legal actions against hospital associations. Emails to Aiken and further documents on nurse shortage spanned from 2004 to 2006 and are held in Bergmann's archive (box 7).

In her June 14, 2004, email, Bergmann sent Aiken a draft of a paper exploring whether local hospital collusion, as suggested by a Department of Justice antitrust suit in Utah, might explain the persistent 'shortage' of nurses.[21] Aiken's detailed reply of July 12, 2004, supported and refined Bergmann's argument by pointing out that hospitals' reluctance to invest in labor-saving technologies implies that nursing labor remains artificially cheap.[22]

[21] She noted that many official reports, including from the Robert Wood Johnson Foundation and the Government Accountability Office (GAO), failed to acknowledge the central role of wage suppression in creating or sustaining the shortage. Bergmann's position reflected her long-standing argument that the so-called shortage was not the result of insufficient nurse education or poor work conditions alone, but rather stemmed from artificially low wages maintained by hospital coordination.

[22] Drawing on her earlier research, Aiken cited her 1987 paper in the *New England Journal of Medicine*, which empirically demonstrated that nurse vacancy rates are inversely related to relative wages, that is, as nurses' pay rises relative to comparable professions such as teaching, vacancies decline. This finding supported Bergmann's economic logic: the market for nurses would clear if wages were allowed to adjust freely. However, Aiken added that higher wages influence both supply and demand, hospitals respond to wage increases not by investing in productivity-enhancing technologies or reorganizing care delivery, but often by attempting to hold wages down instead.

Aiken and Bergmann shared concern about the structural dysfunction of professional nursing organizations, which, in Aiken's words, are 'dysfunctional and compromised by ties to hospital management'. Instead of confronting wage control directly, these organizations focus narrowly on nursing education or shortage advocacy, gaining only minor policy concessions.[23] Aiken also highlighted wage compression as a major problem. New graduates, including those from elite institutions like the University of Pennsylvania, often start at wages higher than any other Penn graduates, including business school alumni. Yet, hospitals fail to reward experience, education, or specialization adequately, leaving veteran nurses underpaid relative to their skill levels. This system discourages long-term retention and professional development, reinforcing turnover and staffing instability.

Finally, Aiken acknowledged Bergmann's conclusion, i.e., that the nurse shortage could be resolved by a truly competitive labor market. Though, she also admitted uncertainty about how such a 'monumental shift' could be achieved given the entrenched structures of wage control and organizational inertia.

Bergmann's commitment to the nursing shortage attracted institutional attention, particularly from the Service Employees International Union (SEIU), which was then expanding its efforts to organize health care workers. A consulting agreement dated June 15, 2005, between Bergmann and SEIU formalized her role in shaping the union's campaign on nursing wages and labor market reform. Under the agreement, Bergmann was to provide consulting services for six months (June–November 2005) at $5000 per month, for a total compensation of $30,000. Her tasks included: publishing her paper "The Mystery of the Nurse Shortage" in a journal such as *Challenge*; writing or co-authoring op-eds and articles on the "artificial wage ceiling" for nurses;

[23] Aiken observed that many leaders within nursing resist the kinds of reforms that would empower bedside nurses economically or organizationally. Her own research, she added, shows that working conditions significantly affect nurse retention and recruitment. Hospitals with better environments can attract nurses even without substantial pay increases, but such institutions are rare: Aiken estimates that only five percent of U.S. hospitals provide work environments that are genuinely attractive to nurses. This imbalance underscores the broader deterioration of the profession's labor standards.

and helping SEIU develop communications and litigation strategies to challenge anticompetitive wage practices among hospitals.[24]

In 2007, Bergmann's expertise on the matter became relevant to ongoing litigation against hospital associations accused of suppressing nurse wages.

In a letter dated February 26, 2007, attorney Michael R. Shumaker of Jones Day notified Bergmann that she was being subpoenaed for two federal cases, *Maderazo v. VHS San Antonio Partners* and *Unger v. Albany Medical Center*, both alleging that health care systems had conspired to suppress nurse compensation between 2002 and 2006. The subpoenas sought materials pertinent to class certification in wage-fixing suits.

In another letter, dated April 23, 2007, attorney Maxwell M. Blecher confirmed Bergmann as a paid expert consultant for Health Temp, a staffing company suing the Arizona Hospital and Healthcare Association and its member hospitals for allegedly similar wage suppression.[25]

Both requests relied on Bergmann's analyses, which aimed at supporting claims that hospital associations coordinated pay-setting practices in violation of antitrust law, reflecting precisely the collusion she and Aiken had discussed years earlier.

Taken together, this correspondence and documentation trace a clear trajectory from academic debate to applied advocacy and legal action. Bergmann's economic framework, which viewed the nurse shortage as a symptom of employer collusion and suppressed wages, was empirically reinforced by Aiken's labor-market research and subsequently operationalized by the SEIU and private plaintiffs. They agreed that the U.S. health care system's chronic understaffing was not due to a lack of qualified nurses, but rather to market distortions stemming from hospital

[24] The contract designated Bergmann as an independent contractor, not an employee, and required her to treat all work products as SEIU intellectual property, 'a work for hire'. It also included strict confidentiality clauses, limiting her ability to produce similar work for any other labor organization for 18 months after the contract's termination. Importantly, the agreement envisioned that part of her work would involve litigation support, under the direction of SEIU's legal counsel, James & Hoffman, P.C. This confirmed the union's intent to pursue legal remedies against hospital wage collusion, directly extending the argument Bergmann had articulated in her 2004 paper and correspondence with Aiken.

[25] Blecher's letter outlined that Bergmann's work would be treated as confidential and privileged, conducted at an hourly rate of $350, and safeguarded under attorney-client and work-product privileges.

behavior. Furthermore, the exchange between Bergmann and Aiken highlights the convergence between economic theory and labor practice: when wages are administratively constrained, shortages persist despite an ample potential workforce. The later contracts and subpoenas illustrate how these ideas influenced union policy and federal litigation, marking a rare instance in which academic inquiry directly shaped real-world legal and labor strategies.

As already mentioned, the last years of Bergmann's research work were devoted to the analysis of the economic and social effects of the decline of marriage (see Chapter 4). Her interest was shared outside academia too.

For instance, in 2007, she wrote an essay, published in *The Times Literary Supplement*, aimed at examining the historical evolution and contemporary decline of marriage, exploring how economic, social, and cultural changes have reshaped this once central human institution. Bergmann began by situating marriage in human history as a social mechanism that bound men to the long-term provision for their offspring, something that distinguished humans from other primates. As human societies grew more complex, with clothing, tools, and shelters requiring cooperation and foresight, marriage became a practical arrangement: men pledged material support to women and their children, while women offered domestic labor and sexual exclusivity, ensuring paternal certainty. Yet, Bergmann observed, beyond this economic contract, marriage also offered emotional stability, companionship, and love, though love, she noted wryly, is notoriously changeable.

Nonetheless, in modern developed societies, Bergmann pointed out, marriage has weakened dramatically. Since the 1960s, marriage rates have steadily declined, divorce has become common, and cohabitation without marriage has risen sharply. By 2005, there were just twelve married couples for every cohabiting couple, compared to ninety-seven in 1960. About one-third of American children were born to unmarried mothers, many of whom struggled to raise children alone. These shifts, Bergmann argued, stem from a combination of new legislation, such as legal divorce and abortion, and new economic and social transformations, such as women's growing participation in paid labor. These factors provide an 'escape hatch' from unhappy unions, weaken the link between sex and marriage, and make single motherhood more economically feasible.

Social scientists, Bergmann explained, remain divided over whether this transformation of marriage and family may be critical for social well-being. Some scholars in the 1970s and 1980s saw divorce as simply replacing death as the typical end of marriage. More recently, other scholars have argued that lone parents, same-sex couples, and cohabiters can perform familial functions just as well as married couples. Yet, she noted, many studies in psychology still suggest that children raised outside of stable marriages tend to fare worse on average. Bergmann summarized their perspectives by comparing three books: Amato et al. (2007), Hymowitz (2007), and Blankenhorn (2007). Bergmann compared three recently published books: Amato et al. (2007), Hymowitz (2007), and Blankenhorn (2007).

Amato et al.'s book, *Alone Together: How Marriage in America Is Changing,* compared survey data from 1980 and 2000. It showed that marital happiness has not significantly declined, while domestic violence and other negative behaviors have decreased modestly. Couples now share housework and childcare more than before, and attitudes favoring gender equality have grown. However, spouses spend less time together due to women's increased laborforce participation. The happiest marriages, according to the authors, are childless ones, while those who cohabited before marriage tend to report lower satisfaction and higher divorce rates, a *non sequitur* conclusion, according to Bergmann.

Hymowitz's *Marriage and Caste in America* blamed the decline of marriage on poorly educated "underclass" groups, especially Black Americans, who, she claimed, had irresponsibly separated marriage from childbearing. Bergmann denounced Hymowitz's argument as racist and unscientific, dismissing the book as right-wing propaganda masquerading as social commentary.

Finally, David Blankenhorn's *The Future of Marriage* focuses on the harm children suffer from the absence of one parent, especially the father. According to Bergmann, Blankenhorn ultimately served as an argument against same-sex marriage, offering few constructive ideas for strengthening family life.

Bergmann concluded the essay by admitting that the institution of marriage continues to erode, reflecting profound changes in gender roles, work, and personal freedom. The persistence of inequality, the pressures of modern life, and the diversification of family forms suggest that marriage, as once known, may never fully recover its central role in human society.

As mentioned in Chapter 2, in 2014, Bergmann was involved as a contributor for the *HuffPost.* She wrote two blog posts which were her last publications.

In the first, published in November 2014, she challenged the popular student-led campaigns urging universities to divest from fossil fuel companies. Although she recognized the moral intent behind these movements, she questioned their practical impact. Drawing a parallel to the South African apartheid divestment campaigns, Bergmann argued that such gestures made only a limited difference to the actual power structures they sought to change. Divestment, she explained, might serve as a moral statement, signaling that fossil fuel companies' actions are reprehensible, but it does little to influence their behavior. Selling stocks simply passes them into the hands of investors less concerned with climate change, thereby reducing pressure for reform. Instead, Bergmann proposed a more effective and strategic form of activism: shareholders should organize collectively to influence corporate decisions from within. She envisioned an association of large investors nominating environmentally conscious candidates to company boards and campaigning for their election. Through such influence, corporations could be pressed to cease opposing carbon taxes and redirect investments toward renewable energy. For Bergmann, meaningful climate action required engagement rather than withdrawal, representing a pragmatic shift from symbolic protest to structural change (Bergmann 2014).

Bergmann had previously discussed environmental issues in an interview published in 2009 where she claimed that global warming is an unprecedented threat and that everything possible must be done to stop it, including reducing our standards of living and challenging the belief that growth is synonymous with prosperity. In that interview she said:

> It is not a matter of maximizing GDP now or GDP in the future, it is a matter of saving the planet. (Bergmann 2009, p. 143)

The second blog post is dated January 3, 2015. It was about the social and economic challenges of family life in contemporary America. Citing data from the Pew Research Center, Bergmann highlighted a striking transformation in family structure: by 2015, 34 percent of American children were living with an unmarried parent, compared with just 9 percent in 1960. The majority lived with single mothers, many of whom struggled with low-paying jobs and little or no support from fathers. For Bergmann, this shift reflected a profound social change, one that could not be reversed by moral appeals to restore traditional family values. Rejecting unrealistic hopes for a return to two-parent households or a religious revival that would curb sex outside marriage, Bergmann insisted that the state must act to protect children, who are not responsible for the conditions into which they were born. She called for a bold, comprehensive system of social support: free, high-quality childcare for all families, expanded financial aid for college, universal healthcare, subsidized housing and direct cash benefits.

She acknowledged the political obstacles, including entrenched resistance to higher taxes and 'big government', but argued that the moral cost of inaction was too great. Without such programs, she warned, the United States risks raising a generation of deprived children, with consequences for society as a whole.[26] For Bergmann, it is only a matter of time before the American electorate recognizes the need for far greater investment in its youngest citizens.

Taken together, these two essays, published two months apart and just a few months before her passing, reveal the consistency of her progressive pragmatism rooted in the rejection of symbolic gestures and moralistic rhetoric in favor of structural and institutional action.

References

Amato, P., Booth, A., Johnson, D., & Rogers, S. (2007). *Alone together: How marriage in America is changing*. Harvard University Press.

Bergmann, B. (1968). Investment in the human resources of negroes. In *Subcommittee on Economic Progress of the Joint Economic Committee Congress of the United States* (pp. 263–266). U.S. Government Printing Office.

Bergmann, B. (1973). A policy agenda for women's economic problems. In *Testimony Before the Joint Economic Committee, Congress of the United States*, July 10.

Bergmann, B. (1974a, July 17). Letter to the editor. *The New York Times*.

Bergmann, B. (1974b, November 3). Economist, poll thy people. *The New York Times*.

Bergmann, B. (1976). Material for amicus brief: *Wetzel vs. Liberty Mutual* (pp. 1–20). Barbara Bergmann's papers, box 7, David M. Rubenstein Rare Book & Manuscript Library. Duke University.

[26] To strengthen her point, Bergmann looked abroad to France and the Scandinavian countries, where generous family benefit systems, funded by taxes that take up to 45 percent of national income, have succeeded in reducing child poverty. By contrast, the United States, with its tax share of around 25 percent, underfunds even its existing programs for childcare, education, housing, and health.

Bergmann, B. (1979). Testimony before the task force on social security and women select committee on aging. U.S. House of Representatives. July 24. Social Security and the Interests of Women (pp. 1–5). Barbara Bergmann's papers, box 4. David M. Rubenstein Rare Book & Manuscript Library. Duke University.

Bergmann, B. (1981a). Hearings before the joint economic committee. In Congress of the United States 97th Congress. First Session. Part 1, January 22, 27, 28, and 29 (pp. 87–91). Barbara Bergmann's papers, box 4. David M. Rubenstein Rare Book & Manuscript Library. Duke University.

Bergmann, B. (1981b, September 20). The economics of expectations. *The New York Times.*

Bergmann, B. (1981c, October 18). A recession could put Reagan in a box. *The New York Times.*

Bergmann, B. (1981d, November 15). Relax, social security is doing its job. *The New York Times.*

Bergmann, B. (1981e, December 13). Charity needs coercion. *The New York Times.*

Bergmann, B. (1982a, January 10). An affirmative look at hiring quotas. *The New York Times.*

Bergmann, B. (1982b, February 7). Here is why you lost your job. *The New York Times.*

Bergmann, B. (1982c, March 7). Investment is the business of business. *The New York Times.*

Bergmann, B. (1982d, April 4). Lobbying: Shakedown on Capitol Hill. *The New York Times.*

Bergmann, B. (1982e, May 2). It's single parents who need help. *The New York Times.*

Bergmann, B. (1982f, May 30). A threat ahead from word processors. *The New York Times.*

Bergmann, B. (1982g, June 27). A vicious cycle of high rates. *The New York Times.*

Bergmann, B. (1982h, July 25). Where deregulation makes no sense. *The New York Times.*

Bergmann, B. (1982i, August 22). The sound and fury over poverty. *The New York Times.*

Bergmann, B. (1982l, September 19). Why the football union can hit hard. *The New York Times.*

Bergmann, B. (1982m, October 17). Who's to blame for the economy? *The New York Times.*

Bergmann, B. (1982n, November 14). Social security's overblown problems. *The New York Times.*

Bergmann, B. (1982o, December 12). The failures of a chair-bound science. *The New York Times*.

Bergmann, B. (1983a). Changes in family and work roles of women and men: The challenge to policy. In *Testimony Before the Joint Economic Committee, Congress of the United States*, October 27 (pp. 1–8). Barbara Bergmann's papers, box 1. David M. Rubenstein Rare Book & Manuscript Library. Duke University.

Bergmann, B. (1983b, June 26). Beware the industry's logics. *The New York Times*.

Bergmann, B. (1983c, June 24). Volcker the economic crippler. *Los Angeles Times*.

Bergmann, B. (1983d, July 14). Sexual harassment keeps women in job ghetto. *Los Angeles Times*.

Bergmann, B. (1984a, July 4). A shortened work week is long in good sense. *Los Angeles Times*.

Bergmann, B. (1984b, August 7). Women, blacks should fight inequality, not each other. *Los Angeles Times*.

Bergmann, B. (1984c, September 4). No one speaks for welfare mothers. *Los Angeles Times*.

Bergmann, B. (1984d, October 21). The economics of abortion. *Los Angeles Times*.

Bergmann, B. (1985a, March 10). The dispute over affirmative action: Whose civil rights? *The New York Times*.

Bergmann, B. (1985b, January 28). Here is the other side of 'great' economic news. *Los Angeles Times*.

Bergmann, B. (1987, October 26). Attuned to the rich, bush offers a warmed-over 'voodoo economics'. *Los Angeles Times*.

Bergmann, B. (1988, July 31). It's 'demogrant reborn, not day care'. *Los Angeles Times*.

Bergmann, B. (1990, October 7). Why America fails its children. *The New York Times*.

Bergmann, B. (1993, February 4). A safety net for children in poverty: The Clinton team has the drive to push programs supplementing work efforts of single mothers. *The Los Angeles Times*.

Bergmann, B. (1995). Folder on Giant Food, including chronology and letters to Avis Sanders, Ellen Vargas, Donna Lenhoff, Barbara Robinson. Barbara Bergmann's papers, box 6. David M. Rubenstein Rare Book & Manuscript Library. Duke University.

Bergmann, B. (1997a, June 10). In France, the grass isn't greener than ours—low child poverty. *The New York Times*.

Bergmann, B. (1997b, December 24). Day-care subsidy only benefits employed; government must pay. *The New York Times*.

Bergmann, B. (1997c, December 29). Paying for day care. *The New York Times.*
Bergmann, B. (1998, July 27). Does it matter who regulates managed care? *The New York Times.*
Bergmann, B. (2000). *Is social security broke?* Illustrated by Jim Bush. University of Michigan Press.
Bergmann, B. (2001, March). Debts and taxes. *The American Prospect Magazine*, 14–16.
Bergmann, B. (2002, May 12). Signing up the littlest. *Focus.*
Bergmann, B. (2003, October 26). Notion building. *The New York Times.*
Bergmann, B. (2004). The mystery of the nurse shortage. Barbara Bergmann's papers, box 7. David M. Rubenstein Rare Book & Manuscript Library. Duke University.
Bergmann, B. (2005, June 22). Paying for social security. *The New York Times.*
Bergmann, B. (2006a). Bad trade. *Foreign Affairs, 85*(4), 202.
Bergmann, B. (2006b). The nurse shortage is a crime. *Challenge, 49*(6), 93–102.
Bergmann, B. (2006c). Importing nurses is not the answer. Barbara Bergmann's papers, box 7. David M. Rubenstein Rare Book & Manuscript Library. Duke University.
Bergmann, B. (2007, June 29). Marriage in America. *The Times Literary Supplement.*
Bergmann, B. (2009). We have to turn the world into Sweden. *European Journal of Economics and Economic Policies, 6*(2), 141–145.
Bergmann, B. (2010a, September 16). How to reduce the trade deficit. *The New York Times.*
Bergmann, B. (2010b). Is prosperity possible without growth? *Challenge, 53*(5), 49–56.
Bergmann, B. (2011, December 20). Climate change and the environment. *The New York Times.*
Bergmann, B. (2014, November 25). Better than disinvestment: A more effective move against climate change. *The Huffington Post.*
Bergmann, B. (2015, January 3). What to do about single parenthood. *The Huffington Post.*
Blankenhorn, D. (2007). *The future of marriage.* Encounter Books.
Blinder, A. S. (2006). *Offshoring: The next industrial revolution? Foreign Affairs* (Enlarged version: Fear of offshoring. CEPS Working Paper No. 119), 113–128.
Bryant J. (1982, December 5). Social security. *The New York Times.*
Celis, W (1992, April 24). Pay of teachers lags at colleges. *The New York Times.*
Chan, S. (2010, October 21). White house promotes economic efforts for women. *The New York Times.*
Daniel, B. (1981, November 29). Pro Bergmann. Letter to the editor. *The New York Times.*

Hogue, C. (1985, March 11). Speaking up for women's rights. *The Montgomery Journal*.
Honan, W. H. (1994, August 7). Professorial nastiness: The academic jungle. *The New York Times*.
Hurd, D. (1982, December 12). Not overblown. *The New York Times*.
Hymowitz, K. (2007). *Marriage and Caste in America: Separate and unequal families in a post-marital age*. Bloomsbury Publishing.
Kaminer, W. (1986, October 26). Books & business; not as easy as it sounds. *The New York Times*.
Lawson, C. (1989, November 9). How France is providing child care to a nation. *The New York Times*.
McNabb, J. (1981, December 20). Whose security? Letter to the editor. *The New York Times*.
Pear, R. (1983, October 3). Earning gap is narrowing slightly for women. *The* New York Times.
Powell, C. (1982, September 19). Sound and fury. *The New York Times*.
Serlin, L. (1982, September 26). Author fumbled. *The New York Times*.
Shanahan E. (1973, July 11). Top Nixon economists say job bias reduces women's wages by 10 to 20%. *The New York Times*.
Shelton, I. (1975a, March 23). Money is women's real problem. *The Washington Star*.
Shelton, I. (1975b, April 16). Women's year group begins countering ERA foes. *The Washington Star*.
Silk, L. (1973, October 17). Peers give Nixon's advisers bad reviews. *The New York Times*.
Silk, L. (1987, February 6). Economic scene; women gain, but at a cost. *The New York Times*.
Tufts, A. J. (1982, December 5). Letter to the editor: Taxing social security benefits fairly. *The New York Times*.
Walshe, W. A. (1982, June 13). Comment: Crying wolf over word processors. *The New York Times*.

CHAPTER 9

Reminiscences and Legacy

Here are collected memories of Barbara Bergmann, as a woman, a mother, a friend, and a colleague.

The first paragraph draws on an interview with her children, Sarah and David, including some excerpts from the eulogy David kindly sent me, which completes the part quoted in Chapter 2. The second paragraph contains memories from her friends and colleagues, shared with me between March and December 2025. The last paragraph presents memories published during Bergmann's lifetime and shortly after her death, including three major obituaries. Testimonies are reported *verbatim*.

The aim of this chapter is to provide a broader overview of what Barbara meant to many people. In fact, these testimonies offer the most vivid and lucid portrait of Barbara's character, providing a more intimate view of her personality in her private sphere that complements her well-known professional achievements and public persona.

9.1 Memories from Barbara's Children

On November 14, 2025, Barbara's children, Sarah and David, kindly made a video call with me to share some of their memories of their mother, which I combined with David's speech at her mother's memorial. We started with some stream of consciousness, followed by some Q&A.

G. Becchio, *Barbara Bergmann*, Great Thinkers in Economics,
https://doi.org/10.1007/978-3-032-18696-6_9

Sarah opened the floor by saying that they found out when they left the house at 18 how unique their family was. In fact, most of the other mothers in their neighborhood did not work, and they were around in the afternoons while Barbara was there with them for dinner and everything, but she was into her career way more than most of the other mothers that they knew. David added that this may be understandable given that he and her sister were born in 1968 and 1967, respectively, when the family structures were a little different. They grew up outside of Washington, DC, in an area that was not a typical slice of the United States in the sense that there were a lot of multicultural families in the area, a lot of diversity.

Barbara (born in 1927) and Fred (born in 1928) were older than other parents around and their life experiences didn't mesh with the experiences of kids growing up in the 1970s and the 1980s. Fred's family had escaped from Germany just before World War II and Fred's teenagerhood was largely about trying to assimilate into the United States culture in the 1940s. He went to college in the 1950s, and "they had a really hard time understanding where we were coming from and vice versa". Sarah added that both their parents had an unusual upbringing, and they did not see a problem with their children having that too. However, David noted that their lives were a lot easier than their parents'. Sarah and David agreed that Barbara and Fred gave them "hard time for how weird they were: very nerdy academic kind of people, eggheads types, ten to fifteen older than most of our friends' parents, who were cool, drove station wagons, and took them to Disney movies", while their parents took them to Europe and to very cerebral movies, "so inappropriate". Sarah and David also agreed in remembering that their parents gave them a lot of freedom. David said: "our parents didn't believe in being helicopter parents, almost the opposite, they used to say 'go out and figure it out'". And Sarah added: "Independence was a big word [for them] (…) They were both really smart and they talked to us a lot. They didn't discipline us a lot, but they talked to us a lot about whatever we wanted".

Then, both Sarah and David started to add some details about their mother's personality. Sarah said: "Barbara was different for sure, in the right sense; she had very strong opinions about everything. She never would say something like 'I don't care'. She would tell you something. Thinking and talking were free". David added: "most of my friends were scared of her", while their father was different; Fred "was much more mild-mannered, more of an introvert, she was more of an extrovert", said Sarah; "he was the yang of her yin", added David.

As mentioned earlier, both Barbara and Fred let their kids explore freely whatever they want. Sarah said: "they let us buy records and listen to whatever music we wanted to and read whatever books and magazines we wanted to. My mom was a feminist economist, so she probably thought that the women's magazines were not helpful, especially *Seventeen*, *Glamour*, and *Vogue*, but she let me have those magazines anyway … I still like them!". And David: "And I loved cars, things that went fast, and boy stuff. And she couldn't fathom. She would always say to me 'A car is just for getting from point A to point B, what's so wonderful about a Porsche or a Ferrari?' However, I would get all the car magazines and read them fervently". Then they both remembered that their mother used to talk with them about diminishing returns. By the way, David never took a course on economics during college, while Sarah took one at the University of Maryland, and "it was the easiest class I have ever taken. Everything came naturally because I had heard it before. It was the whole way of thinking I was used".

After their first thoughts about Barbara, the Q&A began.

GB: Are there any special memories of Barbara's youth in the Bronx that she loved to share with you?

Sarah: She had an aunt, her mother's sister, Lena, whom she loved very much. I think her relationship with her mother was not a bad relationship, but her mother had big expectations, so she loved her aunt very much. Her aunt was a person whom my mom became. She had lots of opinions. She just lived life fully. My mother's mother and her aunt started a business together. And my mom just really respected and loved her aunt Lena (See Chapter 2).

GB: Did she ever miss New York?

David: All the time. She never liked anywhere else.

Sarah: She didn't like suburbia. She wanted to be in a city.

David: We grew up outside of Washington, DC, in suburbia. And then as soon as I went to college, they moved closer to Washington, just inside

DC, where she could walk to the metro, and get on a subway. She could walk to restaurants and to stores.

Sarah: Walk to civilization.

GB: How about Barbara at home?

Sarah: She cooked for us once a week. She didn't make our food or do the cleaning or the laundry. We had other people for that.

GB: I assume that Barbara and Fred were secular Jews, right? Were they in any way connected to the Jewish culture? Did you celebrate the big holidays, for example, or absolutely nothing?

Sarah: We started out celebrating Hanukkah, I was about seven or eight years old or maybe nine. She loved miniature things and she loved stationery. So, we had Hanukkah and we were given a little present and we opened it up and inside for each of us was a mini metal swingline stapler, a baby one. However, we grew up in a really prosperous place, and at school people were going to say, "What did you get for Hanukkah?" And I would be very embarrassed and hate what I got and hate my mother for giving it to me. So I threw a fit, that night, the first night of Hanukkah, as a little girl. And my mother was so angry at me for my ingratitude that it pretty much ruined Hanukkah from then on. And we didn't really do it. And they would just give us money to buy our own presents at that time of the year. So, here's some money so you can have a present.

David: My mom, I think she disavowed all religion pretty young and think that's pretty clear in most of her writings and stuff that cover that. But my dad was raised in quite a religious family. He had a bar mitzvah and when they came over here [in the U.S. from Germany], I think he lived with his mom and dad till he left for college and they continued [to celebrate traditions] and so he brought some of that with him, and he could recite the prayers. Though Hanukkah was the only celebration in our family. We would go to Passover events at other people's houses, I don't think we ever hosted one. I always joke that I've been in more Catholic churches in Europe than I have been in Jewish temples anywhere.

Sarah: We have a lot of Christianity because our parents loved art and architecture, and they took us to Europe one or two times every year, and we would go to churches, cathedrals, and chapels that were painted up in the Middle Ages, in the Renaissance, and we would talk about what was in the paintings. We have a lot of Christian knowledge.

David: Barbara loved that stuff. She lit up with her little red book of the Michelin guide and all the little notes tucked into it. And she loved to travel.

Sarah: She was a great tourist. She would wake up in the morning with a plan, and we would go and look at things, and walk around and eat the food and buy things. She loved Italy the best.

David's words from his mother's eulogy well summarize part of the conversation which took place at this point of our video call. David wrote:

> If spending time with my dad was her number one favorite thing to do, my mom's next most favorite things, in this order, were: 1) eating and 2) travelling; and 3) travelling with the ultimate goal of eating.
> From the time we were very small, my sister and I were packed-up, along with a big box of Pampers, and hustled through airports and onto planes for many family vacations. When we were still toddlers, my mom would usually wrangle some naïve grad-student of hers to come along and run interference, so she and my dad could visit what seemed like every church and museum in all of Western Europe.
> As many of you know, my mom wasn't much of a religious person, quite to the contrary. So, on these trips to Europe I couldn't help but wonder why we were spending so much time in all of these Catholic churches. While my sister and I would run around giggling at all the nude statues and artwork, you could often find my mom feeding coins into the metered spotlights that would turn on for 30 seconds at a time to light up some seemingly obscure sculpture or painting tucked away in the far corner of the church, and she would 'ooh and aah' over what often turned out to be some little known work by one of the Renaissance masters. She had encyclopedic knowledge of classical art and she would always try to stop us and get our attention and try to get us to appreciate what it was we were seeing. Most of the time it was totally lost on me, BUT what I did come to appreciate was the genuine enthusiasm in her voice as she described these works of art to us. And as I grew a little older, even if it still didn't impress me the way it did her, I really came to look forward to these trips; to be able to spend time with her in her element, so she could share with us her appreciation for these things that she loved so much.
> On these trips to Europe, after leaving church, Barbara would pull out her 'bible', which in her case was *The Michelin Red Guide,* and try to find us a worthy restaurant. Very often she would remember one she had eaten at

> on a previous trip and we would have to go there to see if it was still as good as she remembered. She would often boast that she "*rarely forgot a good meal… but she never ever forgot a bad meal*". Together as a family, we ate some amazing meals and travelled to some beautiful places. These trips provided me with some of the most cherished and lasting memories and further impressed upon me, now that I have a family of my own, exactly what it was that my mom loved about travelling so much.

The interview with Sarah and David went on with more Q&A.

GB: Back to the question about the Jewish culture: was she ever worried about anti-Semitism?

Sarah: Yes, very much so, and very much worried about what happened to the Palestinians. She saw what happened to them as very unfair, wasn't handled well. She really felt bad. She visited Israel once, and she stayed in a hotel that was in a very old building, and she asked an Israeli person who used to live here before 1948 and they said no one. And that struck her and she told us about it more than once of how awful it made her feel.

David: She quickly left. I think she cut her trip short and went to Egypt, to Giza and to see the Great Pyramids.

Sarah: She was not sort of like a person who was a hater or anything. I wouldn't call her anti-Zionist. Our family did not have any affinity to Israel; she was very American, and European Jews should have been allowed to stay European.

GB: What kind of book did she like to read besides economics and social sciences?

Sarah: She loved Jane Austen. She really encouraged me from a very young age, maybe 13 or 14 years old, to read *Pride and Prejudice*. And I didn't read it until I went to college and I came back and said, "mom, it was so good. I wish I had read it. I don't know if I could have appreciated it, but thank you". And she liked mysteries.

David: She didn't end up reading books a lot. She loved the book reviews in *The New Yorker*.

Sarah: They were very extensive and involved reviews. And she used to say: "I like to read the reviews and I don't always feel like I have to read the book".

GB: How about the music? Was she an opera lover?

David: Yeah, and she knew how to play the piano, the violin, and the viola. She took classes when she was an adult.

Sarah: She was best at the piano. We had a piano in our house, and so we heard her play. Not a lot, but sometimes she would get in the mood and play, and then we all had a family quartet. David and I played the violin, she played the viola, and our dad took up the cello: we played Baroque chamber music in our quartet in our living room.

David: We had a teacher. This was very much to Sarah's and my dislike, but it was one of the few things I wouldn't say they forced on us. We revolted at about 13 and 14 and gave it up,

Sarah: I was in it through high school pretty much. Yeah, I was in the orchestra.

David: They kind of forced that a bit. They started us when we were, I want to say, five and six, six and seven. We had quarter-size violins. Suzuki method. And it just brought huge smiles to their faces. They thought it was the greatest thing. They would have their friends over and have us play for them. I'll say that Sarah was the first violinist and I was the second violinist.

Sarah: We'd been playing the violin for years. We're pretty good. David was good. And we were playing these classical music quartets, and their friends would say "it's so scary". They just made their hearts explode. And we were just hating it.

David: It was very painful.

Sarah: But one time we got invited to play in a church and at the Wolf Trap, a performing arts venue.

At this point of the conversation, a stream of consciousness from both the siblings came up again. They both started to share what kind of person Barbara was.

Sarah: She was just a person who was very interested in learning. She was ahead of her time in a lot of things, [such as] the personal computer: she adopted it right away. As soon as one came out, we had one for years. Our whole life she had been programming on the mainframe at the University of Maryland. They had one of those big IBM room full of computers—and she would come home and bring us punch cards and computer paper, and we would use it for our work. So as soon as the personal computers came out, she had one, and they evolved so fast that we seem to kind of get a new one every few months and she taught herself all the coding. She knew some of the computing languages, and she knew that databases were going to run the world. She knew this, and she tried to tell me when I was a teenager, and I didn't listen. I should have.

David at this point started to talk about what it was like to have a mom like her and some of the challenges this presented for him growing up, as reported in the eulogy:

> In the 1970s suburbia, as you might have imagined, Barbara often stood out like a sore thumb. I fielded a lot of questions from my friends, like: Why does your mother drive an old beat-up sedan, and not a station-wagon like the rest of the moms? Why does your mom have such short hair? And why does your mom have hair in her armpits? The one I always liked the best was: why doesn't your mom carry a purse?... In fact, is that a men's wallet your mom just pulled-out?... from her bra-strap? Yeah!! And the list goes on.
>
> It even affected me after I grew up and moved out. Everywhere I went, it seemed Barbara had left her mark. One example: I was probably in my early 20s. I'm out to dinner at a local restaurant here in Bethesda with a bunch of friends, and the waiter is taking our order and he gets to me, does a double take, and he says, "I know who you are! Your mom is the reason we don't have a television in the restaurant anymore." Every time we would go there as a family, she would tell the waiter to turn it off. And every time she would admonish them that it wasn't there to entertain the patrons, but rather for the benefit of the employees. Well, eventually I guess they got tired of hearing her complaints. 'Oh yeah' he said, 'I know your mom', and everyone at the table just laughed because they knew her too.
>
> At the time it was hard for me to see the real meaning of her ways and actions, but eventually it clarified for me, and I was able to laugh and make fun of her; to tease her about it, and appreciate her and what she stood for, and ultimately to feel a real sense of pride for what she did, and why she did it. She didn't do it to make a statement. She didn't do it

> to get attention. She did these things because she felt they were the right things to do. She wasn't going to be burdened by a purse, or annoyed by a loud television, and she simply didn't care what anyone else thought. (Bergmann 2015)

Back to Q&A, the discussion went on.

GB: Did she have any particular hobby besides music and traveling?

Sarah: Cook. She was a foodie. She didn't cook our dinners usually because she was working, but on Saturdays she would make something. She was a really good cook.

David: She had a Romanian sort of influence in her, and her aunt Lena and her mom taught her a lot of really good recipes. So, her convention was not three cloves of garlic, but the entire head of garlic, with the top chopped off, thrown in. That was how she used garlic, as an Eastern European person. And her food was delicious. Yeah, she made really good food.

Sarah: She loved the three-star restaurants. We talk about the Michelin stars and try to visit them if we were in the towns where they were.

GB: How about her friends? Mainly colleagues or more outside academia?

Sarah: Colleagues, but she made friends wherever she went. She had a friend in the coat check of the Metropolitan Museum in New York, and for a few years. They would email back and forth and he had this white peacock, and she used to say: "this is my friend. I met him at the coat check at the Metropolitan Museum, and we just fell in love". I want to tell you, speaking of falling in love, just this really strange story that I had regarding Gordon Liddy. Liddy was involved in the Watergate scandal. He was the guy who broke into the Watergate for Nixon, and he was a character, and he had, in the late 1980s, a radio show or maybe early 1990s, he had a syndicated radio show. There was another Republican scandal figure, Oliver North, who was in the Iran scandal during the Reagan administration. And they both had radio shows, conservative radio shows, and I liked them. I listened to them. I've never been a conservative, but I liked listening. So Oliver North's show was on right before Gordon Litty's show. And I did not hear Oliver

North's show. I didn't listen to his show, but I turned on Gordon Litty's show. And Gordon Litty has Oliver North as a guest. And Oliver North mentioned—and I hadn't known about any of this in advance—Oliver North mentioned to Gordon Litty that he had had a very interesting person on his show, Barbara Bergmann, who had a lot of interesting ideas. And I was listening to these two sort of historical Republican right-wing scandal people talk about her. They loved her. So I went over there for dinner and I said: "Mom, I heard Gordon Litty and Oliver North chatting about you", and she said: "Oh yes". [During that period] she was doing the book tour for *Defending Affirmative Action*, which was a big topic for conservatives, and she said: "Oliver North was so cute, and we just liked each other so much, and we fell in love!".

GB: She had a very high sense of humor, right?

David: She, obviously, had her academic side, but she was obviously intelligent and could steer a conversation, listen well, and guide it in an interesting way, while asking questions that would sort of knock you off balance.

Sarah: I think that was good for our intellectual development to grow up with that. I have a silly sense of humor and she loved my sense of humor. The last dinner that I had with her, we went to a Japanese restaurant and we were sitting by a window on the sidewalk and a lady came by with a crazy facelift and she was very interested. She just took a big interest in gender and what people sort of do to perform gender. And so the woman was walking toward me and I said, "Mom, you have to check out this facelift". And she turned around and saw and we just had such a good laugh. It wasn't a laugh like we want to ridicule somebody, but she just took pleasure in the things that people do and how funny we are.

GB: David, which kind of grandmother was she?

David: Owen made up the best name for her. So, that's a good story, real quick. So, she was visiting, he was maybe three, my youngest Owen talking for sure and he kept calling her Mino and when I asked him, he said, "It's cuz Mino knows if she's a boy or a girl". It was his answer, And as she got older, obviously, she became more androgynous but she also kept her hair short and never put a speck of makeup on her face and didn't do all the things that other grandmothers did. No jewelry. She was very honest. Even with us as kids, I don't think she knew how to be sort of super warm and fuzzy.

Sarah: She was very kind and really empathetic and loved people, but she was not particularly soft and nurturing in her manners. She has never been that into children.

David: At the time [grandkids] met her, she was quite old, in her eighties, physically hampered, and so she couldn't get on the floor with them, she would observe them. She loved to watch them. I remember she would watch them and make comments. She wouldn't judge my parenting. She might make a gentle suggestion, maybe not so gentle, direct, but she wouldn't hound you about it. She would say it once, maybe 3 months later, she might suggest the same thing again: "Hey, we talked", but she wasn't overbearing.

Sarah: A lot of her sentences started with "I think".

GB: Did she ever complain at home about her career or academic people? How about Gary Becker? Have you ever met him?

Sarah: She didn't talk about it much to us, but this is interesting: I was accepted to the University of Chicago, and she encouraged me to go. But I didn't.

GB: Did she encourage you to do empirical studies?

Sarah: No, she did not ask us to do empirical studies as in a major. When we were in high school, she preferred academic subjects over soft things. She really objected to home economics because it was pushed on girls.

David: I took home economics. Being a teenage boy, I didn't interpret things for what they were at the time. I remember her pooping the home economic thing very much, but I didn't understand exactly why that was.

Sarah: Also you didn't sign up for only home economics. There were four classes, and you would sign up for them all together, and they were all sort of non-academic classes. So there was home economics, child development (also pushed toward girls), wood shop, and metal shop. There were four classes that went together, shorter than the normal semester, and you either took all of them or two of them. It wasn't that we just particularly signed up for home economics, but we signed up for this group of classes that was non-academic and home economics was in there.

GB: You already told me that she usually started her speech with "I think", right? Was there any motto that she liked to repeat, like a mantra?

Sarah: So many of those growing up. We can tell you some of them: "Nobody's perfect", "Don't spoil my breakfast", "The most important thing is to be a nice person", "Go with the flow".

David: "Don't talk about dessert during dinner".

Sarah: These were all things that we heard endlessly growing up, endlessly. The main thing was to be a nice person.

GB: Is there anything else you would like to add?

David: I think, and it's funny because just a few days ago, I was talking (I am a veterinarian and I had a patient), and I was talking to the owner and it somehow came up that she grew up around Washington DC and her mom worked in the economics department and knew our mom. In fact, she was an administrative assistant, a secretary, and Barbara pushed her to get her degree, which I guess she did. Barbara was apparently advocating for this woman. The other thing this woman said, was that her mother was a student at the University of Maryland as well and ended up taking a course that Barbara was teaching, which didn't happen often. So she took a course—I can't remember what it was—but it was involving the use of computer models in economics, and we had a discussion about Barbara's urgency to transform economics: moving away from theoretical things and using the data that were available to make it more of a hard science. And that, I think, is really something that I remember her talking about a lot.

Sarah: She took an interest in people, individuals who she liked, and wanted to do something for them to help them open their minds to something bigger. She thought that a lot of economics is just sort of people coming up with an idea and it resonates. But it might not be true. She wanted to test it. She was a math person. After she went to American University, they had a math contest every year, and the person who won it was called the Grand Master, and she won it every year that she was there.

GB: Well, I have one more question, and it's the most delicate that I have. Is it fine if I report the way she passed?

Sarah: Yes, it is public information. She was always a member of the Hemlock Society, which later turned into Death With Dignity, and she believed in doing it your way, and doing it her own way and at her own time.

David: She made comments to us for as long as I remember. So that was another thing about her. I was adopted and she told me from before I can remember: "you were adopted and if you ever want to know more about your background and your biological family, we're here to support you", which I thought was really cool. And so I just always knew what was the case and was very comfortable with it. And the same thing with her belief that people should have a say if they're in a terminally ill or in miserable situations. So she made that very clear. She would talk to me about it and she would talk about details. We could talk about delicate stuff as matters of fact. We could talk about it openly. But you just had to understand that was her way of being, just a brutally honest person. And I think you had to respect that. And the last thing I said in that conversation with this woman who took the computer science course or the economics course with Barbara, was that she was a very polarizing personality. People either loved her or people really hated her for her, right?

Sarah: And generally it was the underdog who loved her and the bully who hated her.

David: It was always when Barbara spoke, people listened. and I think we felt that way. When Barbara spoke, as much as we didn't want to listen, we did. She had that innate ability to kind of command a room in a very unassuming way. It was not a mean or forceful or "I am better than you" kind of way.

Sarah: She did not seem to have a big ego at all. I wouldn't call her humble, but just sort of very neutral there. She just wasn't a person who seemed to think highly of herself unduly. She was very modest about her achievements. To me it is so impressive that she came to Washington to work in the White House. She never talked about it. She never brought it up. Never.

9.2 Memories from Her Friends and Colleagues

In this paragraph, reminiscences and memories of Barbara are reported verbatim. I received these messages between March and December 2025, via email, either personally or through the IAFFE mailing list, when I asked Barbara's friends and colleagues to share their memories with me for possible inclusion in this biography.

Memories from Francine Blau

I first came into contact with Barbara Bergmann in 1970 or 1971 when I was stunned and delighted to receive a phone call from her inviting me to present a paper on women at the December 1971 AEA meetings. I was an instructor at Trinity College in Hartford and working on my dissertation on the gender pay gap at Harvard. I don't know any backstory details, but John Kenneth Galbraith was President-Elect of the AEA (and thus the organizer of the meeting) and, as a liberal, likely sympathetic to these issues. It was at these meetings that a group of us banded together to write the motion establishing CSWEP that Carolyn Shaw Bell presented at the Business Meeting. I haven't researched it, but I would think that this was the first session on gender at the AEA meetings.

I think it says a lot about Barbara that she organized this session. Here she was a faculty member at the University of Maryland, a successful woman in an overwhelmingly male field. And she chose to spend some of her capital on organizing a session on women, an area that excited little interest and respect among mainstream economists at that time. And so it was throughout her career. She could have focused solely on attaining and enjoying her own professional success. But, instead, she was deeply involved in efforts to advance women and minorities. Also, in hindsight, I am amazed that she took a flyer on an unproven commodity like me. She also solicited a paper from Harriet Zellner who was working on her dissertation on women at Columbia. She was willing to cast a wide net and take risks. The third [invited] paper was by Charlotte Phelps, a more mature, proven scholar who was on the faculty of Temple University. I think having a session on women at the meetings was an important step in advancing the legitimacy of the field. Inviting Paul Samuelson and other distinguished scholars as discussants was also a step in that direction.

My interactions with Barbara over the years meant a lot to me. As a grad student at that time, I had hardly even met any female Ph.D. economists before the 1971 meetings. And I had never had a female economics professor. In fact, in my whole undergraduate career I had only one female professor, in an English class. It was so inspiring to come in contact with Barbara. She was so impressive. She "walked the walk" and "talked the talk"; she was brilliant and confident; she was quick-witted and articulate; she could hold her own in any setting.

I was kind of a Bergmann groupie. I saw her at those first AEA meetings and caught two seminars she gave near me, at Yale and Wesleyan. After one of the seminars, I was invited to dinner, and she talked about having children and managing that aspect of life, something that never came up in the overwhelmingly male gatherings I was used to. After that, I'd see her speak every time I could, at the meetings or conferences, drawing inspiration each time I heard her.

Barbara was an incredible role model. The only problem was that she was a bit too good, one could not expect to attain her high level. But it was inspiring, nonetheless. This alone for many of us would have been enough, but Barbara didn't stop there. She gave opportunities and encouragement to countless women (as well as criticism—it wouldn't be Barbara otherwise); she devoted much of her research to charting and analyzing inequities and pointing toward solutions; she chaired CSWEP, the AEA committee to advance the status of women in the economics profession; she helped to start an association of feminist economists, international in scope. She was always a few steps ahead of everyone else.

I have one more personal debt to Barbara. In 1991 or 1992 I got a call from Barbara asking me if I would be willing to run for Vice President of the AEA. This was incredibly unexpected, but extremely exciting. I did not expect to win and sincerely thought it was an honor just to be nominated. But to my surprise I won a spot as one of the two VPs. Here again, I don't know the backstory, but Barbara must have been on the nominating committee, and I am sure she had a hand in this.

I have focused on the personal, but of course Barbara had a major impact on me and others intellectually. Of particular importance to me, especially early on when I was formulating my own ideas on understanding the gender pay gap, was her overcrowding model: simple, elegant, insightful. It was published in 1974 but was circulating in draft form prior to that and may have been the paper she presented at those early seminars I attended. This paper was especially significant in providing an explanation of the relationship between occupational segregation (differences in occupational distributions between two groups) and the resulting wage gap. The modern reader may not realize that this emphasis on occupational segregation playing a role in generating pay gaps, beyond the observation that skill levels might differ across occupations, was pathbreaking. In Bergmann's model, employer discrimination which excluded women from "male jobs" generated a gender pay gap as women crowded into "female jobs" depressing wages in the female jobs.

I too had been focusing on employment segregation in my dissertation. I was influenced in part by my reading of sociological literature, where there had long been an emphasis on occupational segregation. But I felt empirical analyses of occupational wage differences between the sexes would likely be fraught with ambiguity regarding the relative role of supply- versus demand-side factors. So, in my dissertation, which became the basis of *Equal Pay in the Office* (1977), I decided to focus on the role of employment segregation by sex in influencing the gender pay gap within narrowly defined occupational categories. Not only did this have the advantage of abstracting from gender differences in occupational preferences, but it also served to highlight an additional dimension of employment segregation that was getting considerably less attention at the time (and indeed still does)—sex segregation by establishment and industry.

I developed a model that posited an internal wage structure that constrained the employer to pay the same base pay rate to all workers within an occupational category, as well as a wage hierarchy of firms for potentially equally productive labor that was consistent across occupational categories. I further assumed that employer tastes for discrimination against women *à la* Becker (1957) were widespread, but the ability to exercise them was constrained by the firm's position in the wage hierarchy. That is, the wages offered by the firm for each occupation were determined by a variety of institutional and market forces and could not easily be altered to accommodate employer preferences for male versus female employees. At the time, my model was grounded in the internal labor market analysis of Doeringer and Piore (1971) and an older institutional literature. The new personnel economics would later greatly expand on within firm analyses (e.g., Lazear 1995) and an extensive later literature utilizing firm-worker matched data would provide considerable empirical support for the assumption of a wage hierarchy of firms, or "firm effects" (e.g., Abowd et al. 1999).

The model predicted that there would be considerable establishment segregation by sex within occupations. Moreover, women would be concentrated in firms which paid lower wages to both men and women, and conversely men would tend to be employed at firms which paid higher wages to both sexes. The gender pay differential within occupations would be due primarily to pay differences among firms rather than pay differences within firms. These predictions were all strongly borne out by the data.

Memories from Amy Cross

Though I did not know Barbara Bergmann personally, I have an intimate connection to her intellectual journey through her professional library, the bulk of which now resides in my home. During the isolation of the pandemic years, Bergmann's books—with occasional sticky notes containing her thoughts—became my intellectual companions as I developed my dissertation on occupational segregation in U.S. history.

One particular book tells a story that captures the connection I feel to my intellectual forebears. On my shelves sit three copies of *The Ideas of the Woman Suffrage Movement 1890–1920* by Aileen S. Kraditor—Bergmann's copy, Heidi Hartmann's copy, and my own copy. In Bergmann's copy, a passage is marked about suffragists' beliefs that women voters would help prevent unnecessary wars. Her only annotation was a sticky note with the female symbol and the word 'peace'. As an economist studying the impact of the military on civilian women workers, I wish Bergmann and I could have discussed that passage with the benefit of a century of hindsight. Having her library as I study is like having a faint trace of an intellectual conversation across time, even if I wish she had written more in the margins.

The physical inheritance of Bergmann's library came to me through Heidi Hartmann and the Institute for Women's Policy Research when they were downsizing their physical holdings in 2020. I carefully cataloged the collection, which included approximately 180 volumes spanning feminist economics, gender studies, labor history, and social policy. Hartmann and I offered volumes to others, particularly young scholars and IAFFE members.

Furthermore, I came to American University specifically because I knew I wanted to center gender in my doctoral education in economics, and our Program on Gender Analysis in Economics (PGAE) was a standout program.

Bergmann developed the initial graduate gender course in the department in the late 1980s (Sex Roles in the Economy), which was used to recruit Ph.D. students. With that course, Bergmann initiated the department's unique graduate specialization in the emerging field. I am sad I never took that course from her, but I feel fortunate to have a tangible connection to her intellectual world through her library.

Memories from Deborah M. Figart

I first met Barbara Bergmann in 1986, shortly after defending my Ph.D. dissertation on women's career ladders and pay inequity at American University in Washington, DC. I was introduced to her by my dissertation advisor, Nancy Smith Barrett. Nancy was instrumental in recruiting and hiring Barbara Bergmann from the University of Maryland to be Distinguished Professor of Economics at American University. In the late 1980s, Nancy Barrett and Barbara Bergmann were two of the only five or six women to be full professors of economics at universities that had Ph.D. programs in economics. They broke several glass ceilings as students at Harvard University and in their careers.

Nancy and Barbara knew each other professionally and through policy circles. Both were labor economists, with experience in academia and the federal government. Both were among the first to focus on gender in the workforce. Bergmann once served on the President's Council of Economic Advisors. Barrett spent two years at the Congressional Budget Office before being appointed Assistant Secretary of Labor in the administration of President Jimmy Carter. It was such an honor for me as a junior cis-gender woman economist to be mentored by such eminent, amazing women.

Barbara's mentorship began within the year that we met, while I remained at American University teaching full-time in the Washington Semester Program. She read a Request for Proposals (RFP) for conducting a study for the Department of Labor on occupational segregation by gender, a topic for which Bergmann became famous with pathbreaking articles on occupational crowding (1971) and (1974). She continued to do research on this topic and pay inequity throughout her career and reached economists, policymakers, and students with the publication of her book, *The Economic Emergence of Women* (Bergmann 1986).

Barbara met with me in person. She showed me the RFP. The sometimes stern and forthright (and unforgettable) Barbara proclaimed "We are doing this study together." During the initial process, Barbara introduced me to the proficiencies of assembling a proposal for a federal government research grant. These skills in grantsmanship have served me well in my career. When our proposal was accepted and funded, Barbara coached me through the reading and writing process. She helped me hone my ability to write for a policy audience, and not just for scholars. We spent over a year working closely together, culminating with publication of our study (one chapter) in the findings of the U.S. Department of Labor's Commission on Workforce Quality and Labor Market Efficiency (Figart & Bergmann, 1989). Since 1989, I have been fortunate to draw upon the tools taught by Barbara to be awarded research grants internal and external to my university, most notably a Fulbright Research Scholar award in Western Europe from 1989–1990.

Fortunately, our professional paths continued to cross for decades after our close work together. Through conference participation at the International Association for Feminist Economics, the Eastern Economic Association, and the Allied Social Science Association, I heard many papers and talks she delivered, and I delivered my own at those conferences. Her energy and enthusiasm for gender equity endure and inspire me. She set an example to risk relocating to another university and to "not let tenure be a trap". She set an example to keep research and writing and fighting for what is right long after retiring from teaching. Upon reflection, Barbara's display of "tough love" has seeped into my teaching philosophy and definitely had a positive impact on my success teaching wide-ranging classes—from principles of microeconomics to senior seminar in economics to general studies courses on gender and work and economic well-being. It is with deep appreciation that Barbara was part of my life.

Memories from Maria "Sergy" Floro

[I remember] Barbara Bergmann as an Activist. Barbara once said: "I have been able to use my standing as an economist and even a bit here and there of my economics training to write on these matters, and, I hope, to make a contribution to the eventual achievement of a more humane world".

She remarkably accomplished this in her capacity not only as a professor and scholar, but also as an activist, one who is not shy in speaking out her mind and her beliefs. It was her strong sense of justice that guided her work and actions.

As a scholar, she contributed significant insights to the issues of poverty, racism, sexism, child care, and the plight of single mothers. She challenged the economics discipline, including its models and methodology, and I quote: "The idea that economists will come closer to the reality...by sitting in their academic offices and making up stories than they might get by observing or talking to people is bizarre. That such story-spinning has persisted as the chosen methodology of our profession ....is beyond bizarre—it is disgraceful."

A frank and direct person, Barbara was in her best form when she was in debates such as defending social security, affirmative action, or the Lilly Ledbetter Fair Pay Act. A former president of the AAUP (American Association of University Professors), she was an outspoken critic of the growing administrative bureaucracy that wasted resources of colleges and universities. Her 1991 essay on this has been widely quoted.

Barbara knew very well that action often speaks louder than words. Her passionate belief on the importance of addressing gender inequities and women's concerns propelled her to do something. She saw the need for feminist economists to gather and discuss together in order to push the boundaries of the discipline. For in her view, "the state of economics has vast practical consequences for humanity's well-being". Together with some people in this audience, here in Washington DC in 1990, she conceived of an IAFFE. When she joined American University in the same year as I did, in 1989, Barbara introduced graduate and undergraduate courses on Women in the Economy and Sex Roles in Economic Life and developed the field in our doctoral program. Barbara thus laid the vital groundwork for the creation of the unique Graduate Program on Gender Analysis in Economics (PGAE) at the Economics Department here in American University.

Over the years, Barbara Bergmann challenged, provoked, and inspired both faculty and students. Her frank remarks made us reflect more deeply on our own ideas and arguments.

That has been her abiding effect on me. Yes, we disagreed at times, but we had mutual respect for each other's opinions.

I want to end by quoting her friend, the late Marianne Ferber, "There are few who have earned as much warm gratitude for generous help to her colleagues, or have gained as much genuine admiration for their dedication as Barbara, of whom it may truly be said that she has made it her mission to comfort the afflicted and afflict the comfortable".

Memories from Thesia Garner

My fondest memories of Barbara were when my little (from ages 2–3 years old) daughter (recently adopted from China) and I visited with her and her husband in their lovely home in Maryland and when we enjoyed our dinners out at their favorite Chinese restaurant. She and her husband also had adopted one of their children; Barbara and I had the inherent bond of mothers. We shared the joys and challenges of being a professional economists when women were not as welcomed as we are today. Barbara would have laughed at that last reference to women not being as welcomed—I can hear her saying "Ha! That would be an understatement!" Barbara shared the joys and challenges of being working moms and the continual striving to do our best in our professional as well as private lives. She challenged me in thought and at the same time encouraged me in her strong but caring way and with great humor. She always stood tall. I will remember Barbara as a leader with a vision to improve our understanding of the contributions of all people, especially those of women.

Memories from Marlene Kim

In graduate school, I was researching comparable worth and gender wage discrimination. A psychology journal had a call for papers for a special issue on comparable worth, so I submitted a paper based on my research regarding how and why women's occupations were underpaid. I received a hard copy of my manuscript back from Barbara Bergmann, a reviewer of my article, marked up with generous comments on what I should include, delete, rephrase, and how. She also said, "Give my best to Clair [Brown, my advisor]." Using Barbara's feedback, I rewrote the article—and it was published. Two years later, I wrote another article around gender and pay and sent it to Barbara, and she emailed me that she didn't know what something that I said in my paper meant, because it was written unclearly or poorly or both. She said that I could visit her for a few days in Washington DC in her home and she would help me.

I took her up on her offer. I wrote all day, received feedback from her, and revised again the next day. For about three days we did this. The first evening, she and her husband Fred cooked and fed me dinner. On the second evening, we went out for excellent Korean food, which they generously paid for. The third evening, I was on my own because they had guests coming over.

I stayed in touch with Barbara through the years. Either the first meeting or the first conference (or both) of the International Association for Feminist Economics (IAFFE) was held in Barbara Bergmann's home, with a cluster of other luminaries, including Heidi Hartmann. Heidi and I served on the first nominating committee for IAFFE: in Barbara's kitchen one morning, we discussed who should fill the roles of President, Vice President, Treasurer, journal editor, etc.

I continued to see Barbara at IAFFE conferences and at Allied Social Science Association (ASSA) meetings. At one IAFFE conference in the Netherlands, I had dinner with her and her daughter, along with my boyfriend at the time (now ex-husband), and I believe other colleagues. Her daughter, who was probably in her early twenties back then, wanted to explore the red-light district. Barbara didn't want to go there, but she refused to let her daughter go alone. Although Barbara had trouble walking back then and wore those thick stockings to help her walk about, she insisted that we accompany her daughter. The four of us toured the red-light district together.

Barbara was one of the few senior feminist economists when I was fresh out of graduate school. Her work paved the way for others to follow, including myself. Simply believing that discrimination existed was anathema to the economics profession at that time. So it was important for those of us who understood that gender bias was crawling around out in the labor market and everywhere else that Barbara existed. Her cogent, clear, great work on how discrimination can thrive and the evidence for this supported our scholarship and affirmed our personal experiences. I cited her Affirmative Action book in my research and used it in my classes for years. It was terrific in its clear explanations, simplicity of arguments, and plethora of solid evidence on how and why discrimination endures.

Barbara was a genius. At one time I was told she was in contention for the Nobel Prize in economics. I hope this anecdote about her reaching out and helping a lowly graduate student publish her first academic paper illustrates how generous she was as well. Not only did she espouse policies that can help women, she also walked the walk: putting these into action in ways that were never compensated nor publicly acknowledged. Until now.

Memories from Mary King

I first "met" Barbara Bergmann when I read her important contributions on the economic status of women and the dynamics of gender in the economy, as well as her messages in the conversations on our IAFFE listserv.

Although, I didn't have the opportunity to spend much time with her I got to know her a little better when Lisa Saunders and I interviewed her and Marianne Ferber, to help later generations of feminist economists also know them and their histories.

She paved the way for me and others, who were able to focus our research and to publish on policies to improve women's economic situations and to teach courses covering the theoretical and empirical work on "Women in the Economy", as well as to start and build IAFFE.

I found her work on crowding in the labor market particularly compelling and useful.

Memories from Myra H. Strober

I first met Barbara when I began my first job as a lecturer and then as assistant professor of economics at the University of Maryland in September 1967. Barbara was 14 years older than I and was already a full professor, but, like me, she had just recently given birth to her first child. We were the only two women faculty members at Maryland, and Barbara became my mentor.

Over the years, Barbara's extremely valuable advice was direct and directive—just like she was. When I told her I was considering moving to a part-time position, she strongly counseled me against it. "You simply cannot have a successful academic career if you go part-time," she said. So, I pushed through with a full-time schedule, despite the absence of any maternity leave (let alone parental leave) and the extraordinary difficulties of finding child care.

I left Maryland after 3 years and stayed in touch with Barbara while I taught at Berkeley and then Stanford; we saw each other at least once a year at the American Economics Association (AEA) annual meetings.

In the 1970s, we both changed our fields of study, she to the economics of racial discrimination and I to women's employment and the economics of child care. But soon, Barbara began studying discrimination against women, as well as occupational segregation by gender and the economics of child care. We were suddenly in the same field.

At the 1990 AEA meetings we were both part of the small group that founded the International Association for Feminist Economics (IAFFE) and its journal, *Feminist Economics*, edited by Diana Strassmann. We both served as associate editors of *Feminist Economics*, and Barbara became the second president of IAFFE and I the third (Marianne Ferber was IAFFE's first president).

During and after our respective terms as presidents of IAFFE, Barbara and I were in close touch and saw each other frequently. After her husband, Fred, died, Barbara was exceedingly depressed, and in 2015, when she was 87, she took her own life. I had the privilege of giving a eulogy at her memorial service, where her friends and colleagues repeatedly acknowledged our intellectual and personal debt to a brilliant, outspoken, and committed feminist economist. We miss her to this day.

9.3 Here's to You, Barbara

As earlier mentioned, this last paragraph summarizes a collection of tributes to Bergmann that were published during her lifetime or shortly after her passing, and it is intended to complement the previous two paragraphs of original materials. It includes a special issue of *Feminist Economics*, with the contributions of M. Strober, M. Ferber, F. Modigliani, N. Folbre, and D. McCloskey, as well as obituaries that appeared in the *newsletter* of the Economics Department at American University, in *The New York Times*, in *The Washington Post*, along with tributes by Peter Riach, and Nancy Folbre on that occasion.

The chapter ends with the final part of David Bergmann's eulogy for his mother.

Feminist Economics special issue.

In 1998, a special issue of *Feminist Economics* was published in honor of Bergmann's work on discrimination, pay equity, occupational segregation, poverty, housework, and women's dignity. In this paragraph, only personal reminiscences published in that issue are reported. The academic articles have been embedded in previous chapters according to their topics.

As Myra Strober pointed out, that special issue was aimed at simultaneously "clarifying, augmenting, extending, and deepening [Bergmann's work]", given the profound influence it had on many feminist economists. Strober underlined how much Bergmann cared about real problems and how to solve them, and she was disappointed by the "unfortunate detour" taken by current economics, which focuses on "mathematical lacunae and elegant theoretical irrelevancies while neglecting the real economic problems of people, especially women and people of color, for whom the economic system does not work equitably or successfully". Strober concluded that:

> There is a lively group of economists and other social scientists planting and sowing precisely in the fields which she has plowed. In the best traditions of feminist scholarship, the volume blends theory, empirical work, and advocacy. Here's to you Barbara, with appreciation, affection, and optimism that the changes about which you care so deeply will be realized in the not-too-distant years of the coming century. (Strober 1998, p. 1)

Marianne Ferber's article was focused on Bergmann's capacity for mentoring students and on being inspirational for both students and colleagues: "a role model, a mentor and to some who were particularly fortunate, a devoted friend". Nonetheless, as Ferber recalled, while many male economists have achieved more recognition within the economic profession than she has. Nevertheless, "there are few who have earned as much warm gratitude for generous help to her colleagues, or have gained as much genuine admiration for their dedication as Barbara" (Ferber 1998, p. 4).

Franco Modigliani's reminiscences of Bergmann are particularly touching (Modigliani 1998). He wrote that it was a pleasure to accept the invitation to write a few lines in honor of Barbara, "because I can never forget how many times she taught me some very important lessons". They met in 1958 when Modigliani spent a year in Harvard as a visiting professor to replace Wassily Leontief on sabbatical. At that time, Bergmann, in her early 20s, was a graduate student working on her thesis. He remembered her "keen powers of observation and her well-developed sense of humor". He continued:

> She proceeded to instruct me, a poor hick from the country, whose previous experience was with primitive and uncouth institutions such as the New School for Social Research, the University of Illinois, and the Carnegie Institute of Technology. Early on, she taught me about the caste system. In the Harvard scheme of things, she explained, the highest caste consisted of the full professors, with the associate professors not altogether outcasts; then came the lower caste of the untenured assistant professors and instructors; and finally the lowest caste, that of the students. (Modigliani 1998, p. 143)

According to Barbara, interaction between castes was not tolerated, except "for some eccentric professor" considered "broad-minded and democratic". Unlike other American universities, where junior faculty were seen as professors "on their way" (as the Italians said, they are "incamminati" which means "those who have started to walk)" (ibid).

Modigliani admitted that he never dared ask her in which caste he fell, "knowing she would have no qualms in answering what she really thought".

In Harvard, Modigliani was teaching macroeconomics for graduate students, which were also open to undergraduates, and Bergmann helped him to prepare the lectures by advising him to be rigorous, without coddling the students by glossing over the hard part of the course. They used to prepare the final exam by writing some questions and then deciding which ones to use. Apparently, Bergmann's questions were rather tough, while she found many of Modigliani's much too easy. He wrote: "she strongly suggested that I was a 'softy'", especially during the process of grading exams for undergraduates.

Modigliani justified himself by claiming that:

> With the graduate students one had to use affirmative action in the form of lower standards! (...) In following her distinguished later career and writings, I have sometimes thought of those Harvard days, and have had a suspicion that her distinction between graduate and undergraduate students applied to the human race, with men playing the role of the graduate students! Might one conclude that the well-known practice of discrimination against women is justifiable as affirmative action to protect inferior male-kind? And on the same grounds of affirmative action, I trust that Barbara will not be given an opportunity to reply. (ibid, p. 144)

Nancy Folbre's reminiscences described Bergmann's personality (Folbre 1998). While preparing her contribution to the special issue in her honor, Folbre sent her an e-mail message and asked for a copy of Bergmann's vita. Bergmann's reply was that in her CV the most important things are missing. More specifically Folbre reported that, according to Barbara, these most important things were:

> My upbringing in the sour-cream-drenched Bronx, God's mistake in failing to answer my prayer when I was 5, my crucial visit to the Russian pavilion at the New York World's Fair in 1938, my maiden air trip in the same year from LaGuardia Airport to Newark Airport and back, my years roaming the Cornell campus in high heels and lipstick in the fruitless quest for a husband, and the time I was accused by an official of the Census Bureau of sabotaging the 1980 Census. (Folbre 1998, p. 160) (see Chapter 2)

Then, Folbre went on by recalling some more personal memories. Without knowing Folbre personally, Bergmann invited her to participate in an American Economics Association session she had organized in Greece. When in Athens, Bergmann invited Folbre to become active in IAFFE while drinking ouzo. Later on, Bergmann helped Folbre to find a place at American University for one semester when Folbre was having some problems in her own university. And then, Folbre recalled, during an IAFFE conference, Barbara accused Folbre of being "Victor Fuchs in drag", as Folbre was insisting that there are some important differences in the supply of men's and women's labor, although, unlike Professor Fuchs, who believed such differences are biologically-given preferences, Folbre considered them culturally constructed and socially contested. In spite of this clarification, Folbre wrote, "Barbara remains suspicious" (ibid, 161).

In her reminiscences, Folbre rightly pointed out that Bergmann belonged to the classical liberal feminist tradition that goes back to John Stuart Mill and Harriet Hardy Taylor Mill, albeit her sex-role caste system is comparable to the notion of patriarchy, adopted by socialist scholars. She wrote:

> While Barbara was optimistic that the forces of economic development, modernization, and increased female labor force participation were undermining this caste system, she also emphasized the need for strong feminist public policies. (ibid, p. 162)

In fact, Folbre continued:

> In a hawk–dove game, the hawks win (until they have rendered the doves extinct). Should we encourage young women to be hawk-like? I think Barbara leans in this direction, because she associates dove-like qualities with, to mix a metaphor, the underdog. (ibid, p. 166)

Finally, Deirdre McCloskey's reminiscences of Bergmann touched on some traits of Barbara's personality as well, such as getting straight to the point, never getting offended, and being eager for confrontation. McCloskey wrote:

> When I saw Barbara in Mexico City in July of 1997 and we wandered through the streets together trying to find the hall for the IAFFE reception, she immediately and with no preliminary social chit-chat started quizzing me on my views about some economic issue – I think it was the minimum wage, but confess that I was so overwhelmed by her eagerness to *Get to Work* that I can't remember. Her attitude was: Here I have a living, breathing member of the Chicago School. What a great opportunity to sharpen my own arguments! Let's see if she has anything to say on the issue. I didn't, but that didn't stop Barbara. (McCloskey 1998, p. 182)

Obituary appeared in the newsletter of the Economics Department of American University

The Economics Department of American University mourns the loss of Professor Emerita Barbara Bergmann. She once said: "I have been able to use my standing as an economist and even a bit here and there of my economics training to write on these matters, and, I hope, to make a contribution to the eventual achievement of a more humane world".

Barbara Bergmann has remarkably accomplished this in her capacity as professor, scholar, colleague, mentor, and active member of the AU community. Since joining American University in 1989 as distinguished professor of economics, she developed graduate and undergraduate courses on gender roles in the economy, drawing students of economics to the understanding of human behavior, economic and social outcomes, and public policy from a gendered lens. As a scholar, she contributed significant insights to a wide range of subfields in economics including macroeconomics, agent-based modelling, and social economic issues of poverty, child care, single mothers, and family. She was active in participating in seminars and debates addressing today's pressing issues and challenges such as unemployment, social security, urban development, discrimination, poverty, woeful lack of childcare support, and women's status.

Over the years, Barbara Bergmann has challenged, inspired, and mentored both faculty and students. She has been an outspoken critic of the current state of higher education in terms of the growing administrative bureaucracy and inefficiencies that have wasted precious financial and human resources of colleges and universities. She has been an inspiration to the creation of the Graduate Program on Gender Analysis in Economics (PGAE) at the Economics Department. Her generosity extended to the establishment of the Barbara and Fred Bergmann Fund to support graduate students in gender research that can help advance the discipline through first-hand investigation and observational methods. In the words of her friend, the late Marianne Ferber, "There are few who have earned as much warm gratitude for generous help to her colleagues, or have gained as much genuine admiration for their dedication as Barbara, of whom it may truly be said that she has made it her mission to comfort the afflicted and afflict the comfortable."

Obituary appeared in The New York Times (Schwartz 2015)

Barbara Bergmann, a pioneer in the study of gender in the economy who herself overcame barriers to women in the world of academic economics, died on April 5 at her home in Bethesda, Md. She was 87.

Her son, David Martin Bergmann, confirmed her death.

Ms. Bergmann was an emeritus professor at both American University and the University of Maryland, and she continued to research, publish and consult until very recently.

Sixty years ago, Ms. Bergmann did not need to sift through economic data to find evidence of discrimination. When she was a graduate student at Harvard in the mid-1950s, one library at the university was off-limits to women, recalled Alice Rivlin, a fellow Ph.D. student who went on to become vice chairwoman of the Federal Reserve and director of the Office of Management and Budget in the 1990s.

Women had just begun to be permitted to work as teaching fellows at the time, Ms. Rivlin added, and took exams separately from their male counterparts.

"It wasn't an atmosphere that was very congenial to women" Ms. Rivlin said. "It was hard to get an academic job unless you wanted to teach at a women's college."

Ms. Bergmann persisted and initially taught at Harvard as an economics instructor after earning her Ph.D. there in 1958 and then joined the White House Council of Economic Advisers in 1961 as a senior staff economist.

After working at Brandeis University and the Brookings Institution, Ms. Bergmann joined the University of Maryland faculty in 1965, teaching there until 1988. She taught economics at American University from 1988 to 1997.

A co-founder of the International Association for Feminist Economics, Ms. Bergmann also contributed columns to the Sunday Business section of The New York Times in the 1980s.

Long a liberal voice in the field, Ms. Bergmann was a fierce critic of the laissez-faire policies then being advocated by the Reagan administration, as well as proposed cuts to social programs dating back to the New Deal.

"We have our Scrooges, and lately the Scrooges have grown bolder in expressing themselves," she wrote in December 1981. "But we are not a nation of Scrooges. On the contrary, we are a nation that, seeing voluntary efforts as commendable but chronically insufficient, has for almost 50 years been relieving social distress through the federal Treasury, using the coercive powers of government to collect the funds."

Some of Ms. Bergmann's columns turned out to be prescient, with an early warning of just how severe the recession of the early 1980s would be, as well as a May 1982 column entitled "A Threat Ahead From Word Processors".

In that piece, she predicted that the advent of computers and "an electronic revolution in the office" would decimate the need for typists, secretaries, and clerical workers, who tended to be women.

She noted the downward pressure this might have on wages in some fields and argued that while technological change and greater productivity might be a good thing economically, existing barriers to women in the workforce might make finding new jobs difficult and worsen poverty.

"Will high-status people be willing to type their own documents in the future?" she asked.

Her answer was: “Though the stigma runs deep, the spreading use of the computer for tasks other than word processing may succeed in removing the stain from the activity of typing on the job.”

In addition to frequent articles in academic journals, Ms. Bergmann was the author of a well- received history of women in the workplace, *The Economic Emergence of Women.* It first appeared in 1986 and was reissued in a new edition in 2005. The book traces how women began joining the labor force in considerable numbers in the nineteenth century and did not start with the rise of modern feminism. Nor was leaving the home and working for hire a result of changing attitudes; Ms. Bergmann concluded that economic forces made women’s labor too valuable to be confined to domestic work.

In the late twentieth century, Ms. Bergmann called for the government to do more in the marketplace on behalf of women and single-parent families, including support for increased access to day care and the passage of legislation mandating comparable pay for women and men.

Whether at Harvard in the 1950s or during the Reagan era, Ms. Bergmann was ready to challenge the prevailing orthodoxies of the time, Ms. Rivlin said. “Barbara was always quite outspoken and forceful in her views,” she said. “She was never shy about them”.

Obituary appeared in The Washington Post (Weil 2015)

Barbara Bergmann, a scholar, author and original thinker who taught for decades at two Washington-area universities and was known as a leader in feminist or gender-based economics, died April 5 at her home in Bethesda. She was 87.

The cause was suicide, said her son David Bergmann.

The holder of a Harvard doctorate in economics, Dr. Bergmann taught at the University of Maryland from 1965 to 1988 and at American University from 1988 to 1997. Afterward, she continued to speak out on public issues, to publish her work, and raise consciousness about women’s issues in economics.

She was “the Betty Friedan of the economics profession,” said economist Heidi Hartmann, president of the Washington-based Institute for Women’s Policy Research.

Over the past half-century, she was known as one of the more influential figures in the economic world, expanding economists’ areas of concern to include the specific and distinctive roles played by women in the world of profit and loss, and getting and spending.

Her aim, once shared by relatively few but now a recognized area of economic thought, was to show how the interests, treatment, and personal characteristics of women might affect the way economies function.

An author of books and papers often seen as visionary or prescient, she was a believer in using economic knowledge for social betterment. She was an enthusiastic and outspoken participant in policy debates and was credited with groundbreaking work on questions of race and gender in the economy, on employment discrimination and on the underlying assumptions held by majorities of those in her profession.

She was mathematically inclined and had worked on computer simulations of economic activity.

Not known for excessive concern for the feelings of colleagues, she often gave interviews disparaging how they reached their conclusions.

Too often, she said, they relied on faulty assumptions that were too readily accepted. As a result, their work "has almost nothing to do with real life," she said.

In particular, she took issue with work purporting to explain why women were paid less than men. In the early 1970s, she published what has become known as her "crowding" theory to explain lower pay for blacks and women.

It was pervasive, systemic discrimination, she said, that often caused blacks and women to crowd into fields that paid less merely because they were available.

She championed methods of the natural sciences, of survey and observation, and of using real-world data to construct models of real-world economics.

Both a feminist and an economist, she was the former before the latter. As a small girl, she said, she recognized what a woman needed for independence.

"I quite quickly perceived," she told an interviewer, "that a woman had to have her own money".

(…) Her doctorate from Harvard, which she received in 1958, created no clamor in academia for her services. "Although I was a star pupil," she once told an interviewer, "I didn't get any offers of academic positions. However, my attitude has always been that anger is bad for the career."

One of her most influential books, *The Economic Emergence of Women*, appeared in 1986 and was regarded as particularly useful for undergraduates.

Obituary By Peter Riach

In Steve Pressman's book *Fifty Major Economists*, there are biographies of 48 men; the two exceptions being Joan Robinson and Barbara Bergmann. It says much about the academic economics profession that neither was awarded a Nobel Prize. Barbara's contemptuous attitude to the Nobel Prize was the subject of her article 'Abolish the Nobel Prize for Economics' (Bergmann 1999). She begins provocatively: "having a Nobel Prize for economics is making the economics profession look ridiculous". She goes on to explain why. Both Joan and Barbara were iconoclastic, and neither resiled from making trenchant and sometimes sarcastic criticisms of leading members of the mainstream academic establishment. Barbara favored direct investigation of economic phenomena as an alternative to statistical inference and expressed her contempt for the perpetrators of new classical economics. She wrote:

> Lucas and Rapping did not, of course, proceed to investigate the factual issues they had raised in the direct way I had suggested would be appropriate. Instead, they proceeded in what I think deserves to be characterized as an insanely indirect way. They got some macro-economic times series data ..., threw the data into a computer and ran some regressions ..., (then) reported that the printout gave only modest support to their ideas, but was not inconsistent with them (the entrails of the next chicken they ate were probably also not inconsistent with the Lucas–Rapping ideas, but they refrained from reporting that). (Bergmann 1989, pp. 35–37)

Barbara made major contributions to the economics of race and gender, including a rigorous advocacy of affirmative action as an indispensable solution to the racial and sexual discrimination which persists in society. The dust jacket of her book *In Defense of Affirmative Action* includes the following endorsement from John Kenneth Galbraith:

> Barbara Bergmann as much as anyone I know combines good compassionate sense with first-rate professional competence and a wonderful capacity for getting and organizing the relevant information. This is evident in this excellent book.

Inter alia in this book, Barbara, with typically robust vigour, attacks Glen Loury's assertion that affirmative action discourages the acquisition of skills by the targets of this policy. Having demolished his argument, she observes:

> Perhaps the reader is beginning to wonder about the appropriateness of Loury's appointment to the Economics Department at Harvard. But the reader should be informed that silly theories are no disqualification there, as long as they are expressed mathematically. (Bergmann 1996, p. 143)

Barbara published in *Econometrica* in 1973; *Journal of Political Economy* in 1979; *American Economic Review* in 1969, 1973, 1981 and 1994; *Journal of Human Resources* in 1971 and 1993; *Feminist Economics* in 1995, 1997 and 2000; *Journal of Economic Perspectives* in 1989 and 1990; and *Journal of Economic Behaviour and Organization* in 1988 and 1990. Probably, her most famous and influential publication was the book she first published in 1986 and reprinted in 2005, *The Economic Emergence of Women*, which has been cited over 1000 times.

Predictably, she had no sympathy for Gary Becker's theory that economic Darwinism would eliminate racial and sexual discrimination. She wrote:

> Most economists are not capable of seeing that wage setting and other employment practices were and are affected by societal systems of status differentials, whether in the harsh regime of the pre-civil rights South, or in the subtler regimes of race and sex favouritism that are still in force everywhere today.

Confirmation that despite Gary Becker, racial and sexual discrimination in employment is persistent and pervasive is to be found in the results of the direct investigation method which Barbara favoured (Riach & Rich 2002). In her article 'Why do most economists know so little about the economy?' Barbara argued that 'the subject matter of economics is a lot closer to anthropology than to mathematics' (Bergmann 1989, p. 33). She recommended that economists should adopt the anthropologists' technique of participant observation. Once in 1988, when I was explaining my current research to a Fellow in a Cambridge Senior Common Room, she replied that I sounded more like a sociologist than an economist. This would have confirmed the disdain which some of my Monash colleagues had for me, but it would have impressed Barbara.

In 1987, Judy Rich and I published the results of our field experiment of sexual discrimination in the Melbourne labor market. Because of Barbara's eminence in the study of sexual discrimination in the labor market, we sent her a copy. At that stage, we were unaware of her campaign for direct investigation of markets, so we were delighted to receive the following reply:

> Thanks a lot for sending me the article that you and Judy Rich wrote on testing discrimination. I think it is a contribution to knowledge to a degree rare in economic research … (W)e should do a great deal more of this kind of work than we do, and maybe yours will inspire some. (Bergmann to Riach 1987, in Riach 2015)

In view of the obstacles we had faced from the Monash hierarchy in conducting this research, Barbara's accolade was particularly welcome. In the past 20 years, the field experiment literature has flourished, as demonstrated by Harrison and List (2004).

In 1994, Judy Rich and I were invited to present our experimental research on sexual discrimination to the conference of the Eastern Economic Association in Boston. Afterwards, we traveled to Washington to meet Barbara for the first time and spent a delightful evening with her and Fred, who introduced us to his collection of 'Dean jokes'.

We met Barbara from time to time at Feminist Economics conferences, and in 1996, I successfully nominated her for an Honorary Doctorate at De Montfort University. I am sure she would have been delighted to know that in 1998, she was joined in the select group of 'Riach-nominated Honorary Doctorates' by Barbara Castle, who had been the Cabinet Minister responsible for the introduction of 'equal pay for equal work' in the United Kingdom.

It has been one of the great privileges of my academic life to have had both Joan Robinson and Barbara Bergmann as friends, mentors, and referees.

Nancy Folbre's Tribute After Barbara's Passing (2016)

Folbre paid a wonderful homage to Bergmann a few months after her passing, during a session "Inequality, Public Policy, and the Future of Economics: In Memory of Barbara Bergmann," organized by Diana Strassmann, at the meetings of the American Economic Association in San Francisco, on January 5, 2016, later published in Folbre's blog.[1] Below, an excerpt from Folbre's words:

[1] Retrieved November 25, 2025, from https://www.revaluingcare.org/heroine-of-the-noisy-revolution/. I own this information to David Bergmann, who kindly shared the text with me.

Claudia Goldin famously described the dramatic movement of women into paid employment over the course of the twentieth century as a "quiet" revolution of cumulative labor supply decisions. But this revolution had its noisy moments, and its noisy advocates, among them the magnificently noisy Barbara Bergmann. Barbara never denied the relevance of individual choice. But she emphasized the institutional structures and cultural norms that have traditionally constricted women's choices, and she chose to challenge them.

In *The Economic Emergence of Women*, she described a literal caste system in which people were labeled "pink" or "blue" and those labels determined not only their roles in the economy, but the ways they were taught to accept those roles. She never agreed with the notion that economists should take individual preferences as a "given." In fact, she often suggested that women were hoodwinked into internalizing some very expensive preferences of care and concern for others.

The feminist movement of the 1970s relied heavily on a term that has now fallen out of fashion: consciousness raising. Barbara believed, to her dying day, that consciousness could and should be raised. She described a social structure of discrimination against women that could and should be dismantled by collective action and public policy.

She also believed in the power of individual indignation, and she knew how to exercise it on a daily basis. For instance, she loved to eat fine food, but hated the conspicuous division of labor largely based on gender and race evident in most upscale restaurants.

She had a little card printed—the size and shape of a business card—saying something like this: "Your business appears to allocate tasks based on race and gender. I hope you are aware that you may be in violation of federal anti-discrimination law and you may also be alienating valuable customers like myself." She would sometimes ask a waiter to send the manager over to her table. He usually came expecting praise for the cuisine. Instead she would hand him the card with a stern glance, usually leaving him speechless.

Of all Barbara's important contributions to economic theory, my favorite is the short "The Economic Risks of Being a Housewife", which appeared in the *American Economic Review* in 1981. In it, she explained why housewives should be considered members of a particularly disempowered and risky occupation. Whatever benefits it offered, it left them vulnerable to the economic insecurity typically resulting from divorce.

Much of my own work builds on this argument, focusing on the economic risks of being a paid or unpaid caregiver. Gender inequality cannot be reduced to inequalities between men and women in the same household or the same workplace. It also encompasses profound gender inequalities in the costs of caring for dependents—inequalities that can be measured in both time and money.

As Barbara intuited, care for others is a costly preference. As the angry Cersei in the HBO melodrama *Game of Thrones* put it "the more people you love, the weaker you are." In my view, caring preferences have contradictory consequences—punishing in some respects, rewarding in others; costly for individuals, valuable for society.

Barbara often warned me not to idealize caring preferences. She worried that more public support for family work would, by reducing its costs, encourage women to take on more responsibilities for it than men. In his 1988 book *Women's Quest for Economic Equality*, Victor Fuchs suggested that single mothers were more vulnerable than fathers to poverty because they derived so much satisfaction from taking custody of their children. This was, after all, a revealed preference. If they wanted to, they could have relinquished their children to foster care.

Barbara once accused me of being Victor Fuchs in drag. I don't think this is true. But I am pretty sure Victor Fuchs would have been more horrified by the suggestion than I was.

I miss Barbara. No one sharpened my thinking more, or set a better example of testing the edge. Every time I am tempted to whine about the sorry state of the world or succumb to slightly girly sentimentality I give myself a little slap in the face to remind myself of a formidable and fearless heroine of the noisy revolution.

The final part of David Bergmann's eulogy for his mother (Bergmann D., 2015)

The last words of this chapter are from Barbara's son, David, who concluded his eulogy with this wonderful tribute:

> My mom was the most forthright and pragmatic person I have yet to meet. She was a person who often said exactly what she thought, whether you wanted to hear it or not. A lot of times that was pretty hard to take. But again, as I grew older, I came to realize the value in that. I never had to question where I stood with her; it was always right there, out in the open. There were no mind games, no mental duress. She was a truthful and sometimes brutally honest person, but she carried no ill will in her heart. You always knew where you stood with her, for better or worse, but there was never any doubt that her criticisms and comments were borne from a desire to see me succeed, or to be happy and healthy, or just to try to make the world a better place (…). By default, being my mother, she was a huge part of my life, as all mothers are, but on top of that she was one of the most brilliant, and kind, caring, and genuinely honest human

beings I've ever known (...). Thank you for everything! Now, if Barbara were here, she'd be the first to say, enough talking, let's eat! (Bergmann D., 2015)

To conclude I invite the reader to echo David's words in thanking Barbara for what she accomplished in her life and in her profession as well as David's invitation to work and live by following Barbara's constant and tireless example of integrity and commitment.

References

Abowd, J., Kramarz, F., & Margolis, D. (1999). High wage workers and high wage firms. *Econometrica 67*(2), 251–333.

Bergmann, B. (1986). *The economic emergence of women*. Basic Books.

Bergmann, B. (1989). Why do most economists know so little about the economy? In Bowles, S. & Shepard, W. (Eds.). *Unconventional wisdom: Essays on economics in honor of John Kenneth Galbraith* (pp. 29–37). Houghton Mifflin Company.

Bergmann, B. (1996). *In defense of affirmative action*. Basic Books.

Bergmann, B. (1999). Abolish the Nobel Prize for economics. *Challenge, 42*(2), 52–57.

Bergmann, D. (2015). Barbara Rose Bergmann Eulogy. Unpublished.

Blau, F. (1997). *Equal pay in the office*. Lexington Books.

Doeringer P, & Piore, M. (1971). *Internal labour markets and manpower analysis*. M.E. Sharpe, Inc.

Ferber, M. (1998). Barbara Bergmann: Scholar, mentor and activist. *Feminist Economic, 4*(3), 3–4.

Figart, D. & . Bergmann, B. (1989). Facilitating women's occupational integration. U.S. Department of Labor, Commission on Workforce Quality and Labor Market Efficiency, 26. Available at: https://scispace.com/pdf/facilitating-women-s-occupational-integration-background-2k0836sp18.pdf.

Folbre, N. (1998). Barbara, the market and the state. *Feminist Economics, 4*(3), 159–168.

Folbre, N. (2016). Heroine of the noisy revolution. Retrieved November 11, 2025, from https://www.revaluingcare.org/heroine-of-the-noisy-revolution/

Harrison, G., & List, J. (2004). Field experiments. *Journal of Economic Literature, 42*(4), 1009–1055.

Kraditor, A. (1965). *The ideas of the woman suffrage movement 1890–1920*. Columbia University Press.

Lazear, E. (1995). A jobs-based analysis of labor markets. The *American Economic Review, 85*(2), 260–265.

McCloskey, D. (1998). Simulating Barbara. *Feminist Economics, 4*(3), 181–186.
Modigliani, F. (1998). Lessons learned from Barbara. *Feminist Economics, 4*(3), 143–144.
Riach, P. (2015). Barbara Bergmann (20 July 1927–5 April 2015). *The Economic and Labour Relations Review, 26*(3), 493–495.
Riach, P. & Rich, J. (1987). Testing for sexual discrimination in the labour market. *Australian Economic Papers, 26*, 165–178.
Riach, P. & Rich, J. (2002). Field experiments of discrimination in the market place. *The Economic Journal, 112*(483), F480–F518.
Schwartz, N. (2015, April 11). Barbara Bergmann, trailblazer for study of gender in economics, is dead at 87. *The New York Times*.
Strober, M. (1998). This one's for you, Barbara. *Feminist Economics, 4*(3), 1.
Weil, M. (2015, April, 15). Barbara Bergmann, leader in gender-based economics, dies at 87. *The Washington Post*.

CHAPTER 10

Bergmann's Place in the History of Economic Thought

Historians of economic thought commonly situate economists either within distinct schools, such as the classical school, marginalism, the various neoclassical schools based in Cambridge and Lausanne, the Austrian school, institutionalism, monetarism, and so forth, or within specific research fields, including game theory, feminist and gender economics, experimental economics, and many more (Backhouse 2002; Blaug 1997).

These categories are neither exhaustive nor mutually exclusive. Nonetheless, schools and research programs help historians to understand the genesis and development of theoretical models. For example, classical economists such as Smith, Ricardo, and Marx engaged deeply with value theory and the origins of profits, rents, and wages (Schumpeter 1954), adopting a macro approach based on class dynamics. Early neoclassical economists such as Marshall, Pareto, and Clark, by contrast, concentrated on marginal analysis, the structure of market equilibria, and the conditions under which distributive outcomes emerge, adopting a micro approach based on the decision-making of economic agents (Stigler 1982).

Beyond the identification of schools and fields, historians of economics also examine the methodological frameworks through which economists construct theoretical explanations for economic phenomena. As a matter

G. Becchio, *Barbara Bergmann*, Great Thinkers in Economics, https://doi.org/10.1007/978-3-032-18696-6_10

of fact, methodological disputes have a prominent place in the history of economic thought.[1]

In the late twentieth and early twenty-first centuries, a major divide emerged between mainstream (often described as neoclassical or orthodox) and heterodox approaches to economics. The *Journal of Economic Literature* (JEL) classification codes reinforced this divide by assigning heterodox methodologies to category B, while the remaining alphabetical categories correspond primarily to mainstream research areas (American Economic Association 2025). Mainstream economics is generally characterized by highly formalized mathematical modeling based on optimization and by econometric analysis grounded in statistical inference. These approaches imply the adoption of methodological assumptions on which rational choice theory is grounded (Weintraub 2002).

Following Robbins's (1932) definition of economics as the science of choice under conditions of given ends and scarce means, mainstream economics traditionally leaves little room for psychological, sociological, ethical, and cultural dimensions (Hausman & McPherson 2006).[2]

Regardless of whether an economist is mainstream or heterodox, as Schumpeter (1954) famously observed, every economist is guided by an underlying vision, which can be regarded as a pre-analytic cognitive framework, shaped by philosophical, political, and cultural factors. This vision influences an economist's selection of research questions, methodological preferences, and interpretive lenses. Complementing this notion is the idea of an analytical toolbox, which refers to the formal techniques, conceptual apparatuses, and empirical strategies employed in economic analysis.

Hence, the place of an economist within the history of economic thought depends on a complex array of factors: their analytical tools and methodological commitments; their intellectual vision; the schools and research fields to which they belong; and the evolution of their ideas over time, including potential paradigm shifts or revisions of earlier positions.

[1] For instance, the *Methodenstreit* between Menger and Schmoller in the 1880s concerned the nature of economic agents as well as the origin of institutions, while the debate between Pareto and Croce at the beginning of the twentieth century reflected deeper tensions regarding the scientific status of economics and its general laws.

[2] Gary Becker's work was particularly influential in defining the core elements of the neoclassical toolbox, i.e., maximizing behavior, stable preferences, and equilibrium outcomes, and in extending these principles to domains outside traditional economics, including discrimination, family decisions, and crime (Becker 1976, 1981).

Biographical context also plays an essential role. Personal experiences, socio-political frameworks, and historical events frequently shape the theoretical concerns and methodological orientations of economists. Here are some examples. Keynes's monetary theory as well as his *General Theory* cannot be fully understood without reference to the historical context of the Great Depression and the subsequent unemployment which emerged in the United States (Skidelsky, 1983). The debate on a planned economy versus a free market economy cannot be understood without considering the Bolshevik Revolution that actualized a planned economy. Feminist economics is inevitably connected with the rise of the so-called second wave of feminism, which included sexual and cultural revolutions. The phenomena mentioned above represent only one aspect of a more complex set of factors that usually lead to the formation of new theories in any discipline, including economics.

Hence, Barbara Bergmann's place in the history of economic thought must be examined within this broader conceptual and historiographical framework. As with other major figures in the discipline, situating Bergmann historically demands a synthesis of biographical factors, methodological analysis, and theoretical interpretation in order to understand the distinctive role she played within the evolving landscape of economic thought.

Bergmann stands as a paradigmatic case of an economist whose work emerged from a distinctive synthesis of normative commitment, empirical realism, and methodological challenges to mainstream economics.

Her life experience shaped her intellectual priorities. She faced discrimination from her youth as both a Jew and a woman, and it was undeniable that she had to work harder than many male colleagues of hers in order to secure her place within the discipline. Her adult life, spanning from American McCarthyism to the progressivism of the JFK era, from the struggle for civil rights for Black Americans to the feminist fight for women's empowerment, and from Reaganomics to the election of the first Black president, informed her research as well as her public engagement. Her personal and unwavering commitment to social justice made her an economist on duty, aiming to change what was wrong, not merely observe, explain or justify the *status quo* (see Chapter 2).

Her methodological writings explicitly challenged the excessive formalism and empirical detachment of mainstream economics that had been consolidated during the second half of the twentieth century. She sharply diverged from the dominant neoclassical framework, which she believed systematically abstracted away from real-world inequalities. Her critique extended to the profession's neglect of discrimination, inequity, and institutional constraints. Bergmann argued that economic analysis requires direct engagement with normative concerns, rejecting the view that economists should build up positive science rooted in formal and abstract models without considering the real problems affecting individuals and the economy. She consistently maintained that critical social problems, such as poverty and discrimination, were not peripheral anomalies that a free market could adjust away but rather structural features of the economy that deserved to be properly measured, understood, and solved, rather than merely described by theoretical models built on a priori assumptions.

Hence, she championed the use of microsimulation models and showed an interest in the development of experimental economics as methods to analyze labor markets, discrimination, and the effects of social security, among other topics. Her use and promotion of simulations allowed her to model complexity and feedback effects beyond the traditional formalized analytic systems adopted by mainstream economists and their obsession with technique over substance, long before methodological pluralism became an academic concern. She frequently reflected on the shortcomings of economic policy advice derived from overly abstract models. Perhaps her most provocative institutional critique came in her proposal to eliminate the Nobel Prize in economics, arguing that it reinforces a cult of mathematical elegance over relevance (Bergmann 1999) (see Chapter 5).

Regarding Bergmann's vision, her rejection of Marxism led her to consider solutions to economic discrimination within a capitalist system that, in her view, continually required affirmative action to function more fairly. Her egalitarian liberal feminism made the struggle for women's emancipation, both in the public and private spheres, a matter of individual rights to be achieved through an androgynous model that implied equality in the job market and within households (see Chapter 6). Her concern for poverty and for the economic and social conditions of the most vulnerable groups led her to consistently prioritize policies and solutions aimed at reducing inequality and injustice over producing endless refinements of her own theoretical contributions. Therefore, her research went beyond theoretical contribution, given her enduring concern for social justice, particularly for women, children, racial minorities, and economically vulnerable individuals (see Chapter 8).

From the perspective of economists' analytical toolbox, Bergmann's work in the economics of discrimination was original and remains fundamental: her occupational crowding model explained how discriminatory processes push women and racial minorities into segregated, low-wage occupations, not because of productivity differences, but because restricted entry forces them into oversupplied job categories. This insight provided a structural alternative to the mainstream taste-based theory of discrimination *à la* Becker (see Chapters 3, 4, and 7). Her sustained efforts to build a feminist economics capable of challenging household and family models that ignored power dynamics, as well as her involvement in founding IAFFE and the journal *Feminist Economics*, secured her a primary role in the history of the discipline and underscore her commitment to institutional change within the discipline (see Chapter 6).

Bergmann's vision and analysis, as well as her personality and life experience, placed her among those economists who expanded not only the content but also the scope of economics by redefining economics as a social science deeply connected to political responsibility. By confronting the limits of neoclassical methodology, she challenged its claims to normative neutrality. By creating institutional support for a feminist approach to economic theory and policy, she helped economics to become a more human science. And her legacy persists.

References

American Economic Association. (2025). JEL classification codes guide. Retrieved November 22, 2025, from https://www.aeaweb.org/jel/guide/jel.php

Backhouse, R. (2002). *The ordinary business of life: A history of economics from the ancient world to the twenty-first century*. Princeton University Press.

Becker, G. (1976). *The economic approach to human behavior*. University of Chicago Press.

Becker, G. (1981). *A treatise on the family*. University of Chicago Press.

Bergmann, B. (1999). Abolish the Nobel Prize for economics. *Challenge, 42*(5), 26–31.

Blaug, M. (1997). *Economic theory in retrospect*. Cambridge University Press.

Hausman, D., & McPherson, M. (2006). *Economic analysis, moral philosophy, and public policy*. Cambridge University Press.

Robbins, L. (1932). *An essay on the nature and significance of economic science*. Macmillan.

Schumpeter, J. A. (1954). *History of economic analysis*. Oxford University Press.

Skidelsky, R. (1983). *John Maynard Keynes, 1883–1946: Economist, philosopher, statesman*. Macmillan.

Stigler, G. (1982). *The economist as preacher and other essays*. University of Chicago Press.

Weintraub, E. R. (2002). *How economics became a mathematical science*. Duke University Press.

Index

G. Becchio, *Barbara Bergmann*, Great Thinkers in Economics,
https://doi.org/10.1007/978-3-032-18696-6

I

J

T

Kolibri 360 GmbH
Ferdinand-Jühlke-Straße 7
99095 Erfurt, Deutschland
produktsicherheit@kolibri360.de